# Asian versus Western Management Thinking

# Asian versus Western Management Thinking

## Its Culture-Bound Nature

Kimio Kase
*IESE Business School*

Alesia Slocum
*St Louis University*

and

Ying Ying Zhang
*CUNEF, Complutense University of Madrid*

First published 2011 by
PALGRAVE MACMILLAN

Palgrave Macmillan in the UK is an imprint of Macmillan Publishers Limited,
registered in England, company number 785998, of Houndmills, Basingstoke,
Hampshire RG21 6XS.

Palgrave Macmillan in the US is a division of St Martin's Press LLC,
175 Fifth Avenue, New York, NY 10010.

Palgrave Macmillan is the global academic imprint of the above companies
and has companies and representatives throughout the world.

Palgrave® and Macmillan® are registered trademarks in the United States,
the United Kingdom, Europe and other countries.

ISBN: 978–0–230–27293–4

This book is printed on paper suitable for recycling and made from fully
managed and sustained forest sources. Logging, pulping and manufacturing
processes are expected to conform to the environmental regulations of the
country of origin.

A catalogue record for this book is available from the British Library.

Library of Congress Cataloging-in-Publication Data

Kase, Kimio, 1949–
    Asian versus Western management thinking : its culture-bound nature /
Kimio Kase, Alesia Slocum, Yingying Zhang.
        p. cm.
    Includes bibliographical references and index.
    ISBN 978–0–230–27293–4 (hardback)
        1. Management – Cross-cultural studies. 2. Cognition and culture. 3. East and
West. 4. Diversity in the workplace. 5. Cultural intelligence. 6. Organizational
behavior – Cross-cultural studies. I. Slocum, Alesia. II. Zhang, Yingying. III. Title.
HD30.19.K37 2011
658—dc22                                                          2011011823

10  9  8  7  6  5  4  3  2  1
20  19  18  17  16  15  14  13  12  11

Printed and bound by CPI Group (UK) Ltd, Croydon, CR0 4YY

*To Mercedes and in tender memory of Gabriel; and to Miguel and Grita – KK*

*To my beloved, cross-cultural, global-spirited family – AS*

*To Lee, to illustrate a world that he may get to know more – YYZ*

# Contents

# Illustrations

**Tables**

## Figures

# Acknowledgements

This long-standing book project has finally materialized after Kimio Kase's two attempts in five years to conduct and report his research on the analysis of cognitive differences between Asian and Western managers, working with two different teams of academics.

We feel greatly indebted to our contributing authors, who helped us gather case research materials and write up the cases, especially to Bangor University's Professor Bernardo Bátiz-Lazo (Annex 2.7, Virgin Group's Richard Branson) and to Mr Antonio Guerrero (Annex 2.1, Acer's Stan Shih).

The Universidad Complutense de Madrid's Dr José Antonio Ruiz and Dr Nuria Villagra kindly assisted us in preparing the survey questionnaire described in Annex 1, and IESE Business School's Dr Lourdes Susaeta was instrumental in collecting the survey data. Bunkyo University's Dr Noriko Takai and Yonsei University's Professor Il Im also extended their valuable help in gathering data from Japan and Korea.

We are grateful to Dr César G. Cantón of the Universitat Pompeu Fabra, who conscientiously critiqued (and suggested improvement on) our literature review on philosophy and epistemology as well as other parts of the book; to the Universidad Complutense de Madrid and CUNEF's Professor Luis Carretero, who meticulously perused Chapter 6 on the theoretical framework; to IESE Business School's Dr Roberto García, who brought to our notice some points that, to facilitate understanding for readers, needed to be re-addressed in Chapter 6; to the Universidad Complutense de Madrid's Professor Vicente Bermejo, who kindly checked Chapter 4 on cognition psychology; and to CUNEF's Sylvia Rohlfer, for her insightful and constructive critiques on the book's cross-cultural and inductive and deductive aspects. Special thanks go to Professor Álvaro Cuervo, the director of CUNEF, for fully supporting our research activities.

Marcos Sáenz and Juan Ignacio Cantarero are two of the many people who encouraged us with their kind comments and feedback to continue in our endeavour to write this book.

All the authors wish to thank their colleagues at IESE Business School, CUNEF, and St Louis University in Madrid for their continual support and encouragement as well as for their advice and friendship throughout the process of writing this book. They also wish to thank their former business colleagues as well as diverse groups of students, all of whom have been exemplars of a multi-cultural approach to learning and thinking about business.

Finally we would like to warmly express our gratitude to IESE Business School, especially to Silvia Jiménez for having financed the task of correcting the draft by assigning an editor. The same gratitude goes to Josefinna Portella and her colleagues, who reviewed and corrected the style of our draft. Our thanks also go to CUNEF for financing the index.

*Kimio Kase*
*Alesia Slocum*
*Ying Ying Zhang*

# Foreword

To what extent are the theories of management universally applicable principles and to what extent are they specific to particular cultural, national and temporal contexts?

Business enterprises and the people who inhabit them are both products and members of the societies and the economic systems in which they are situated. As these societies and economic systems vary across countries, so the business sectors show distinctive national characteristics.

Among the English-speaking nations, business sectors tend to be dominated by large corporations with dispersed ownership whose shares are stock exchange listed. In China, state-owned companies dominate industrial activity. In Italy and some other southern European companies, family-owned businesses account for a major proportion of economic activity. In many emerging economies, the business sector features two distinct segments: a set of large, highly diversified business groups, and a wide range of industries (including agriculture and most service industries) composed of small, unincorporated family businesses.

Differences in firm strategy are also apparent across countries. During the early years of the twentieth century, Alfred Chandler observed how US and German industrial companies were willing to make massive investments in technology, industrial plants, and systems of marketing and distribution necessary to exploit economies of scale and vertical integration, while British companies followed more short-term, opportunistic strategies.[1] During the 1970s and 1980s, Japanese corporations such as YKK, Honda, and Toyota pursued international strategies based on global products, heavy investment in new product development, and exploitation of economies of volume and learning on an unprecedented scale. More recently, Chinese and Indian companies have emerged on the world stage pursuing strategies that we have yet to recognize and understand. In the case of Indian companies, Capelli et al. identify an orientation towards social goals and a commitment to employee welfare and development.[2]

However, these characteristics of firms and their strategies that differentiate the business sectors of different countries seem quite superficial as compared with the cultural and social features of countries that are reflected in the behaviour and cognition of their organizational members. As Hofstede and subsequent writers have shown, individual attitudes, characteristics of social relationships, and norms of perception vary substantially between different countries. These differences have far-reaching consequences for the nature of leadership, the design of incentives, the characteristics of hierarchical and peer relationships, patterns of communication, and a host of other management issues and practices.

The implication is that management is different in Italy from what it is in Ireland; in Thailand from what it is in Taiwan. As Kase and his colleagues clearly reveal, there are some distinctive differences in cognition, attitudes towards knowledge and learning, and patterns of sensemaking between Asian and Western managers. But what do these differences imply both for our theories of management as predictors of the characteristics of organization and management under different circumstances and for our principles of management as a prescriptive science?

The fact that different national circumstances produce differences in firm characteristics and management processes does not necessarily imply that management theories and principles are inevitably culturally and geographically bounded. Consider some of the differences in firms' strategy and structure between countries. In the US and UK, conglomerate firms, especially those organized around holding company structures, have all but disappeared. In emerging market countries (India, Indonesia, Brazil, and Thailand) and some advanced industrial nations (South Korea), the leading companies are widely diversified business groups.

Some four decades ago, Alfred Chandler and Richard Rumelt pointed to the superiority of related over unrelated diversification and the advantages of the divisional corporation. But, clearly, these findings have limited validity outside the advanced industrialized nations. The key issue here is whether the theory that explains these phenomena embodies implicit assumptions that limit its domain of applicability. Thus, implicit in the prediction that related diversification outperforms unrelated are the assumptions that, first, securities markets are reasonably efficient and, second, that factor markets – especially those for capital and labour – are not subject to substantial transactions. Once the presence of such market inefficiencies is recognized, the rationale for conglomerate companies in emerging market counties becomes apparent.[3] Thus, by viewing these national differences not as the result of unique national circumstances but as quantitative variations within particular contextual variables, observed international differences can be explained by existing theory.

The implication then is that, in order to recognize the extent to which theories are geographically or culturally bounded, we need to identify the assumptions that are implicit within them. Once we can recognize and then relax some of these assumptions, there is the potential to extend the domain of applicability of the theory.

In relation to issues of institutional structure, such implicit assumptions are relatively easy to recognize. Much more elusive are the psychological assumptions that underlie individual behaviour. If we return to our transaction cost explanation for the propensity for conglomerate forms to persist in emerging market countries, these explanations are rooted in assumptions of individual behaviour that presume opportunism. The assumption of opportunistic behaviour is based upon notions of human behaviour that themselves rest upon premises concerning individualism and self-interest that are related to Western rather than Eastern cultural norms. Indeed, even with the context of Western society these implicit assumptions have been criticized.[4]

To the extent that all management theory rests upon microfoundations that comprise assumptions about individual behaviour and individual cognition, the cultural boundaries of established management theory become apparent. The great opportunity is that by recognizing the cognitive and behavioural assumptions that are implicit in our theories we become able, first, to identify the boundaries of theory and, second, to begin extending those boundaries by considering the implications of relaxing or broadening some of these assumptions. The recent work on open source communities offers some indication of this potential: evidence of production by unpaid volunteers is forcing reconsideration of our theories of motivation.[5]

It is this role of international differences in individual cognition and behaviour in limiting the universality of management theory and management practice that gives this book its interest and importance. By addressing differences in management thinking between the West and the East, the authors embark on an exciting journey with the hope of expanding the scope and depth of management theory and practice by inquiring into its cultural specificity. Progress along this path is unlikely to be fast. Two decades ago a special issue of *Academy of Management Review* addressed the international dimensions of management theory. The editors observed that:

> most of the theories and literature that we in North America are familiar with and uphold as universal were primarily developed and applicable to a North American context. We now know enough about other cultures to realize that this assumption is incorrect, and it is time to move beyond the exclusive emphasis we have had in our research and writing on the North American perspective.[6]

As the balance of activity in the global economy shifts from the West to the East, so challenges arise, first of recognizing the distinctive management practices and management thinking of Asian companies and second of the increasing urgency of building culture-free theories of management.

*Robert M. Grant*
*Full Professor of Strategic Management*
*The ENI Chair of Strategic Management in the Energy Sector*
*Università Bocconi*

# Prologue

As a proponent of the knowledge-based view of the firm or the Knowledge School of Management I heartily support the thesis advanced by Kase, Slocum and Zhang in this book. I emphasized in my book entitled *Managing Flow*, co-authored with Professor Ryoko Toyama and Toru Hirata in 2008, that strategy is the creation of the future and that management's role is reading the flow of change, taking timely decisions and continually innovating.

I am firmly convinced that the view considering firms as a means for the earning of profit and the pursuit of the maximization of shareholders' economic value as the ultimate *raison d'être* of for-profit organizations fails to fathom the most fundamental meaning of firms: that they are not a mere aggregate of production functions, transactions and resources, but are entities centred on the creation of knowledge.

In other words, my view of the firm is *human-centric*. How and why so?

My research these last few years has mainly focused on the elucidation of the intricate process mechanism regarding the dynamic creation and use of organizational knowledge through interaction with environmental forces, that is to say, on the establishment of a dynamic theory of knowledge-based management predicated on dynamic management process.

The emphasis on the processual aspect of management entails the capturing of (1) the knowledge as a product that is born of dynamic relationships among individual workers and (2) the firm as a dialectical existence immersed in its relationships with the environment. From this viewpoint we do not dissociate the individuals and the knowledge, and individuals and their firms on the one hand from their environment on the other.

Individual humans are analysed and appreciated in the dynamic theory of knowledge management as leading actors who develop and play their role as change agents of environment, firms and society at large, availing themselves of their own judgement criteria and world-view.

In line with this thought Kase, Slocum and Zhang delve into the working of information processing and decision-making from the angle of cognition. Their thesis that between (Eastern) Asians and Westerners there is a difference in thought process, that is to say, the former using the inductive way and the latter the deductive way, certainly sheds light on the problem of why Asians do not seem to have strategy as understood by Westerners, which has always puzzled Western managers and academics. Other implications of their findings are discussed in their concluding chapter.

In summary, my endorsement of this book is derived from the fact that (1) their approach is human-centric, (2) their contribution signifies a step forward in our understanding of knowledge in its various manifestations (tacit and implicit), (3) their thesis cautions the blanket use of management concepts regardless of their cultural provenance, and (4) the phenomenological instead of the reductionist interpretation of management phenomena is emphasized.

*Ikujiro Nonaka*
*Professor Emeritus*
*Hitotsubashi University*

# 1
# Introduction

When West meets East, cultures collide and minds can be opened to different viewpoints. In the business world, on the one hand, Asians have learned much about management systems from Westerners since World War II regarding how to develop their industries; on the other hand, Westerners have also been influenced by contemporary Asian management styles.

Starting from the 1960s and accelerating into the 1970s in the aftermath of the two energy crises, diverse Japanese multinational companies (MNCs) have gained relevant positions in the US market first, and then all over the world. The Japanese flourished not only in the automobile industry but also in consumer electronics, heavy equipment, photocopiers and steel, among others. The rise of Japanese enterprises took most of their American competitors by surprise, who then rushed to learn about just-in-time (JIT), Total Quality Management (TQM), Kanban or Kaizen.

Theoretical contributions from practice and observation of Japanese management include William Ouchi's 'Theory Z' and M-form companies (Ouchi, 1981, 1984; Ouchi & Jaeger, 1978) in the 1970s and 1980s, and Ikujiro Nonaka's *Knowledge Management* (Nonaka & Takeuchi, 1995), or redundant management (Nonaka, 1990), in the 1990s. Many of these concepts and theories already form an essential part of mainstream management thinking around the world.

The surge of interest on the part of practitioners and academics in Chinese management is due not only to its economic power and growth potential but also to the inroads made by Chinese MNCs in the international competitive arena. Huawei, Lenovo, Haier, and TCL are some of the companies that are penetrating the international market with different strategies – strategic alliances, acquisitions, or setting up their own laboratories and distribution channels. Nevertheless, Chinese (or Korean) management practices have not made a prominent theoretical contribution to management, barring the application of some classic theories or concepts to modern management such as 'the art of war', 'guanxi', and 'yin–yang'.

The differences in management styles seem to be obvious between the West and the East. However, this divergence is not the only trend. Convergence has also played a part in this process of West meeting East, referring specifically to the market share gained by the Western way of being and Western management systems in Asia (Abegglen, 1973; Aoki, 2003; Apospori & Papalexandris, 2008; Dore, 1973; Dunphy, 1987; Hickson, 1968; Jackson & Miyajima, 2007; Olivier, Thoenig & Verdier, 2008).

Since Japan opened its doors to the outside world in the mid-19th century under pressure from the US and Europe, it has been inundated by Western civilization, encompassing all branches of its sciences, both natural and humanistic. To cope with this overwhelming influence of the West, the Japanese gave vent to their frustration by coining phrases such as 'Japanese spirit and Western learning'. When forced to choose between traditional Chinese and Western medicines, Mori Ogai, at that time Surgeon General of the Imperial Army of Japan and a Germany-trained medical doctor as well as one of the founders of modern Japanese literature, declared that there were not two medicines but one, and that Western medicine was the right one.

Similar decisions in favour of Western technology, sciences, and political systems were taken by China, Korea, and other Asian countries. China's 'Self-Strengthening Movement'[1] in 1861–1895 is one such example. The West also thought then, and still thinks now, that if scientific facts are neither paradoxical nor conflicting, then there cannot be two ways of attaining scientific truth. School curricula and systems therefore follow the Western model. Mathematics, physics, chemistry, and logic are taught according to Western thinking.

Management teaching is no exception. Business schools have mushroomed everywhere in recent times. In China, schools such as China Europe International Business School (CEIBS) were established with the help of European management schools, including Spain's IESE Business School. In Japan, schools such as the International University of Japan opened with the collaboration of the US Tuck School. These schools are now assiduously teaching and educating future managers by diffusing the latest, albeit Western, management tools. Discounted cash flow technique, Porter's model for strategy, Kotler's marketing textbook, Hill's textbook on international trade, among others, are examples of the thinking that frames the minds of executives throughout the world.

However, the very assumption that management phenomena can or should be addressed by using a uniform set of management tools and concepts worldwide was challenged at the time of Japan's halcyon days, namely, two or three decades ago in the 1970s and 1980s. As a consequence of Japanese companies' apparent success over their competition from the West, and despite their lack of clear strategic orientation – apart from gaining market share in the world (Abegglen & Stalker, 1985; Chuma, 2006; Fruin, 1992; Hamel & Prahalad,

1989), demonstrating the value of emerging strategy concepts in contrast to designed or planned strategy (Mintzberg, 1990; Mintzberg & Waters, 1985), showing the importance of muddling through (Lindblom, 1959), using incrementalism in general management (Pucik & Hatvany, 1988; Quinn, 1980a, 1980b), emphasizing the importance of soft skills (Peters & Waterman, 1982), and highlighting the value of a corporate culture (Deal & Kennedy, 1982; Goffee & Jones, 1996; Hirota, Kubo & Miyajima, 2007; Kono, 1990) – these techniques were 'discovered' and ended up forming an essential part of what continued to be *Western* management teaching.

The subsequent lapses of Japan as well as its lacklustre economic performance during the Lost Decade (the 1990s) made it lose its 'sheen' and the world retracted its praise of Japan, transiting from 'Japan bashing' to 'Japan passing'. Academia's interest returned to its fold and both management academics and practising managers again turned their attention to Western management wisdom.

The emergence of China (and of Korea a decade ago) as world economic (and political) powers may be tipping the balance again in favour of divergence theory. In other words, the world may be ready soon to accommodate different ways of doing business, instead of converging on one type of management, namely, the Western management style. The emerging discussion of what Chinese management means, whether it is a contextual factor for the application of Western theories or whether we can talk of a Chinese theory of management (Barney & Zhang, 2009), is a proof of this movement.

Between this tension of convergence and divergence in Western and Asian management, our intention in writing this book is to elaborate on *how* business done can differ between or across cultures. We assert that, when faced by that unknown future, managers use their cognitive frameworks, gained from their past experience, their habits of mind, and/or their tacitly or explicitly learned 'cultures', to frame, understand, and then act upon the challenges they confront. The implication is, of course, that different people use a different 'how' to comprehend and act in their managerial environments.

Our book explores this by identifying two different approaches to understanding and acting that we assert are used by managers when making sense of the world around them, through philosophy, epistemology, cognition, and culture. We term these 'inductive thinking' and 'deductive thinking' (see our Appendix on the making of this book). We also argue that these two approaches can be identified as general tendencies in the way that Asian managers, as opposed to Western managers, strategically think and manage. We then propose a framework for how managers can first identify these different 'how's in others, and then embrace elements from both ways of thinking to create better strategic and managerial solutions across borders. By providing our readers with a variety of cases, written by and about both Asians and Westerners, we hope that they can begin to identify and apply 'inductive' and 'deductive' thinking themselves as a way to better understand managerial situations and to strategically approach broader solutions. Finally, the implication of divergence and convergence in Asian and Western management thinking is discussed, exploring the workings of inductive and deductive integration in the cognitive process.

## Objectives

We have tried to fulfil three major objectives in writing this book. Initially, we have sought to evaluate old and new theories of culture, knowledge, and cognition, exploring the differences between how these originated and are perceived in Asia[2] and how they originated and are perceived in the Western world,[3] and as they apply to the way in which different managers manage.

To some degree, in doing this we have taken into account Nisbett (2003), who elaborated on the substantial differences in the way that Asians and Westerners think. However, we have also taken his approach a step further into the realm of management, by writing a literature review and summary of what we consider to be the relevant philosophical origins, epistemological approaches, advances in cognitive science, and advances in cross-cultural management perspectives that might apply to an analysis and understanding of how different international managers think and act.

To do this, we have also compared and contrasted the prevalence of some of these theories in Western and Asian management cultures, and then provided very specific cases (forming Annex 2) upon which to evaluate these theories.

Our second objective has been to propose a theoretical framework for understanding the differences in thinking by Asian and Western managers, by defining what we call 'inductive' and 'deductive' approaches to managerial cognition (by taking Boisot and McKelvey (2010), as well as others, a step further).

Because of its systematic approach to learning and its potential to provide a more complete understanding of content at various levels of performance, we have used Swanson and Law's (1993) 'Whole–Part–Whole' model to identify, deconstruct, and then reconstruct a definition of what we mean by 'inductive and deductive thinking', and have developed example tables of some major cognitive 'schemas' that could be considered to be held by different inductive or deductive thinkers.

Our third objective is pedagogical, that is to provide researchers, students, and practitioners with a book of international cases and a framework for working through these cases, using an 'inductive/deductive' lens and elaborating upon this in an 'open content' way. We have proposed an analogical framework for helping students, researchers, and managers to evaluate and apply the myriad theories they are faced with for themselves.

## Questions addressed in this book

Based on the earlier view of Asian and Western differences in management, we also observe the divergence in terms of business diversification. Diversification is an important corporate-level decision for companies: should they diversify or not; if so, in what fields, related field or new ones, and so on.

From multiple observations, we can see many examples of unrelated diversification in Asia. *Zaibatsu, keiretsu* and *chaebols* are typical formats in Japan and Korea. Similar groups can be found in the West, too. Sweden's Wallenberg group is one example. Corporate-level strategy attributes the emergence of these diversified corporations to value creation by plutocrats or well-connected people with access to sources of finance or political networks in underdeveloped economies.

However, the phenomenon of unrelated diversification probably is much more extended in Asia, and the base of their decision-making is more than mere financial and political resources. The thesis of this book is, as mentioned above, that there is a cultural difference in the cognitive processes which influence the way Asians and Westerners construct their discourse: Asians follow an inductive approach and Westerners follow a deductive approach.

Accordingly, we phrase our questions as follows (they will be repeated and analysed in Chapter 7):

1. Assuming that there are differences in philosophical and epistemological background which are reflected in cognitive processes, doubt may be felt as to how much this is due to a collective phenomenon or whether it can be put down to personal traits.
2. Accepting that the difference in cognitive processes can be captured on a collective basis, to what degree can such a trait provide an explanation for the behaviour of incumbent executives? Does it fully explain the most important phenomena of the executives analysed?
3. Is the division between induction and deduction a permanent one? Or can a person change his/her way of approaching management phenomena, for example, from induction to deduction, or vice versa? And, related to point 2, is a person always inductive or is he/she sometimes inductive and on other occasions deductive?

Related to these questions are others, such as:

4. Are the perceived differences between Westerners and Asians due more to personal traits or may we use collectives of Asians and Westerners as units for analysis?
5. Can a person or a group of like-minded people switch from induction to deduction or vice versa?

6. Further to these questions, what implications for management exist, if our thesis is deemed to be grounded in reason? This could be subdivided into the following sub-questions:

- If the basic understanding and cognition of management phenomena differs from one region to the other, how can we teach the same business models?
- If the competitive environment undergoes change, is it possible to continue using a way of thinking that, until now, has provided success?
- If the environmental changes require another, different treatment of human resources, can we do this? And how?
- If the two ways of thinking (inductive and deductive) meet, how can each cope with competition from the other?
- If the business environment remains more or less the same, can we infer that one way of thinking is better adapted to it?

## Methodological approach

Following the method used in Kase, Sáez-Martínez and Riquelme (2005), we ultimately used heuristics, as shown in Figure 1.1.

For the case writing, Kase et al. (2005) was followed as to the method of gathering information and data. Figure 1.2 illustrates the procedure.

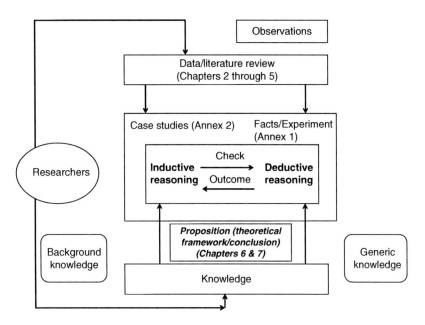

*Figure 1.1*  Methodological approach

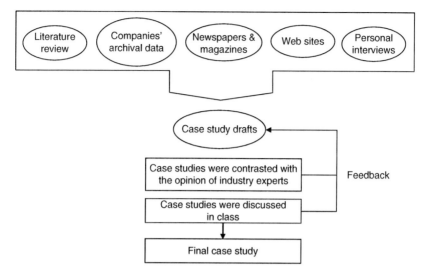

*Figure 1.2* Methodology for case study elaboration
*Source*: Adapted from Kase et al. (2005: p. 7).

## Structure of the book

We begin by providing a literature review in four chapters.

Chapter 2 reviews the literature in philosophy concerning cognition and knowledge both in the West and the East, focusing on how induction and deduction are treated in both regions. In consideration of its reduced accessibility, more space is devoted to Asian philosophy, comprising Buddhism and Confucianism in their different tracks and schools.

Chapter 3 centres more on the epistemological analysis of induction, deduction, and abduction.

Chapter 4 discusses the literature in the area of cognitive psychology, where there exists a large body of research literature on cognition and language learning in different languages and regions of the world.

Chapter 5 treats the literature on cross-cultural management in support of our thesis that management decisions and phenomena can be analysed taking regional cultures as analytical units, as well as considering the trend of convergence and divergence of management thinking and practice in the global business world.

Chapter 6 epitomizes our thesis on the difference of cognitive and thought processes between Asia and the West by proposing a theoretical framework for better understanding the workings of the two ways of thought. The Asian and Western cases in Annex 2 are analysed in the first part and a theoretical framework is advanced in the second part.

Chapter 7 summarizes and concludes our exposition and suggests a direction for future studies after analysing the limitations that our own study may have.

Annex 1 replicates some of the empirical surveys conducted in the field of cognitive psychology to analyse the cognitive differences between Asians and Westerners, as a verification of our thesis.

Annex 2 comprises eight case studies we have carried out as a basis for our inference embodied in Chapter 6.

Figure 1.3 graphically represents the structure of the book and its flow of argument.

### Suggestion for executive readers

For those readers who do not wish to or do not have the time to dwell on the intricacy of our arguments and counterarguments, on the clarification of 'subtle' shades of meaning in different affirmations, we advise the following steps, which will help them quickly capture the message we aspire to convey.

First, read through Chapter 1 'Introduction', and then proceed to Chapter 6 on the theoretical and practical frameworks that can be used for

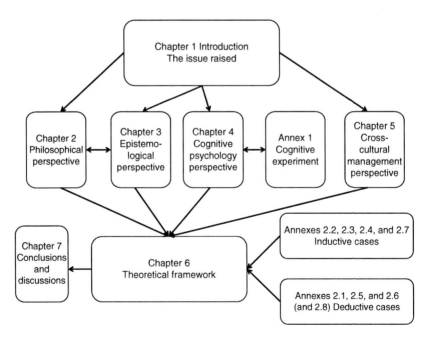

*Figure 1.3*   The structure of the book and its argument flow

the case analyses. Chapter 7 'Conclusions and Discussion' may also help their understanding.

Annex 2 may be visited if the reader wishes to gain greater depth on the basis of viewing the situations more in the round. It may not be necessary to read them all. One or two cases from each category (inductive and deductive) may be sufficient for a thorough understanding.

## Appendix: the making of this book

The idea that there is a difference between Asian and Western approaches to management has always been intuitively felt and tacitly shared by the authors throughout the process of writing this book.

The background of each of the authors is international in many senses. Each of us has faced frictions and difficulties in our personal and business challenges. This is, most probably, due to the different ways that we approach problems and to the different viewpoints we cherish. These may derive from the differing cognitive processes we have found to exist between different cultural origins, which are quite different from what we regard as personal traits. Our individual profiles are also diverse, including our family structure: all of us are married to a spouse from a different cultural background from our own.

One of the authors, of Japanese nationality, worked for a Japanese company for 10 years, for a British international audit and consultancy firm for nearly a decade, for a multilateral development bank based in Washington, DC, for two years, and taught in schools in Spain, Bolivia, Japan, and Peru, among others. He has therefore participated in negotiations and transactions involving various nationalities over many years. Another author, of Spanish nationality but Chinese origin, worked for several companies operating in Spain and doing business with China before entering her academic career. She has also pursued learning and knowledge-sharing in different nations such as Singapore, the UK, Denmark, Peru, and the USA. Still another, a US citizen, worked for an international audit and consultancy firm in Spain, and then for various multinational firms in the UK, where she was responsible for projects that spanned four continents and covered over 30 countries at any one time. All of the authors were educated in their own countries up to their undergraduate studies, and then obtained their doctorates either in Spain or in the UK.

In writing this book, we encountered problems similar to the different inductive or deductive approaches we have been studying in this book. Our Japanese author launched the basic idea for the book about two years ago. He proposed a generic idea based upon his intuition and sense that the same facts may be interpreted differently by different general groups or cultures. Accordingly, the sense-making process itself bifurcated when two people from different geographic areas, in this case Asia and the West, were involved.

The original team was composed of an East Asian with a Swiss PhD, a European with a Swiss PhD, and the above three members. Landmark dates were set for progress of the writing and the division of tasks was decided. After six months, it was discovered that the work had not progressed. Lack of time, no serious dedication to the assignments, and other personal reasons were alleged. Finally, these two members of the team left. The remaining three pushed forward. But in the last stage, in which the theory part was to be written, we reached an impasse and little progress was made for some months.

It has taken many months of impasse and lack of advance to produce the book. Finally, we identified the cause of these difficulties: it appeared to us to be linked to the topic of the book itself – the great 'divide' between deductive and inductive approaches.

While the Japanese author's proposal was in favour of each one working on an assigned part based on a general idea so that the contributions from each individual could be put together at a later stage and discussed and analysed by all, the US author insisted on a clear picture of the entire work with a specific model established from the beginning and sought a thorough thrashing-out of viewpoints before even starting the project. Meanwhile, the Chinese author was more familiar with the inductive way and appeared to deal with it with a certain ease.

These personal perceptions from our own daily lives are not just anecdotal, but also confirm our conjecture that the way a Chinese or Japanese person thinks is very different compared with a Spaniard or North American person, and that this is not due only to personal character traits. Without performing a meticulous analysis of our behaviour and cognition in this process, we recognized that we may have to examine our own personal trajectories in more detail in the future, in order to specifically distinguish which elements contribute to our deductive system and which to our inductive system for functioning. This may also offer interesting insights regarding the questions raised.

As all three authors claim to have this combination of inductive and deductive thinking, integrating these two apparent opposites seems to have been the key to finishing this book. Ultimately, we could argue that a 'middle way' – that is, combining in some way both the deductive and inductive approaches – is probably the best way to address a rapidly globalizing world.

# 2
# Literature Review: Philosophical Perspectives on Knowledge and Cognition

In Chapter 1, we proposed exploring the difference between cognition processes used by Westerners and those used by Asians. We also elaborated on a list of issues to be addressed in relation to this.

Before discussion of our main topic (that is the difference between how Asians and Westerners use inductive and deductive thinking in strategic business situations), as well as various ancillary issues related to this (discussed in Chapters 6 and 7), we conducted a literature review. Our purpose has been to examine the issue from various angles, which, albeit not exhaustive of all possible approaches, will shed light on the aspects we consider relevant to our study. Thus, the chapters on our literature survey will comprise the following four perspectives:

- Chapter 2: philosophical perspective;
- Chapter 3: epistemological perspective;
- Chapter 4: cognitive psychology perspective;
- Chapter 5: cross-cultural management perspective.

In this chapter, therefore, we survey the literature on the issues of cognition and knowledge (specifically, induction and deduction) from the philosophical viewpoint, in the belief that the different approaches to the analysis of this reality must be influenced by the mental framework prevalent in one's country or the milieu where one has been brought up. Chapter 3 reviews the literature on epistemology in more detail.

We contend that the survey of philosophy in this chapter bears upon the subject of this book in that: (1) Western philosophical thought gave rise to different epistemological approaches from those produced in Asia. These have, therefore, given rise to different degrees of dependence on deduction, as is obvious from the influence exerted by empiricism on science and technology. Essentially, Westerners avoid the construal of reality from purely theoretical speculation. (2) Both in Europe and in Asia, there exists a divide between those who believe that we can comprehend reality through speculation and those who insist that this must be achieved through the use of sensory data.

(3) In Asia, highly speculative Buddhist thinking was converted into a more intuitive, and therefore perhaps more inductive (and even, perhaps, more practicable) thought system, above all, in China and Japan, though both ways of thinking coexist side by side in modern times. And (4) a similar process seems to have taken place in Neo-Confucianism, as evidenced by the transition of the systematic and highly speculative *Songxue* to the more practical *Yang-Ming School*.

However, from points (1) and (2), and as an explanation of Asian and Western approaches, we will settle for the presumption that we can describe these differences by applying the generalized terms 'deductive and inductive thinking' to the also generalized categories of people, 'Westerners' and 'Asians', albeit with the caveat that all Western people may not necessarily be deductive thinkers (see Annex 2.7, the Richard Branson case). Similarly, from (3) and (4) we may conjecture that all Asians may not be given totally to the inductive approach. We do assert, however, that they are more often than not, 'inductive thinkers'.

Without aspiring to be exhaustive, in our first section we review Western philosophies where a dichotomy between the two opposing viewpoints has always existed. In the second section, we analyse the highly speculative and deductive Indian philosophy embodied as Buddhist teaching, that we later synthesize into an approach that is more intuitive and inductive. Pure Land Buddhist and Zen schools, as well as Chinese autochthonous Confucianist teaching, are reviewed. More space is also dedicated to the Asian philosophy because in management literature it is not frequently accessed for relevant information.

## Review of Western thought

### Dichotomy in Western philosophy

A common thread throughout most of Western philosophy, we argue, is the contrast made between induction and deduction. These are also conceived as universals (or mind) and particulars (or reality). In essence, the individuation of phenomena is either subsumed into universals or affirms itself in the form of particulars. In the West, this process takes shape through philosophies such as Plato's stance on moving from the general to the particular, that is 'in order from that position to elucidate and explain the data of experience' or Aristotle's proposal that we move from the particular to the general, that is through 'derivation of general inferences and results from a sum of given facts and phenomena' (Schwegler, 2010: p. 97). Induction gives relevance to the particulars whereas deduction concedes importance to the universals.

Nominalism and Realism are the second forms of this contrast, which originated in the Middle Ages. The nominalists did not believe in universal concepts (*universalia*), holding that they were mere names or *flatus*[1] *vocis*[2] without reality (Schwegler, 2010: p. 145). Therefore, with nominalism there were no general notions or *genera*. 'All that is, exists only as a singular in its pure individuality' (Schwegler, 2010: p. 145). Nominalism fostered empiricism, which then led to experimental science (Watanabe, 2005: pp. 218–219). Roscellinus (c. 1050–1125) and William of Occam (c. 1285–1349) are examples of its principal proponents (Shimizu, 1994).

The realists, disciples of Plato, 'held firm to the objective reality of the universals – universalia ante res' (Schwegler, 2010: p. 145; Marías, 2008). Thomas Aquinas (1224–1274) and John Duns Scotus (c. 1266–1308) represented this school (Shimizu, 1994).

Both Aristotle and Aquinas held an intermediate position between Plato and Scotus, on the one hand, and Occam, on the other (Schwegler, 2010; Russell, 1995). For Aristotle and Aquinas, universals had no existence independently from the things they were embodied in (contrarily to Duns Scotus); and they only had existence in the *cognoscens*'s mind. The difference with nominalism consists of the view that there is something in 'things' (essence) that is a sufficient basis for the rationality of the universals we have in our minds (Marías, 2008).

The third form settles on Idealism and Realism (Marías, 2008; Miller, 2010; Schwegler, 2010): 'idealism is the philosophical theory which maintains that the ultimate nature of reality is based on the mind or ideas. In the philosophy of perception, idealism is contrasted with realism in which the external world is said to have an apparent absolute existence.'[3] Realism in this context represents empiricism, sensualism or materialism (Schwegler, 2010: p. 177). Therefore, idealism approximates deduction, while realism makes use of induction.

The fourth form of dichotomy[4] encompasses Empiricism and Rationalism (Lacey, 2005a, 2005b). The former view holds that our knowledge is based on experience through the five senses (Locke, 1997). Rationalism, on the contrary, stresses the role of reason, and includes intuition in contrast to sensory experience (Descartes, 1968a, 1996; Lacey, 2005b).

Fifth, we note that this dichotomy also occurs in Asia. Apart from the general differences between Asian and Western philosophies (practice-orientation vs. theory-orientation, religion-basedness vs. logic-basedness) (Nishitani, 1982; Suzuki, 2002), even within Asian or Chinese thinking, for example, if we look at Confucianism, we find two different streams: the subjectiveness school vs. the objectiveness school. The former, which is theory-oriented, attaches importance to the attainment of virtue (*ren*) through reflection, while the latter, practice-oriented, sets store by acts and the exercise of propriety (*li*) for the same purpose (Watanabe, 2005: pp. 148–149).

Out of the above-mentioned dichotomies, and by virtue of its relevance to our research, we centre on deductive and inductive thinking as represented by Plato and Aristotle (and by the latter's interpreter, Thomas Aquinas), though we also review very briefly the contrast between continental rationalism and British empiricism as represented by Descartes and Locke.

## Deduction versus induction

### Plato: deduction

Rowe (2006: p. 13) holds that the interpretation of other philosophers is easier than that of Plato, since Plato addresses his readers indirectly, not appearing as a character himself in his *Dialogues*. Moreover, Socrates, who is the main character in the majority of *Dialogues*, is represented as heard by 'someone' or some named individuals.

With this caveat, we can then follow the line set out by Russell (1995: p. 163) who contends that in Plato 'there is a doctrine that there is nothing worthy of being called "knowledge" to be derived from the senses, and that the only real knowledge has to do with concepts'. He also points out that 'Theaetetus' and its enquiry of 'what knowledge is' (Plato, 1989) is a work which deals with Plato's strong criticism of the view that knowledge could be the same thing as perception (Hamilton, 1989).

Regarding knowledge (Guthrie, 1986; Plato 1989: 145d8–145e5) advances the following arguments:

1. What makes people wise is wisdom (145d11).
2. Learning about something means becoming wiser in that matter (145d8–9).
3. People are wise in the things of which they have knowledge (145e5)

Silverman (2009) considers (1) as being circular, while he thinks that (2) implies (3), and poses the question: 'what is knowledge?'

Runciman (1962) cited by Chappel (2009) raises the question of whether Plato distinguished (1) knowledge of objects (knowledge by acquaintance or objectual knowledge) – 'knowing what' –, from (2) knowledge techniques (tekhnē) – 'knowing how' –, and (3) knowledge of propositions – 'knowing that'.

Chappel (2009) argues that Plato considers tekhnē to be incidental to a discussion of epistēmē. He conjectures that the Greeks treat propositional knowledge as a special case in objectual knowledge, due to its grammatical structure. Here, instead of using a 'that'–clause, it treats the object of propositional knowledge as a 'thing considered as having a quality'. Therefore, a sentence such as 'I know that Socrates is wise' becomes 'I know wise Socrates', as it would also be in Latin – *cognosco Socratem* and *scio Socratem (esse) erudītum*.

To Socrates's question ('what is knowledge?'), Theaetetus's first response is to offer examples. This is rejected by Socrates on the argument that for any x, examples of x are neither necessary nor sufficient for a definition of x, because they are irrelevant and not sufficient (because they presuppose understanding of a definition to be sought) (Chappel, 2009).

Chappel points out that 'for the Platonist, definition by examples is never even possible; for the empiricists, definition by examples is the natural method', which suggests that Theaetetus's argument is levelled against empiricism.

From Plato (1989: 151–187), Chappel (2009) identifies the definition of knowledge (D1) as perception following the word of Theaetetus who opines that 'knowledge is perception' (Plato, 1989: 151e4).

This opinion leads to (a) PS (phenomenal subjectivism) – things are to any human just as they appear to him or her – in (Plato, 1989: 151d–e) and (b) the theory of flux – things are not stably existing objects with stably enduring qualities – in (Plato, 1989: 152a–160e), both of which are ultimately rejected by Socrates.

D1 is criticized on the ground of several arguments (Chappel, 2009).

The first objection holds that if all perceptions are true, then there is no reason to think that animal perceptions are inferior to a human being's perceptions, which Socrates finds absurd (Plato, 1989: 160e–161d).

Chappel (2009) argues, however, that this objection ought to be considered to be against judgements about perceptions rather than about perceptions *in sensu stricto*, since many animal perceptions are superior to human perceptions.

The second objection (Plato, 1989: 161d–162a) criticizes the implication that no-one is wiser than anyone else.

The third objection (Plato, 1989: 162c2–6) relates to the implication that animal perceptions are not inferior to human perceptions, as all perceptions are true, which Chappel (2009) qualifies on the grounds that Greek gods may not be different from humans with respect to their perceptions, but they may be different in their power of judgement about perceptions.

The fourth objection (Plato, 1989: 163a–169c) holds that, if perception is knowledge, then anyone perceiving an utterance in an unknown language should understand (know) that utterance.

The fifth objection (Plato, 1989: 163a–169c) is based on the relations between memory and perception: remembering is knowing them, but not perceiving them.

The sixth objection (Plato, 1989: 163a–169c) argues that, if perception is knowledge, seeing an object with one eye and not seeing it with the other would mean knowing it and not knowing it.

The final objection by Socrates to D1 (Chappel, 2009; Plato, 1989: 183c4–187a9) states that the mind makes use of a range of concepts which it could not have acquired through the senses: existence, sameness and difference, for example; and therefore knowledge is not perception.

The second definition (D2) according to Chappel (2009), based on Plato (Plato, 1989: 187b–202c), proposes that 'knowledge is judgement about immediate sensory awareness', which begs the question of how judgements or beliefs can emerge from immediate sensory awareness.

Plato argues that there is no way for the empiricist to construct 'contentful' belief from sensory awareness alone and that we need something else beside sensory awareness to explain belief, since empiricists claim that sensation is the source of all beliefs (Chappel, 2009).

Plato (1989: 200d–201c) refutes the thesis that knowledge is true belief with the example that a skilled lawyer can bring jurymen to a state of true belief without bringing them to a state of knowledge, thus showing that knowledge and true belief are different states.

The third definition (D3) proposed by Plato (1989: 201d–211a) is that 'knowledge is true belief with an account (logos), and where no account can be given of a thing, it is not "knowable".'

Several interpretations of what logos is are advanced: (a) logos as 'speech' or 'statement'; (b) 'logos of O' as 'enumeration of the elements of O'; (c) logos of O which signifies the sign or diagnostic feature (wherein x differs from everything else or everything else of O's own kind) wherefore knowledge of Theaetetus consists of true belief about Theaetetus plus an account of what differentiates him from every other human being (Silverman, 2008).

Chappel (2009) contends that D3 does not solve the problem faced by D2; that the jurymen example applies to D3 as well; and that we cannot define knowledge as true belief unless we have an account of false belief.

Socrates in Plato (1989: 210a–211b) states that:

> [N]othing could be sillier than to say that it is correct belief together with a *knowledge* of differentness ... So ... neither perception, nor true belief, nor the addition of an 'account' to true belief can be knowledge.

By way of summary, Harvey (1986: p. 332l) may be cited:

> [I]n some of his earlier dialogues is found one of his principal contributions to philosophical thought, the Theory of Ideas. The Idea or form of a thing ... is something of the nature of our abstract conception of that thing, but having a real existence outside the world of sense; it is the unchanging reality behind the changing appearance. The knowledge of these ideas is to be attained only by pure reason (*nous* or *dianoia*[5]) unaffected by sensation, and proceeding by dialectic. The supreme idea is that of the Good, on which all the others are ultimately founded ... virtue is knowledge, knowledge of this supreme idea. Plato's later doctrines ... appear to have included a system of logical categories and a tentative identification of the ideas with numbers.

*Aristotle: induction*

Aristotle (2001a: I.1 71a1–3) postulates that 'all teaching and all intellectual learning come about from already existing knowledge'. Ferejohn (2009) attempts to clarify this seemingly anti-foundationalist[6] principle. Ferejohn (2009: pp. 66–67) sustains that Aristotle refers to 'knowledge *simpliciter*', the highest form of knowledge, when he expresses the above postulation, which is ultimately demonstrated knowledge.

Regarding demonstrated knowledge and otherwise Guthrie (1990); Aristotle (2001a: i.1 72b3–10) compares two schools (sceptic and circular arguments): those holding that there is no scientific knowledge because of the need to know the primary premises; and those who think that there is, but that all truths are demonstrable.

The first school assumes that there is no way of knowing but by demonstration and that if behind the prior stands no primary knowledge, we fall into an infinite regress; but if there are primary premises, and if they are not knowable by demonstration, then they are not scientific knowledge but are based on mere supposition. The second school holds that demonstration can be circular and therefore that all truths are demonstrated (Aristotle, 2001a: I.1 72b10–20).

Aristotle's own doctrine is that 'not all knowledge is demonstrative...knowledge of the immediate premises is independent of demonstration' (Aristotle, 2001a: I.1 71a4).

In this connection, Ferejohn (2009: p. 69) argues that Aristotle recognizes the existence of undemonstrated knowledge arising from *some cognitive capacity*. Aristotle (2001: 99b35–6) calls this 'perception' and explains (Aristotle, 2001a: 101a) that out of sense-perception we have memory, out of repeated memories we develop experience, out of experience we develop the skill of the craftsman and the knowledge of the man of science. He concludes that these states of knowledge are neither innate nor developed from other higher states but are from sense-perception.

However, Aristotle states that there are first principles that cannot be induced (but rather, we are born with). We find these principles in our consciousness by way of intuitive knowledge – they work as a condition of possibility in every other thought and are the principle of no contradiction (for theory) and the *synderesis*[7] ('do good and no evil', for practical reasons) (Aristotle, 2001b). However, nothing can be derived from the first principles; they work instead, as stated, as a background against which all other thinking is possible (Aquinas, 1993).

Aristotle (2001a: 71b9–13) defines science as knowledge of the causes of why things must be as they are. For Aristotle (2001a: 71b 18–19), science depends on demonstration, which is a 'scientific syllogism', namely, 'a syllogism such that we have science by virtue of possessing it' (Smith, 2009b: p. 51).

Accordingly, Aristotle's logic revolves around one notion: deduction (*sullogismos*) (Smith, 2009a).

Aristotle says:

> A deduction is a discourse in which, certain things having been stated, something other than what is stated follows of necessity from their being so. (Aristotle, 1984: I.2, 24b18–21)

> Anything stated is a premise of the argument, and what follows of necessity is the conclusion: the core of the definition is the notion of following from necessity and this corresponds to logical consequence, namely, X results of necessity from Y and Z, it being impossible for X to be false when Y and Z are true. (Smith, 2009)

Aristotle's logic is restricted to assertions or statements that are true or false, and only deals with subject–predicate or categorical statements (Keyt, 2009: p. 32).

Categorical statements relate to quantity, quality and modality; while in modality statements are assertoric (assertive), necessary, or possible, in quality they are affirmative or negative, and in quantity they are universal (all), particular (in part), singular, or indefinite or indeterminate (Aristotle, 1984: 25a1–5).

Excluding singular statements and indefinite statements,

> ...one is left with four types of assertoric categorical statement: (i) universal affirmative (P belongs to every S), (ii) universal negative (P belongs to no S), (iii) particular affirmative (P belongs to some S), and (iv) particular negative (P does not belong to some S). (Keyt, 2009: p. 33)

Statements of indeterminate or indefinite quantity (for example, 'Pleasure is good') are not much heeded in Aristotle's syllogistic, which may show Aristotle's sympathy for non-Procrustean logic (Keyt, 2009: p. 33).

As discussed before, therefore, the goals of science are attained by scientific deduction or demonstrative syllogism, and Aristotelian demonstrative science consists of primitive and demonstrable principles (which are known non-inferentially) (Anagnostopoulos, 2009: pp. 103–104).

The question now to address is: how do we arrive at the primitive or first principles? We have mentioned above the sceptical and circular arguments. Aristotle agrees with the sceptics in the need for there to be some kind of cognition of the first principles, but rejects the Platonic view of innate knowledge, and expresses his view that our knowledge of universals from particulars is predicated on induction (Anagnostopoulos, 2009: pp. 105–107).

Anagnostopoulos (2009: p. 107) summarizes the relationships between cognition, method and state of cognition in Table 2.1.

*Table 2.1* Summary of the relationships among cognition, method and state of cognition

| Type of things cognized | Method | State of cognition |
|---|---|---|
| Principles (axioms) | Induction (epagôgê) | Comprehension (nous) |
| Theorems | Demonstration | Understanding (epistêmê[1]) |

*Note:* [1] 'The subject of the *Posterior Analytics* is *epistêmê*. This is one of several Greek words that can reasonably be translated "knowledge", but Aristotle is concerned only with knowledge of a certain type (as will be explained below). There is a long tradition of translating *epistêmê* in this technical sense as science.' (http://plato.stanford.edu/entries/aristotle-logic/ accessed on March 17, 2010). In Chapter 3, we orient our work towards translating episteme as science, and therefore the study of how, more than the 'what' of knowledge. Some of this difference may be in translation, as pointed out above, for example, where our main argument about cognition ends up being that, although philosophy and schools of thought originated the bifurcation between induction and deduction, we think it is the 'how' that they are used that creates the main point of our contribution in this book – i.e., we are looking at how entire groups of Asians and Westerners perceive things differently based on how they tend to think in the first place.

*Source:* Anagnostopoulos (2009: p. 107).

*Nous* is understood as rational intuition, or mental vision grasping non-inferentially that some propositions are true, and Aristotle viewed that we cannot discern cognize nous as being true by any cognition but by induction (Anagnostopoulos, 2009: p. 107).

In summary,[8] although Aristotle used and really invented the concept of deduction, he was insistent that there was no way to have new knowledge that was not also innate (which he rejected). Therefore, philosophically, we have argued that there is a bifurcation between those who use induction vs. deduction, based upon the philosophical activity of arguing about, and accepting whether, knowledge is innate or not.

Derived from this is also the ontological discussion about whether a culture tends to accept something as true or not, again separating out those who see deduction as demonstrated, and therefore reliably true, or not. This should then segue into the next section on major schools of thought, pointing out that this original philosophy of separating inductive and deductive led to major schools that had to choose, or take a stand, on inductive and deductive thinking, as shown below.

### Rationalism vs. empiricism

*René Descartes: rationalism and mind-body dualism*

Unlike Aristotle, who proceeded from complex reality to unifying principles, Descartes goes from the idea to the thing, in other words, his method is deductive (Sutcliffe, 1968: p. 18).

The deductive path followed by Descartes begins with the idea of God, since he 'himself believed that if he could get as far as establishing the existence of God ... he could proceed to establish a systematic physical science ... From the uniformity and constancy of God, Descartes proceeds to deduce important general principles' (Cottingham, 2005: p. 203). God in Descartes' system plays a role as guarantor of the reliability of human cognition (Cottingham, 2005: p. 202).

His famous '*cogito ergo sum*' ('I think therefore I am') is based on this belief in God as a guarantor of reliability and the Cogito is 'a first principle from which Descartes ... deduces all that follows' (Sutcliffe, 1968: p. 19). Descartes casts doubt on everything and 'the first truth to emerge unscathed ... is the meditator's certainty' (Cottingham, 2005, p. 200).

In terms of the doubts thus cast, Descartes defines knowledge, distinguishing *scientia* (knowledge) and *persuasio* (conviction) (Newman, 2008).

Regarding knowledge, Descartes breaks away from the Aristotelian tradition in two ways. The first is his rejection of substantial form[9] as an explanatory principle in physics, as this is deemed incapable of discovering any new or useful knowledge. Second is his denial of the thesis that all knowledge comes from sensation, on the grounds that sensation cannot be a reliable source for knowledge (Skirry, 2008).

As mentioned in *supra*, Aristotle sets out a set of argumentative forms known as 'syllogisms' composed of a major premise, a minor premise and a conclusion. Descartes considers them to offer truth if the premises are true, but he argues that they are faulty if these premises are based on mere beliefs, expressing only probabilities based on sensation (Skirry, 2008).

In his *First Meditation*, Descartes (1968c: p. 96) recognizes that 'everything I have accepted up to now as being absolutely true and assured, I have learned from or through the senses. But I have sometimes found that these senses played me false ...'

Even if our senses deceive us sometimes, Skirry (2008) wonders what basis for doubt exists for the immediate belief that you are doing what you are doing now, for example, reading this book. He also wonders how we can know if this is not based on the false sensations found in dreams. This is called 'internalist justification' and is predicated on the view that justifying factors must be accessible to the knower's conscious awareness (Newman, 2008).

In his *Second Meditation* (Descartes, 1968c: pp. 105–107), Descartes attempts to establish absolute certainty by reasoning that 'I am, I exist' (Cogito, *ergo sum*) and discourses on it:

> I am ... only a thing which thinks ... a mind, understanding, or reason ... but what else? ... I am not this assemblage of limbs ... I am not a wind ... I find I am nevertheless certain that I am something.

The discussion here takes place in the first person. The mere fact that 'I am thinking' implies that there must be something engaged in that activity.

Hence, 'I exist' is an absolute certainty that serves as an axiom from which certain truths can be deduced (Skirry, 2008).

Also in his *Second Meditation* (Descartes, 1968c: p. 107), Descartes concludes that 'What...am I? A thing that thinks...a thing that doubts, perceives, affirms, denies, wills, does not will, that imagines also, and which feels'. Descartes distinguishes intellectual perception and volition as belonging to the nature of mind. He contrasts this with imagination and sensation as also being faculties of the mind insofar as they are united with a body, and then implies that imagination and sensation are lesser faculties of mind (Skirry, 2008).

In the *Third Meditation* (Descartes, 1968c: p. 116), Descartes classifies his ideas into three categories: (1) innate, (2) adventitious and (3) invented. The first is taught by nature, and the second, 'my experience tells me that these ideas do not depend on my will; for often they come to me despite myself...I am persuaded that this sensation or idea of heat is produced in me by something different from me, viz., by the heat of the fire by which I sit'[10] (Descartes, 1968c: p. 117). Examples of innate ideas are metaphysical principles such as the idea of the mind and the idea of God (Skirry, 2008).

The truths[11] reached in the Second Meditation such as 'I am or exist'[12] and 'I am a thinking thing', guaranteed by God's existence and used to conclude that God exists in the *Third Meditation,* cannot be absolutely certain, since the premises of the argument for God's existence are not absolutely certain and are based on the conclusion, which gives birth to what is known as the Cartesian Circle (Skirry, 2008).

In the same *Third Meditation* (Descartes, 1968c: pp. 116–118), mention is made of the ideas called 'judgements' subject to being true or false, because 'it is only in making a judgement that the resemblance, conformity or correspondence of the idea to things themselves is affirmed or denied' (Skirry, 2008).

Judgement is dealt with depth in the *Fourth Meditation* (Descartes, 1968c: pp. 133–135) and described as a faculty of the mind resulting from the interaction of the faculties of intellect and will. Descartes (1968c: p. 139) asserts that the intellect is limited in humans and that humans do not know everything. This limitation, combined with one's will, is the source of human error.

Mind–body relation is discussed in the *Fifth Meditation* (Descartes, 1968c: pp. 150–169). According to Skirry (2008), Descartes argues that (1) mind is a substance (*res cogitans*); (2) it can be clearly understood without any other substance, including bodies, and (3) that God could create a mental substance all by itself without any other created substance.

Mind and body[13] are argued to be distinct[14] (namely, mind–body dualism or Cartesian Split) by Descartes through two arguments: (1) the mind is understood as a thinking, non-extended thing, whereas the body is understood as an extended, non-thinking thing; and (2) the nature of body is divisible into parts, while the nature of mind is not composed of parts and is indivisible (Skirry, 2008).

The mind–body or dualism debate opened by Descartes posed the problem of how the soul and the body causally interact. Therefore, the desire to avoid dualism has been the 'driving force' of much of contemporary philosophical work (Nagel, 2005: p. 221).

In the *Sixth Meditation* (Descartes, 1968c: p. 150), the question of the existence of material things is discussed, about which Descartes expresses his view that 'I know already that [material things] may exist in so far as they are considered as the object of geometrical proofs, seeing that in this way I perceive them very clearly and distinctly.'

Skirry (2008) elaborates on this view and explains:

> Descartes recognizes that sensation is a passive faculty that receives sensory ideas from something else. But what is this 'something else'? According to the Causal Adequacy Principle of the *Third Meditation*, this cause must have at least as much reality either formally or eminently as is contained objectively in the sensory idea produced. It, therefore, must be either Descartes himself, a body or extended thing that actually has what is contained objectively in the sensory idea, or God or some creature nobler than a body, who would possess that reality eminently. It cannot be Descartes, since he has no control over these ideas. It cannot be God or some other creature ..., for if this were so, then God would be a deceiver, because the very strong inclination to believe that bodies are the cause of sensory ideas would then be wrong; and if it is wrong, there is no faculty that could discover the error. Accordingly, God would be the source of the mistake and not human beings, which means that he would be a deceiver. So bodies must be the cause of the ideas of them, and therefore bodies exist externally to the mind.

Ultimately Descartes aspires to achieve the unity of science and proposes four rules: (1) intuition or the use of 'the pure light of the mind' as opposed to the evidence of the senses or of the imagination; (2) the rule of analysis, enjoining us to decompose complex issues into issues as simple as possible; (3) the rule of synthesis, as applied to the truths reached by the two preceding rules; and (4) the rule based on deduction supported by memory. However, in order to avoid the failure or defect of memory, the link between the first principles and their ultimate consequences is established in deductive reasoning, in which Cogito is a first principle from which Descartes will deduce all that follows (Sutcliffe, 1968: pp. 15–17).

Basart Muñoz (2004: p. 106) concludes that Descartes' objective is the method, not a specific strategy but a general procedure that may have validity for each and every issue.

### Locke: empiricism

Woolhouse (1997) asserts that John Locke's opinion about our limited and finite understanding is optimistic in the sense that for Locke 'God has provided for us sufficiently' and 'what we cannot know we have no need to know'.

Within this limit, Locke (1997: p. 109) presents a systematic account of the nature and activities of human understanding, leading to empiricism in that 'all our knowledge is founded; and...ultimately derive(s) itself (from)...Our observation employed...about external sensible objects or about the internal operations of our minds...(it) is that which supplies our understanding...'

Locke (1997: p. 467) defines knowledge as 'the perception of the connexion and agreement, or disagreement and repugnancy of any of our ideas'.

Locke (1997) maintains that no human knowledge is innate and that all our ideas are derived from experience. Such ideas are only the materials of reason and knowledge, but knowledge itself has not been 'made out to us by our senses' but is a product of reason connecting these ideas. Thus, Locke's 'empiricism' about ideas is combined with rationalism (Honderich, 2005: pp. 526–527).

What experience provides is not knowledge, but its materiality or ideas (perception, memory, association) presented to us in experience. Knowledge is the result of the interplay between ideas and our understanding. And, knowledge is not the result of mere observation of empirical correlations among our experience-given ideas, as this can only lead to belief or opinion (Woolhouse, 1997, 2005).

In support of empiricism, Locke (1997: p. 59) rejects the *innate principles* which the 'soul receives in its very first being; and brings into the world with it'. Among such principles supposed to be innate to the human mind are moral precepts and speculative axioms such as the law of non-contradiction (that is, it is not possible that something be both true and not true at the same time and in the same context).

Locke denies any special source other than the use of our natural faculty of reason, which means that there is no epistemic priority or 'first principles' (Woolhouse, 1997: p. xiv).

Derived from Aristotle, Scholastic philosophy believes in 'first principles' such as (1) a belief in substantial forms and essences, (2) an insistence on syllogism, (3) the acceptance of Aristotle as an unexamined authority (Woolhouse, 1997).

The first principles in Aristotle and Scholastic philosophy serve as the starting-point for 'demonstrative' knowledge, namely, 'the demonstration from certain starting-points that the property is a characteristic of human beings as such' (Woolhouse, 1997: p. xv).

## Attempt at synthesis

The dichotomy between rationalism and empiricism led Kant (Allison, 2006; Bird, 2006a, 2006b; Guyer, 2000; Kant, 2003; Schönfeld, 2006; Sellars, 1967; Waxman, 2006; Wood, 2006) to carry out an attempt at synthesis. He accepted that 'the basis of knowledge is experience but did not accept the argument that experience is the sole source of all knowledge' (Nonaka and Takeuchi, 1995: p. 24). According to Kant (2003), we can only guess the thing-in-itself through our sensory perception that captures the phenomena.

The polarities or dialectics perceived between two opposing arguments regarding schools of thought have led Westerners to continually question both induction and deduction as insufficient for arriving at all truth, and therefore it is the synthesis of those who compare schools of thought that has led to advances in knowledge in the West, that is a built-in need for compare-and-contrast dialectics has potentially led to the method being the answer.[15]

## Review of Asian thought

### India: Buddhism and epistemology

Perhaps no other classical philosophical tradition, East or West, offers a more complex and counter-intuitive account of mind and mental phenomena than Buddhism … they do not associate mental phenomena with the activity of a substantial, independent, and enduring self or agent. Rather, Buddhist theories of mind centre on the doctrine of no-self (Pāli *anatta*, Skt. *anātma*), which postulates that human beings are reducible to the physical and psychological constituents and processes which comprise them. (Coseru, 2010)

*Theravada and Mahayana*

After the Second Council about 100 years after the death of the Buddha, eighteen or twenty schools arose, of which those that taught that the elements, namely, the five aggregates (skandhāh[16]), are real entities, were called Hīnayāna or Theravāda (for example, the Sarvāstivādin). To combat these the *prajña* appeared, giving rise to branches of the Mahāyāna including Mādhyamika and Yogācāra (Japanese English Buddhist Dictionary, 1999: p. 23r).

Theravada has a widespread following in Sri Lanka and Southeast Asia, and Mahayana is found throughout East Asia.[17]

Based on his three concepts employed for the analysis of Buddhism, Tominaga Nakamoto[18] (1973), an 18th-century scholar in Japan, called into question the veracity of the Mahayana school of Buddhism. Tominaga's (1973) three concepts, especially *kajo* (putting something on another), were used to explain the way in which new theories are added to go beyond previous ones. This led to the conclusion that the Mahayana sutras were created after the Buddha's death.

Thus, Kato (1981b: pp. 132–133) cites the development of 'limitless knowledge' to 'neither think nor know' or the 'conception of non-existence' to be superseded by 'neither conception nor non-conception'.

In essence, the kajo theory holds that newer theories try to demonstrate their supremacy over old ones by adding new components, which means that the documentary evidence for new elements is likely to be even newer ones (Sueki, 2003: p. 46). Despite this, however, the Mahayana School exerted an immense influence on the way of life and thought of people in Japan, China and Korea. This continued in spite of the fact that in China, Buddhism would eventually be dropped from the main current of ideas after the Middle Ages, and in Korea, government oppression during the Joseon Dynasty (1392–1897) would eventually stymie its vigour. This was in strong contrast to Japan, where Buddhism continued to influence the population (Sueki, 2003: p. 147).

## Madhyamika and Yogacara

The two major groups in the Mahayana School of Buddhism are (1) Mādhyamika, founded by Nāgārjuna[19]; and (2) Yogācāra, founded by Maitreya[20] (Nagao, 1967: p. 44).

## Madhyamika

Nagarjuna's Madhyamika school revolves around the idea of Śūnyatāvāda (Nagao, 1978: p. 4). Śūnya or śūnyatā may be translated as 'void, nothingness or relativity'; it does not deny the concept of existence as such, but maintains that all existence and the constituent elements (skandhas) that make it up are dependent on causation. Sunyata denies the possibility of any form of phenomenal static existence (Japanese English Buddhist Dictionary, 1999: p. 204r).

Gyonen[21] (2006: p. 32) gives voice to this idea of voidness or emptiness by stating that:

[i]n the way that there is no water within a pot, there is no self (pudgala or ātman) within the five skandhas. This then is insight into the emptiness of the self... there is insight into selflessness. In the way that there is no substantial reality in the nature of the pot, all the dharmas of the five skandhas are only provisional names. This then is insight into the emptiness of the dharmas.

Nagarjuna (1995: p. 2) articulates this as 'whatever is dependently arisen is unceasing, unborn, unannihilated, not permanent, not coming, not going'. Garfield (1995: p. 101) interprets this verse and holds that:

[d]ependent arising amounts to emptiness, and emptiness amounts to non-existence... While... Nagarjuna defends the conventional existence of phenomena, he will urge that none of them ultimately exist–that none of them exist independently of convention with identities... that they possess in themselves... nothing ultimately is born, and from the ultimate standpoint there is nothing to cease.

*Yogacara and Vijñapti-matrata*

For the purposes of this book, and regarding cognition and cognitive processes, Yogacara is more relevant to our objective of carrying out a literature review, as evidenced by the fact that it is also called Vijñapti-mātratā or Consciousness-only. This can be summarized as 'the doctrine that all phenomena are produced from seeds (shūji) stored in the ālaya-vijñāna (Japanese English Buddhist Dictionary, 1999: p. 369l); and as a view that all existing things in the world are empty and their existence is a mere illusion lodged in one's consciousness (Nakamura et al., 2000: p. 810r).

The Buddhist's credo is that 'all is pain and all is ephemeral'.[22] The fundamental obstacle to a life of liberation from the sufferings of this world, then, is ignorance. This requires systematic clarification of the mechanisms of ignorance as well as of the process of liberation from it (Cook, 1999: p. 2; Vasubandhu, 1999a, 1999b; Hsüan-tsang,[23] 1999), his commentarist, attempt to answer this question by demonstrating that the seemingly real external objects of perception (dharma) and the seemingly real self (ātman) that perceives these objects are mental fabrications that do not exist apart from consciousness (Cook, 1999: p. 3).

Hsuan-tsang[24] (1999: p. 10) argues that the self and dharmas are metaphors based on nothing but false delusions and that an external realm is established on the basis of delusion. All conditioned phenomena are produced from ālaya-vijñāna, the stored consciousness (Vasubandhu, 1999a), which stores the shūji (seeds) of all dharmas, falsely taken as one's atman or soul by individuals (Japanese English Buddhist Dictionary, 1999: p. 11r).

Consciousness is a constant interplay between the latent container consciousness with all the defiled seeds of past action, and the manifested, active consciousnesses of thinking, perceiving, and sensing, which bring to maturation those seeds and in turn plant new karmic seeds in the container consciousness (Keenan, 2003: p. xiv). Therefore, all the various dharmas are cognizing-only (consciousness-only), and there is no dharma that exists outside of the mind (Gyonen, 2006: p. 68).

The container consciousness appropriates all the physical sense organs and is the support for taking up all the experiences of rebirth (Asanga, 2003: p. 14). Therefore, the teaching of Buddhism centres, through meditations on consciousness-only, on the realization that all dharmas or phenomena are illusions and the self is a fabrication of the container consciousness to destroy the seeds of rebirths, which could only be achieved by bodhisattva, conscious beings of or for the great intelligence, or enlightenment (Ui, 1974: p. 429).

Having reviewed the overall panorama of Buddhism, in order to touch more on cognition within it, a comparison of two aspects of it are made below: logic and intuition or anti-intellection. The first concerns Indian syllogism and the second, Zen Buddhism.

*Buddhism: 'Intellection' – its logic and epistemology*

Indian logic (hetu-vidyā) is for enlightening others in addition to self-enlightenment:

> the methods are of two kinds: the fivefold formula and the threefold formula. The latter was perfected by Dignaga ... According to the former, the formula consists of: proposition (pratijñā), reason (hetu), example (dṛṣṭānta), application (upanaya), and conclusion (nigamana). For example: I) A voice is impermanent; II) because it is produced by causes; III) it is like ceramics; IV) ceramics are produced by causes and are impermanent–in the same manner a voice is also; V) therefore, a voice is impermanent. In the threefold formula, IV) and V) are omitted. (Japanese English Buddhist Dictionary, 1999: p. 139r)

There are two concepts essential for Buddhist logic – (1) trairūpya (the triple character of evidence) and (2) apoha (exclusion) – and they are related to the problems of inductive logic and those of meaning and universals (Bimal K. Matilaland Masson, 1986: p. ix).

Dignāga (陳那), the great Buddhist logician, a native of southern India, living in circa 500 or 550 AD, founder of the new logic,[25] a member of Vasubandhu's school,[26] proposed a theory of inference that could be stated as follows:

> When we infer some fact or item or characteristic belonging to some object on the basis of our knowledge of some other characteristic belonging to the same object, the second characteristic ('liṅga' or 'hetu', 'inferential sign' or 'indicator-reason') must have the 'triple-character'. The first characteristic is called the 'inferable'... or the fact to be proven or the characteristic to be established as belonging to the object in question. The object in question is called the pakṣa... the subject of the inferred conclusion... or intended object... Similarly I shall call the 'indicator-reason' the obvious or evidential characteristic... the 'triple-character' of the evidential characteristic... is:
>
> 1. The evidential characteristic must belong to the intended object.
> 2. It must belong to (at least) one similar object.
> 3. It must not belong to any dissimilar object. (Bimal Krishna Matilal, 1986: p. 1)

The Apoha (exclusion) theory of meaning points out that 'this is a cow' does not assert the cowhood of the subject, but it denies that anything apart from cowhood can be a predicate of the subject (Matilal, 1986: p. 2).

The Buddhist view of knowledge distinguishes two kinds of knowledge – perceptual and non-perceptual, both of which are understood to be episodes of awareness within us; however, there is no ownership of such episodes, for an individual is a mere aggregate of such episodes (Matilal, 1986: p. 3).

Exclusion theory is connected with the confirmation of induction. Dignāga confirms that all ravens are black and so each green leaf, being a non-black non-raven, should mean that all non-black things are non-ravens (equivalent to saying that all ravens are black) (Matilal, 1986: p. 10). For Matilal (1986: 10), Dignāga's response that 'all ravens are black' may not imply 'all non-black things are non-ravens'.

## Influence of Buddhism in Japan

In Japan, there were 73,000 Buddhist temples in 1959 according to Oda (2003: p. 44), which compares to 22,700 churches plus 905 monasteries in Spain as of 2007.[27] Assuming that the number of temples did not change since 1959, and the population estimate for 2010 of Japan being 127,430,000,[28] each temple in Japan has 1,746 people associated with it. With Spain's population estimate in the same period being 45,989,016,[29] each church (including monasteries) has 1,948 people associated with it; that is a similar level of population density for each temple as for each church. From this, we can broadly assume that access to the influence of religious facilities in Japan (Eastern Asia) and Spain (Western Europe) might have been similar.

The classification of Buddhist schools with significant presence is shown in Table 2.2.

The quadrants correspond to the schools that have followers in Japan, of which there are eight: (a) Kusha or Abhidharma School, (b) Jojitsu or Satyasiddhi School, (c) Ritsu or Vinaya School, (d) Hosso, Faxiang or Dharmalaksana School, (e) Sanron Sanlun, Madhyamika, or Middle School, (f) Tendai o Tiantai school, (g) Kegon or Huayan School, and (h) Shingon School, and two new additions, namely, (i) Zen School and (j) Jodo or Pure Land School (Gyonen, 2006). The Nichiren School is not included in Gyonen's analysis, perhaps because it was considered to be a part of Tendai School at the time of his writing.

Kusha School may correspond to quadrant (1) of Table 1, Jojitsu School to quadrant (2), Hosso, Ritsu and Sanron Schools to (3)–(5). Tendai, Kegon, Shingon, Zen and Jodo Schools to (5) and (6).

The distribution of temples by school in Table 2.3 is an estimate by Oda (2003).

From Table 2.3 it is obvious that as many as 77 per cent of Buddhist temples in Japan belong to the Jodo (40 per cent), Zen (28 per cent) and Nichiren (9 per cent) Schools with the remainder corresponding to the Tendai and Shingon Schools. Given that the parishioner system in Japan was institutionalized in the Tokugawa period (The World Great Encyclopaedia (Sekai Hyakka Jiten), 1998), it is likely that the number of temples may reflect that of parishioners or followers.

Therefore, we may not be too wide of the mark if we conclude that the Jodoshu or Pure Land School and the Zen School wield the greatest influence in the religious mind of the Japanese.

*Table 2.2* Classification of Buddhist schools by Ui (1974)

| | Teaching of existence (youmen) | Teaching of emptiness (kongmen) | Madhyamika (yiyouyi-wumen) | Ekayana (yicheng) |
|---|---|---|---|---|
| Jirikikyo (Theravada) | (1) Sarvastivada | (2) Satyasiddhi sect (Jap. Jojitsu-shu), based upon the Satyasiddhisastra of Harivarman | | |
| Tarikikyo (Mahayana) | (3) Vidya-matrasiddhisastra (zhengweishilun) | (4) Mahayana-samparigraha-sastra (The Summary of Great Vehicle) | (5) Mahayana-sraddhotpadasastra (Awakening of Faith), The Sanlun, Madhyamika, or Middle School | (6) Tiantai, Huayian, Shingon, Zen, Pure Land |

*Source:* Based on (Ui 1974: pp. 120–121).

*Table 2.3*   Distribution of Buddhist temples by school

| | No of Buddhist temples as of 1959 | |
|---|---|---|
| Tendaishu, Shingonshu | 16,718 | 23% |
| Jodoshu, Shinshu | 29,324 | 40% |
| Zen | 20,694 | 28% |
| Nichiren | 6,233 | 9% |
| Others | 263 | 0% |
| Total | 73,232 | 100% |

*Source*: Oda (2003: p. 43).

## *Jodo and Jodo Shinshu: Pure Land School*

Kato (1981a: 218–219) stresses that the Pure Land and Zen Schools are branches of Buddhism that developed in China and that Pure Land Buddhism further evolved in Japan independent of 'its Chinese parent'. In addition, Zen 'inspired some of the greatest masterpieces of Buddhist doctrinal writing ever produced in the Japanese language'.

Pure Land Buddhism revolves around 'the desire to be reborn after death into the Western Paradise, the concentration of belief in the Amida Buddha, and the emphasis on the Nembutsu as a means of achieving rebirth' (Kato, 1981a: p. 219). Nembutsu means 'adoration of the Buddha of Infinite Light' (Suzuki, 2002: p. 145).

Honen (1971), the founder of Japanese Pure Land Buddhism, made a single great contribution to Pure Land thought through his doctrine that 'the Nembutsu was … the only and best one' for achieving rebirth in the Western Paradise, 'rendering all other devotions unnecessary' (Kato, 1981a: p. 220).

Amida made his 'original vow' to save all those who prayed for their rebirth in Western Paradise by invoking his name (Gómez, 1996: p. 71). Shinran, Honen's disciple and the founder of Jodo Shinshu, emphasizes that salvation depends on Amida's vow to save, and not on deeds conducted by men to achieve the rebirth (Shinran, 1972), similar to the credo in Christianity that salvation depends on the will of Almighty God (Kato, 1981a: p. 223).

Overall Pure Land Buddhism is similar to Zen Buddhism in that its philosophy is not speculative, but more intuitive, not intellectual but more practical (Yanagi, 1997).

### *Buddhism: 'intuition' – Zen Buddhism*

Citing Rudolf Otto, Jung (1964) contends that 'Zen is anything but a philosophy in the Western sense of the word' and qualifies its central issue, *satori* or enlightenment, as *mysterium ineffabile*.

Suzuki (1949: p. 230) defines satori as 'an intuitive looking into the nature of things in contraposition to the analytical or logical understanding of it' and emphasizes that 'with satori our entire surroundings are viewed from quite an unexpected angle of perception', suggesting the possibility of a kind of reviewing or re-/de-codification of one's worldview.

Herrigel (1984: p. 16) conjectures that the *unio mystica* and detachment (*abegescheidenheit*) advocated by Meister Eckhart, a German mystic, are one and the same with satori. Meister Eckhart (n.d.: 343) equates true detachment with 'a mind as little moved by what befalls, by joy and sorrow, honour and disgrace, as a broad mountain by a gentle breeze'.

For Suzuki (2002: p. 11), detachment is 'pure nothingness' (and satori) seemingly the same concept as 'suchness' or 'thusness' (tathatā).

Suzuki (2000: pp. 343–344) enumerates three means of realization by which to reach it: (1) practical, (2) intellectual, (3) intuitional. The third method of appealing to our intuitive faculty is Zen and it 'refuses to resort to verbal explanations, or logical analysis, or to ritualism' proposing to 'grasp it without intellection, imagination, accumulation of merit, etc.' Buddhists always practised Dhyāna (meditation), but Zen does it more systematically (Suzuki, 2000: p. 345).

## China: Confucianist epistemology: Zhu Xi and Wang Yang-Ming

### Confucianism, Taoism and Buddhism

In his book, written in an ornate classic Chinese entitled *Indicators of the Goals of the Three Teachings*, Kukai (1972), an eighth/ninth-century Japanese Buddhist monk, refers to and compares three teachings as the main ideologies of his days in Eastern Asia, namely, Confucianism, Taoism and Buddhism, deeming them to be self-contained systems of thought.

However, the influence of Taoism was limited to China and never exerted a serious influence in Japan[30] despite the fact that Taoist titles such as *Zhuangzi*[31] and *Huinanzi*[32] enjoyed vast popularity in Japan.

As to Korea, 'during the Joseon Dynasty...Confucianism was the primary system of belief among the scholarly yangban classes and generals. Koreans historically have found religions natural and easy...thus (they) restrained Buddhism, maintained shamanism in rural areas, but encouraged Confucianism for its use in administration and social regulation' (Wikipedia, 2010a).

In fact, Taylor (2004: p. 85) argues that 'in societies in which Confucianism played a part, there was virtually no aspect of society unaffected by Confucian teachings and values'.

Accordingly, we will focus here on Confucianism, with special regard to its epistemological methods, and more specifically on the Songxue and Wang Yangming Schools of Neo-Confucianism, as they exerted a profound influence on metaphysical thinking in Eastern Asia, according to the writings of Confucianist scholars such as Fujiwara Seika, Hayashi Razan, Yamaga Soko,

Nakai Toju, Arai Hakuseki, Ito Jinsai, Ogyu Sorai and more (some of whom are referred to below) (Tomoeda, 1971).

## The theory of Tiyong

Before entering upon the actual disquisition, we would like to call attention to the particularity of a Chinese Confucianist philosophy called *tiyong*,[33] that should not be confused with a causal relationship. According to the Buddhist Asvaghosha (2001: 83), it is like 'water showing the symptoms of disturbance when stirred up by the wind' with the wind and the disturbance being the cause and the effect, respectively. In contrast, the Confucianist tiyong relationship points to the water (ti) in relation to the disturbance (yong), in that it concerns the substance and effect, or the substance and phenomenon (Shimada, 2004: pp. 3–4).

Shimada (2004: pp. 9–10) conjectures that the implications of the tiyong-based way of thinking are, for example, that (1) pantheism fits better than monotheism, which may presuppose a cause-effect relationship to the exclusion of a reliance on an absolute godhead, and (2) this creates a trend of relying on a kind of circular argument despite the development of a highly metaphysical thought system such as Neo-Confucianism, mentioned below.

## Songxue or Neo-Confucianism

Wong (2009) argues that Confucius and Mencius did not feel the need to explain the assumption on which the reality of the world is founded, but the influence of Buddhism forced the Confucian scholars into developing a metaphysical system to account for the reality of the world by proposing two concepts: a generative substantial force, qi[34] (Japanese: ki) and the rational principle (Chinese: li;[35] Japanese: ri) (of which we will detail more later).

This new development was called Neo-Confucian[36] philosophy or Songxue,[37] 'the learning of the Song dynasty', xinglixue,[38] the learning of human nature and principle', xinxue,[39] 'the learning of the mind', and lixue,[40] the learning of principle' (Wong, 2009).

## Songxue

Songxue expounded by Zhu Xi[41] following Zhou Lianqi,[42] Brothers Cheng,[43] comprises *in grosso modo* five aspects: (1) the ontological theory of li and qi;[44] (2) the ethical theory of xing ji li;[45] (3) the epistemological and methodological theory of jujing jiuli;[46] (4) the hermeneutics of the Classics; and (5) politics (Shimada, 2004: p. 79).

In order to centre on the relevant points for us, we will focus below on the first and the third aspects.

With respect to the first aspect, all things are brought into being by the union of two universal aspects of reality: qi, sometimes translated as vital (or physical, material) force; and li, sometimes translated as rational principle (or law) (Wikipedia, 2010d).

Qi and li[47] operate together in mutual dependence and these two aspects are manifested in the creation of substantial entities (Wikipedia, 2010d). When their activity is waxing, it is in the yang energy mode; when their activity is waning, it is in the yin energy mode (Shimada, 2004: p. 81). In the process of the waxing and waning, the alternation of these fundamental vibrations, the so-called five elements[48] (fire, water, wood, metal and earth) evolve. When the yang energy concentrates, it becomes wood and fire elements, and when the yin concentrates, it becomes metal and water elements (Shimada, 2004: p. 81).

The combination of the five elements determines the disposition and character of everything, including time and seasons, since, for example, the seasons with strong yang mode are spring and summer and those with strong yin mode are autumn and winter (Shimada, 2004: p. 82).

We now address the third aspect, namely, the theory of jujing jiuli. Some interpret that, according to Zhu Xi's epistemology, knowledge and action were indivisible components of truly intelligent activity (Wikipedia, 2010d), while Shimada (2004: p. 101) categorically states that Songxue concerns a method of searching for a way to become a holy man[49] or an unworldly person (or sage).

There are two ways to achieve this: (1) jujing and (2) juili, namely, pursuit of high ethical standing (subjective option) and pursuit of intellectual standing (objective option) (Shimada, 2004: p. 101).

Jujing – cherishing a reverential feeling and being easy about small matters (Legge, 1986: Book VI Yung Yey) – signifies the focusing of the mind on the keeping of one's inborn nature (Shimada, 2004: p. 102). Kaibara Ekiken, a 17th-century Japanese Confucianist, contends that qi is all and li, depending upon it, disappears upon death. Therefore, there 'exists no duality between li and man's endowment' from which it follows that 'man is not imperfect, in that there is no perfect Principle (li) against which his imperfections can be judged', meaning that man is ethically perfect (Kato, 1981b: p. 57).

Jiuli – reaching one's destiny by understanding li perfectly and exhausting one's potential (Takada and Goto, 2000: p. ii 287) – which is explained as *gewu zhizhi*,[50] namely, the perfection of knowledge depends upon the investigation of things, by Zhu Xi in his commentary on the Great Learning (Fu, 1995: p. 23).

'How to investigate and what these things are is the source of much debate. To Zhu Xi, the things are moral principles and the investigation involves paying attention to everything in both books and affairs because "moral principles are quite inexhaustible"' (Wikipedia, 2010d).

In his commentary on the Great Learning known as 'the Supplementary Comment on Gewu', Zhu Xi (Fu, 1995: p. 23) expresses his idea:

[i]f I intend to perfect my knowledge, I have to study assiduously the ways of things. All minds are so keen that there is not one mind that

does not have senses and perceptions inborn, and all things have their way. If one does not study things diligently, his knowledge will be limited and he will be not able to understand things fully and thoroughly. So if we as beginners start education with The Great Learning, when in contact with things, we must use the knowledge we have already acquired to study the way of all things until we reach the acme of knowledge...

Shimada (2004: p. 104) deduces from this that li is not only the internal rationality of man but also the external rationality of the nature between which there is continuum, and therefore that to become a holy man signifies the possession of li itself inside himself.

Suzuki's (1995: p. 227) interpretation is (1) that the nature of men comprises li pointing to the absolute goodness that is the pristine nature of men and qi that can embody different emotions and sentiments; (2) that therefore men are good viewed from li but qi can move them away from this goodness depending on how qi is formed; (3) that moral virtue ought to be an effort to move away from qi to return to li; and (4) that men must build up their moral character by gewu zhizhi.

Kato (1999: p.jo 464) recapitulates Songxue by stating that Songxue offers a theoretical support to secularism, since it is composed of li and qi that are considered to exist within this world and that dominate the world, and it therefore does not require any supernatural power or existence and may give a systematic explanation to the way of the world.

## Songxue's influence in Japan

Wong (2009) points out the Neo-Confucianist influence on the belief held in Japan and 'shared generally by orthodox and heterodox thinkers, that education, whether practical or discursive or both, was a necessary ingredient in the life of all persons who might hope to realize their full potential'. This resulted in 'the proliferation of education in early-modern Japan, producing mid-19th-century literacy rates comparable to those of the most advanced Western nations'.

Apart from Kaibara Ekiken, others include Ito Jinsai (1627–1705), Ogyu Sorai (1666–1728) and Arai Hakuseki (1657–1725) as some of the outstanding Confucianists in the Tokugawa-period Japan (17th to 19th centuries) (Kato, 1981b: pp. 54–70).

Kato (1981b: pp. 48–50) supports the idea that it was in 17th-century Japan that the 'Japanization' of the highly metaphysical Songxue took place. This consisted of discarding its metaphysical element and using its conceptual tools in the study of the natural sciences, ethics, politics and economics.

*Wang Yang-Ming School*

Wang Yang-Ming[51] raises several objections to Songxue (Shimada, 2004: pp. 127–128):

1. How can one attain the understanding of all and everything despite Zhu Xi's theory of gewu zhizhi (Wang, 1972: pp. xia 1 II–III)?
2. If we believe in what Zhu Xi says, do mind and things, or heart and li become two separate and opposed things? How does this relate to the real meaning of Learning?
3. Zhu Xi defines the mind (xin) as something that is always subject and never object, but if, on the other hand, as Zhu Xi emphasizes, the mind, despite having an absolute existence, needs to be perfected by external 'hearings and learnings', it does not seem to have such an absolute existence (Wang, 1972: pp. zhong 6–7).

As Wang Yangming's maximum contribution, Feng (1989: pp. 32–33) extols the concept of *zhiliangzhi*,[52] namely, the attainment of good knowledge.

Following this line of thinking, Kondo (1972: pp. 7–14) argues that, for Wang Yanming, the problem of Songxue is its separation of xin (mind) and li and its search of li outside one's mind. In its lieu, Wang Yangming pursues the subjective side of Zhu Xi's philosophy.

Kondo (1972: pp. 7–14) enumerates seven components of Wang's philosophy, of which we will refer to four as relevant to our literature review on cognition:

1. **Attainment of the good knowledge**
   Based on Mencius' (Legge, 1986: p. 943) statement that 'the ability possessed by men without having been acquired by learning is intuitive ability (that is *liangzhi*[53] or *liangneng*[54])' Wang attributes to men the possession of good knowledge (liangzhi) which he considers to be a natural instinct inherent and inborn in men, which allows them to discern the good from the bad; unlike Zhu Xi, who viewed men's minds as being subject to improvement, Wang affirms that lianzhi is perfect from the beginning.

2. **Gewu zhizhi**
   Whereas Zhu Xi insists on the attainment of knowledge by means of the search for the li of things, Wang Yangming argues against him on the grounds that if you follow Zhu Xi's indication you may never be able to attain knowledge and therefore never will attain perfection of body and mind. Accordingly, Wang interprets gewu as the correction of things, meaning the corrections of wrongs when attention is turned to them. This signifies more a process of mental and spiritual exercise. Wang interprets zhizhi as the realization of knowledge equipping you

for the discernment of good and bad without being hindered by vicious desires.

3. **Xinjili**[55]

Wang asserts that xin or mind is the same as li and denies the existence of li outside of your mind, in contrast to Zhu Xi's belief that there are mind's li and things' li.

4. **Knowledge as action**[56]

'Wang rejects the investigation of knowledge (as is the case with Songxue) based on the traditional view of Chinese thought that once one had gained knowledge, he had a duty to put that knowledge into action. Wang believed that only through simultaneous action could one gain knowledge, and he denied all other ways of gaining it. To him, there was no way to use knowledge after gaining it because he believed that knowledge and action were unified as one. Any knowledge that had been gained and *then put* into action was considered delusion or false' (Wikipedia, 2010c).

*Influence of Wang Yangming School in Japan*[57]

Wong (2009) maintains that:

An important legacy of Confucian philosophy in modern Japanese history derives from Confucian understandings of the philosophy of history. This is evident in the transition from the Tokugawa period, dominated politically by a samurai regime led by a shogun, to the Meiji period (1868–1912), billed at least as a restoration of imperial rule. Rather than assuming that history was progressing ever forward to incrementally better levels, Confucians tended to see ideals in the past... The political transformation giving rise to the Meiji imperial regime, at least in terms of its philosophical presentation as a return to an ancient, supposedly more ideal model, was characteristically Confucian...

Among the revolutionaries of the Meiji Restoration under the influence of the School of Wang Yangming are Yoshida Shoin, Saigo Takamori, Takasugi Shinsaku and others (Wikipedia, 2010c) who followed the teachings of Nakae Toju, Kumazawa Banzan and Miwa Shissai (Otagiand Terada, 1998: p. 367).

Shimada (2001) cited by Otagi and Terada (1998: pp. 364–365) opines of the Wang Yangming School (1) that before Wang's School men's worldly desires were an impediment for them to reach the status of holy men, which Wang considered unnecessary and accepted; (2) that the equality of men qua possessors of liangzhi, which urges men to adopt an active stance towards life; (3) that the focus on liangzhi liberates the constraints traditionally imposed on technology and on free intellectual activities; (4) that a critical view of traditionally accepted authority has been born, since the belief in the goodness of your li residing inside you ceases to accept an external authority; (5) that heterodoxy is now viewed more positively, if it is based on liangzhi; and (6) that the consideration of the Classic Books, until now considered to be the maximum authority, ceases to exist, since learning does not mean reading and interpreting them but rather bringing yourself to the reality of the li residing internally.

This contrasts with the situation in China where Ming loyalists blamed individualistic decadence on Wang Yangming for 'causing an internal enervation of Chinese society' (Fogel, 1984: pp. 159–160). Even at the present time, mainland China seems to be not much in favour of the Wang Yangming School, due principally to its subjective Mentalism or xinjili (which goes counter to Materialism) (Otagiand Terada, 1998).

### China: deduction or induction?

Before concluding this part of our literature review on the philosophical underpinnings of cognition in Asia and the West, we wish to discuss two additional questions: the commensurability, or lack of it, of Chinese and Western thoughts, and the inferential method in China.

Are Chinese and Western philosophies commensurable or not? Wong (2009) holds that:

[O]ne common portrait of the difference between the Chinese and Western traditions posits ... Chinese philosophy is 'wisdom' literature, composed primarily of stories and sayings designed to move the audience to adopt a way of life or to confirm its adoption of that way of life. Western philosophy is systematic argumentation and theory. Is there such a difference? One reason to think so is the fairly widespread wariness in Chinese philosophy of a discursive rationality that operates by deduction of conclusions about the particular from high-level generalizations. The seventeenth chapter of the *Zhuangzi*[58] notes that ... Tang and Wu were kings who fought and conquered. But Duke Bo also acted on that rule, fought, and lost ... it is impossible to establish 'any constant rule.' Inspired by the achievement of insight or wisdom in some particular cases, we create general rules that we believe will work for many other cases in the future ... Confucians are more willing to articulate their teachings in the form of principles, but such principles seem to function as designators of values or general considerations that ought to be given weight in judgments about what to do ... The best rules lose applicability in unusual circumstances ... there are no 'super-principles' to supply ready answers. The appropriate resolution to each conflict depends very much on the situation.

From the above citation we may conjecture that the inference is conducted on the basis of deduction from high-level generalizations applied to particular phenomena. Yoshikawa (1971: p. 565) asserts that Confucianist scholars derive their theories and thoughts from ancient Chinese thinking, especially from Confucius's thinking, by means of deduction.

However, at the same time we may also conjecture that such an inferential process is not actually grounded on a purely deductive method, but rather on an inductive one, within the framework of the general guidance or justification provided by the principles.

Ziporyn (n.d.: pp. 2–4) may provide a clue in this regard by her reference to the lack of two-tier metaphysics in the Chinese tradition. She refers to this in the sense that the Platonic type of logic is based upon rules and their instantiation, that is, a transcendent realm of determinate forms and eternal normative principles. This, she argues, makes it difficult for European philosophers to grasp the meaning of Chinese philosophy.

Ziporyn (n.d.: pp. 4–6) wonders how 'did the traditional Chinese thinkers conceive of regularities in nature and of the binding normativity of behavioural patterns without reference to an immaterial and immutable realm?'

This 'bewilderment' (according to Ziporyn) may point to the basic difference in the inferential process between Westerners and the Chinese (or East Asians).

## Conclusion and discussion

This chapter has afforded ground for subsequent chapters of our literature review by comparing some of the roots of Western and Eastern philosophical thought regarding cognition and knowledge.

As anticipated at the beginning of this chapter, Western thought comprises different approaches and shows different degrees of dependence on deduction and/or induction. Empiricism and rationalism tend to advocate deduction as being of prime importance, opting for the construal of 'reality' from observations and empirical data. This is in contrast to other more inductive Western approaches, where emphasis is placed on purely theoretical speculation to create new knowledge. We argue that the tensions created by these dialectically opposed philosophies, and the simple process of juxtaposing them in the first place, have given rise to high expectations of exactitude with regard to deductive processes in the West, while somewhat de-legitimizing exploration with inductive processes.

On the other hand, we find the Easterners to be generally more inductive, since even the highly speculative Buddhist thinking born in India ended up being more focused on universal issues such as 'balance', 'moral and religious values', and 'the way of all things'. Empirical data, or particulars, were used as a conclusion in the case of the Zen School and Pure Land Buddhism, not only in Japan but also in China and Korea. Likewise, the highly speculative Songxue founded by Zhuxi led to the more inductive and practical Ming Yang School.

Chapter 3 will elaborate further on the issue of induction and deduction.

# 3
# Literature Review: Epistemological Perspective – Inductive and Deductive Thinking

## Introduction: inductive and deductive logic in management thinking

In Chapter 2, we analysed some of the differences between Asian and Western thought by examining their philosophical underpinnings. Through this literature review we obtained a general framework that begins to identify some of the ontological origins of the dichotomies we assert exist in cognition and knowledge-related concepts between the West and the East.

As regards the West, we included a review of the influence of early Greek philosophers, such as Aristotle and Plato, and showed how the continual and paradoxical tension created between an inductive and deductive approach has created some fundamental, and yet unresolved, differences in the way Westerners understand what is true.

Regarding the East, we reviewed the reduction of highly-speculative Buddhist thinking to a more synthetic and intuitive Pure Land and Zen Buddhism in China, showing how Easterners have tended to view all activity as a continually changing, yet mysteriously combined, whole. We also reviewed how the Confucianist schools varied from the highly abstract and deductive Songxue to the practice-oriented Yang Ming School. Overall, our philosophical analysis has pointed to fundamental differences in the ontological origins of shared Western vs. shared Asian thought on the 'truths' to be found in our surroundings.

In this chapter, we develop our argument from an epistemological perspective. For this purpose, we will define epistemology as encompassing the process of reasoning used in order to arrive at an understanding of what is true. We also focus on epistemology as a method of judgement, that is as the way that opinions are formed, through the process of distinguishing and evaluating strategic options. Once again, we have based our argument upon a review of the literature, as well as upon our conviction that managers do not all think in the same way, and that cultural differences do influence how they think.

While numerous international studies already exist, as reviewed in Chapter 5, which show how the cultural environment has a substantial effect on how managers act, and we agree with many of these, including Nisbett (2003); Hofstede (2001); Lewis (1997, 2010); and Hofstede and Bond (1988), we also argue that there are internal, *cognitive* reasons that lead managers to approach strategic problems, and arrive at conclusions about outcomes, differently.

We argue that it is the process of thinking used by Asian managers that is different from the process of thought used by Western managers. In other words, it is also (at least partially) the 'how' of their cognitive processes that leads to their 'what', that is their differing strategic management approaches.

We then define a 'shorthand' way to identify these different epistemological approaches to thinking, referring to them as 'inductive' or 'deductive' thinking. To address how inductive and deductive thinking are related, we begin by defining epistemology as 'the science of knowing', taking a theoretical stance that seeks to uncover how our method or grounds for knowing what we know in the first place affects our ultimate thought frameworks. This is especially important in understanding strategic business decisions. We would like to know how a businessperson arrives at the conclusions he or she does.

Therefore, in looking at cognition, we are seeking to understand the processes managers use to make their strategic decisions. In this chapter, then, we assert that these processes can be grouped into two basic categories: (1) what we refer to as 'inductive thinking' and (2) what we refer to as 'deductive thinking'. (See Table 3.1 for the comparisons between management philosophies, what needs to be studied and their scientific rationale.)

## Epistemology and science

Much of management education is based on the assumption that the underlying process of managerial thinking or cognition is similarly 'scientific' for most managers, and therefore can be taken for granted when comparing other aspects of international business. The typical focus of international business researchers, then, has traditionally been one of identifying other, more environmentally-based differences, such as those to be found when comparing cultures, languages, structures, creeds and laws across international borders (Hofstede & Bond, 1988) (see Chapter 5 for more details).

The tacit assumption behind this is (1) that the different management strategies used by these groups and subgroups must necessarily be reduced to one common scientific approach, and (2) that we have only to identify the differences between empirical phenomena and situational contexts in order to arrive at a good understanding of international business outcomes.

*Table 3.1*  Approaches to management thinking

| What managers do | What needs to be studied | Scientific base | Philosophical base |
|---|---|---|---|
| **Under current mainstream MBA teaching** | | | |
| All Managers carry out Actions | outcomes | 'proof' (generally deductive) | Greek, UK, French, Renaissance, etc. |
| Why Western vs Asian Managers act differently in adapting to their strategic challenges | differences in environment | assumed same | assumed irrelevant or separate issue |
| **Our Argument** | | | |
| When Western vs Asian managers act | why they think in a certain way | can be inductive or deductive | Is relevant |
| Managers also use their OWN COGNITIVE Approach | how they think | we categorise and identify inductive or deductive schemas (as we define them below) | we differentiate between Asian (Confucius, Tao, etc.) vs. Western (Greek, etc.) |

*Source*: Authors.

However, our proposal in this book is to question this assumption, and to dig more deeply into the assumptions underlying philosophically opposed ontologies and epistemologies. Different groups, we argue, interpret and understand the 'truths' in the world around them differently, and do so while thinking in fundamentally different ways. Our goal in this chapter is to focus upon the epistemological aspects, and therefore to identify patterns regarding what may be occurring cognitively among and between individuals with different (but shared) backgrounds, environments, accumulated experience and knowledge.

Based on our literature survey that has been described in Chapter 4 as well as on the experiment mentioned in Annex 1, we assert that people, and therefore managers, can be grouped into two major descriptive categories:

1. Eastern thinkers – those who generally approach strategic managerial challenges from an 'inductive thinking' approach.
2. Western thinkers – those who generally approach strategic managerial challenges from a 'deductive thinking' approach.

In this section, then, we begin by identifying 'types' or segments of individuals who think in an identifiably different way from other segments, and do so on both a 'macro' level (that is as a response to stimuli such as culture or religion) and on a more 'micro' level (that is as a response to inherently held or accepted cognitive habits).

Our overall proposition in this book is that these 'types' can then potentially be grouped into the macro-level terms of 'Eastern' (or Eastern Asian including China, Japan, Korea, Taiwan) and 'Western' (Europe and North America) approaches to management. However, in this section, we also propose that these patterns and differences can be reduced to a more 'shorthand' and cognitive, or micro-level definition by referring to them as 'inductive' and 'deductive' approaches to thinking.

Our method in addressing this task has involved carrying out a selectively *inductive* research strategy, focusing on the analysis of texts, and allowing, as Blaikie (1993: p. 100) states, for 'the possibility that other ideal typical research strategies may have existed in the past, and may exist now or in the future'.

While it is true that we could have chosen many different methodologies for evaluating the epistemological differences between Eastern and Western thinking, we have chosen to evaluate what we consider to be relevant literature, which is clearly a selective process on our part. However, we approach this review in a way suggested by Hart, who states that '... knowledge generation and understanding is an emergent process and not a universal product. In order to know the nature and character of the implications of a development you need to know the intellectual context of that development' (Hart, 1998: p. 27).

Our goal, therefore, has been to provide a broad overview of the major concepts related to the cognitive aspects of how large segments of the world's population approach strategic management differently, while recognizing that in an even broader world, our resources constrain us to select what is relevant rather than to attempt to exhaustively cover all that might be or has been said about our topics. As our method is inductive, we have observed and evaluated data, and then projected a theory that might explain some observed patterns around those data.

We have begun by identifying some key terms and logics used within the philosophical and cognitive management literatures (Chapters 2 and 4). After initially establishing comparisons between these terms, we then break them down into generally shared schemas and sub-schemas that we have observed to be held in common by managers within these groups.

Finally, we re-categorize these smaller parts back into the larger general categories of 'inductive' and 'deductive' (where we merge 'abductive' thinking back into the overall concept of 'induction'), having specified how our definition of these terms allows us to better understand differences in managerial thinking across regional borders.

Our inductive review process of defining terms, establishing links and comparisons, breaking the concepts down, and then categorizing them again into re-grouped wholes is very similar to a process established in the field of psychology which relates to learning. Originally based upon Tolman's concept of 'purposive-behaviorism' (Tolman, 1959) it is an approach that seeks to integrate the Behaviourist and Gestaltist camps in Psychology where behaviour is juxtaposed with holistic views, using whole-part and part-whole comparisons (Swanson & Law, 1993). Swanson and Law then developed what they term the 'Whole-Part-Whole' (WPW) model as a way to identify the process that human beings go through in starting with a generically understood (or sometimes, misunderstood) term, then breaking it down into more meaningful individual components, and then unifying the components again into a better understood whole (Swanson & Law, 1993). Because we also start with the generically understood (or misunderstood) terms of 'induction' and 'deduction,' we too have chosen to base our method of conceptual analysis upon the WPW approach to learning.

This technique serves to help groups of people with differing starting points to 'end up' at a more commonly shared point of understanding. For us, the WPW model serves as a basis to first identify an accepted central conceptual term which most individuals describe, ascribe meaning to, or refer to in a holistic, common way, such as the words 'deductive' and 'inductive'. We can then examine in more detail the components of these terms, such that a 'shorthand' use of either term will invoke a better understanding of its meaning in the context of our book.

To allow the reader to group and compare how these terms are affected by some of their more obviously considered influences (such as culture, religion, geography, governments, history, or nationally accepted structures), we have presented various international business cases elsewhere in this book. Each case allows the reader to examine a real, strategic business scenario that was approached by a thoughtful individual with either an Asian or a Western background.

In this section, however, we seek to further explore the thought processes of international managers. Therefore, we propose that the terms 'deductive' and 'inductive' thinking be categorized (Holland, Holyoak, Nisbett & Thagard, 1987; Mervis & Rosch, 1981) into smaller groups or categories, which we will refer to as schemas, or mental frameworks, that are cognitively based (Holland et al., 1989).

By examining in more depth some of these schemas, and through a process of dialectic comparison (Morgan, 1997; Blaikie, 1993; Yin, 1994) within the literature, we have begun to identify some examples of what we propose are relevant and shared, yet tacit and internally held, categorizations and assumptions related to the way two different types of international managers think.

We have also begun to identify some potentially relevant patterns within these shared tacit assumptions (which we have grouped into general sub-categories), that we assert are managers' tacitly held frameworks that affect the way they strategically manage. These include concepts such as temporality, expectations, materiality, predictability, causality, recursivity and approaches to learning. We then regroup these elements back into larger categories (Swanson and Law's final 'whole'), which we then refer to, now redefined, as our definitions of 'inductive' and 'deductive' managerial thinking and approaches to problem solving. (See Figure 3.1, showing how the WPW model has been applied.)

To summarize some of our 'micro' level, and cognitive, findings we propose that deductive thinking would imply, under our new definitions, such things as a general anticipation of the predictability and linearity of time, guarantees in expectations, tangibility of the material, numeric and demonstrable falsifiability of propositions and observability of actions.

Inductive thinking, however, would imply such things as a general anticipation of the unpredictability and circularity of time, probable truth in expectations, equal validity placed on tangible and intangible materiality, degrees of 'likelihood' of propositions, and a real existence of unobservable actions.

While there is clearly a risk that we could lapse into unnecessarily stereotyping groups of individuals by highlighting these elements as categories, our objective is to clarify our definitions and give examples of these categories in the hope that some of the patterns we identify can provide researchers with an additional set of concepts upon which to base studies related to the 'why' and 'how' of certain international business practices, and the cognitive understandings, thoughts and actions of different international managers underlying them (Mervis & Rosch, 1981; Morgan, 1997; Holland et al., 1987).

Our proposition is that there are identifiable epistemological differences between what we refer to as 'inductive thinkers' and 'deductive thinkers'. In this section, therefore, we first carry out a literature review of the terms

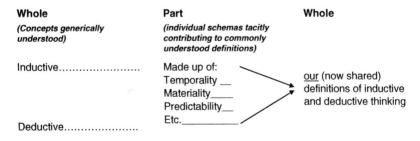

*Figure 3.1*   Application of WPW model

*Source*: Adapted from Swanson and Law, 1993, and elaborated by authors.

and definitions used, most specifically related to the use of the terms 'induction' and 'deduction'. We, secondly, explore these in greater depth, using a comparative and dialectic enquiry between and among literature where we believe inductive and deductive thinking can be identified (Blaikie, 1993; Morgan, 1997; Yin, 1989), highlighting the similarities and differences between the two cognitive approaches to management.

Third, we break this down even further by analysing some of the cognitive categories and sub-categories that have been identified in this literature as explicitly or implicitly associated with one approach or the other. Finally, we propose a framework for understanding each approach, and put forth some suggestions as to how the nuances in our definitions can be used to perceive international business situations and cases from a point of view that adds a slightly different dimension of understanding.

## Philosophy as the basis for inductive and deductive epistemology

When we think, we also reason. Reasoning, simply put, is the process of drawing from existing knowledge to arrive at conclusions, make predictions, or construct explanations. In general, most scientists agree that there are two basic methods of reasoning: inductive and deductive. As we discussed in Chapter 2, one consists of proving whether something is true, that is deduction, while the other relies on 'strong inference', otherwise known as induction, to advance what is not yet known as a proposition (Platt, 1964). This division serves a purpose: it allows us to observe the differences between the two concepts as polar comparisons, thereby facilitating a dialectic analysis.

We also know that the perception of a clear difference between inductive and deductive thinking has its roots in the early philosophical logic of the Greeks, beginning with Aristotle and Plato (Locke, 2007), as we discussed in Chapter 2. As Stadtler points out, 'ever since Aristotle, it has been accepted that there exists a combination of inductive and deductive reasoning and a sort of unified inductive-deductive methodology' (Stadtler, 2004: p. 1).

Indeed, Aristotle proposed these two concepts as the most fundamental, but opposing, methods for scientific enquiry. To arrive at truths in mankind's existence, he said, it is necessary to progress back and forth from observations to general principles, and back to observations, using what he defined as dialectic enquiry (Schweiger, Sandberg & Rechner, 1989). We begin by inducing explanatory principles from the phenomena to be explained, and then deducing statements about these phenomena from premises which include these principles (Losee, 2001). These processes are at the heart of logical inference, and tend to involve oppositional as well as complementary aspects of epistemology, leading us to better understand how we can know something is true.

The 'opposition' and 'complementarity' of these basic elements has led to extensive development of further theories related to them, which have also then been juxtaposed as complementarities or opposites. These include scientific concepts such as explanation vs. empiricism, or discovery vs. justification. However, in spite of a continually fierce debate about each side's merits and faults over the centuries, induction and deduction remain the philosophical bases of any scientific approach.

And, as we also discovered in Chapter 2, philosophy itself is a major part of what can be traced as the basis from which we are willing to understand something as true in the first place. Philosophy has been described as 'more a rigorous and enquiring attitude of mind than an academic discipline. In philosophical enquiry, the facts, the theory, the alternatives and the ideals are brought together and weighed against each other in the creation of knowledge' (Chia, 2002: p. 2). Our philosophical attitudes, therefore, shape us and orient us towards the strategies we use to produce and act upon knowledge.

But we also know that our perceptions and actions are in their turn inherited phenomena, in that our culturally-based mindsets place order on the types of things that we think or do, and influence how we interpret concepts. This can vary substantially according to the 'embedded collective histories and cultural traditions within which our own individual identities have emerged' (Chia, 2002: p. 3).

What we consider to be legitimate and reliable knowledge, therefore, can vary according to how our cultural origins guide us to interpret it, such as how it is delivered, including aurally or in writing, or how it is communicated, including verbally or in an unspoken way. Our priorities, too, can vary, from our roles as observers, where we attempt to try to understand and explain, to our roles as practitioners, where we attempt to actively elicit consequences and effects. We assert that each of these elements relating to how we acquire, communicate and use our knowledge, then, is also a deeply embedded method that affects our understanding, it is also, we argue, our epistemological approach that will define how we understand and act upon the world around us.

In essence, therefore, we all have a deeply embedded set of assumptions that underpin our thinking, and these can be grouped into cultural and philosophical, as well as ontological and epistemological, categories. It is our assertion, following on from this, that a better understanding of what we define as our 'epistemological attitudes' can then lead to a better understanding of the bases for many of our managerial actions.

After having concluded that philosophies can be 'an attitude of mind', we can then examine in greater depth the cognitively held epistemologies of induction and deduction. While Aristotle's method of gleaning knowledge 'entails the breaking down, fixing, locating and naming of all experienced phenomena' (Chia, 2002: p. 6), this also leads him to imply that our focus should be on empiricism, that is we seek to obtain universal laws from particular facts, and that we can legitimately do this through personal experience and observation.

Plato, on the other hand, was considered a rationalist, more concerned with using logic and reason to arrive at abstract principles. His classic 'Allegory of the Cave'[1] asks us to question whether we are focusing on the 'correct' reality, and implies that only logic and reason can lead us around our somewhat blind focus on an 'incorrect' reality. However, what is now considered the modern scientific method is a result of Aristotle's attempts to combine Platonic rationalism with his own focus on empirical observation, resulting in the establishment of the inductive and deductive epistemological strategies of scientific research still in effect today (Lawson & Appignanesi, 1989).

Nevertheless, in spite of the fact that inductive and deductive logic had similar roots and can be integrated effectively, over the last century there has been a tendency for these approaches to be polarized, defended and used by groups of people who think very differently from each other. Plato-based rationalists (such as Karl Popper or René Descartes) tended to focus on logic, reason, symbols, concepts and idealized objects, while Aristotle-influenced empiricists (such as John Locke and David Hume) tended to focus on specific observations that allowed them to formulate and justify their views while playing down the significance of tacit generalizations. In effect, each area was defending an ability to know the truth that could not, by definition, ever be complete, and therefore could not be easily compared on a like-for-like basis.

This dichotomy, known as 'incommensurability', sparked debate over many centuries (Stadtler, 2004), and led to the creation of new philosophical terms such as 'logical positivism' (a research doctrine created by a group referred to as 'the Vienna Circle' in the 1920s which focused on the need to verify all assertions with hard facts) or 'radical empiricism' (a step in the opposite direction by William James, advocating the 'lived experience' as most important and incorporating 'phenomenology' by Husserl and 'intuitionism' by Bergson) (Lawson & Appignanesi, 1989).

Researchers and philosophers began to branch out into combinations of ontological and epistemological approaches that they increasingly exhorted as incommensurable, or lacking in a common measure or comparison base with other approaches (Weaver & Gioia, 1994). For our purposes, the most important concept to recognize here is that, over the centuries since Aristotle and Plato began to think about inductivism and deductivism, there has been a generalized bifurcation between the two approaches that separates large groups of individuals in the way they think about what is real, existing, or true, and most importantly, *how* we can legitimately arrive at these conclusions.

Hence, it behoves us now to define and compare more carefully just what our epistemological conceptualizations of 'induction' and 'deduction' really mean. To do so, we will refer to Table 3.1, which provides a summarized comparison of the two forms of reasoning that we will now discuss. As a first step, however, we turn to a dictionary. The Webster's New Collegiate Dictionary defines induction as 'the act, process or result or an instance of reasoning from a part to a whole, from particulars to generals, or from the individual to the universal' (Woolf, 1977). Likewise, it defines deduction as 'the deriving of a conclusion by reasoning, or specifically, an inference in which the conclusion follows necessarily from the premises' (Woolf, 1977).

## Induction

Inductive reasoning, then, is a process of seeking new knowledge which starts with a generalization and concludes with a particular. According to Blaikie, 'the inductive strategy starts with data collection, followed by data analysis, and then the development of generalisations that, with further testing, can become law-like propositions to be used to explain aspects of social life' (Blaikie, 1993: p. 100).

Therefore, a manager who is thinking inductively, we argue, is seeking to 'determine the rule' about something that he or she can observe happening in his or her environment. It is an effort to justify a conclusion by collecting empirical data to support it, perhaps because the empirical data creates a pattern of generalities. It assumes that a reasonable theory is one that can be demonstrated to be probable and relevant enough to be studied further. And, of course, it implies that a conclusion can be postulated before the law or pattern exists to explain it.

Symbolically, induction can be represented as follows:

A1, A2, A3 ... A100 are B.
A1, A2, A3 ... A100 are C.
Therefore, B is C

A finite set of data is identified and named to represent something (A or B). Then, a generalization is developed (therefore B is C) which can be later tested to evaluate its validity as a law-like proposition (is B always C?). Verbally, we can represent the same thing by saying 'Young swans are white, old swans are white; all observed swans are white; therefore, all swans are white' (Locke, 2007).

Intrinsically involved in all of this is the concept that analogies can be drawn, linking an observed phenomenon to an unobserved one, in a process that Shelley calls 'shared abstraction'. 'Analogous objects do not share necessarily a relation, but also an idea, a pattern, a regularity, an attribute, an effect or a function ... comparisons, metaphors and images can also be used as valid arguments ... and analogies' (Thagard & Shelley, 2003).

Typically, and according to Platt (1964), (a physicist), inductive inference involves the following steps that must be necessarily applied to every problem in science:

1. Devising alternative hypotheses;
2. Devising a crucial experiment (or several of them), with alternative possible outcomes, each of which will, as nearly as possible, exclude one or more of the hypotheses;
3. Carrying out the experiment so as to get a clean result;
   (1') *Recycling the procedure, making subhypotheses or sequential hypotheses to refine the possibilities that remain, and so on.*

While critics such as Karl Popper (Popper, 1957; Chalmers, 1999) criticize inductive methods, precisely because they may be false and therefore need to be falsifiable, they also recognize that all science, especially that related to new knowledge, does proceed inductively at some point, from observation or experiment of the world around us (Ketokivi & Mantere, 2010). By using the above steps in a formal and explicit and regular way, however, Platt argued that science would move forward faster (Platt, 1964).

Popper qualifies that, however, by saying that observation is selective, and therefore it presupposes the adoption of a frame of reference that automatically colours our observation of the world around us. For him, a good scientific approach allows us to jump to conclusions, but only if we also strive to refute them (Popper, 1953, 1974). Proponents of induction, however, such as Hume, point out that induction cannot ever be logically justified, and attempts to do so would only lead to infinite regress (Hume, 1969). In other words, drawing conclusions from that of which we have experience to inform us on that of which we have no experience is not a logical or rationally justifiable process, although even deductivists admit it is a reality in our on-going world.

Some very typical methods of jumping from the known to the unknown in inductive research are to use techniques including: metaphor (Gannon, Locke, Gupta, Audia & Kristof-Brown, 2005/2006; Jacobs & Heracleous, 2006), storytelling (Boje, 1991), symbols (Johnson, 1992), rites (Trice & Beyer, 1984), verbal vs. non-verbal communication (Engstrom & Middleton, 1988), the drawing of paradoxes (Pettigrew, Woodman & Cameron, 2001; Taylor-Bianco & Schemerhorn, 2006), dialectic enquiry (Seo & Creed, 2002), and 'devil's advocacy' (Okhuysen & Eisenhardt, 2002), among many others.

However, as all of these techniques only pose possible knowledge to be considered at further length, they are often criticized as unscientific by deductivists, who continue to base their assertions on whether the new knowledge is falsifiable and/or follows irrefutable (and therefore deductivist) logic. In essence, all of these methods are deemed to be illogical precisely because they involve jumping to a conclusion before it has been scientifically or logically verified.

Popper's response to the illogic of induction, for example, was to use it to draw an analogy himself, thereby showing what is both an inductive and a deductive example of how we create our own internal mental frameworks. He therefore used an inductive technique to claim that induction could have no scientific validity:

> To sum up this logical criticism of Hume's psychology of induction we may consider the idea of building an induction machine. Placed in a simplified 'world' (for example, one of sequences of    c o l o u r e d counters) such a machine may, through repetition, 'learn', or even 'formulate', laws of succession which hold on to its 'world'. If such a machine can be constructed (and I have no doubt that it can) then, it might be argued, my theory must be wrong; for if a machine is capable of performing inductions on the basis of repetition, there can be no logical reasons preventing us from doing the same.
>
> The argument sounds convincing, but it is mistaken. In constructing an induction machine we, the architects of the machine, must decide a priori what constitutes its 'world'; what things are to be taken as similar or equal, and what kind of 'laws' we wish the machine to be able to 'discover' in its 'world'. In other words, we must build into the machine a framework determining what is relevant or interesting in its world: the machine will have its 'inborn' selection principles. The problem of similarity will have been solved for it by its makers who thus have interpreted 'the world' for the machine. (Popper, 1957: p. 74)

For Popper, hence, cognition and cognitively created frameworks exist, but are not valid sources of scientific information, as they will always, by definition, interpret the data through framing it, before its analysis in a logical structure. Crucially, however, we must ask ourselves if our cognition and cognitively created frameworks can provide useful scientific advance in some way, by helping us to pose the right new questions. Do our cognitive frameworks limit us to what is already known, or is there some way we can advance into a realm of new knowledge by understanding the limitations of our cognition a little bit better? In other words, is our selective interpretation by definition an insurmountable problem?

Edwin Locke and other inductivists have addressed the issue of cognitive frameworks and selective interpretation by embracing them as elements that are part of valid approaches to the generation of new knowledge. Locke asserts that good examples of inductive thinking involve 'proximal rather than remote causes of actions', starting and staying with a 'core idea', and the recognition that 'consciousness has causal efficacy', none of which necessarily involves falsification (Locke, 2007: p. 25).

He recommends focusing on the probability of certainty in its context, where a large degree of positive evidence and no negative evidence can support a reasonable conclusion, all of which therefore makes claims of knowledge possible and allows science to progress (Locke, 2007). He also points out that this is an approach shared by many, saying 'Aristotle, Bacon and Rand were advocates of the primacy of existence and believed that knowledge was discovered starting with observation by the senses followed by the inductive integration of sensory material by reason' (Locke, 2007: p. 40). For Locke, there is a sequential course where knowledge is obtained via observation and then validated via reason, logic and evidence.

Locke, too, then used an analogy to illustrate the validity of induction:

Professor X looks everywhere for new bird species and discovers white swans. He forms the concept swan and describes them as birds having webbed feet, a long slender neck, and white plumage. He generalises that swans are white not only on the basis of his observations but on the basis that bird species are widely classified on the basis of colour (e.g., crows are black, cardinals are red – though male and female members of the species may differ). Then someone discovers black swans in another country. This, it is typically claimed, shows the futility of induction, viz. 'You can't claim swans are white unless you have seen every swan in existence, which means you can't generalise at all.'

What's wrong with this conclusion? It ignores the fact that concepts are open-ended. The original definition was contextually valid (certain) and the concept of swan includes all yet to be discovered knowledge. Discovering black swans does not invalidate the concept of swan but simply adds to what we know. The definition could be changed to 'usually white' or 'white or black'. The new definition is again contextually valid. If green swans were then discovered, we would have learned more and the definition would again be modified. But the concept of swan would not be invalidated. We have not progressed by falsification as such, but by learning more. This is the model for the whole history of science. (Locke, 2007: pp. 37–38)

Ultimately, induction can be and is used quite effectively, especially in the social sciences, as it provides us with a way to advance within a subjective, relative and unpredictable social environment (Stadtler, 2004). However, it is precisely in regard to the cognitive frameworks that underpin our use of induction as a scientific method that we think Popper and Locke and others may have had a point worth investigating, and which we will develop further in this chapter.

## Deduction

Deductive reasoning can be defined as a process of drawing logical consequences from premises. In this way, consequences or outcomes are derived from what is assumed. Essentially, it can be said to work in reverse order from induction. 'It begins with an observed regularity that needs to be explained; a tentative theory is acquired or constructed; then hypotheses are deduced and then tested by collecting appropriate data' (Blaikie, 2000: p. 100). Through deductive reasoning, we are seeking to determine a conclusion or outcome, and our role is to evaluate and refine hypotheses in doing so, based, of course, on having established other plausible premises in the first place.

We can also use symbols to describe deduction, saying, for example:

All As are Bs
C is B
Therefore, C is A

Our symbolic statement is true if our premises are true, and we can verify them through falsifiability, that is if we can show that there is an example of them being false, then they are not true. Our task, then, is to evaluate empirical data (in this case, the value of these letters), using other concepts and premises we know to be true.

The same can be stated with words, such that we can say:

All men are mortal.
Joe is a man.
Therefore, Joe is mortal.

The logic of deductive reasoning is straightforward: to test theories, to eliminate false theories and to corroborate the surviving theory. This is done by borrowing or constructing a theory and expressing it as an argument, deducing the hypotheses, and then testing the hypotheses by matching them with data (Blaikie, 200: p. 101).

Deduction assumes that, to be scientific, theories must be reducible, refutable, falsifiable and testable (Popper, 1953). First, the process of deduction should be capable of representation by a process of explanatory reduction, where one theory should be reducible to another via logic functions that establish identities on two sides of an equation. For example, 'heat = molecular motion'. These 'identities' are reduced, such that 'a term on one side of the identity sign belongs to a theory that is explanatorily more basic than the theory to which the other term belongs. Successful reductions increase a reducing theory's explanatory power, for they expand the theory's domain while retaining its simplicity' (Gertler, 2002: p. 23).

Second and third, the theory must be refutable, in that if it can be proven to be wrong in some instance (refuted), it is then shown to be wholly false (falsified). Fourth, through deduction a theory must be testable, with empirical data or premises that provide a guarantee of the truth of the conclusion.

In other words, if the premises are correct, it should be impossible for the theoretical conclusion to be false.

Deduction is generally associated with Critical Rationalism, a philosophy of science developed by Popper in the 1930s, which assumes that nature and life consist of essential uniformities where scientists must discover what these are and develop statements that truly describe them.

However, he also claimed that scientific certainty about the real world was impossible, and therefore the process of induction was superfluous and inconsistent (Locke, 2007). 'Rationalism is the tendency to explain particulars in terms of universalistic and idealized categories' (Chia, 2002). And it follows that, to the proponents of deduction, reality is assumed to exist regardless of whether scientists can discover it or not. Plato, Descartes and Kant, among others, believed that 'ideas were implanted in the mind independently of experience' and that therefore only consciousness could deduce this (Locke, 2007: p. 40).

Popper's arguments for a deductive strategy (as opposed to induction) are based on his assertion that observations cannot be considered a reliable source of scientific theories, that inductive logic is flawed, and that since data collection is necessarily selective, it should be used only to test tentative answers posed by initial hypotheses (Blaikie, 2000).

Ontologically, deduction agrees that undiscovered realities do exist, but epistemologically 'the use of the senses is rejected as a secure foundation for scientific theories' (Blaikie, 2000: p. 105). This also relates back to Plato's concept that the senses cannot be counted upon fully as they do not always and reliably perceive truth, and to Kant's assertion that we can only know the world as it appears to us (Locke, 2007).

In sum, Popper rejected not only induction but everything that makes induction possible: reality (specifically, the ability to know it), causality and objective concept formation. Popper rejected the whole concept of proof and claimed that science only advances by disproving theories. This brings up the question: where do theories come from, if not from integrating observation and discoveries by induction? Popper had no real answer to this, '...there is no such thing as a logical method of having new ideas, or a logical reconstruction of this process. My view may be expressed by saying that every discovery contains 'an irrational element', or a 'creative intuition'. (Locke, 2007: p. 4, quoting Popper, 2003)

Ultimately, one of the greatest challenges with deduction is that it can only use information that already exists, and yet, somehow, new knowledge has to come from somewhere. Induction, on the other hand, is essentially any inferential process that *can* expand knowledge in the face of uncertainty (Holland et al., 1989). However, *how* it does so is often unclear. The 'incompleteness of inductive reasoning presents an enduring dilemma for organizational researchers' (Ketokivi & Mantere, 2010: p. 315).

This lack of methodological clarity leads many, such as Popper, to call the inductive process 'pseudo-empirical...that is to say, a method which, although it appeals to observation and experiment, nevertheless does not come up to scientific standards' (Popper, 1953: p. 1). Nevertheless, many researchers do insist that it can be helpful to perceive deduction more as a process of discovering the truth, while induction should be perceived as the process of creating it.

Table 3.2 summarizes some of the major differences between induction and deduction. It also shows where the term 'abduction' fits in with these concepts. 'Abduction', as we will argue in our next section, is basically a type of induction.

### Addition of abductive logic

Another term for a type of logic, abduction, was originally developed by Charles S. Peirce in the early 1900s, and is particularly applicable to the social sciences (Pierce, 1903). Abduction can be defined as 'the process of looking for a pattern in a phenomenon and suggesting a hypothesis' (Yu, 1994).

Blaikie uses a slightly more specific definition for abduction in social sciences research, as 'the process used to generate social scientific accounts from social actors' accounts; for deriving technical concepts and theories from lay concepts and accounts of social life' (Blaikie, 2000: p. 114).

In management, abduction allows us to explore a wide variety of data and find patterns in them that may be plausible but have not yet advanced far enough to be more than a proposed idea or a new way of understanding.

A symbolic example of abduction might be:

The surprising phenomenon, X, is observed.
Among hypotheses A, B, and C, A is capable of explaining X.
Hence, there is a reason to pursue A.

(Yu, 1994)

Or, a verbal example might be:

It has been observed that when it is very cold, the pond freezes.
The pond is frozen now,
therefore, it may be very cold.

As a metaphor, abduction can be compared with definitions of rational decision-making (Kaufman, 1990; Skidd, 1992). From a purely rational perspective, managerial choices should always be made quickly, with full

*Table 3.2*  Definitions and examples of inductive/deductive reasoning

| Definition type | Abductive | Inductive | Deductive |
|---|---|---|---|
| Meaning | The process of looking for a pattern in a phenomenon and suggesting a hypothesis | The process of generalizing from a sample to conclude about a population | The process of drawing logical consequences from premises |
| And... | Explore data, find a pattern, suggest plausible hypotheses using categories | Reach conclusions about unobserved things on the basis of what has been observed | Derive the consequences of what is assumed |
| To do what? | Determine the precondition | Determine the rule | Determine the conclusion |
| Role | Generate new ideas or hypotheses | Justify hypotheses with empirical data | Evaluate hypotheses |
| Goal | Explore data, find a pattern, suggest plausible hypotheses using categories | Empirically substantiate | Refine hypothesis based upon other plausible premises |
| Symbolic example | The surprising phenomenon, X, is observed. Among hypotheses A, B, and C, A is capable of explaining X. Hence, there is a reason to pursue A | A1, A2, A3 ... A100 are B. A1, A2, A3 ... A100 are C. Therefore, B is C | All As are Bs C is B Therefore, C is A |
| Verbal example | 'When it is very cold, the pond freezes. The pond is frozen, therefore, it may be very cold.' | All observed crows are black; therefore, all crows are black | All men are mortal. Joe is a man. Therefore, Joe is mortal. |
| New knowledge | Seeks new knowledge through the generation of hypotheses | Induces the universal from the particular, but may be false | Cannot lead to new knowledge because conclusion already embedded in premise |

Continued

*Table 3.2*   Continued

| Definition type | Abductive | Inductive | Deductive |
|---|---|---|---|
| Knowledge | Knowledge is cumulative and self-corrective, but fallible | Socially constructed | New frameworks overthrow old frameworks (paradigm shifts) |
| Truth | Exploratory and plausible only | Probable, but not definite | Always, falsifiably, true, by definition, and independent of sense experience |
| Contribution to our knowledge of a phenomenon | Contributes to our conceptual understanding | Adds quantitative details to our conceptual knowledge | Soundly valid if the conclusion follows necessarily from the premises |
| In short | Creates | Creates and verifies | Explicates, proves or discovers |

*Source*: Authors.

information available and best economic interests at heart. However, from a practical point of view, we know that this is often not done, and, in many instances, it is not even possible.

Managers must, therefore, act in a 'boundedly rational' way, as they are limited in time, scope, information and ultimate political interests. Just as bounded rationality relates with pure rationalism, abduction 'softens' the process of knowledge creation into a more practical and useable approach. It generally creates new knowledge from fewer facts than might otherwise be desired, and provides a means for us to make do with the information we realistically have access to (as would a doctor making a diagnosis or a juror judging the evidence he or she is presented with) (Thagard and Shelley, 1997).

Albert Einstein, for example, was able to go well beyond a 'standard' deductive or inductive process to make an exceptionally creative leap into a new realm of thought in proposing his theory of relativity (Salam, 1990). Like Einstein, however, most people often cannot explain *how* they may have arrived at an unsubstantiated idea through either deduction or induction. Einstein was careful to specify that certainty (deduction) cannot be achieved in science (Adam, 2006). Nevertheless, in his 1919 paper on 'Induction and Deduction in Physics' Albert Einstein also explained that, although (a standard definition of) induction does seem like an important step in science, often events work in an opposite fashion:

> The really great progress of natural science arose in a way which is almost diametrically opposed to induction. Intuitive comprehension of the

essentials about the large complex facts leads the researcher to construct one of several hypothetical fundamental laws...both the fundamental law (axioms) and the consequences form what we call a theory...But he (the researcher) does not arrive at his system of thought in a methodical, inductive way, rather he snuggles to the facts by intuitive choice among the imaginable axiomatic theories. (McPhee, 2008, quoting Einstein)

While 'snuggling to the facts by intuitive choice among what is imaginable' may strike a manager as unscientific, it is nevertheless often a reality in the way he or she attains new knowledge. Somehow, human beings carry out a process of making an undefined 'leap' to a new idea or managerial solution, in a way that defies logic and cannot be easily written or duplicated by a machine or process (Suchman, 2007).

While it may be unexplainable, it is still real. We argue that abduction should therefore be accepted as a legitimate way of thinking, and that once the managerial world has accepted it as legitimate, it should be viewed as simply another variety of inductive reasoning (Ketokivi & Mantere, 2010).

The typical logic of 'induction' proceeds with a set of observations that leads to a highly likely conclusion, but abduction takes this even further, often beginning with an *incomplete* set of observations and leading to a *possible* explanation (Thagard & Shelley, 1997).

Abduction is a more speculative process, but essentially can still be categorized into the same overall process as induction, since it is still a generic category comprising anything that is not yet proven, nor falsified, nor even possibly falsifiable, and yet still allows us to propose new theories and new knowledge (Nisbett, 1992). Much is a question of sequence – on a time continuum, induction and abduction are just before and just after their deductive proof, that is neither are proven when a proposition is made.

We assert, therefore, that because abduction still moves from data to a conclusion about that data, or from a lack of knowledge to new or proposed knowledge, it is 'similar enough' to induction to still be categorized in that overall field. We admit, however, that often it is the process of categorization itself that can lead us astray.

This is especially important in (East-)Asian cultures, where the 'whole' is perceived to be of greater importance than its 'parts', and therefore too much focus on a category of a 'part' is considered to lead one away from the 'big picture'. For example, the Chinese Taoist philosopher Chuang Tzu once said:

...the problem of...how terms and attributes are to be delimited, leads one in precisely the wrong direction. Classifying or limiting knowledge fractures the greater knowledge. (quoted in Nisbett, 2003: p. 138)

We propose, however, that categorizing abduction with induction simply allows us to place deduction in opposition. We can then categorize knowledge creation, while knowledge discovery can be balanced. In doing so, we have identified the fundamental polarization of the major epistemological approaches, namely that in obtaining our knowledge, human beings are either creating new knowledge *or* discovering and elaborating upon knowledge that already exists.

Regardless of the ontological implications behind this (the difference between those who believe that a truth exists, whether or not we are aware of it, and those who don't), both epistemological approaches ask us to *make* a decision, something that is intrinsic to the field of business; and also to act in an uncertain environment, something that is intrinsic to strategy. In addition, we argue that it is choosing the degree to which we will be more inductive or deductive that allows us to seek a more balanced approach in addressing strategic managerial decisions.

Categorizing abduction within the overall inductive approach can help managers identify and understand how an inductive 'lens' can be used to analyse people, cases and situations. With abduction, the scientist's task is essentially to explore data, identify a pattern, and suggest plausible hypotheses, using categorization as a technique to uncover something not previously known (Mervish & Rosch, 2004). And, in keeping with the Greek approach, a focus on categorization can also help induce at least some new knowledge from a single case or metaphor. It is also possible to apply the Chinese holistic view of data, which provides an additional way to interpret the new data once identified patterns have been highlighted (Nisbett, 2003: p. 139). What an abductive approach essentially adds is the ability to determine the preconditions for a theory, by generating new ideas or hypotheses from data (Yu, 1994).

For the purposes of our arguments, we will therefore consider abduction to be a simple variation on induction, and will consider culturally derived abduction to be a form or subset of inductive thought processes. In seeking new knowledge through the generation of hypotheses, it still moves from the general to the particular. It is self-correcting and plausible, rather than socially constructed and probable.

In essence, abduction contributes to our conceptual understanding of a phenomenon by creating the first step of what induction then verifies and adds quantitative details to. For its part, when possible, deduction then proves it in some way that is beyond doubt.

From a more 'macro' point of view, abduction is generally associated with 'interpretive' approaches to social enquiry. An interpretivist approach to social science:

> seeks to discover why people do what they do by uncovering the largely tacit, mutual knowledge, the symbolic meanings, motives and rules, which provide the orientations for their actions. Mutual knowledge is background knowledge that is largely unarticulated; it is constantly being

used and modified by social actors as they interact with each other; and it is produced and reproduced by them in the course of their lives together. It is the everyday beliefs and practices, mundane and taken for granted, which have to be grasped and articulated by the social researcher in order to provide an understanding of these actions. (Blaikie, 2000: p. 115)

Overall, we agree with Ketokivi and Mantere in their injunction that authors 'make a choice and defend it' (Ketokivi & Mantere, 2010: p. 329). Having established a difference between what they term 'contextualization' (inference to the best explanation, or what we refer to as 'abduction') and 'idealization' (eliminative, enumerative, what we term 'standard' and rule-based induction), they state that we must 'either separate inference and explanation, or treat the two as one' (Ketokivi & Mantere, 2010: p. 329).

## Cognition, schemas and induction/deduction

Cognition is increasingly used as a focal point for studying how strategies are produced and problems are solved in a managerial environment (Schwenk, 1988). Indeed, organizations are often seen as the locus for the creation of a community of shared meaning. Eisenberg and Riley, for example, go even further, stating that 'investigations of organizations should explore the potential for multiple or competing meaning systems, and the degree to which they are shared across time and space, in order to better understand the maintenance and transformation of organizational reality' (Eisenberg & Riley, 1988: p. 321).

### Gestalt and association

One early approach to the study of cognition was called 'Gestalt', which emphasized the importance of context in reasoning (Kohler, 1947). Essentially, Gestalt holds that if the context of a cognitive task can be understood, then meaningful solutions will also follow. If, on the other hand, no relevant contextual data are used, then people will revert to mindlessness, be wrong, or possibly focus on a range of information that will be too narrow to be useful (Grisson, 1987; Sharps, Hess, Casner, Ranes & Jones, 2007).

In addition, according to Mayer, 'people get stuck solving problems because they cannot change their problem solving set – since they cannot look at the situation in a new way, they cannot see a new way to fit the elements together' (Mayer, 1992: p. 40). Gestaltists argue that, if people can insightfully find a way to reorganize the basic elements of a problem, they will then be able to solve it.

Opposed to this is the cognitive approach known as 'Associationist'. Instead of creating new solutions, Associationists use different elements of past experience, trying out possibilities until one works, and carrying out their thinking tasks by associating stimuli and responses (Mayer, 1992).

The important element here is that many psychologists differentiate between two kinds of thinking. One reproduces old types of thinking, and the other generates new solutions via new organization (Mayer, 1992; Wertheimer, 1959). As Mayer points out, both the Gestalt and Associationist schools served to foreshadow what has later been termed 'the cognitive revolution', where a whole new domain of 'cognition' has been carved out on the academic landscape, using new tools and techniques for gathering data about cognitive processes (Mayer, 1992).

While cognition is now an entire, and rather broad, field, it is still somewhat disperse and ethereal. For our purposes, we will focus on some epistemological aspects of cognition that enable us to better understand how managers might think differently across cultures.

A wide number of researchers in the cognitive sciences have studied different meaning systems across boundaries or countries. Imai and Gentner (1997), for example, carried out various clinical psychological studies and showed that language influences the different categories and boundaries perceived in words by children. These differences showed that people, and especially children, in Japan had a very different epistemological approach to learning and using their language than people in America, and that the nature of the categories they perceived (objects vs. substances) and the boundaries around them, differed substantially between the two cultures (Imai & Gentner, 1997) (of which more in Chapter 4 and Annex 1). Nisbett then suggested that evidence such as this, 'taken at face value'... indicates that 'Westerners and Asians literally see different worlds' (Nisbett, 2003: p. 82).

Hutchins, in a very different study, looked at cognitive activity in its context (what he referred to as 'the wild') in trying to understand how individuals sailing together on a Navy ship managed to understand each other in complex situations (Hutchins, 1996). While recognizing that these individuals had similar internal frameworks and training in understanding navigation, that is they shared organizational knowledge, he also proposed that it was important to look at how cognition was situated within a complex sociocultural world 'where context is not a fixed set of surrounding conditions but a wider dynamical process of which the cognition of an individual is only a part'. 'Human cognition', he said, 'differs from the cognition of all other animals, primarily because it is intrinsically a cultural phenomenon' (Hutchins, 1995: p. xiii).

Taking all of the above into account, we propose that the same dichotomies that exist in the realm of psychology, differentiating between Gestaltist and Associationist thinking, between objects vs. subjects, or between organizational knowledge vs. dynamical cultural processes, are also similar to the differences between inductive and deductive thinking. One works by falsifying a concrete dataset, while the other works by seeing things in a new way. One involves a static set of data while the other involves a dynamic and complex exchange of information. One involves organizational knowledge that has already been gathered while the other involves interpretation of a tacit and constantly changing environment.

We take this further to argue that the bases of modern MBA or business strategy teaching show that most educators have chosen one type of thinking, namely what we call 'deductive', as the best way to approach a strategic or business problem (of which more in Chapter 7). However, while recognizing that internal cognitive processes can be very different from a mainstream approach, it would be wise to also recognize that the reasons behind making different strategic decisions could be even more important than the outcome or chosen path. As Allison points out, this is because different ways of thinking will necessarily lead to different understandings of the outcomes (Allison, 1971).

Following on from this, then, we propose that it is very possible that managers will benefit from better understanding of how and when other managers might be using different cognitive approaches to solve problems, as a first step to better understanding managerial decisions from different cultures. The challenge, of course, is not only to show thinkers how they could potentially have different options for thinking, but also to teach them how to do it differently in order to be more effective managers.

## Schemas as a basis of analysis

But how can we ever really know what someone was or is thinking? While action is something that is generally observable in some form, cognition remains elusive. One way researchers such as Bartunek (1984), Bartunek and Moch (1987), Harris (1994), Labianca, Gray and Brass (2000), Holland et al. (2004), Schwenk (1988), Axelrod (1976), Taylor and Crocker, (1981), Hunt (1989), Balogun and Johnson (2004) have operationalized the study of cognition has been to identify and compare schemas.

If a schema, which can be defined as 'a cognitive framework that gives meaning to experience' (Labianca et al., 2000: p. 238), can be distinguished, then it can serve as an operative way to identify a phenomenon that takes place mentally. Schemas are used to mentally identify repeatable patterns and to associate these with unidentified new knowledge. Essentially, a schema is a thought that is 'driven by pattern recognition' (Hunt, 1989). Most important to us, perhaps, is the fact that schemas can be identified as cognitive structures and processes in themselves, which can then be shared in some way by multiple individuals as they interpret the world around them (Schwenk, 1988).

> The cognitive sciences suggest that the world as it is experienced does not consist of events that are meaningful in themselves. Rather, cognitions, interpretations, or ways of understanding events are guided by organizing frameworks – or schemata. (Bartunek & Moch, 1987: p. 483)

From the viewpoint of a deductive thinker, managers and strategists carry an inherently biased framework within their minds. This then becomes, they argue, an insurmountable problem, negatively affecting the frames of reference that managers use to make strategic decisions, and therefore their ability to be 'scientific' in solving problems. However, inductive thinkers disagree, and simply seek to comprehend what these frames of reference are, in order to better understand how problems are formulated (Schwenk, 1988).

From among many examples that could be given, Weick describes framing as the 'worldviews, fields of vision, or perspectives for managing meaning, both mental and social and linked to the labels members assign to situations' (Weick, 1979). Axelrod (1976) shows how there can be shared assumptions across a group of strategic decision makers, and then demonstrates how an entire group can attribute cause to specific policies (Axelrod, 1976). Taylor and Crocker show how previously developed schemas can be applied to new problems (Taylor & Crocker, 1983). Orlikowski and Gash (1994) were among the first to identify the concept of a specific technological frame, which sets out the mental schemas of a group studied in Information Technology, and how these are shared. Balogun and Johnson (2004) show how shared group schemas can change over time.

Instead of turning different cognitive frameworks into a problem, inductive thinkers are able to embrace a non-tangible concept and use it to theorize, classify and gather data about the world around them. Indeed, Holland et al. (1989) go so far as to say that induction itself is simply the process by which the units that make up mental models are generated, constructed and revised. 'Cognitive systems construct models of the problem space that are then mentally "run", or manipulated to produce expectations about the environment' (Holland et al, 1989: p. 12).

### Inductive and deductive schemas identified

If we then do the same, we can identify a number of schemas that relate to what we can define as generalized ways of thinking, from within management and organizational literature. We have summarized this in Table 3.3, where we identify some of what we consider to be relevant mental schemas. We then posit that these can be viewed as polarities, and can be associated with either inductive or deductive thinkers, although here, we are clearly making what could be called an 'abductive leap'.

We then re-aggregate all of these polarized schemas back into our overall proposal of what we mean by 'inductive or deductive thinking' and thereby providing the reader with a clarified definition of the cognitive 'inductive/deductive lens' that we suggest can be applied to better understand the cases in this book. In essence, we propose that the process of identifying these general schemas can help to better understand the approaches managers take to resolve some of their strategic challenges when they originate from

*Table 3.3* Schemas related to inductive and deductive thinking

| Schema sub-categories | Deductive | Inductive |
|---|---|---|
| Temporality | Anticipation of predictability and linearity of time | Anticipation of unpredictability and circularity of time |
| Predictability | Guarantees in projected future | Probable truth in projected future |
| Materiality | Tangibility of the material | Equal validity of tangible and intangible materiality |
| Falsifiability | Numeric and demonstrable falsifiability of propositions | Degrees of likelihood of propositions and alternative scenarios |
| Recursivity | Not admitted: there must be observability of linear actions | Real existence of unobservable and recursive actions |
| Approach to learning | Behaviourist (connectionist): learn by memorizing | Gestalt (cognitive): learn by understanding |
| Approach to thinking and restructuring of problems | Associationist: reproductive, stimulus-response linked, and precise (apply solution habits from past experience, try till it works, associate stimuli and responses) | Gestaltist: productive, reorganizative, organization fades, and vague (create new solution to new situation, rearrange problem elements, mental structures are units of thought) |
| Approach to categorization | Categories are determinate, with definite boundaries and clear structures | Categories are an experimental epistemology (a) categories are internally structured by gradients of representativeness (b) boundaries are not necessarily definite (c) there is a close relation between attribute clusters and structure and formation of categories |
| Cognition of empiricism | To be legitimate, key decision makers' perceptions and role in issue diagnosis and problem formulation must represent innate, real, and demonstrable capability | Links between environment, strategy, structure can legitimately be cognitive and socially constructed |
| Use of analogy | Analogy is not an autonomous mode of thought or inference, and therefore is not valid to advance scientific truth | Analogy can be a relation, idea, pattern, regularity, attribute, effect or function, and comparisons of these are valid arguments that facilitate understanding |
| Perception of Reality | Objective – absolute | Subjective – relative |

*Source*: Elaborated by authors.

different backgrounds or form part of different groups who have a shared set of assumptions about the world around them.

## Categories of inductive and deductive schemas

In this section, we elaborate on 12 of the categories we have identified that could help our readers classify managers as 'inductive thinkers' or 'deductive thinkers.' These include: (1) Temporality (2) Predictability (3) Materiality (4) Falsifiability and proof (5) Recursivity (6) Approach to Learning (7) Approach to Thinking and Restructuring of Problems and (8) Approach to Categorization (9) Cognition of social surroundings (10) Metaphor (11) Analogy (12) Perception of reality. We have identified these as prevalent categories used in the literature we have reviewed. This is NOT intended to be a comprehensive list of all the categories that could be included, but rather it is a starting point for readers to begin to identify elements of these and other categories that could contribute to providing important indicators of a manager's 'inductive thinking' or 'deductive thinking'.

### 1. Temporality

One of the first schemas for classifying different types of thinking is that associated with how managers and strategists perceive time. As Adam (2006) states, 'Culture is inescapably tied to human beings' relationship with time: to death and the boundedness of human existence, to change, transience, ephemerality and contingence, and to the rhythmicity of the physical and living environment' (Adam, 2006: p. 119).

In the managerial sciences, time is considered a basic element that must be understood when working with different cultures. Edward T Hall, for example, identified time as one of the great differentiators between cultures. In proposing a difference between 'monochronic' and 'polychronic' perceptions of time, he established a way to understand how separate cultures use time differently in managerial situations (Bluedorn, 2002; Hall, 1976).

Sahay took this even further, identifying trends in the management and use of technology that were moving away from the classical functional and reductionist viewpoint and towards a more integrative, interpretivist perspective (Sahay, 1997).

> Time and space are crucial for understanding the context and also for describing social processes... Social processes such as learning or communication are always situated in a particular time and space context, which provide both enabling and constraining influences on these processes. In the natural sciences, the Newtonian view of the world conceptualised time and space as absolute entities, where space was like an empty container that was independent of the physical phenomenon occurring in it. Changes in the physical world were described in terms of a separate

dimension; time, which again was absolute, flowed smoothly onwards, having no connection with the material world. Einstein's relativity theory changed these absolute conceptualizations of time and space, forcing them to be viewed as relative concepts in a unified continuum ... emphasizing a holistic and integrative view of the world ... understood in terms of dynamic patterns rather than objects; as events rather than as things or substances. ... Organizational culture ... has groups' dominant assumptions of time and space embedded within it. (Sahay, 1997: p. 230)

Orlikowski and Yates (2002) also added to this conversation, discussing temporal structuring as a way to 'understand and study time as an enacted phenomenon in organisations. ... A focus on temporal structuring, combined with a practice perspective, allows us to bridge the subjective-objective dichotomy that underlies much of the existing research on time in organizations' (Orlikowski & Yates, 2002: p. 684). Numerous other researchers have addressed the need to conceptualize time differently including Bluedorn (2002), Standifer and Bluedorn (2006), Yakura (2002), Webb and Pettigrew, (1999). Even Michael Porter (1991) has suggested the need to have a new theory incorporating dynamism into the way strategy is carried out.

Time has also been firmly linked with culture in business strategy, where managers are asked to interpret the past, identify the present, and ultimately, predict and manage the future. As regards the past, Rowlinson, Booth, Clark, Delahave and Proctor (2010) point out that

...the dominant model of memory...is that of a storage bin. But this model has been rejected by psychologists because it overlooks the distinctly human subjective experience of remembering.... (and)...fails to take account of the specific social and historical contexts of organizational memory. (Rowlinson, Booth, Clark, Delahave & Proctor, 2010)

As regards the future, Bluedorn, in his book, *The Human Organisation of Time*, 2002, suggests that 'we begin thinking of the future as a temporal commons – a collectively constructed, owned and managed resource, optimally balanced in terms of temporal practices and past, present and future foci...to help us think more deeply about how our own views of time permeate not only how we approach life but how future generations will as well' (Bluedorn, 2002).

We argue that many deductive thinkers show a clear tendency to perceive time as linear, as 'conceptually stoppable', as consistent and constant, and as commonly shared. For these thinkers, time is a given, a fixed assumption that will remain constant in any situation. For them, time is also linear and consistent, and applies equally to everybody and every situation (Bluedorn, 2002).

Their analysis often focuses on conceptual 'points in time' that they regard as a standardizing element, such that in a chaotic or unpredictable situation, a definition of a point in time or a fixed episode with a beginning, middle and end, will serve to create a more manageable context (Hendry & Seidl, 2003; Lewin, 1951).

Inductive thinkers we propose, on the other hand, are generally associated with ideas relating to constant change (Hamel, 2001), chaos (Allen, 2001: p. 3980) (Allen, 2001), recursivity (Giddens, 1984), dynamism (Sahay, 1997) the circularity of time (Orlikowski & Yates, 2002), the recurrent social practices of social actors (Orlikowski & Yates, 2002), and the 'pacing' of time (Gersick, 1994).

## 2. Predictability

The concept of predictability is linked to that of temporality, in that, by definition, it deals with the future. We propose that the uncertainty associated with the future, and of not knowing what may happen in any given situation, leads deductive thinkers to expect a high degree of 'guarantee' in what current or past data tells them, and to then extrapolate these guarantees to highly reliable predictions of future behaviour.

To do this, they must first assume that time is linear, in order to ensure that what they are holding constant continues to have the same values and properties in all future times.

In contrast, some, more inductive, thinkers embrace the unpredictable, alleging that this enables us to better deal with uncertain and dynamic environments. This is precisely because, they argue, uncertainty is a better description of the real, social world than constancy is. To advance knowledge in a realistic manner, they argue, we only need to have some level of probable truth in our projected future. This allows us to manage alternative scenarios and glean possible patterns from chaos (Chermack & van der Merwe, 2003; Chermack, Lynham & Ruona, 2001).

## 3. Materiality

Materiality can be described as the perception that the basic elements or components that make up our world are made up of, or directly derived from, physical matter. The opposite of this, then, would be that which is immaterial, namely elements exist that have no substance and/or do not consist of matter, and yet are consequential to our understanding of the universe. One end of this spectrum of thinkers might assert that thinking is the movement of one neuron from point A to point B, while the other end would accept that thought exists (however it is produced physically) and should therefore be studied as if it were material. In other words, this end of the spectrum places equal validity on tangible as well as intangible materiality (Orlikowski, 2006; Leonardi & Barley, 2008).

## 4. Falsifiability and 'proof'

Falsifiability is one of Popper's basic tenets, and is therefore an easily identifiable schema used by a deductive thinker. If a theory can be proven to be wrong, then it is not universally and always right, and this makes it an 'illegitimate' concept. A fully rational decision maker will, for example, try to falsify his or her propositions, and will often attempt to do so with quantitative data, studying a static point or set of points in what is by definition a past 'time', and then using that to predict a future event or behaviour. The management sciences are replete with research and examples of how the technique of falsification is and can be used to arrive at helpful knowledge (Popper, 1953, for example).

The problem comes, however, when a deductive concept that has not been falsified is applied in the social sciences. Other than in clinical testing situations, it tends to be difficult (if not impossible in some instances) to identify all the variables that might affect outcomes in the social sciences, especially those that relate to individuals' characteristics and thought processes. Inductive thinkers do not necessarily believe that most social concepts can ever be 'always right', and therefore tend to content themselves with focusing on the degrees of likelihood of propositions and alternative scenarios. The management sciences are also replete with research and examples of how non-falsifiable information can be used to generate new knowledge and practical solutions to managerial challenges (Hume, 1969, for example).

## 5. Recursivity

Recursivity is defined as something that is produced and changed by an action that is or has also been used to produce and change that same action at a different time (Giddens, 1984). It is, in other words, something that builds upon itself or repeats itself indefinitely in creating what it is. Social constructivists define social phenomena in this way, stating that when humans interact, they build upon their own ideas and actions (Giddens, 1984). However, while the concept is clear, there are two ends of the spectrum in interpreting recursivity. Inductive thinkers will say that this procedure shows a valid truth, and will support it with the perception that there is indeed a real existence of unobservable actions that may have been built upon in order for the phenomena to have come into being. However, we would argue that at the other end of the spectrum, deductive thinkers are not comfortable with recursivity, and do not recognize it as a valid way of arriving at the truth. For them, there must be observable action, somewhere, and this should be reducible to linear time (Orlikowski & Yates, 1994).

## 6. Approach to learning

While learning is a broad and yet disputed field, we would nevertheless argue that individuals perceive how learning comes about from two major, and different, viewpoints. Behaviourists (also known as connectionists) tend to learn by memorizing the rules of a given situation. However, opposed to this is Gestalt Theory, where people are perceived to learn by understanding (Mayer, 1992). The concept of understanding, however, varies in more than the procedure used to learn (memorizing), as the concept of understanding moves people into the realm of cognition, which is already unacceptably intangible for deductivists (Crossan, Lane & White, 1999).

## 7. Approach to thinking and restructuring of problems

It could then be said that there are also two 'poles' related to the schemas that people use to think and restructure problems. An Associationist would be an individual who thinks based on reproductive, stimulus-response links. This person tends to be very precise about knowledge, attempting to apply knowledge from past experience, 'try it till it works', and associates stimuli and responses to structure the problem into a solution. In contrast to this are the Gestaltists, who tend to restructure problems based on productive, reorganizational, organization. As explored alternatives fade and become more vague, they search for ways to create new solutions to new situations. This is often based on rearranging problem elements into uses and solutions not considered before addressing the problem. Essentially, these individuals use their mental structures as units of thought or building blocks to create new thought (Mayer, 1992).

## 8. Approach to categorization

One typical 'pole' in thinking is that of how individuals and groups categorize their social surroundings (Mervis & Rosch, 1981). We would argue that, for deductive thinkers, categories are determinate, with definite boundaries and clear structures. However, for inductive thinkers, categories are an experimental epistemology. For these types of thinkers, (a) categories are internally structured by gradients of representativeness, (b) boundaries are not necessarily definite, (c) there is a close relation between attribute clusters and the structure and formation of categories.

See Table 3.3 below for a summary of the different categories that we recommend considering when evaluating the degree to which an individual may use 'inductive' or 'deductive' thinking to approach their strategic decisions.

## 9. Cognition of empiricism

The current stand-off between reductionists and anti-reductionists about the mental has sparked a long-overdue re-examination of key issues in philosophical methodology. The resulting debate promises to advance our understanding of how empirical discoveries bear on the numerous philosophical problems which involve the analysis or reduction of kinds. The parties to this debate disagree about how, and to what extent, conceptual facts contribute to justifying explanatory reductions. (Gertler, 2002: p. 22)

One of the main points on which inductive thinkers and deductive thinkers disagree is the validity of empirical facts derived from the mental realm. Deductive thinkers would argue, we assert, that to be legitimate, key decision makers' perceptions and roles in issue diagnosis and problem solving must be tangible enough to be observed by all parties.

Inductive thinkers, however, expect that 'human cognitive limitations introduce biases into the development of strategic assumptions and may lead to simplification in strategic schemata. These biases and simplifications affect strategic decisions when decision-makers' existing schemata are used to diagnose and frame new strategic problems' (Schwenk 2001: p. 47).

Formulation must represent an innate, real and demonstrable capability, for deductive thinkers. Inductive thinkers, on the other hand, will look for links between an environment, strategy or structure, that seem to relate to the problem at hand, and therefore could just as easily be cognitive as physical. For them, it is legitimate to reduce knowledge to a cognitive and socially constructed level.

## 10. Use of analogy

An analogy can be defined as something that embodies the essential relationships of the thing that it represents (Cornelissen & Clark, 2010). Or, to put it another way, analogy is the cognitive process of transferring information or meaning from a source to a target (Holland et al., 1986). In relation to induction and deduction, it is the process of inferring or arguing from one particular to another, without having used the premises or conclusions normally involved in the induction or deduction process to arrive at that inference. Analogical reasoning is, therefore, another manner in which managers arrive at their conclusions and actions related to strategic management.

Numerous authors have examined how analogical reasoning contributes to the way that some managers think and act (Cornelissen & Clark, 2010; Baron & Ward, 2004; Gentner, 1998; Robichaud, Giroux & Taylor, 2004; Thagard & Shelley, 1997).

For deductive thinkers, we would argue that analogy is perceived NOT to be an autonomous mode of thought or inference, and therefore is not valid to advance scientific truth. For inductive thinkers, on the other hand, analogy can be a relation, idea, pattern, regularity, attribute, effect or function, and comparisons of these are valid scientific arguments that facilitate understanding (Holyoak & Thagard, 1997; Cornelissen & Clarke, 2010).

## 11.  Use of metaphor

In a similar vein, we also propose that the use of metaphor can be considered a category that can provide us with insight into how Asian vs. Western managers think. The word 'metaphor' can be understood to be a figure of speech, a word or a phrase denoting one thing used in place of another to suggest a likeness between them (Woolf, 1977). When a metaphor is used by a manager, we can evaluate it in terms not only of what the manager is trying to communicate, but more importantly, of how the use of certain metaphors will provide that manager with an a priori perspective.

As Morgan points out, '... all theories of organization and management are based on implicit images or metaphors that lead us to see, understand and manage organizations in distinctive yet partial ways' (Morgan, 1997: p. 4). Managers draw metaphors to illustrate their points, aiming for insight while trying to avoid distortion, and therefore creating a paradox that allows them to see some things while ignoring or not seeing others (Morgan, 1997). Metaphor, therefore, is a strategic tool used by managers to shape the managerial situations they face. However, viewed from an epistemological standpoint, we assert that how a manager uses metaphor will also define many aspects of what the manager will do and think. Ultimately, we agree with Morgan (1997: p. 350) in that, reality has a tendency to reveal itself in accordance to the perspectives through which it is engaged.

Much research has been done on the relation between figurative language, such as metaphors, and other cognitive actions such as stimulus, imagery and response. Paivio, for example, writes that learning is best when the words that are being presented are very concrete and evoke a strong level of imagery, while it is worst when the words used are very abstract (Paivio, 1991). He then proposes a 'dual-coding' theory, in which he identifies whether words are coded mentally into verbal or non-verbal systems, alleging a difference between the left and right hemisphere brain functions. While neuroscience has since gone well beyond what is referred to as the 'left brain, right brain' theory, it still highlights the different ways that individuals can use and interpret metaphorical language (Katz, Paivio & Marschark, 1985). Our point here is that metaphors can also be applied to the differentiation between inductive and deductive thinking, as they can serve to highlight the process by which an intended or strategic use of language can be interpreted differently by different individuals (Cornelissen & Clarke, 2010).

## 12.  Perception of reality

Ultimately, we argue that deductive thinkers start with a different perception of reality from inductive thinkers. This relates back to Chapter 2, where we discuss the two different types of philosophical approaches that underpin Asian thinking vs. Western thinking. We also make reference to some of the philosophical points elaborated above in this chapter, where we point out, for example, the polarities between 'Rationalists' such as Popper, and 'Empiricists' such as Hume. We argue that, potentially, these ontological assumptions can also be used as ways to identify and differentiate between the epistemological processes used by their proponents to perceive reality. For deductive thinkers, for example, there appears to be a tendency for them to see reality as objective and absolute, while for inductive thinkers, reality tends to be perceived as subjective and relative (Holyoak & Thagard, 1997; Cornelissen & Clarke, 2010) (see Table 3.3).

## Conclusion and discussion

We believe there is a case for identifying a group of schemas or sub-schemas typically related to inductive or deductive thinking that potentially serve as general criteria that can be applied to many different situations or environments or people. Although, clearly, there are many combinations of the above schemas, as well as many other schemas that could be considered, we nevertheless propose that these can be grouped into polarized 'inductive' and 'deductive' types or categories, which are used by individuals to approach problems and decisions on a cognitive level. These schema groupings can then serve to provide readers with an additional, but cognitive, set of categories with which to understand the differences between groups or cultures.

In effect, these can then each be generalized to encompass a view of how Western or Eastern managers tend to think when they approach management problems, allowing us a more specific understanding of how other managers tend to think, and therefore enabling us to improve the management of cross-border business situations as well as predictions of potential scenarios or outcomes. In doing this we try to provide the reader with a tool (in addition to many other tools that are associated with other non-cognitive elements of management across borders) for better understanding groups of other people with whom they may work or come into contact.

These schemas are simply a starting point for combining the two different approaches. On the Eastern side, there are specific processes of attention, perception and reasoning that focus in a specific way on detecting important events and discerning relationships among complex systems. These are in contrast to the Western viewpoint, which tends to use different rules and categories to isolate an object from its context, infer categories of which the object is a member, and then infer how rules apply to those categories. While both can be equally valid, they are different epistemological approaches that, by definition, can lead to different conclusions.

Our categories have been proposed and discussed, not as definitive content, but as examples of content that could be identified as relevant to individuals and cases analysed across cultures. We propose that these, and many other categories that the reader could think of, could be put onto a spider diagram, allowing us to identify how we analyse a case, person or situation. Using this method, we can compare whether we think others are thinking in an inductive or deductive manner.

By putting these onto a spider diagram, and having established what we think are the 'poles' at either end that relevantly apply to these different categories, in the context of different cases or individuals studied, and having weighted the categories that are most relevant for us, we can then draw a helpful 'picture' of a managerial thinking process, that can help us use both induction and deduction to arrive at how to address these managerial situations. This is elaborated further in our chapter on theory and framework (Chapter 6). In effect, we are proposing a framework that allows students to both categorize and holistically analyse a case or event or person, and then use that analysis in an integrated fashion to better deal with whatever managerial situation they may be facing, including an uncertain future.

Essentially, we have provided a proposed 'lens' and group of 'sub lenses' which can be used by managers to interpret and act upon the worlds they find themselves in. As a 'shorthand' term, 'inductive thinking' and 'deductive thinking' describe a set of schemas that serve to give us much more insight into the cognitive processes of different groups of international managers, and how they have decided to approach the challenges they face. We assert that the implications are more important here than the exactitude or comprehensiveness of the categories, namely that how managers think can vary strikingly between one group and another, and these differences seem to indicate that researchers' usual assumptions about the basic sharedness of ultimately valid scientific ontologies and epistemologies are not as shared as might have been thought. In other words, inside their heads, groups of managers do come from different thought worlds, where their thought processes and perceptions of scientific, ontological or managerial validity can vary substantially.

Having reviewed relevant literature from philosophical and epistemological perspectives in Chapters 2 and 3, respectively, we will now further reconnoitre literature on cognitive psychology in Chapter 4 and cross-cultural management in Chapter 5. This will facilitate our comprehension of national-level and regional-level behavioural patterns before ultimately undertaking the main task of this book, namely, the schematic understanding of the workings of the two different cognitive epistemologies in the West and Asia in Chapter 6.

# 4
# Literature Review: Cognitive Science Perspective

Though Chapter 2 reviewed different philosophical schools regarding induction and deduction, which were further elaborated in Chapter 3 from a more epistemological perspective, psychology, especially, cognitive psychology may offer a better approach to deductive or inductive ways of thinking than philosophy for the following two reasons:

1. Inductive or deductive thinking may not be at the forefront of the problems addressed by some of the schools of philosophy discussed in Chapter 2. For instance, Plato and Aristotle seek above all to explain the opposition between change and permanence of things (as mentioned in Chapter 2). Idealism does not deal with the opposition of universals and particulars, deduction and induction, but forms part of a higher-level attempt at determining the substance of reality as rational.
2. The problem of inductive and deductive thinking arises with the emerging natural sciences. Although Plato, Aristotle or nominalism could be seen as Descartes' and Locke's antecedents, and even share some of their general topics, their principal concerns seem to lie elsewhere. For instance, the understanding that Aristotle and Locke have of induction is very different, because the former (contrarily to the latter) does not think at all that general laws result from accumulating single cases, but rather from determining the essence of one particular object or phenomenon – although for that the observation of several single cases is considered necessary, albeit not to the exclusion of the possibility that, at least ideally, a general rule (that is the essence of 'tree') could be extracted from the observation of a single case (that is an oak).

Therefore, considering that different approaches to the business situation under study in this book may be better addressed from the viewpoint of cognition and its process, we will now turn to the perspective offered by cognitive science and cognitive psychology.

Cognitive science studies reasoning, perception and other cognitive processes and involves interdisciplinary investigation by psychology, linguistics, neuroscience, artificial intelligence and philosophy (Crane, 2005). It addresses the interdisciplinary study of mind and intelligence and its conclusions about how the mind works must be grounded on experimentation (Thagard, 2008).

Norman (1980: pp. 13–14) specifies that all cognitive systems, both general and animate, interpret and identify the information received by receptors, control the actions to be performed, and guide the allocation of cognitive resources, and enumerates 12 items to be studied that include belief systems, development, language, learning , memory, thought and so on.

Some contend that the main topics with which cognitive science is concerned are (1) artificial intelligence (AI) – the study of cognitive phenomena in machines, (2) attention – the selection of important information, (3) knowledge, and processing, of language (theoretical linguistics, cognitive linguistics and psycholinguistics), (4) learning and development (learning and developmental psychology), (5) memory, (6) perception and action (perception) (Wikipedia, 2010a).

Given that cognitive science covers such a vast range of topics, in this chapter we will centre our attention on the two that seem most relevant to us, namely, memory and cognitive (and, very briefly, developmental) psychology.

In the section on memory, we will first review different definitions and classifications of memory and, second, we will review the relations between memory, generalization and induction.

In the section on cognitive and developmental psychology, we will illustrate and discuss what is implied by the individuation and generalization of words or concepts and how this may influence thought.

## Memory

### Varieties of memory

Zemach (1968: 526) asserts that remembering that p (namely, remembering that something is the case) can serve as a basic definition of the concept of memory in general, since 'all other forms of the said concept (*remembering the...*, *remembering how to...*) can be viewed as merely adding one or more extra conditions to those already included in the original definition'.

Malcolm (1963) cited by Zemach (1968) calls 'remembering that p' factual memory. Zemach (1968: p. 30) contends that 'knowing how to – called habit memory by A. J. Ayer – can be defined through *knowing that p*, since "remembering how necessarily involves remembering *that* something is the case".'

Holland (1954) distinguishes memory-knowledge – the knowledge we have in recollecting – from perceptual knowledge by stating that the former is 'memory-knowledge of the past' and the latter is 'perceptual knowledge of the present'.

Wikipedia (2010a) classifies memory: between (1) a long-term and short-term store, (2) declarative (memory for facts and specific knowledge, specific meanings and specific experiences) and procedural forms (actions and motor sequences such as how to ride a bicycle, often called implicit knowledge).

Thagard (2008) lists (1) habit memory – a range of phenomena from 'simpler forms of associative learning through to kinesthetic, skill, and sequence memory'; (2) propositional memory or semantic memory, namely, 'memory for facts, the vast network of conceptual information underlying our general knowledge of the world: this is naturally expressed as "remembering *that*"'; (3) recollective memory or episodic memory, sometimes called personal memory, experiential memory, or direct memory – memory for experienced events and episodes, such as a conversation this morning or the death of a friend eight years ago ('episodic memories are naturally expressed with a direct object: I remember arguing about Descartes yesterday, and I remember my feelings as we talked'); (4) declarative memory in contrast to non-declarative memory; (5) explicit (accessible verbally) memory and implicit (memory without awareness) memory.

### Memory and causal connectedness

Genuine episodic memories causally depend on the remembered experiences (Sutton, 2010) – namely, memory and causal connectedness. Martin and Deutscher (1966) cited by Sutton (2010) argue that 'the past experience itself must have been causally operative in producing (intervening) states which are in turn causally operative in producing the present collective experience'.

In autobiographical memory, we assign causal significance to specific events so that 'we incorporate a sense of the uniqueness and potential significance of particular choices and actions into our...conceptions of how to live' (Sutton, 2010).

The causal theory of memory, however, does not require that the original experience be entirely traced and allows some transformation at the time of recollection, such as taking a position of onlooker, viewing oneself from the outside (Sutton, 2010).

### Metamemory

Our memory capabilities and strategies aid memory as well as the processes involved in memory self-monitoring (Wikipedia, 2010c). The main theories are (1) cue familiarity hypothesis, (2) accessibility hypothesis, (3) competition hypothesis and (4) interactive hypothesis (Metcalfe & Shimamura, 1994).

Cue familiarity hypothesis implies that judgements about metamemory are dependent on an individual's familiarity with the information provided in the cue (or question) and therefore we are more likely to think that we know the answer to a question if we are familiar with the topic (Reder & Ritter, 1992).

Accessibility hypothesis contends that people base their judgement on retrieved information rather than on the familiarity of the cues (Koriat, 1993).

Competition hypothesis holds that brain systems are activated by different inputs that compete for processing access, which occurs in multiple brain systems and is integrated among the individual systems, and competition can be accessed based on the relevant characteristics of the object (Wikipedia, 2010c).

Interactive hypothesis combines cue familiarity and accessibility hypothesis and suggests that cue familiarity is employed initially and, upon its failure, accessibility gains weight (Koriat & Levy-Sadot, 2001).

### Generalization

The cognitive process and cognition in relation to inductive, deductive and abductive approaches to mentation or intellection may correlate with the generalization at the word or concept level.

The following story will serve as a starting point for a discussion of the role of memory in the inferential process.

Jorge Luis Borges, an Argentinean novelist recounts a strange story of a man named Funes *el Memorioso* or the Memorious (Borges, 1989). This illustration may refer to both declarative and procedural memories mentioned before or only to declarative memory. What interests us is that this story shows that there does not seem to exist any thought process in the absence of generalization, since Pothos (2006: p. 212) argues that inductive inference occurs when generalization by the simplicity principle ('Occam's Razor'[1]) takes place through similarity (Nosofsky, 1992), rules (Hahn & Chater, 1998) and parts of stimuli (Knowlton & Squire, 1996).

According to the summary made by Wikipedia (the italics are the authors'):

> 'Funes the Memorious' tells the story of a fictional version of Borges himself when he meets Ireneo Funes, a teenage boy who lives in Fray Bentos, Uruguay, in 1884. Borges's cousin asks the boy for the time, and Funes replies instantly, without the aid of a watch and accurate to the minute.
>
> Borges...in 1887 comes back to Fray Bentos, intending to relax and study some Latin. He learns that Ireneo Funes has meanwhile suffered a horse-riding accident and is now hopelessly crippled. Soon enough, Borges receives a note from Funes, asking him to lend him some of his Latin books and a dictionary. Borges, disconcerted, sends Funes what he deems the most difficult works[2] 'in order fully to undeceive him'.

Days later, Borges receives a telegram from Buenos Aires calling for his return due to his father's ill health. As he packs, he remembers the books and goes to Funes's house. Funes's mother escorts him to a patio where the youth usually spends his dark hours. As he enters, Borges is greeted by Funes's voice speaking perfect Latin, reciting 'the first paragraph of the twenty-fourth chapter of the seventh book of the Historia Naturalis'.[3]

Funes enumerates to Borges the cases of prodigious memory cited in the Historia Naturalis... reveals that, since his fall from the horse, *he perceives everything in full detail and remembers it all.*[4] *He remembers, for example, the shape of clouds at all given moments, as well as the associated perceptions (muscular, thermal, etc.) of each moment. Funes has an immediate intuition of the mane of a horse or the form of a constantly changing flame that is comparable to our (normal people's) intuition of a simple geometric shape such as a triangle or square.*

In order to pass the time, Funes has engaged in projects such as reconstructing a full day's worth of past memories (an effort which, he finds, takes him another full day), and constructing a 'system of enumeration' that gives each number a different, arbitrary name.[5] Borges correctly points out to him that this is precisely the opposite of a system of enumeration, but Funes is incapable of such understanding... Funes, we are told, is incapable of Platonic ideas, of generalities, of abstraction; his world is one of intolerably uncountable details.[6] He finds it very difficult to sleep, since he recalls 'every crevice and every moulding of the various houses which [surround] him'.

Borges spends the whole night talking to Funes in the dark. When dawn reveals Funes's face, only 19 years old, Borges sees him 'as monumental as bronze, more ancient than Egypt, anterior to the prophecies and the pyramids'.

Later Borges learns that Funes died of natural causes a couple of years after their meeting.[7]

In reminiscence of procedural memory, Borges (1989: p. 490) further adds that '[Funes] had learnt without effort English, French, Portuguese, and Latin. I suspect, however, that he was not very capable of thinking. To think is to forget differences; it concerns generalizing, abstracting. In Funes' crammed world there wasn't but details...'

Because of the absence of the bounded rationality problem (March, 1978), Funes does not seem to need narrowing down his thinking. Theoretically, the novel's hero could beat a computer if he plays a chess game as he is likely to have learnt by heart all possible moves and their consequences. Regarding the role of strategy, the situation is similar to that of perfect competition (namely, everybody holds perfect information).

Because Funes can distinguish every physical object at every distinct time of viewing, he has no clear need of generalization (or detail-suppression) for the management of sense impressions. The narrator claims that this prevents abstract thought, given that induction and deduction rely on this ability. (http://en.wikipedia.org/wiki/Funes_the_Memorious accessed 3 June 2009)

This history raises the issue of what the thinking process is like. Some of the questions that arise are:

1. Absence of generalization: The individuality of each phenomenon in Funes' brain may mean that he does not need to make an abstraction of it and find the commonality among a set of phenomena. He may be viewing the world as it is. On the other hand, it is to be doubted whether the identity of each object can exist if an apple I have in front of me at 20:44 on June 5th 2009 is different in Funes' mind from the same apple at 20:45 on the same day.

   Borges, the author, states that generalities cannot exist in the hero's mind. If there are no generalities there may not exist any possibility or need to find a law linking them together, first, because the phenomena are seen as they are and, second, because the number of linkages between two specific phenomena will become so large that the human mind will not be able to comprehend them simultaneously.

2. Absence of an induction and deduction process: Both deductive and inductive arguments presuppose the existence of premises. In the former, 'the premises provide a guarantee of the truth of the conclusion and support for the conclusion that is so strong that, if the premises are true, it would be impossible for the conclusion to be false'. In the latter, 'the premises provide reasons for supporting the probable truth of the conclusion ... the premises are intended only to be so strong that ... it is unlikely that the conclusion is false.'[8] Mere enumeration of data and facts may not stimulate the induction or deduction thought process.

3. Tacit knowledge: The tacit knowing defined by Polanyi (1966: p. 3) as an act of integration that takes place by reducing 'our focal awareness of observation into a subsidiary awareness of them, by shifting our attention from them to their theoretical coherence' will not be accommodated in Funes' mind. Therefore, there cannot be a tacit apprehension of coherence that is so essential for 'scientific' discovery.

4. Data gathering: The Asians, especially the Japanese, tend to gather data (Nisbett, Peng, Choi & Norenzayan, 2001: p. 299). Their decision-making takes place in the process in which the data collected are taken out one by one during their analysis. What remains in the process constitutes the very decision (Kase, 1996). The data gathering effort may be grounded on a belief in 'complete' data as the guarantor of the quality of processed information. Funes' crammed mind map could be the ideal situation for the Japanese for the wrong reason.

The relations between memory and inferential, especially inductive, thought processes, points 1 and 2 above, have been addressed by a host of researchers. We will review some of them. Our conjecture is that procedural, recollective, explicit and implicit memories, according to the classification of various authors we reviewed above, ought to intervene in this thought process.

According to Fisher and Sloutsky (2005), there are several views about the relations between memory and induction: (a) the naïve theory – even young children conduct induction on the basis of a set of conceptual assumptions about language and the world; (b) the similarity view – induction is a generalization process and young children do it on the basis of multiple commonalities or similarities.

Fisher and Sloutsky (2005) and Sloutsky and Lo (2001) hold that (1) induction is based either on similarity or category, (2) the former is usual among young children (11-year-olds or younger) and the latter among adults, and (3) even adults perform better similarity-based induction with high memory accuracy. In this inductive process, some kind of recognition heuristic may be established when based on memory (Pachur, Broder & Marewski, 2008), influenced by the structure of knowledge and memory (Wilensky, 1983). An argument is category-based if 'the premises and conclusions are of the form All members of C have property P... an example is grizzly bears love onions. Therefore, all bears love onions...' (Osherson, Smith, Wilkie, López & Shafir, 1990: p. 185).

## Developmental psychology: the social world and cognitive development

The psychological changes that take place during the course of human lives are studied by developmental psychology, which is concerned with the explanation and modification of developmental processes (Baltes, Reese & Lipsitt, 1980), studying issues such as whether development occurs by gradual accumulation of knowledge or occurs in stages; and whether children are born with innate mental structures or they learn through experience (Wikipedia, 2010b).

Vygotsky (Tudge & Winterhoff, 1993), Piaget (1999) and Bandura (1971, 1986, 1989, 2001) focus on the social world and its relations with cognitive development from different angles.

Piaget (1968) proposes genetic epistemology to 'explain knowledge on the basis of its history, its sociogenesis, and especially psychological origins of the notions and operations upon which it is based'. It takes into account logical formalizations applied to equilibrated thought structures. Piaget emphasizes that, unlike the traditional philosophical view of epistemology that studies knowledge as it exists at the present moment, genetic epistemology deals with the analysis of knowledge 'for its own sake and within its own framework without regard for its development'.

Genetic epistemology deals with the formation and the meaning of knowledge; its fundamental hypothesis is that 'there is a parallelism between the progress made in the logical and rational organisation of knowledge and the corresponding formative psychological processes' (Piaget, 1968). Piaget defines the field of study by genetic epistemology as the reconstitution of human history and for that purpose, ontogenesis (the origin and development of an individual organism from embryo to adult) is useful. This is the reason why studying children (Bermejo & Rodríguez, 1987) can offer the possibility of learning about the 'development of logical knowledge, mathematical knowledge, physical knowledge, and so forth' (Piaget, 1968).

In this connection, Piaget (1999) analyses the relationships between the acquisition of causality, the advent of speech and representative thought, and the emergence of the concepts of time and space from the first months of life to the eleventh or twelfth year, through children's hands-on experience. Piaget (2008: p. 157) stresses the linkage between language and symbolic play and mental imagery, that is the semiotic function which leads to representative thought.

In addition to children's learning through hands-on experience, Vygotsky emphasizes the importance of timely and sensitive intervention by adults, named 'scaffolding' by Vigotsky (Tudge & Winterhoff, 1993; Wikipedia, 2010a).

However, major topics in cognitive development are the study of language acquisition and the development of perceptual and motor skills (Wikipedia, 2010b). Accordingly, we will proceed in the following section to a review of the cognitive psychology literature on linguistic learning.

## Cognitive psychology: universal ontology, linguistic influence and cognition

Cognitive psychology is a field that may be essential for understanding the different approaches to management we are discussing in the book. Discussion and analysis of experiments conducted by some researchers on language learning may shed light on the relationships between 'substance names' and 'object names' and the Whorfian question of whether linguistic categories affect thought (Quine, 1960, 1968), (Whorf, 1940, 1962, 1997), and therefore, the ways that Asians and Europeans manage their discursive processes.

### Quine's ontological difference between objects and substance

Quine (1968) calls attention to the problems children encounter in learning the ontological difference between entities having a discrete reference (objects or countable nouns) and those having 'scattered' or 'cumulative' reference (substances and attributes, or uncountable nouns).

The learning of a word has two parts: knowing its sound, which is easily attained, and knowing how to use the word, which is more complex, since there may be a problem of 'determinancy', related to a 'system for translating...pluralizations, pronouns, numerals, identity and related devices contextually...' (Quine, 1968: pp. 187–189).

It derives from the inscrutability of reference and the ostensive indistinguishability of the abstract singular from the concrete general, opposing what is called 'deferred ostension' to direct ostension (Quine, 1968: pp. 193–195). Inscrutability of reference refers to the impossibility to discern whether a word is referring to a countable or uncountable noun.

There are two kinds of ostension: 'deferred ostension' and 'direct ostension', with the latter signifying 'the truth or falseness of the term being ostensively explained', whereas the former signifies things such as the gauge in contrast to the gasoline which is shown by the gauge (Quine, 1968: p. 195).

We can distinguish the abstract singular from the concrete general by apparatus individuation thanks to the signs of ostension, namely, 'whether a word takes an indefinite article, whether it takes a plural ending, whether it stands as singular subject, whether it stands as a modifier, as predicate complement, etc.' (Quine, 1968: p. 194).

The indeterminacy may be due not to the meaning (intension) but to reference (extension), that is to say, that perhaps 'reference, extension, has been the firm thing; meaning, intension, the infirm' (Quine, 1968: p. 191).

Quine also points to the existence of a language such as Japanese in which the ontological difference between entities does not exist and 'classifiers' are used as ostensive means (for example, *hiki* in *go-hiki no ushi*, five oxen or five 'units' of ox) (Quine, 1968: pp. 191–912).

## The Whorfian theory of habitual thought and behaviour to language

Whorf (1997: pp. 197, 201) hypothesizes that an accepted pattern of using words is in place before lines of thinking and forms of behaviour and, therefore (1) our concepts of time, space and matter are in part conditioned by a given language's structure, (2) there are tractable affinities between (a) cultural and behavioural norms and (b) large-scale linguistic patter.

Languages differ in how they build their sentences and in how they break down nature to secure the elements to put in those sentences. Thus, English and similar languages lead their native speakers to think of the universe as a collection of distinct objects and events corresponding to words (Whorf, 1955: 240).

Hunt and Agnoli (1991) qualify the Whorfian hypothesis and conclude that 'the weaker form of the hypothesis, which states that language influences thought, has been held to be so vague that it is unprovable' but 'there appears to be a great deal of truth to the linguistic relativity hypothesis', wherefore 'in many ways the language people speak is a guide to the language in which they think'.

## Universal ontology and linguistic influence

Soja, Carey and Spelke (1991) argue that the data of their three experiments go counter to Quine's conjecture, because their two-year-old subjects' projection of the novel word to new objects respected the shape and number of the original referent, while their projection of new words for non-solid substances ignored shape and number, which means that there were no effects on the child's knowledge of count/mass syntax.

Boroditsky (2001) finds a difference between Mandarin speakers and English speakers regarding the conception of time and how language shapes thought about abstract domains and how one's native language influences habitual thought (for example, how one tends to think about time) although it may not entirely determine thought in the strong Whorfian sense.

Imai and Gentner (1997) replicate Soja et al.'s research with Japanese and American children, with the following steps:

1. *Experiment 1a*: adult ratings of shape complexity and meaningfulness: 20 American adults (not participating in the main experiment) rated the complexity of the shapes using a 7-point scale with the result that complex objects received the highest ratings (M = 5.41, SD = 0.74), followed by substances (M = 3.85, SD = 1.04) and finally simple objects (M = 3.31, SD = 1.04);
2. *Experiment 1b*: children's extension of novel words: 43 Japanese-speaking and 42 English-speaking American children aged 2–4 years, and 18 adult Japanese and 18 adult Americans were tested individually, showing each individual four types of complex objects, simple objects and substances ('standard') with shape and material alternatives, making up in total 12 (4*3 = 12) tests for each child. A non-sense name was given to the standard (dax). The subject children were asked, 'Point to the tray that also has the "dax" on it'.

The results of Experiment 1b were:

1. The two language groups showed ontologically-differentiated word meaning projections from the two-year-olds up to the adults.
2. The word meaning projection patterns were largely different across the two language groups: American subjects made a higher proportion of shape responses than Japanese subjects in both the simple object and substance trials; above all, in the substance trials, Japanese subjects consistently projected novel words based on material identity while American subjects failed to show such preference for material-based extension.

3. ANOVA was conducted based on language (2) *age (4) *entity type (3) = 24 variations. There was a significant language effect that indicates that American subjects made more shape responses at p < 0.001.

An interesting point drawn from this experiment is that 'language requires that their speakers pay attention to different dimensions', since 'English count/mass syntax requires speakers to make a dichotomous decision' and therefore 'the structure of English leads to its speakers paying "habitual attention to shape"' (Imai & Gentner, 1997: p. 190). (See Annex 1 that replicates and verifies the object individuation,[9] namely, shape or material recognition, difference between Westerners and Asians.)

Imai and Gentner (1997) and Imai (2002), above all, the former, respond to the ideas advanced by Quine and Whorf and conclude that:

1. The universal use of ontological knowledge in early word learning exists;
2. There are early cross-linguistic differences where American and Japanese children generalize the simple object instances and the substance instances differently;
3. It may be speculated that children universally make a distinction between individuals and not individuals in word learning but that the nature of the categories and the boundary between them are influenced by language.

## Context sensitivity

On the hypotheses that (a) East Asians attend to field information more than Americans and (b) East Asians' perception of objects is more 'bound' to the context in which they were initially encountered than that of Americans, Masuda and Nisbett (2001) conducted two experimental studies with about 150 Japanese and American students showing a variety of objects and backgrounds and discovered that (1) the Japanese tend to refer to field more than Americans, (2) the Japanese reported more statements about relationships between the objects and the background information, and (3) the Japanese recognized more accurately previously seen objects when combined with the original background than when associated with novel backgrounds.

Nisbett, Peng, Choi, and Norenzayan (2001) compare a wider grouping, including Chinese and Koreans, and reason that East Asians' holistic and Americans' analytic cognition are, inter alia, due to the following factors:

1. Relationships and similarities versus rules and categories: among Asians, relationships are used for grouping (for example, shown a photo of a man, a woman and a child, Chinese people would group the woman and the children together as the mother taking care of her children while Americans would group the man and the woman together as adults.

2. Relationships versus categories as the basis for the judgement of association: Chinese people were found to justify more by relationship ('the sun is in the sky') while Americans justify more by category membership ('the sun and the sky are both in the heavens').

3. Family resemblance versus rules as the basis for judgements of similarity: asked to select an object in view of two groups (objects resembling each other; and objects sharing a unidimensional deterministic rule such as a curved stem), East Asians tended to pick the 'family resemblance' group, whereas Americans picked the 'rule' group.

4. Categories and induction: unlike Osherson, Smith, Wilkie, López and Shafir's (1990) statement that people generalize in part depending on the extent to which premise categories cover the lowest-level category (for example, lions and giraffes give the idea of rabbits sharing the same category). Koreans make less use of categories for inductive inference purposes than Americans.

5. Category learning: East Asians are relatively unlikely to use explicit rules for assigning attributes to objects and objects to categories, which makes it more difficult for them to learn how to classify objects by rule systems.

Using two studies, Kitayama, Duffy, Kawamura, and Larsen (2003) support the hypothesis that 'individuals engaging in Asian cultures are more capable of incorporating contextual information and those engaging in North American culture are more capable of ignoring contextual information'.

It may be deduced from these researchers that relationships or context may be one element on which inductive processes are predicated in the East Asian mind.

## Conclusion and discussion

In this chapter, we have reviewed different branches of cognitive science in search of illustration regarding cognition and cognitive process in the belief that it may help us understand more about inductive and deductive ways of thinking.

Memory plays a key role in the cognition process. Generalization, tacit knowledge, data gathering and others have been analysed. Relations of memory with induction and deduction have been reviewed.

In the review of development psychology literature, we have studied the question of whether children are born with innate mental structures or they learn through experience.

But more importantly, the literature survey of cognitive psychology highlights several interesting points such as the role of language, context, relationships among objects and so on in the inductive thinking process.

The key finding here is that the object individuation is different between Asians and Westerners, and it has been confirmed by our empirical experiment in Annex 1. Westerners tend to establish the identity of a new object and 'individuate' it by comparing it with a model or some kind of pattern they have before viewing the object. Form (shape, size, pattern) is the criterion (Wilcox, 1999: p. 130). Asians care more about substance than form. Substance is not a discrete entity and is considered to be uncountable in European languages. We guess that if more attention is paid to substance than to form, Asians must intuitively see something (for them) lying behind each object. Thus, Asians may not need so much to individuate it in order to capture its essence. Substance is the essence.

This carries the implication that Asians cognize objects or phenomena as an entity 'representing' a given substance and, as such, do not need to individuate them. As the substance is captured ex ante, there is no need to generalize the observed phenomena into laws, theories and the like.

This leads to our thesis that Asians have a penchant for inductive ways to approaching business situations, unlike Europeans or Americans (who address a given situation using deductive ways of processing data).

This thesis is amply discussed in Chapter 6, The Theoretical Framework.

# 5
# Literature Review: Cross-Cultural Management Perspective

Markus and Kitayama (1991: p. 224) hold that 'people in different cultures have strikingly different construals of the self, of others, and of the interdependence of the two', which 'can influence, and in many cases determine, the very nature of individual experience, including cognition, emotion, and motivation'.

In this section, we explore Asian and Western cognitive differences from the viewpoint of cross-cultural management (CCM). We start from the assumption that (1) cultural differences that form the base of people's worldview exist, (2) culture works as a cohesive power to cement people's individual and collective action, and (3) culture provides an additional explanation for management to make a sense of different behaviours encountered.'

Our earlier review of the literature on epistemology and cognition provided an overview of these differences between Asians and Westerners in general. Even though any definition of culture per se could be considered arguable, we assert that there are clear cultural differences to be found at regional level, and we will discuss this further in this section. As an expression of collective behaviour, culture can be reflected at the individual, group, or other dimensional levels such as professional or industrial. Given the book's purpose, we argue that the influence of these regional culture differences affect leaders, who then design or refine a firm's strategy. This creates certain differences that we attribute to culture and what we term 'knowledge management style' between Asian and Western enterprises.'

Therefore, in this chapter, we first give some definitions of culture, followed by a review of the methodological approaches to management theory related to culture. This leads us to a discussion of the individualistic and collective approaches to management. After reviewing the applicability of management theories to different cultures, we highlight the issue of convergence and divergence in the globalizing business world. Finally, we conclude and discuss the paradigm shift in cross-cultural management studies.

## Definitions of culture

Academic studies show a considerable variety in their definitions of culture, taking many different approaches and perspectives. In this section, we present a generic review illustrated with examples to help in our readers understanding this complexity in its diversity of definitions, and while addressing its relevance in strategic management studies.'

Cultural issues have been the centre of focus for business scholars for decades (Adler, 1983b; Apospori & Papalexandris, 2008; Azumi, 1974; Bartlett & Ghoshal, 1989; Chinese Culture Connection, 1987; T. Deal & Kennedy, 1982; T. E. Deal & Kennedy, 1999; Dunphy, 1987; Furuya, 2006; G. Hofstede, 1980; Geert Hofstede, 1980; Hofstede, 1993, 2001; Hofstede, Neuijen, Ohavy & Sanders, 1990; Kitayama, Duffy, Kawamura & Larsen, 2003; Markus & Kitayama, 1991; Nisbett, Peng, Choi & Norenzayan, 2001; Fons Trompenaars, 2006; Zhu & Han, 2008). Culture helps us understand and explain apparent differences in the approach taken by managers and entrepreneurs from different cultural backgrounds and nationalities. And we assert that it may also help explain the differences in the way these managers and entrepreneurs perceive of, and then act upon, their strategic managerial tasks.

Therefore, we will explore culture from the viewpoint of cognition processes, centring on its relationship with inductive and deductive ways of thinking (discussed in Chapters 3 and 4).

Understanding culture per se is not a simple matter, because 'culture uses and transforms life to realise a synthesis of a higher order' (Lévi-Strauss, 1969). Thus, it is understandable that culture has been defined in many different ways by different scholars. Some examples of the definition of culture are:

Culture ... is that complex whole which includes knowledge, belief, art, morals, law, custom, and other capabilities and habits acquired by man as a member of society. (Edward Tylor 1903/1988: p. 64)
We have designated as 'cultural sciences' those disciplines which analyse the phenomena of life in terms of their cultural significance. The significance of a configuration of cultural phenomena and the basis of this significance cannot, however, be derived and rendered intelligible by a system of analytical laws, however perfect it may be, since the significance of cultural events presupposes a value orientation towards these events. (Max Weber 1904/1949: p. 75)
Culture consists of patterns, explicit and implicit, of and for behaviour acquired and transmitted by symbols, constituting the distinctive achievement of human groups, including their embodiment in artefacts; the essential core of culture consists of traditional (i.e. historically derived and selected) ideas and especially their attached values; culture systems may, on the one hand, be considered as products of action, on the other

as conditioning elements of further action. (Kroeber and Kluckhohn 1952: p. 357)

Kroeber and Kluckhohn (1952), in their extensive work, compile hundreds of definitions of culture with their critical review of the concept. This compilation provides a catalogue of elements for understanding the concept of culture by dividing them into different definition groups. For example,

• The group of descriptive culture definitions emphasizes 'enumeration of content' (p. 81);
• Historical definitions stress 'social heritage or tradition' (p. 105);
• Normative definitions accentuate 'rule or way' (p. 95);
• Psychological definitions with 'culture as a problem-solving device' (p. 105);
• Structural definitions as 'patterning or organization of culture' (p. 118);
• The group of genetic definitions view 'culture as a product or artefact' (p. 125).

Among other recent influential cultural definitions in management research, there is the often-cited definition by Hofstede (1980a): 'The collective programming of the mind which distinguishes the members of one human group from another…the interactive aggregate of common characteristics that influence a human group's response to its environment.' In this definition, people are seen as being from different cultures if their ways of being and acting as a group differ significantly from other groups.

Even though most scholars might agree with this definition, management scholars vary significantly in how they approach the study of culture and its differences. In the next section, we present six different approaches to culture.

## Approaches to cultural differences

In order to define the relationship between cross-culture and management, Adler (1983a,b) performs a methodological review and describes a typology of six approaches in management studies involving culture: parochial, ethnocentric, polycentric, comparative, geocentric and synergistic. For each approach, there are different assumptions and premises concerning similarities and differences across cultures, and the extent to which management phenomena are or are not universal.

Parochial studies are single-culture studies, many of which have been produced in the United States (Adler, 1983a). In parochial research, universality is assumed in a study's design, ignoring other cultures, even though most of the time this assumption is implicit. By definition, parochial studies do not consider culture as a factor in the research project but treat it as a constant. Therefore, no matter how good the research is, the result's applicability is limited to the domestic environment. That is, if the research is carried out in the United States, the results are, 'at best, applicable to the United States. They may or may not be applicable to Africa, Asia, Europe, or Central and South America' (Adler, 1983b: p. 32).

Before the globalization of business, an extensive domestic market was often considered sufficient and many companies did not need to go abroad. Thus, parochial research worked well in this domestic domain even though it is no longer applicable to many managers' concerns.

Ethnocentric research represents a further step in parochial research, which is originally designed and conducted in one culture but then replicated in another culture. Like parochial research, most ethnocentric research is American-based and is then replicated outside the United States. Moreover, it often implicitly assumes that the home country is superior to another culture in the replicated research and learning comes from extending the research from the home country to another culture (Adler, 1983b).

This approach is interested in extending theories to apply them in other cultural contexts, attempting to confirm or reject whether the theory is culturally dependent or universal. Replication of the research often follows standardization of the project, only differing in the language used. When translating the research instruments and administration, the emphasis is on standardization rather than on assuring the same meaning in each of the target populations.

Thus, differences in meaning are often treated as a result of the study rather than incorporating them into the project's design. Consequently, the results of replicating the study from the first culture may or may not have meaning or importance in another cultural context.

Polycentric research interprets management within a specific culture. In this approach, universality is generally denied, based on two assumptions: one is the equifinality 'that there are many culturally distinct ways to reach any particular management goal'; and the other is the cultural relativity that 'no culture's way of reaching a goal is any better than any other's' (Adler, 1983b: p. 34).

Based on these assumptions, polycentric research is generally carried out following an inductive methodological approach rather than a deductive approach. This minimizes the research process's impact on the culture and allows a pattern to emerge from the data used to generate the models or theories (Adler, 1983b: p. 35). In the process, the researchers' intervention may consciously or unconsciously add their own culture (i.e. design, data collection, interpretation and analysis).

Therefore, researchers not only need to beware of imposing their cultural perspective, but they must also cooperate with local researchers from the target cultural context in order to become more familiar with the cultural conditioning studied (Stening & Zhang, 2007).

The comparative studies approach is designed to identify similarities and differences in a specific field or theory between two or more cultural contexts.

Accordingly, researchers attempt to identify which aspects are universal and which are culturally specific. Unlike ethnocentric or polycentric studies, where the former imposes the theories of one culture on another culture as universal and the latter denies the possibility of universality, comparative studies assume that there is no dominant culture (Hesseling, 1973).

Besides recognizing differences in cultural specificity, this approach also searches for similarities across cultures in order to propose universal theories, even though this is a research outcome rather than a pre-study assumption (Adler, 1983b). The methodology for comparative management studies is complex and faces many challenges, the first being to decide which definition of culture is used.

Echoing what has been described in an earlier section regarding the definition of culture, Ajiferuke and Boddewyn (1970) and Roberts (1970) note that there is no single definition of culture which is generally accepted by most management researchers. Also, the potential bias of a researcher's own culture requires that comparative management studies be carried out by multicultural research teams (Triandis, 1972).

Furthermore, unlike ethnocentric studies in which standardization is used as the crucial criterion for replicating the research in another cultural context, comparative researchers must design the study in such a way as to ensure that the meaning in two or more cultures is similar. Even then, since the results could be confounded by an interaction between the culture and experimental variables Brislin, Lonner & Thorndike (1973) suggest multiple approaches and multiple methods for determining effects other than cultural effects.

Given the complexity presented by comparative management studies, especially in the methodological issues regarding the development of equivalent research, it is difficult to apply the level of rigour of the domestic or ethnocentric studies to comparative studies. Since it is still in its infancy compared with domestic organizational studies, considerable work is still required to develop in the field of comparative studies (Adler, 1983b).

The fifth approach, geocentric studies, focuses on the management of multinational organizations operating in more than one nation. This approach implicitly looks for similarities across cultures. To differentiate from traditional international management studies, geocentric studies go beyond the individual nation (transnational).

Both Child (1981) and Laurent (1983) suggest that the transcultural approach based on individual skills and organizational goals (geocentric) may be most appropriate for macro-level organizational studies. This approach tends to have no problem with translation since English often is the common language used in the company, but distance adds complexity in the research.

Finally, the sixth approach, synergistic research is concerned with people's behaviour within multinational and transnational organizations. It seeks to understand the patterns of relationships and the theories to apply when people from different cultures interact in the workplace. Initially, most of these studies query whether culture is an influence in organizational management. With acceptance of its causation (Child and Tayeb, 1982–83), the issue becomes the extent to which culture is influential relative to other environmental factors. Overall, these six different approaches by scholars to the concept of culture show the reader how very difficult it is, indeed, to use just one definition of culture in an academic study, and how much these definitions can vary by level of analysis. However, we assert that these very differences also serve to highlight our points in other parts of this book. We argue that while cultural differences do exist, these discernible differences can be understood better by evaluating them as philosophically and cognitively based epistemologies. In essence, we are proposing a 'seventh approach' to culture studies, exhorting our readers to consider these cultural differences as indicators of a how managers in two different regions tend to think.

## Comparative culture: individualism and collectivism

After introducing these different approaches to cross-cultural studies, we now concentrate on comparative culture to discuss the cultural differences between Asians and Westerners, illustrating them with the specific dimensions of individualism and collectivism.

Inspired by his Chinese students, Nisbett (2003a) converted from a lifelong universalistic scholar to a comparative scholar. In his work *The Geography of Thought,* he compares the different ways of thinking between Asians and Westerners and seeks to explain why these differences exist. Going back to the origin of the two cultures, ancient philosophy, science and society in Greece and China were compared, represented by syllogism and the Tao for Western and East Asian societies, respectively.

To start with, the ancient Greeks, unlike other ancient peoples, 'had a sense of personal agency, being in charge of their own lives and free to act as they chose' (Nisbett, 2003a: p. 2). This implies that individual identity accompanied this sense of personal agency, which also fuelled the tradition of debate. On the other hand, the ancient Chinese centred on Harmony. This implies collective behaviour rather than the individual behaviour of the Greeks.

As philosopher Henry Rosemont wrote: '... For the early Confucians, there can be no me in isolation, to be considered abstractly: I am the totality of roles I live in relation to specific others...' (cited by Nisbett, 2003: p. 5). Self-control was important in Chinese culture to minimize friction with others and make it easier to abide by other people's requirements. From the Tao as the main philosophy for harmonious society as a whole, to the system of government built on Confucianism, the Chinese had a sense of 'collective agency' (Nisbett, 2003: p. 6).

This difference between individualism and collectivism was also highlighted by Hofstede (1980a) and Trompenaars and Hampden-Turner (1997), even though these authors have focused more on the country level (e.g. Chinese versus Greek) rather than the regional level (e.g. Asians versus Westerners). The first of the four dimensions that Hofstede (1980a) identified as having the same pattern of differences between countries is individualism versus collectivism. The other three are large or small power distance, strong or weak uncertainty avoidance, masculinity versus femininity.

This dimension of individualism versus collectivism is also presented in the seven-dimension model of national culture differences of Trompenaars (1993), with correlation and factor analysis at the country level. However, the latter's work has been criticized because the results have only statistically confirmed two of the seven dimensions: Individualism/Achievement and Universalism/Diffuse. Moreover, 'both [dimensions] are correlated with Hofstede's Individualism dimension' (Hofstede, 1996).

While other dimensions presented in Hofstede's and Trompenaars' works have appeared to be arguable, the dimension of individualism has been generally accepted. In this sense, individualism versus collectivism could be considered one of the main indicators of cultural differences, with special relevance for the inference of relations between self and others.

In the definition of Hofstede (1983), the fundamental issue involved in individualism versus collectivism 'is the relation between an individual and his or her fellow individuals'. Therefore, in the continuum of the scale, we can find loosely integrated societies at one end, with individuals who 'look after his or her own self-interest and maybe the interest of his or her immediate family'; and tightly integrated societies at the other end, with individuals who 'are born into collectives or in-groups which may be their extended family (including grandparents, uncles, aunts and so on), their tribe, or their village'.

In loosely integrated societies, individuals have a large amount of freedom to act; in tightly integrated societies, people are given less freedom but have a large amount of commitment, since they are 'supposed to look after the interest of his or her in-group and to have no other opinions and beliefs than the opinions and beliefs of their in-group'.

Nisbett (1992, 1998, 2003b: p. 52; 2003a, 2001) presents a figure to illustrate the Eastern and Western views of the relations among self, in-group and out-group. In this illustration, the distance between in-group and out-group is highlighted. Thus, in the Eastern view, there is a large distance between two groups; in the Western view, the distance is shorter. Nisbett (1998) also highlights the relation between self and in-group. Thus, in the Eastern view, the self is close and more pertaining to the in-group; in the Western view, the self is more distant from the in-group. In this figure, Nisbett (2001) presents each (self, in-group and out-group) as a single unit. Following the logic of an inclusive and exclusive relation, respectively, 'between the self and in-group' and 'between the self and out-group', we draw Figure 5.1 to present these two different perspectives (i.e. Asian and Western) on the self and others to illustrate the origin of the different mindsets.

In the illustration presented, since the self is part of a group (in-group) and all outsiders (outside of the group) are out-group members, the out-group is no longer presented in a single circle. As Nesbitt (2003: p. 51) considers the in-group as the 'close circle of friends and family', only Asians really give a strong meaning of (extended) family to this group, in which they feel a strong tie with other members in the 'family'. The group relation among Westerners is actually the concept of family for most Asians or, at any rate, most Chinese. Consequently, we use the term 'family' to place the general term of 'in-group' in the Asian perspective.

The definition of family is extended from the blood relation family to a broader family with strong ties in different circumstances. The self is a part of this big family; the frontier between the two becomes fuzzy since one is for others and others supposedly will also take care of each individual.

Therefore, we use a dotted line for the circle of the self in the Asian perspective to describe this fuzzy connection between the self and the family.

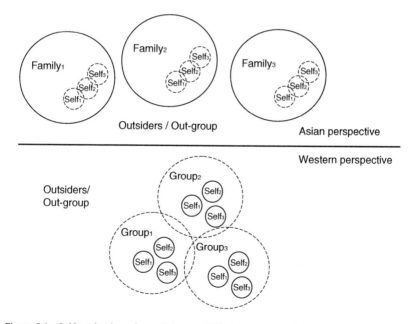

*Figure 5.1*  Self and others from Asian and Western perspectives

*Note*: The subscripts refer to the unit of analysis, i.e., self₁, self₂, etc., correspond to different individuals as units of analysis.

*Source*: Authors.

Meanwhile, in a Western-defined group concept, the self is the centre and there are many different layers whose frontier with self is strictly delimited. Thus, the group organization is relatively more open to other outsiders and the group organization per se is more flexible and unstable than the concept of family in Asia. Hence, we draw a solid line for the circle of the self and a dotted line for the group in the Western perspective.

The strong personal ties between and among family members for each individual (i.e. $self_1$, $self_2$, $self_3$ ...) in Asian societies create interdependence for individuals from their childhood onwards. However, most Western children are often encouraged quite explicitly to be independent (Nisbett, 2003). The interdependence of Asian family members makes the family unit solid but also builds a fence around the family unit for better internal protection and to impede access from outside. Therefore, the circle of the family is drawn with a solid line, and the frontier between families (i.e. $family_1$, $family_2$, $family_3$ ...) is much clearer than the frontier between groups (i.e. $group_1$, $group_2$, $group_3$ ...) from the Western perspective.

### Differences in cognition

As it may be argued that individualism and collectivism are the fundamental parameters for distinguishing between Asian and Western cultures, the next question is how this pattern is formed. It has long been believed that culture plays an important role in the formation of the cognitive mental procedure for perceiving, interpreting and constructing reality as well as for identifying and solving issues.

Another of the often cited and deployed definitions of culture in organization studies performed from the psychological perspective is: 'a pattern of shared basic assumptions that the group learned as it solved its problems of external adaptation and internal integration, that has worked well enough to be considered valid and, therefore, to be taught to new members as the correct way to perceive, think, and feel in relation to these problems' (Schein, 1992).

But if we accept this definition that culture is 'learned', then 'its ultimate locus must be in individuals rather than in groups ... then cultural theory must explain in what sense we can speak of culture as being shared or as the property of groups at all, and it must explain what the processes are by which "sharing arises"' (Goodenough, 1971). Accordingly, this cognitive perspective of culture helps build our rationale for analysing different ways that entrepreneurs manage their businesses in different environments.

As a consequence of the above, entrepreneurs and managers in these different regions behave differently in different situations. How individuals perceive problems and solve them depends on what they learned during the early years in their education and even in their language training. In the cross-linguistic study performed by Imai and Gentner (1997: p. 169), they suggested that there is 'a universal use of ontological knowledge in early word learning, but the nature of the categories and the boundary between them is [much] influenced by language'.

An individual gains culture through a lifetime's learning experience and the projection of word meanings is a part of collective culture for those who share the same culture. Imai and Gentner (1997: p. 197) conclude that 'the projection of word meaning is determined by an interplay of cognitive and language-specific factors' even though further studies are needed to discover which kind of categories are most likely influenced by language and how the development is manifested (of which more in Chapter 4).

Nonetheless, Nisbett (2003) is also aware of the generalization of two large cultural blocs as Asian and Western, where billions of people are simply labelled with these single terms and treated as if they were identical. Indeed, in his early work, Hofstede (1980a: p. 11) already 'explores the differences in thinking and social actions that exist between members of 40 different modern nations'.

Irrespective of whether the cross-cultural study is performed at regional or national level, the truth is that since the landmark work of Hofstede (1980a), the focus of cultural studies has shifted from organizational level to national level (most of the time). The current state of the art in the field of cross-cultural management is much more complex. Zhang, Dolan & Zhou (2009) argued that the current cultural studies undergo a paradigm shift at this stage of complexity (see Figure 5.2).

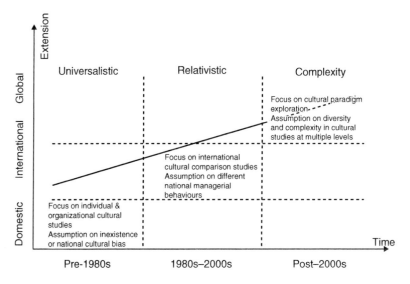

*Figure 5.2* Evolution of cultural studies in organization theory

*Source*: Adapted from Zhang, Dolan and Zhou (2009: p. 278).

## Management theories on culture

As illustrated in the Figure 5.2 above, the studies of management theory have gone through the evolution from culture-free (universalistic) to relativistic (contingent), and are now introducing complexity theory into today's globalized business world with regard to national cultures (Zhang, Dolan & Zhou, 2009). Research in comparative studies in international business has surged dramatically following Hofstede's *Culture's Consequences* (1980a). As a result, studies on culture have become mainstream instead of a past fad in managerial research (Hofstede, Neuijen, Ohavy & Sanders, 1990).

From different perspectives of culture, we can observe that most of the leading modern management theories have been generated and studied within the context of the Western corporate world. These theories generally assume the universality of their applicability in the world, irrespective of any cultural differences. However, the applicability of these managerial theories in other cultural contexts such as Asia is questionable.

Even though the definition of culture is arguable, as discussed earlier, this debate could continue as an extension of geography. The first question Adler (1983b: p. 40) raises on the definition of culture in the field of comparative management is 'can a country, or nation-state, be used as a surrogate definition for culture?' Given that national boundaries are often non-explicitly used or accepted as 'operational definitions of culturally distinct units', in most comparative management studies, this definition has also been adopted here to incorporate culture in the evolution of organizational studies.

If culture is understood in terms of national culture, then most management theories are culture-free since the main scope of these theories was domestic business. Thus, management theories were systematically assumed to be universal and applicable to the entire world (Hofstede, 1994). As business has become increasingly international, managers and entrepreneurs have also become more aware of national cultural differences and international business theories, and have demanded that culture be taken into consideration.

Hofstede's *Culture's Consequences* (1980a) and his later articles on national cultural differences (Hofstede, 1983, 1984) marked a reference point that set the course for international business studies. Thus, cultural relativity has gained popularity in management theories and various instruments have been developed for cross-cultural measurement studies and training, building a foundation for this line of research. Examples are the Survey conducted in *Culture's Consequences* (CCS) by Hofstede (1980a), and the further developed fifth dimension added from the Chinese Value Survey (CVS; Chinese Culture Connection, 1987).

Geert Hofstede and his colleagues such as Michael Bond use five cultural dimensions to measure cultural differences between different countries: power distance index, individualism, masculinity, uncertainty avoidance index, and long-term orientation (e.g. Hofstede & Bond, 1988).

Some researchers have attributed this cultural difference to the distinction between the self and the others as, for example, proposed by Markus and Kitayama (1991). In their conception, many Asian cultures insist more on the 'fundamental relatedness of individuals to each other', while American culture or Western culture in general 'neither assumes nor values such an overt connectedness among individuals'. In other words, there is a difference in the definition 'between a construal of the self as independent and a construal of the self as interdependent' and 'each of these divergent construals should have a set of specific consequences for cognition, emotion, and motivation' (Markus & Kitayama, 1991: p. 224).

In their work, they gave several examples to illustrate that people in the US stress attention to the self, the relevance of oneself to differentiate from others, and of asserting their self; for their part, Japanese people attempt to fit in with others, emphasizing attention to others, and the relevance of a harmonious interdependence with them.

Hence, we take a stance that culture is a basic unit of our analysis. However, instead of taking it at each national level, we capture it at a higher level of categorization, namely, the regions, (East) Asia and the West, in a similar vein to Toynbee (1946a,b), who manages the civilizations as his basic units of analysis, as 'the forces in action are not national but proceed from wider causes...and not intelligible in their partial operation unless a comprehensive view is taken...' (Toynbee, 1946a: p. 3).

In support of the argument that the world will be shaped by the interaction of seven or eight civilizations or groups of countries, Huntington (1993) enumerates several reasons: their differences are real; the process of modernization is separating people from traditional local identities; civilization-consciousness is growing; cultural characteristics are less mutable than political and economic characteristics, among others.

There are other management scholars who use cultural studies in different ways: for example, Farh, Hackett and Liang (2007) use cultural differences to account for the perceived organizational support-employee outcomes relationships; Huang and Dastmalchian (2006) for the implications of trust and distrust for organizations; Hutchings (2002) for the selection process for expatriates; and Liu, Friedman and Chi (2005) for specific relationships between individual differences and distributive negotiations. Similarly, we also have argued earlier that there are substantial differences between Asian and Western philosophies, which have influenced the culture and the way of being managers and entrepreneurs.

## Convergence or divergence: globalization and national culture change

By saying that we are focusing in this book on a higher level of cultural studies, specifically, between Asians and Westerners, we recognize that this is also based on globalization trends and national culture changes. Cross-cultural knowledge management has even been suggested to reconcile the imbalance between global and local concerns in the global organizations (Paulee, Rooney & Holden, 2010).

Another term used by scholars to express universality or contextuality is convergence and divergence (Dunphy, 1987; Tregaskis & Brewster, 2006; Apospori & Papalexandris, 2008). Based on the example of Japanese enterprises and their management, Dunphy (1987) has discussed convergence or divergence in a temporal review. In the analysis by Tregaskis and Brewster (2006) of the contingent employment practice in Europe over a decade, a limited convergence by the institutional embeddedness of organizations is suggested. The convergence/divergence trend could shift when managers gain more experience and enterprises succeed in the global market.

Coinciding with the premise of comparative cultural studies defined by Adler (1983b), no full convergence or divergence has been confirmed in management reality. There has always been a co-existence between the two. Even though we hypothesize a tendency by Asians towards induction and by Westerners towards deduction, this pattern of co-existence may change. As business becomes more globally diverse and uncertainty increases, Asians and Westerners may learn from each other to adapt to new circumstances.

Thus, not only the universalistic perspective is coming under additional criticism, but also the national cultural paradigm in cultural studies is being questioned (see Gerhart, 2009). As Williams (1981) said, '...in highly developed and complex societies there are [...] many levels of social and material transformation... [Culture] is indeed in the area of these complex transformations that the signifying system is itself developed and must be analyzed' (p. 210); a new paradigm of cultural studies and international/global business is needed to fulfil this demand in a complex society.

Even though most of Hofstede and his colleagues' studies are at national level, considering that cultural differences are the 'most recognizable' at this level, they accept that the cultural relativity of any managerial theory can be found not only across countries but possibly even within them (Hofstede, 1994: p. 4). The second question that Adler (1983b: p. 40) raises in relation with culture definition is precisely that 'should populations within a national boundary be considered as culturally homogeneous or as multi-cultural (Adler, 1983b)?'

This has also been empirically confirmed by scholars such as Dolan, Díez, Fernández, Martín & Martínez, (2004) in their studies of regional cultural differences within a single country. To test whether geographical factors affect culture more than linguistic factors, Zhang, Straub and Kusyk (2007) studied the same linguistic group in different regions across countries and found that there were significant cultural differences in two very different geographical locations (Europe and North America) in spite of using the same language, French. Various other approaches have been employed in the studies. For instance, studies on cultural differences based on gender (Maddock & Parkin, 1993; Powell, 1993; Rosener, 1990) and religion are booming (Biberman & Altman, 2004).

Thus, even though cultural differences at the national level are a topic of ongoing research, different orders and priorities are evidence of different research directions. Complexity suggests multiple intricacies for dealing with turbulent environments; 'order and construct [may] emerge after chaos is guided and led towards one defined direction in accordance with natural rules' (Dolan, Garcia & Auerbach, 2003).

This inner generated complexity in cultural studies also echoes the external environmental complexity in globalizing business. Not only managers and entrepreneurs who go abroad to do international business are facing cultural challenges, but also the continuous movement of international talent and immigrants is creating cultural diversity in the workplace.

However, a simple application of national cultural differences may constitute more a stereotype than effective cultural understanding. This is especially relevant and true when we can easily get in touch with other cultures, experience them and merge them with the traditional culture.

Thus, an individual's acculturation process may change the typical traditional cultural pattern (Pool, 1965; Kim, 1977; Tung, 1998; Peñaloza & Gilly, 1999; Safdar, Lay & Struthers, 2003; Rahman & Rollock, 2004). In their edited book, *Cross-Cultural Management*, Tjosvold & Leung (2003) suggest that managers and researchers in Western countries 'alike increasingly recognize the limitations of traditional organizational theories and management approaches that assume individual and cultural homogeneity'; therefore, they are also willing 'to move away from reliance on Western ideas and approaches to incorporate those from Asian and other cultures'. In this sense, Western managers and entrepreneurs are also 'experimenting with new ways of organizing and managing...' (p. 2).

This dynamic acculturation perspective of culture adds an additional complexity in the studies of cross-cultural management. Thus, culture is not only static but also dynamic, evolving contingently to other factors. The third question that Adler (1983b: p. 40) raises regarding the definition of culture is that 'should culture be treated as an independent variable, a constant, a dependent variable, or a residual variable?'

In the universalistic or ethnocentric perspective of management theory, culture is often treated as a constant or a residual variable. When culture is addressed comparatively across nations, it is often treated as static and unchangeable. Hence, in most of the studies cited in the section above, it is treated as an independent variable. However, if a dynamic perspective of culture definition is taken, then most probably it needs to be treated as a dependent variable in order to observe which factors constitute a different culture and how it is changed. Culture could also be treated as an intervening variable modifying and being modified by other phenomena (Roberts, 1970: p. 331).

## Conclusion and discussion

As mentioned above, the cultural paradigm has been changing while globalization has become a commonplace process. In the social science, the paradigm has been treated as relevant to understanding collective scholarly thinking. In *The Structure of Scientific Revolutions*, Kuhn (1996) characterized science by the dominance of succeeding paradigms as models for thinking or 'a constellation of concepts, values, perceptions and practices shared by a community which forms a particular vision of reality that is the way a community organizes itself'. When a certain 'vision of the reality' is generally accepted by the scholarly community, it forms a paradigm in theory building and testing. This established paradigm helps scholars to see certain things in a certain way within it. However, it also makes it difficult to see other certain things that do not belong within the paradigm (Clarke & Clegg, 2000).

In the cultural paradigm that management scholars have been exploring, it has shifted from a universalistic perspective to a relativistic perspective. While at the national level, cultural differences have been at the core of cross-cultural management studies for decades, rising critics have pushed the field towards a new paradigm shift into complexity. Until a new established paradigm is built, the former will retain its functionality and influence (Kuhn, 1996).

Since the culturally 'underlying intellectual, economic and technological dynamics seem too powerful to reverse ... [one also needs] to understand, approach and handle our cultural differences' (Tjosvold & Leung, 2003: p. 2). The difference in the native cultures embedded in the researchers adds an additional difficulty in advancing cross-cultural differences.

In this process of cultural paradigm shift, we face the challenge of exploring a new paradigm: How does the interaction between different cultures affect the cross-cultural paradigm? Will the national-level cultural differences still be the most significant in global business as during the international business stage? What will be the new elements of the cultural studies in the new paradigm? How do cultural differences influence inductive and deductive management logic among Asian and Western managers and entrepreneurs?

In the complex organizational context that business is facing, cultural issues appear to be situated in a complex array of multidimensional, multileveled and multilayered constructs (Leung, Bhagat, Buchan, Erez & Gibson, 2005) in order to achieve and maintain competitive advantages. In this context, the dividing line between the analytical units of cultural studies becomes fuzzy.

Within the complexity perspective of the cultural paradigm, organizational culture regains weight in cultural studies. For instance, organizations viewed in terms of complexity theory help leaders to fine-tune managerial philosophies within a culture of organized chaos (Dolan, Garcia & Auerbach, 2003). How to balance the organizational culture with the national culture within the global business context is one of the critical issues in the new paradigm. In accordance with complexity theory, the situation often self-organizes. In the complexity of cross-cultural management, it represents the fact that managers and entrepreneurs need to be inductive and creative to adapt to new contextual situations implying active learning.

At the same time, they also need to be deductive and efficient to apply current knowledge. This corresponds to the exploration and exploitation theory of knowledge as March (1991) suggests for organizational learning. Exploration is the creative process of inducing general phenomena from realities and exploitation is the efficient process of deducing and maximizing the utility of existing knowledge. This combination of inductive exploration and deductive exploitation becomes important at different times in the company's and industry's lifecycle. Moreover, culturally coded knowledge needs to be managed within the global context in order to achieve better reconciliation at different units and levels (Pauleen, Rooney & Holden, 2010).

In conclusion we confirm the assumption mentioned at the beginning of the chapter in that (1) cultural differences that form the base of people's world-view exist, (2) culture works as a cohesive power to cement people's individual and collective action, and (3) culture provides an explanation for management to make sense of different behaviours.

Such assumption, however, ought to be qualified to some extent in the sense that, after reviewing cross-cultural management literature, we employ a dynamic perspective of culture as explained above to approach and reconcile two extremes of inductive and deductive management style, which are viewed as opposites and therefore traditionally confront each other.

When the relativistic cultural paradigm was established decades ago, it broke the old universalistic cultural paradigm. Even though it is generally agreed that culture is the cement for people to act cohesively, the critical analytical unit of culture per se is questioned in a complex cultural paradigm. If culture is viewed as a dynamic object, then it is only treated as an independent or dependent variable, that also plays a role in bringing in change, and self-organizing.

# 6
# Theoretical Framework

This chapter is the central part of the book. To facilitate the reader's understanding we anticipate here by way of executive summary the main points to be addressed.

- In accordance with the different perspectives advanced in Chapters 2, 3, 4 and 5 we propose a theoretical framework to analyse and interpret our thesis: (1) that there is a difference in the management thinking used by (Eastern) Asians and Westerners and (2) that such a difference is explicable if we view it from the angle of inductive and deductive ways of thinking.
- Our thesis is based, apart from the literature review we have carried out on the different perspectives, on the case studies we have attached on eight Western and Asian entrepreneurs/organizations. These cases are focused mainly on the figures of their leaders, and the analyses are included below.
- First, after a brief introduction to the theories on inductive and deductive ways of thinking, we proceed to analysing the cases. Different epistemological categories explained in Chapter 3 are made use of for better understanding.
- Second, after using the case analyses as examples of our thesis, we propose a theoretical framework regarding the difference in cognitive and inferential approaches used by Asians and Westerners.
- Finally, their relation with the concepts of tacit and explicit knowledge are discussed.

## Introduction: theories for analysing cases from an inductive or deductive viewpoint

In our Introduction in Chapter 1, we asked whether there were any differences in the cognitive processes used by Asians (mainly Japanese, Chinese and Koreans) vs. those used by Westerners. The question arises from the differences observed in behavioural phenomena regarding the ways managers in each group tend to carry out decision-making and strategic diversification.

Despite accepted wisdom in the West, as well as findings by management researchers (Rumelt, 1974, 1982; Ginsberg, 1990; Keats, 1990; Keats & Hitt, 1988; Khanna & Papelu, 1997; Markides & Wiliamson, 1994; Montgomery & Wernerfelt, 1988; Montgomery, 1982; Palich, Cardinal & Miller, 2000; Park, 2003; Peng, Lee & Wang, 2005; Ramanujam & Varadarajan, 1989; Rumelt, 1982; Singh & Montgomery, 1987) that emphasize the importance of diversification into businesses related to the firm's core business and to the firm's dominant logic (Bettis & Prahalad, 1995; Grant, 1996), we have observed that Asian entrepreneurs are more daring and tend to take up business opportunities that may not offer the kinds of guarantee of success that Western management dicta would demand to be taken into account.

Japan's Sony, for example, covers extremely divergent areas, such as consumer electronics, insurance and banking. Korea's Lotte Group is engaged in candy manufacturing, retail, financial services, heavy chemicals, entertainment and more.

What could be the underlying dominant logic that would justify such dispersion? Is it possible that such a logic does not exist? If there is one, what is it? And why are there behavioural patterns in Asia so divergent from those of the West?

With these questions in mind, we first wrote and collected in-depth case studies on Asian and Western management, which we have included in Annex 2. Secondly, we conducted literature reviews in Chapters 2, 3, 4 and 5 of relevant debates on cognition and knowledge in philosophy, especially epistemology, cognitive psychology and cross-cultural management.

Likewise, in pursuing the findings presented in Chapter 4, we have carried out an experimental survey with Asians and Westerners to focus on their different cognitive approaches, as well as replicating and adapting to our study the findings and analysis by other researchers in linguistic and cognitive psychology (Gentner, Imai & Boroditsky, 2002; Imai, 2002; Imai & Gentner, 1997), whose outcome is described in Annex 1.

Accordingly, we are now in a position to advance our proposition concerning the working of the cognitive process in the minds of Asians and Westerners.

This chapter will consist of two sections: first we present our analysis of the cases, and describe some theoretical frameworks that can be used to interpret the workings of Asians' and Westerners' mental schemes; and second, we further discuss the dimensions of induction and deduction as well as how they relate to tacit and explicit concepts, a central theme in the field of cognition and knowledge.

Centring on the research topic of this book, both the analysis of practical examples and the theoretical framework attempt to demonstrate our proposition that Asians (Eastern Asians) and Westerners differ from each other in their cognition process; and that the former have a penchant for inductive thinking and the latter for deductive thinking.[1]

In support of our proposition, we will avail ourselves of 12 schema categories as illustrated in Table 6.1,[2] related to inductive and deductive thinking (explained in Chapter 3)

In the light of previous studies by Kase, Sáez & Riquelme (2005) that developed a leadership category in terms of cognition, we have added an Appendix at the end of this chapter that compares induction/deduction with these models (long-term oriented PIF and short-term oriented PA concepts in leadership) in order to present a more rounded picture.

## Induction and deduction

As our analytical focus concerns inductive and deductive ways of thinking, this section is divided into two. First, the analysis of inductive cases and deductive cases are both conducted in Annex 2. Then we (1) propose a theoretical framework that explains these different reasoning and inferential processes, which, we argue, follow the inductive and deductive ways that build upon an induction and deduction paradigm and (2) describe the factors affecting these two processes or approaches in management.

### 1. Induction and deduction in operation: illustrations from the cases

The case studies carried out for this book represent various countries as well as two regions of origin. As Table 6.2 summarizes, four examples come from Asia and four from the West. Three of these are classified as deductive and four as inductive, with the remaining study illustrating a combination of the two approaches within a firm and the conflict derived from the resulting divergence in management focus.

We have defined the country of origin for each case either as the home base of the case companies' CEOs or as the home country where the protagonists grew up. Two cases run against this definition: Lenovo and Dr Richner. Though the former's headquarters is now in the US, we have classified this as a Chinese case since Liu Chuanzhi, its founder and the protagonist of the case, developed his entrepreneurial activities in China. Second, Dr Beat Richner, who founded four children's hospitals in Cambodia, has had Asia as his usual place of residence for the last two decades. Nevertheless, we assert that he thinks and behaves as a European professional.

We now proceed to analyse and identify different management thought processes based on the above case studies. Although we assert that Asians are basically inductive thinkers, we also identify one of the Asian cases as an example of deductive thinking (Acer's Stan Shih). Likewise we have a Western exception (Virgin Group's Richard Branson[3]) that follows an inductive management approach. Finally, the Logico case illustrates the

*Table 6.1* Twelve schema categories related to inductive and deductive thinking

| Schema categories | Deductive | Inductive |
|---|---|---|
| Temporality (how time is perceived) | Anticipation of predictability and linearity of time | Anticipation of unpredictability and circularity of time |
| Predictability (how future uncertainty is coped with) | Guarantees in projected future | Probable truth in projected future |
| Materiality (perception about whether the world is only physical or contains non-substance) | Tangibility of the material | Equal validity of tangible and intangible materiality |
| Falsifiability (statement as open to error or as absolute truth) | Numeric and demonstrable falsifiability of propositions | Degrees of likelihood of propositions and alternative scenarios |
| Recursivity (repetition of itself) | Not admitted: there must be observability of linear actions | Real existence of unobservable and recursive actions |
| Approach to learning | Behaviourist (connectionist): learn by memorizing | Gestalt (cognitive): learn by understanding |
| Approach to thinking and restructuring of problems | Associationist: reproductive, stimulus-response linked, and precise (apply solution habits from past experience, try till it works, associate stimuli and responses) | Gestaltist: productive, reorganizative, organization fades, and vague (create new solution to new situation, rearrange problem elements, mental structures are units of thought) |
| Approach to categorization (of social surroundings) | Categories are determinate, with definite boundaries and clear structures | Categories are an experimental epistemology (a) categories are internally structured by gradients of representativeness (b) boundaries are not necessarily definite (c) there is a close relation between attribute clusters and structure and formation of categories |

Continued

*Table 6.1* Continued

| Schema categories | Deductive | Inductive |
|---|---|---|
| Cognition (about the validity of empirical facts derived from the mental realm) | To be legitimate, key decision makers' perceptions and role in issue diagnosis and problem formulation must represent innate, real, and demonstrable capability | Links between environment, strategy, structure can legitimately be cognitive and socially constructed |
| Use of Analogy | Analogy is not an autonomous mode of thought or inference, and therefore is not valid to advance scientific truth | Analogy can be a relation, idea, pattern, regularity, attribute, effect or function, and comparisons of these are valid arguments that facilitate understanding |
| Use of Metaphor | Metaphors are concrete and verbally coded | Metaphors can be abstract, and verbally or non verbally coded |
| Perception of Reality | Objective–absolute | Subjective–relative |

*Source*: Authors.

combination of both inductive and deductive approaches. Therefore, we first describe some inductive approaches that are prevalent among Asian executives and firms (including the exceptional Western case). An Asian case (Allen Lee) is added as it illustrates some traits of an inductive manager's typical behaviour pattern. And then we follow that with a description of deductive approaches taken by Western executives and firms (including this Asian exceptional case). Finally the combined approach in the Logico case is presented.

### Case analysis: an inductive management approach

Within the inductive management approach, two different patterns have been identified in the decision-making process: (a) One group of top decision makers places more emphasis on the analysis of situations and decision-making based on a set of highly abstract principles, (b) while the other group shows that they capture the situation and address it as a long series or continuum of fine-tuning of short-term actions. We would argue, however, that (a) and (b) are not mutually exclusive approaches, as each merely shows where more of the emphasis is placed – that is, either top-heavy or bottom-heavy.

*Table 6.2*   List of the cases in Annex 2

|  | Examples | Deductive | Inductive | Combination deductive/ inductive |
|---|---|---|---|---|
| Asians (4) | Taiwan: Stan Shih (ACER) SM-1557-E Annex 2.1 | √ | | |
| | Japan: Imperial Japanese Army SM-1558-E Annex 2.2 | | √ | |
| | China: Liu Chuanzhi (Lenovo) DG-1521-E Annex 2.3 | | √ | |
| | China: Ren Zhengfei (Hua Wei) SM-1560 Annex 2.4 | | √ | |
| Westerners (4) | Switzerland: Dr Beat Richner SM-1548-E Annex 2.5 | √ | | |
| | Spain: Emilio Botin and Aflredo Sáenz (Banco Santander) SM-1534-E Annex 2.6 | √ | | |
| | UK: Richard Branson (Virgin Group) SM-1559 Annex 2.7 | | √ | |
| | US: Logico SM-1563 Annex 2.8 | | | √ |
| | Number of Examples | 3 | 4 | 1 |

*Source*: Authors.

Table 6.3 relates the schema categories to inductive thinking. Our thesis is that the aforementioned (a) and (b) help define the stance towards the 12 schema categories by inductive managers.

**(a) Highly abstract principles and ideas guiding thought patterns**

*Lenovo's Liu Chuanzhi (Annex 2.3)*

Liu Chuanzhi's management philosophy in Lenovo is grounded on values that are deeply rooted in the minds of the Chinese, such as the middle way (*zhongyong*), magnanimity (*hongyi*), perfect virtue (*ren*) and trust (*xin*).[4]

The middle way concept helps a person to avoid extremes and balance his relationships between shareholders and employees. Magnanimity guides him in the handling of extreme situations, such as the revolt of one of his executives who tried to oust him from the firm. Against the belief in China that no merchant is beyond committing fraud are the concepts of ren and xin, or the combined concept renxin, which state that virtue and trust together are the only viable measures for the long term.

These principles' high degree of abstractness is offset by concrete operational concepts. The product technology concept tilts Lenovo towards

*Table 6.3*  Schema categories and inductive thinking

| Schema categories | Inductive |
| --- | --- |
| Temporality (how time is perceived) | Anticipation of unpredictability and circularity of time |
| Predictability (how future uncertainty is coped with) | Probable truth in projected future |
| Materiality (perception about whether the world is only physical or contains non-substance) | Equal validity of tangible and intangible materiality |
| Falsifiability (statement as open to error or as absolute truth) | Degrees of likelihood of propositions and alternative scenarios |
| Recursivity (repetition of itself) | Real existence of unobservable and recursive actions |
| Approach to learning | Gestalt (cognitive): learn by understanding |
| Approach to thinking and restructuring of problems | Gestaltist: productive, reorganizative, organization fades, and vague (create new solution to new situation, rearrange problem elements, mental structures are units of thought) |
| Approach to categorization (of social surroundings) | Categories are an experimental epistemology (a) categories are internally structured by gradients of representativeness (b) boundaries are not necessarily definite (c) there is a close relation between attribute clusters and structure and formation of categories |
| Cognition (about the validity of empirical facts derived from the mental realm) | Links between environment, strategy, structure can legitimately be cognitive and socially constructed |
| Use of analogy | Analogy can be a relation, idea, pattern, regularity, attribute, effect or function, and comparisons of these are valid arguments that facilitate understanding |
| Use of metaphor | Metaphors can be abstract, and verbally or non-verbally coded |
| Perception of reality | Subjective–relative |

products that are user-friendly, as evidenced by the adoption of specifications that allow its customers to adapt different voltages in China. Cost reduction is considered to be of the essence when it refers to keeping the total cost under control. Lenovo's priority is to minimize finished and semi-finished products and the basis of Lenovo's organizational functioning is the autonomy given to the business units. Liu calls it the 'convoy model' in which business units work in a similar fashion to independent companies. Liu diversified from the PC business into venture capital, real estate and financial industries on the grounds that he felt that Lenovo needed to create new businesses to leverage their managers' skills and capabilities and to prevent managers from leaving the firm due to lack of promotion opportunities. Obviously, Liu viewed new business development from his own perspective (from within Lenovo and its group), and not from the theoretically deductive viewpoint that takes into account core competence, relatedness of businesses, value creation or the possible subtraction of value for shareholders through diversification.

*Allen Lee (additional case)*

Allen Lee's case (Fernandez & Willendrup Jenster, 2010) epitomizes the way abstract or generic ideas influence decision-making. Allen Lee, a successful IT entrepreneur, one day met on a flight a business man who told him that he ran a chain of foot massage parlours and planned to expand it. At that moment, Allen had enough cash to invest in new business opportunities and decided to ally himself with this entrepreneur.

What propelled Lee into the foot massage business was:

1. Lee's business had had exponential growth in the past five years and therefore he had enough cash to invest in new business opportunities.
2. Because of an improvement in living standards, Lee was convinced that people would pay greater attention to their health in the future.
3. Lee was impressed by the confidence and ambition of Zhang, the owner of the spa chain with whom he had struck the acquaintance on a flight.
4. Zhang informed Lee that his spa chain enjoyed a good brand recognition.
5. Lee's gut feeling was that Zhang's management could be improved, with his help, to become more profitable and to grow in size.
6. Lee thought that he and his co-investors could introduce effective management techniques, such as business planning and cash-flow analysis to modernize the chain.
7. Lee analysed the organizational structure of the chain as being too dated but amenable to improvements.
8. Lee thought that introducing standardization to the spas' service quality would increase success.

Lee ultimately failed in the new business because:

1. Basically Lee and his colleagues did not understand the nature of the new business – unlike the IT business, it is closely controlled by

public authorities and obtaining licences is a complicated and difficult business.

2. Lee did not understand that the only possible value created by him was the injection of money. Lee did not realize that the so-called new management techniques, such as business planning, was not a key success factor: it might improve operations but would not provide strategic value creation. He lacked what could be considered the fundamental factor for success – a keen insight into the nature of the business.

3. Lee did not seem to have counted on any external advice from professional advisory firms such as lawyers and auditors, who could have helped him carry out due diligence before investing his money. He simply did not call into question what he heard from Zhang.

4. Zhang did not have control of his chain. The brand was not protected by patent. His employees, after having learnt the basic massaging technique became independent but continued to use the chain's brand, converting themselves into competitors, and without paying any royalties.

The key point in this case is to look at Lee's analysis of his failure:

1. Lee was aware that he and his co-investors were clumsy enough 'to give the money', believing that Zhang was an expert.
2. Lee held that they had learnt their lesson the hard way after losing RMB 20 million.
3. It was not until Zhang's failings became obvious that Lee visited the country and discovered that Zhang had not registered the chain's brand nor was he the owner of the chain's shops.
4. Lee considered this failure to be a precious learning experience: (1) never to make any future investment blindly and (2) to stick to 'proper' (deductive) procedures (hiring audit firms, lawyers, and other experts).
5. Lee was still persuaded that, well managed, the spa business could still be profitable.

His analysis led to the conclusion that it was, in a way, a 'technical' or operational failure. No strategic shortcoming was brought out as the main cause of the failure.

Lee's original argument to take part in the new business was 'opportunity-based', not resource-based. Management resources such as the ability to understand the market better than anybody, the minimization of risk from related diversification, assessment of one's own business acumen, and the injunction not to have any invisible assets other than the brand were neither discussed nor paid due heed.

Deep down in his mind we conjecture that his intuition assured him that there was some commonality between the IT business and the spa business. For Lee, hard work, astuteness in business, and connections were what he considered to be the key success factors in business. Growth potential was the key indicator by which the investment decision was made, but he simply did not realize that the question was not whether the potential was there but rather, whether he was better prepared to take advantage of it.

The individuality of the new business itself, as well as the differing traits and characteristics of his other business in comparison, may not have been the points to which Lee gave attention.

Thus, generic features may prevail over the individuality or uniqueness of each business.

*Virgin Group's Richard Branson (Annex 2.7)*

Virgin Group's Richard Branson is an example of a type of manager who is quite an exception to the norm in the West, in that his behaviour and public statements clearly support our conjecture that his management style is based upon the inductive way of thinking.

The management thoughts explained on the group's website (see Annex 2.7 Richard Branson case) express the view that the company can be considered a branded venture capital organization. Essentially, this means that it is a private equity concern where the companies operate under the Virgin brand. They then create value in industries where consumers are badly served, and are aided in achieving success thanks to Branson's reputation, which comprises a commonwealth of shared ideas, values and goals.

One thing that ought to be considered an essential part of the statement is Branson's belief in having 'fun' at work as a guiding principle (Branson, 2008: p. 34). In line with Southwest Airline's Herb Kelleher's dictum, his argument runs that if the staff is motivated they will deliver quality service and products, which the Virgin brand can then guarantee to its customers. They call it the 'Virgin experience' (Branson, 2008: p. 44).

The Virgin experience, namely, quality service and products offered in an industry where competitors fail to deliver them, is the common thread that goes through this diversified business group. It ranges from categories 45 through 81 in NAICS[5] – the North American Industry Classification System – and therefore has a 44.7 per cent dispersion rate over the entire range of industries classified, with the minimum and the maximum being 11 and 92, respectively. This is considered by deductive theorists to be a range that is too widely dispersed. Branson (2008: pp. 45–46), however, stresses that his business group is 'as focused as any great company', because of one common factor, namely, the customer and his/her satisfaction.

Branson's idea of the Virgin Group corresponds to that of a 'hands-off keiretsu'. It has venture capital corporate governance, which binds the group companies together through the Virgin headquarters, and it invests in all its companies much like Western venture capitalists do (Branson, 2008: p. 85).

Branson's idea and belief system, and the guiding principles that emanate from it, are different from the deductive model in that (1) they are more deeply rooted in an individual person's belief, (2) they are very personal and cannot be separated from the figure of the 'ideologue', (3) they are more a 'rule of thumb' than a model which requires precision of input to produce specific output.

Common to all of these cases are the way abstract principles such as traditionally accepted ethical codes (Liu), aspirations for gain (Lee) and a 'play hard-work hard' culture (Branson) help assimilate cognitively held schemas such as temporality, predictability, materiality, falsifiability, recursivity and approaches to learning. In thinking these schemas through and structuring and categorizing the challenges they are faced with, we assert that each of the above cases represents an example of how the managers depicted in them have tended towards using an inductive mindset.

### (b) Continuum of short-term decision-making and implementation

Emerging strategy, in contrast to planned and intended strategy (Mintzberg, 1990; Mintzberg, Raisinghani & Théorêt, 1976; Mintzberg and Waters, 1985), fills the gap left by traditional strategy theory that has not been able to explain why Japanese firms, apparently lacking a designed strategy, successfully deploy their operational ideas (Grant, 1991).

We call this an 'operational continuum' since an Asian CEO may depend on this variety of inductive thinking to address the emerging and changing elements of his business situation by adapting to each new issue as it develops. Although a CEO may have learned highly abstract principles to use in dealing with business situations, the mainstay is nevertheless a flexible capability.

*Hua Wei's Ren Zhengfei (Annex 2.4)*

Hua Wei's Ren emphasizes his firm's 'wolf' culture. The traits highlighted in the wolf culture are group action, collective power, each team member carrying out personal responsibilities, tactful understanding of each person's goals, collaboration among team members, keen powers of observation, curiosity, patience, attention to detail and perseverance.

A former export manager for Hua Wei points out the firm's lack of specific strategic and marketing goals but marvels at its invincible spirit and cultural resilience. He indicates that the firm is good at adapting itself to changing situations without preconceived biases. Constant innovation and continuous improvement are keys to Hua Wei's success, with 10 per cent of the firm's revenues being ploughed back into R&D. In Ren's words, 'we need to work hard to support the globalization of our products'. Working hard, however, does not specify how and to what degree. A Westerner might consider this a typical platitude or 'motherhood' statement, but obviously the firm's staff draw meaning from it and use it as a shared sense-making device.

Compared with Japanese firms, Hua Wei is more proactive in adopting modern management tools. It consults the Hay Group for its HRM transformation and redesigned job descriptions, rewards systems, practices assessment and appraisal, performance management, and systems for recruitment, training and retention of personnel.

The emphasis here is typically placed on the need to improve the company's operational aspects. Incentives for managers stress their front-line experience, including overseas assignments and development of professional skills. Because of his military working experience, Ren's management style is authoritative and the way employees develop their career is based on order and strict discipline.

### Imperial Japanese Army (Annex 2.2)

Unlike other inductive cases in Annex 2 that demonstrate success, the case study of the Imperial Japanese Army attributes failure precisely to the inductive way of thinking used by this organization. It analyses six battles fought by the Japanese Army against the US Army during the Second World War. It identifies six causes for their failure: ambiguous objectives, lack of grand design, preference for short-term decisive battles, subjective and inductive strategic planning dominated by the 'mood' reigning among the top echelon of commanding officers, narrow strategic options and the imbalance between high-level technology and 'primitive' organizational design.

We assert that the Imperial Japanese Army lacked a conceptual apparatus to generalize the results obtained from the battles that were fought, and therefore they were not able to learn generalizable lessons from them. Both the Army and the Navy remained enmeshed in their 'accepted wisdom', such as the value of hand-to-hand battle or the usefulness of pursuing victory with artillery. No channel or loop existed to renew or shift such tacitly held 'strategic paradigms'. Convictions cherished by the most vociferous members of staff prevailed over the logical thinking of the minority. Overall, the Japanese Army set store by (1) the ability to 'learn by doing' without underpinning this with theoretical support, (2) decisions were based on previous experience and there were no contingency plans in case they turned out to be wrong, and (3) there was no ability to re-design a new strategy in case of failure.

Many of the worst aspects of the inductive way of thinking are present in this case. The heavy dependence on personal networks led to an avoidance of punishment for those who made a blunder, especially if that person belonged to the élite corps. The 'person principle', namely, decisions being taken not on the basis of systems, rules, but by people within the context of their relationships with others, resulted in a process where differences of opinion were resolved in situ. Part of this process was a fine-tuning of perceived intentions, in which priority was given to ensuring that nobody lost face. Since objectives were ambiguous and strategy was based on the inductive method, the real situation was taken into account, based on *incrementalism* (Quinn, 1980), in taking decisions.

Appraisal of personnel was based on process and motivation or intention. The sincerity of intentions rather than results was considered more important. No objective, 'black-and-white' assessment was performed. After the catastrophic Battle of Khalkhin Gol (the Nomonhan Incident) initiated against the better judgement of Tokyo, those people responsible were not punished. Clearly, the personal network helped many to avoid receiving blame, and therefore to avoid being obligated to learn how to develop a better process afterward.

We assert that many of the traits shown by the Imperial Army coincide with typical characteristics of Japanese companies, including the inductive way of thinking and the narrowness of strategic options considered.

In summary, in terms of the categories of schema described in Table 6.1 (and further analysed below), the inductive cases presented here address inductively the 12 schema categories by means of abstract (and often high-minded) internal guiding principles and/or a continuum of short-term decision-making and implementation. Some examples are presented below.

1. Temporality ⇒ High on short-termism,[6] incrementalism, and lack of alternative scenarios considered.
2. Predictability ⇒ Too much emphasis on an inability to see ahead, as well as a blind acceptance that this could be resolved by spur-of-the-moment improvisation and social manoeuvring that would necessarily imply no loss of face or negative consequences for strategy makers.
3. Materiality ⇒ More decisions based on intangible and tacitly held perceptions (loss of face, accrual of blame, internal convictions) than on tangible and material results (number of deaths in a battle, effectiveness of actions already taken).
4. Falsifiability ⇒ Expectations very low in thinking that deductively demonstrable results can 'prove' internally held convictions or accepted wisdom to have been wrong.
5. Recursivity ⇒ High dependence on the element of recursivity that takes a 'wait and see' attitude in these cases. Those at the top tend to try a solution and hope after the fact that it works, rather than choose the best of a number of foreseen alternatives ahead of time, thereby intentionally not pushing in a specific long-term direction.
6. Approach to learning ⇒ Need to learn by understanding, where understanding implies a unified, holistic and coherent picture of forms or configurations, based upon experience.
7. Approach to thinking and restructuring of problems ⇒ Very dependent on 'aha!' moments of insight.

8. Approach to categorization of social surroundings ⇒ Words such as 'flexibility' and 'continuums' and 'intuition' converge to represent the impermanence of the boundaries and structure that might apply to any categories established, as well as different levels of representativeness.
9. Cognition of the validity of empirical facts derived from the mental realm ⇒ Most of the 'action' is happening mentally or in different perceptions of what is being communicated.
10. Use of analogy ⇒ Heavy use of analogies such as 'wolf culture' and 'hard work' to facilitate shared understanding of future goals.
11. Use of metaphor ⇒ Metaphorical words used include 'primitive', 'mood', and 'fun' to elicit more abstract concepts.
12. Perception of reality ⇒ In general, all of these cases show examples of individuals who are willing to see the reality that surrounds them as something acceptably subjective. In addition, they accept this reality as something that produces results that are relative to the changing circumstances and social interactions of the people around them.

### Case analysis: deductive management approach

The common feature amongst ACER's Stan Shih (Annex 2.1), Dr Beat Richner (Annex 2.5) and Banco Santander's Emilio Botín and Alfredo Sáenz (Annex 2.6) lies in the fact that their behaviour pattern is amenable to systemic analysis with relative ease because they tend to reduce the variables for control and strategic decisions to a finite and previously established number. Business models are, more often than not, easily discernible. These deductive and model-based entrepreneurs stand out for the predictability of their behaviour, although this may not necessarily mean that they are easily imitable. Table 6.4 relates the schema categories to deductive thinking.

*Reductionism*

One way by which we can identify the 'deductive' way of thinking is to examine behaviour patterns and find that they are reducible to a set of objectively defined variables with relations amongst them that can be clearly set out.

*Dr Beat Richner (Annex 2.5)*

Dr Beat Richner is a Swiss paediatrician who runs and manages four children's hospitals in Cambodia. In these hospitals, no fees are charged to patients or their parents. Dr Richner raises $US22 million per year, mainly from private donations, to keep these hospitals running. Though he did not have any formal training in management, Dr Richner has been capable of designing a precise control and management system for his organization.

*Table 6.4*   Schema categories and deductive thinking

| Schema categories | Deductive |
|---|---|
| Temporality (how time is perceived) | Anticipation of predictability and linearity of time |
| Predictability (how future uncertainty is coped with) | Guarantees in projected future |
| Materiality (perception about whether the world is only physical or contains non-substance) | Tangibility of the material |
| Falsifiability (statement as open to error or as absolute truth) | Numeric and demonstrable falsifiability of propositions |
| Recursivity (repetition of itself) | Not admitted: there must be observability of linear actions |
| Approach to learning | Behaviourist (connectionist): learn by memorizing |
| Approach to thinking and restructuring of problems | Associationist: reproductive, stimulus-response linked, and precise (apply solution habits from past experience, try till it works, associate stimuli and responses) |
| Approach to categorization (of social surroundings) | Categories are determinate, with definite boundaries and clear structures |
| Cognition (about the validity of empirical facts derived from the mental realm) | To be legitimate, key decision-makers' perceptions and role in issue diagnosis and problem formulation must represent innate, real, and demonstrable capability |
| Use of analogy | Analogy is not an autonomous mode of thought or inference, and therefore is not valid to advance scientific truth |
| Use of metaphor | Metaphors are concrete and verbally coded |
| Perception of reality | Objective–absolute |

With the Swiss and Cambodian governments' contribution representing only a small portion of the hospitals' budget, funds are sought among private donors in Europe in general and in Switzerland in particular. Accordingly, it is vital that the overall system for the organization's management be able to satisfy and convince donors about how their monetary contributions are being used. This means that Dr Richner must attain two objectives: (1) he must transmit a message to his donors that their money is being used directly and solely for sick children in Cambodia, a country famous for rampant corruption in its public sector; and (2) he must convey the information that the money is being used efficiently.

The scheme designed by Dr Richner consists of:

1. Foundation in Switzerland:
   - Represented by reputable professionals.
   - The actual collection of funds through its bank accounts and their management.
   - The money provided by the Cambodian government is paid into the Foundation's account in Switzerland.
   - The hospital personnel's salaries are administered by the Foundation and paid directly into an account in a Thai bank, from which they can withdraw money using their passbooks.
   - The accounting books of the Foundation are audited by a major international audit firm.
   - The medicines produced by top-tier pharmaceutical companies are procured by the Foundation from a German trader in Thailand, who offers more competitive prices.

2. Public relations, communications:
   - Public relations are handled in Switzerland.
   - Dr Richner travels to his home country several times a year to seek funds through his concerts (as a cellist).
   - Dr Richner personally sends a letter every year to all who donate more than €100.

3. Other management system components:
   - Dr Richner is involved in the recruitment of all his personnel.
   - Dr Richner is informed of the situation of each of the four hospitals by eight o'clock each morning.
   - The staff are paid salaries that are far better than those in the local labour market, perhaps 20–30 times more. Thus, the hospitals' and the personnel's interests are aligned – doctors will perform their duties in order to keep their positions and the hospitals can avoid malpractices such as the theft of expensive medicines to sell them in the black market.
   - The hospitals also serve as teaching hospitals, training the medical staff of other hospitals in Cambodia and abroad.
   - Dr Richner focuses on the achievement of high efficiency, namely, the ratio between output (the number of children attended) and input (money used to attend to them), unlike multilateral aid organizations such as UNICEF, WHO and other NGOs that prioritize effectiveness in other ways, namely, by focusing upon the ratio between achievement (the number of laws legislated by a local government for its health system) and their own purpose (the improvement of health systems in the world).

## Model-based, systematic behavioural patterns

*Banco Santander's Emilio Botín and Alfredo Sáenz (Annex 2.6)*

Banco Santander grew from being one of the smallest city banks in Spain to becoming the largest retail bank in the European Union in terms of its market capitalization. The key figure in this achievement was Emilio Botín, an exceptional banker who has revolutionized and helped in transforming the dormant Spanish banking industry into a world leader over the last 30 years. His business model (Kase & Jacopin, 2007) has a two-tier system:

1. At a higher level, the model depends on three-pronged pillars:
   - The macro-economic policy by Spain's monetary authorities that facilitated the banking system's modernization by requiring it to be on a par with that of the most competitive nations.
   - A visionary business leader (in this case, Emilio Botín)
   - The efficient and capable implementation of the leader's ideas (in this case, Alfredo Sáenz).

2. At a more operational and implementational level, the model hinges on three interrelated elements:
   - The operational efficiency ratio between expenses and costs and income; that is, for each €100 of income the bank receives, it calculates how much was needed to generate it. Spanish banks in general have very low ratios. Banco Santander and its group run at around 40 over 100.
   - IT systems that facilitate the cross-sharing of information on operations and transactions among subsidiaries and business units and help to achieve higher operational efficiencies. They make it possible to transfer know-how and skills from one local market to another, sharing similar products already tried in Spain or abroad. As implementation of IT systems poses significant technical and organizational difficulties, the systems create a high entry barrier for competitors.
   - Economies of scale that enable the group to enjoy lower costs in the development of IT systems. These were garnered when the bank diversified into Latin America by acquiring local banks, leveraging both the operational know-how already embedded there and the advantages of combining to create a larger operational scale of efficiency.
   - Thus, schematically, the working of this model goes as follows: IT systems ⇒ operational efficiency ⇒ geographical diversification/economies of scale ⇒ more R&D on IT systems and improvement ⇒ operational efficiency and so on.

*Acer's Stan Shih (Annex 2.1)*

Though belonging to the same PC industry, Stan Shih at Taiwan's ACER largely differs from Liu Chuanzhi at China's Lenovo in that it is possible to identify the former's model and strategic vision in a schematic form. We can also attach more importance to one representation it has produced, known as the Smile Curve. Likewise the former does not champion highly abstract principles, and eschews his broader strategy in favour of daily implementational operations.

Shih's statement about his work ethic, as defined by the American Heritage Dictionary, is 'an idea or moral belief that influences the behaviour, attitudes, and philosophy of a group of people'. He thereby avoids high-minded philosophical principles and centres upon plain ideas such as managing a company, controlling it in the common interest of the people inside it, and sharing his common vision and common goals, which are for mutual benefit and express his belief that human nature is basically good.

Early on in his life, Shih helped his widowed mother in selling stationery and duck eggs and showed his penchant for trying to analyse situations and identify the critical success factors for businesses. He theorized that, even if the stationery business yielded a hefty 50 per cent profit margin, with its inventory turnover at two or three months, this was in negative contrast to the egg business, which had only a 10 per cent profit margin but its inventory turned over every two or three days, so he decided his focus must go to the egg business.

Likewise, based on his experience, Shih realized that in the value chain the most profitable parts are its two ends. For him, the PC industry's value chain is broken down, from upstream to downstream, into R&D, key components, component assembly, sales and after-sales services. When the profitability curve is plotted from downstream to upstream, it shows a U shape like the smile graphic.

Until then, ACER's main business was sales to original equipment manufacturers (OEM) and therefore it was positioned on a lower part of the curve. Shih decided to reorient his business towards original design manufacturing (ODM) with emphasis on its own brand. But the traditional OEM business was not jettisoned and was established as a separate business, rechristened Wistron Corporation.

Following his analysis based on the Smile Curve model, Shih redirected the entire business system towards more focus on the dealer channels, eliminating direct sales, in an effort to keep the inventory level to eight weeks of sales. He was rewarded by year-to-year sales growth of 30.6 per cent, for example, in 2006.

Overall, Shih's strategy is supported by (1) a multi-brand strategy, (2) a sustainable and profitable business model, (3) overall efficiency of operations, (4) marketing strength, (5) growth and size.

### Case analysis: a combined management approach

*Logico (Annex 2.8)*

As shown by the Logico case, different management groups and echelons may produce different cognitive patterns and one business unit may be guided by an inductive way of thinking while another may be guided by deduction in its decisions.

The Logico case identifies and analyses a conflictive situation in the supply chain business, that between the IT department (an internal cost centre) and the freight management (FM) unit (a profit and loss centre that attends to customers in a variety of industries, especially the high-tech sector, which represents 35 per cent of its revenues).

The friction occurs when the IT unit is called upon to help implement an IT system that will control the sales people's activities as well as manage information flows about customers so that they can be shared across different national territories and business units.

This friction is derived from several causes: (1) organizational inertia, (2) a remuneration system that does not foster exchange of information, (3) personal conflicts worsened by the fact that IT managers (supported by a board-level director) expect immediate and measurable results whereas the FM unit regards more personal relationships with customers to be fluid and unpredictable, and (4) both therefore have different ways of thinking.

The IT specialists diagnose and identify issues on the basis of established procedures, diagnosis manuals and check lists. The solutions they propose likewise follow a pre-established mental scheme, as evidenced by the opinion of a young IT consultant who diagnoses the Sales situation as chaotic after only a couple of visits made with one salesman to three customers. His diagnosis has possibly been preconceived and established as valid even before the visits.

The Sales people, meanwhile, focus on specific customers (not enough, perhaps) and tend to be focused only upon the region they are personally in charge of. The overall customer needs outside his/her territory is not considered to be his or her concern. For them, concrete customers in their portfolio are their 'customers'.

Hence, in Logico the problem is twofold: (1) some managers act deductively while some act inductively and (2) there is a bifurcation between what is perceived as a generalized problem vs. what is seen as a localized view of it. In both instances, managers from different groups tend not to understand each other very well, which makes working together very difficult.

In summary, in terms of the categories of schema described in Table 6.1 (and further analysed below) the deductive cases presented here also address the 12-schema categories in a deductive way by means of concrete, measured and specific internal guiding principles based on careful calculation of likely long-term options. Some examples are presented below:

1. Temporality $\Rightarrow$ Deductivists tend to focus more on the long term,[7] as well as on carefully planned alternatives and scenarios. Time is seen as linear, and concrete results are expected in specific periods.
2. Predictability $\Rightarrow$ There is a strong tendency to expect that unknown conditions can indeed be planned and predicted ahead, and that even the most impromptu situation should have been foreseen, for example, such as the turnover of inventory as an indicator of future profit.

3. Materiality ⇒ Most decisions are based on tangible, external, and/or explicitly held perceptions (the Smile Curve model, 'immediate and measurable results' or the use of an international audit firm).
4. Falsifiability ⇒ Here, deductively demonstrable results can always 'prove' internally held convictions or accepted wisdom to have been right or wrong.
5. Recursivity ⇒ Low dependence on the element of recursivity means that those at the top tend to discard the possibility that something could define itself, and do so by choosing the best of a number of foreseen alternatives ahead of time and intentionally pushing in a specific long-term direction. This happens in the Richner case, where a perception of corruption in Cambodia is combated by managing and controlling the finances from outside of the country.
6. Approach to learning ⇒ Need to learn by association, that is associating a person or an event with an already learned model or framework, or assuming that the whole is the sum of its parts. Deductive thinkers, therefore, may tend to jump to erroneous conclusions if they are basing their conclusion on an erroneous fact (the IT consultant in Logico who arrives at the conclusion that Logico has no established sales processes).
7. Approach to thinking and restructuring of problems ⇒ Very focused on arriving at a specific conclusion based upon concrete facts.
8. Approach to categorization of social surroundings ⇒ Words such as 'best choice' and 'long term' and 'fact' converge to represent the tangibility of the established categories and all structures and processes have explicit boundaries.
9. Cognition of the validity of empirical facts derived from the mental realm ⇒ Most of the 'action' is happening physically or what is being communicated is considered very concrete.
10. Use of analogy ⇒ Heavy use of analogies such as 'planning' and 'achievement' and 'results' to facilitate shared understanding of future goals.
11. Use of metaphor ⇒ Metaphorical words used to elicit concrete concepts include 'reputable', 'authority', 'audit', 'eliminating', to specify concrete examples and objectives.
12. Perception of reality ⇒ In general, all of these cases show examples of individuals who see the reality that surrounds them as something very objective, concrete and/or material.

## 2. Theoretical framework for the interpretation of Asian and Western cognition

*The induction and deduction paradigm*

In conjunction with our literature review (Chapters 2 through 5) and empirical survey (Annex 1), we developed a thesis in our previous section that Asians basically tend to behave in an inductive way whereas

Westerners tend to behave in a deductive way. It should be noted, however, that in the Asians' inductive way, there is little 'corollary' or generalization, that is, generalization from observations tends to be conspicuous by its absence.

Apart from some of the observations and interpretations we have made in the case studies, the core of our proposition is derived from the findings of our empirical survey (see Annex 1), that demonstrate that the individuation of objects runs along different tracks for Asians and Westerners. When faced with a new object, it was discovered that Westerners set more store by its 'form', by trying to establish its identity, comparing it with a pre-established model, and reviewing the coincidence of the traits and characteristics borne by the object. The Asians, on the other hand, pay heed to its 'substance' and they stop short of establishing its individuality.

We postulate that Western cognition processes discourse on the basis of deductive thinking, namely, by going from generic to individual phenomena, while Asian cognition processes discourse on the basis of inductive thinking, with the particularity that (1) possibly there is not much effort or desire to generalize from each phenomenon or object observed and (2) there is possibly an intuitive capturing of the object's substance, meaning that it does not go through conscious and intellectual analysis.

Therefore, taking overall the concept we have just mentioned, it can be illustrated as in Figures 6.1a, 6.1b, 6.2a and 6.2b.

As described in Annex 1, the individuation process takes different turns between Asians and Westerners. The latter pay attention to the 'form' and capture the individuality of an object by contrasting its attributes and traits with those of a model or 'idea' they already possess, and then they decide on it. The former, in contrast, take heed of the 'substance' and establish a judgement about an object by drawing some kind of interpretation on a high-level abstract idea or teaching. Sometimes such an idea may be based on a highly moralized teaching such as the Confucian credo (such as Lenovo's Liu) or a more down-to-earth idea such as the pursuit of profit (Allen Lee, a Chinese IT entrepreneur who invested in a chain of foot massage parlours in quest of growth and profitability).

*Inductive reasoning*

As shown in Figure 6.1a, inductive reasoning is predicated on (1) a large number of observations, (2) which are repeated, (3) and which do not conflict with a derived law or universal statement (Chalmers, 1985: p. 4).

Our cases in Annex 2 deviate from the pure form of induction (inference of a general statement on the basis of a large number of examples) due to specificities such as (a) a relatively small number of observations or examples, (b) the repetition of what may be observed in past experience and (c) the inference that a universal statement or conflicts with it will not be an issue.

> **Induction**
> 1. The number of observation statements for a generalization is large.
> 2. The observations are repeated under a variety of conditions.
> 3. No accepted observation statement conflicts with the derived law.

*Figure 6.1a* Inductive reasoning
Source: Chalmers (1985: p. 4).

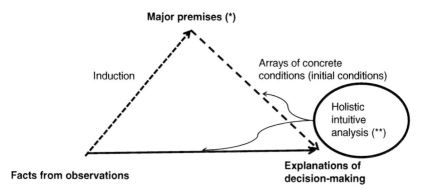

(*) Highly abstract principles, accepted management wisdom, 'essence', 'substance', experience (Major premises).
(**) Logic difficult to trace from outside.

*Figure 6.1b* Explanation for inductive decision-making process
Source: Adapted and modified from Chalmers (1985: p. 6).

In this connection, Figure 6.1b graphically illustrates the working of inductive reasoning in the managerial context. The essential part of inductive thinking in Asian management is how it helps managers to make predictions and explanations (or make decisions on the choices presented) from a universal statement or general principles. Thus:

1. Prediction and explanations are based on general principles (highly abstract principles, accepted management wisdom) that are 'derived from experience by induction' (Chalmers, 1985: p. 8).
2. The attainment of a conclusion is achieved (Chalmers, 1999: p. 8) by:
   Major premise (Fairly pure water freezes at about 0°C);

Initial conditions (My car radiator contains fairly pure water);
Prediction or conclusion (If the temperature falls below 0°C, the water in
my car radiator will freeze).
3. The minor premise in the case of deduction is replaced by initial con-
ditions, for example, 'the details of the set-up under investigation'
(Chalmers, 1999: p. 8).
4. In addition to general principles or universal statements, the particulari-
ties consist of any of the following methods used to make predictions
(Aamodt & Plaza, 1994; Wikipedia, 2010):
  • Inductive generalization (the proportion Q of the sample has attribute
  A; therefore, the proportion Q of the population has attribute A);
  • Statistical syllogism (a proportion Q of population P has attribute A; an
  individual X is a member of P; therefore, there is a probability which
  corresponds to Q that X has A);
  • Simple induction (a proportion Q of the known instances of population
  P has attribute A; individual I is another member of P; therefore, there
  is a probability corresponding to Q that I has A).

In other words, induction that is carried out in the Asian mind (or in the
mind of some inductive managers) may run the following course.

When an inductive Asian manager is challenged to take a decision regarding a strategic option, he makes use of some highly abstract principles
derived from accepted wisdom such as Confucian teaching or past experiences embodied as a credo in the organization (Virgin's Branson) or a set of
values (Hua Wei's 'wolf culture'). Vision (Peters & Waterman, 1982), long-
term orientation or strategic intent (Hamel and Prahalad, 1989), and moral
standards (Andrews, 1983; Etzioni, 1961; Ghoshal & Nohria, 1989) could be
other examples of highly abstract principles. Cases or situations are used not
so much as a means for inferring some general statement or general principles but rather to confirm them (Lenovo's Liu).

These principles or credo are so deeply rooted in an inductive person's
mind that he will hardly call them into question unless an extreme situation contradicting them arises (the Imperial Japanese Army). Predictions of
results are made from general principles and not grounded on major and
minor premises but on major premises and initial conditions (a variety of
conditions; Hua Wei's Ren).

Based on these major premises and arrays of concrete conditions, inductive managers apply their holistic view of the world with intuitive analysis
to reach an explanation which forms their decision-making process. As this
analysis process is highly abstract and often tacit, it is not easily observable
for outsiders, and they therefore find it difficult to identify the underlying
logic for an analysis. Consequently, the decision process that goes from certain observed facts is much more visible, in that we can draw it in a linear
fashion. The induction process, going from observed facts to major premises

and then to the decisions based on arrays of other factors, tends to be much more submerged, and hence we draw them in dotted lines. We also use dotted lines to express the idea that the inductive decision-making process is an open system, and that new elements must be incorporated from the external environment in order to generate new ideas and be creative.

The mental steps taken from the observation of a given situation requiring decision-making, to the predictions and explanations derived by going through the evaluation based on the general principles, are almost instantaneous. The very process may seem intuitive and lack an analytical basis in many cases. However, the authors' personal experiences point to a rather contradictory phenomenon – the Japanese are well-known for their thorough numerical analysis at the time of decision-making. An explanation may be that the analysis, when conducted, is not placed in a wider, general panorama but it is confirmatory of often foregone conclusions reached on the grounds of this shared credo.

*Deductive reasoning*

The explanation of the deductive examples we have studied is straightforward, since they fit in with what we understand as a generically deductive way of thinking. They also avail themselves of a syllogism as illustrated in Figure 6.2a, namely, of the major and minor premises which help managers reach a conclusion.

Predictions and explanations therefore fulfil the steps shown in Figure 6.2b. Laws and theories that may have otherwise been reached from inference or induction are assumed to already exist as fact. They then support the deductive objective of seeking foundations in the facts garnered from many tangible and/or provable observations.

When the major premises are constituted by induction from observed facts, they are then generalized as universal laws and theories, which are often transformed into universal business models in management. Once this process is complete, it is a closed system, in which deductive managers apply analytical logical analysis, adding other minor premises to reach certain predictions for decision-making. In this sense, these universal laws are deductively applied to observed facts, which can eventually and incrementally contribute minor modifications to the established universal laws, namely, theories or models. Since the modifications and application process in these types of decision-making is much more efficient, according to deductive logic, managers could achieve their objectives of a high degree of control within this closed system. In the case of Dr Richner, we can observe that the application of an established business model and controlling procedure implemented by Dr Richner in his hospitals in Cambodia is very successful. Since his deductive way of decision-making based on prediction is a closed system, all the lines drawn are continuous.

Deductive thinking pursues rational business opportunities and attempts to avoid risks by basing itself on models, theories and past experience which

> **Deduction**
> 1. Major premise: all books on philosophy are boring.
> 2. Minor premise: This book is a book on philosophy.
> 3. Conclusion: This book is boring.

*Figure 6.2a*    Deductive reasoning
Source: Chalmers (1985: p. 6).

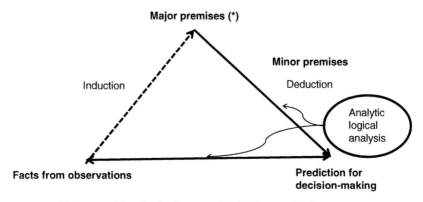

(*) Laws and theories/business models (Major premises)

*Figure 6.2b*    Predictions for deductive decision-making process
Source: Adapted and modified from Chalmers (1985: p. 6).

have been duly classified and analysed. This application of previous knowledge provides better control, high efficiency and less risk-taking for deductionists. Nonetheless, its full advantages must be viewed with caution since the use of a specialist approach rather than a holistic approach, such as that used by Asian inductive leaders, may also lead to a narrowed strategic focus, limited innovation and follower behaviour.

*Factors influencing inductive and deductive approaches*

Evidence is adduced to the trend that inductive and deductive approaches are relative in the sense that elements such as education, a lengthy stay abroad (especially Asians staying in the US, EU and elsewhere), may affect the typical cognitive patterns used. We postulate that this can cause, especially in Asians, a move away from an inductive approach towards a deductive one. As a matter of fact, our findings from the empirical survey discussed in Annex 1 highlight the positive influence of education on the individuation of objects, namely, the fostering of a deductive way of thinking when more extensively trained in higher education.

The culture from which you hail may also have a strong influence. Intuition, holistic comprehension, Nishida's (1987) pure experience, Zen Buddhism's enlightenment or jianxing (Suzuki, 1949, 1964, 2000a, 2000b), point to a less rationalized form of capturing reality which is more conducive to inductive thinking. This is certainly not exclusive to Asia, as is obvious from the case on UK's Richard Branson (see Annex 2.7). Be that as it may, we often meet Asians more given to synthesizing a situation by framing a cohesive story around it, based on an interpretation of a highly abstract idea such as di (virtue or moral excellence) or 'fun' in work (for example, Richard Branson), rather than by providing a coherent analysis on the basis of modern management tools.

No one, we assert, is 100 per cent deductive or inductive (see Figure 6.3). The proportion of inductiveness to that of deductiveness may form a balancing trade-off. The higher the one is, the lower the other will be. In our survey, we could not find a level of statistical significance in the difference by gender regarding the use of inductiveness or deductiveness, though popular wisdom identifies intuitiveness with females. The passage of time may affect this combination in favour of one tendency or another. It may also be that the life-cycle thesis could apply here, which means that the degree

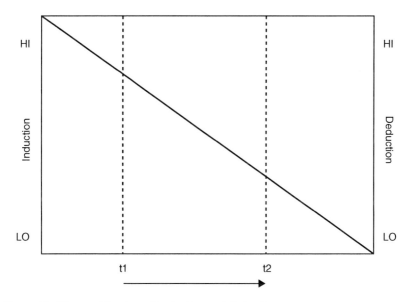

*Figure 6.3* The combination of induction and deduction
*Source*: Authors.

to which a person may be deductive or inductive is not fixed, and it may change over time.

A penchant for tacitness in the handling of management resources, especially capabilities, core competencies, is influenced by the group to which a manager belongs. Asian managers may find themselves at odds with overt explicitness and prefer a more tacit approach. This is often exemplified by such instances as 'I will think it over', 'it's good but perhaps you can come up with another offer', by way of not giving a flat 'no' to a proposal in Japan and China. The reverse may be proved in analysing Western managers who dislike tacitness and consider 'fuzzy' borders to be an evil in management scenarios, though we may detect some differences in this respect between managers from Anglo-Saxon countries (England and North America) vs. Latin countries (France, Italy and Spain) (Figure 6.4).

## Practicalities for measuring and visualizing different dimensions of inductive and deductive ways of thinking

In Chapter 3, in our literature review regarding epistemology, we have analysed some schemas related to inductive and deductive thinking that can be broken down into 12 attributes, namely, temporality, predictability, materiality, falsifiability, recursivity, approaches to learning, approaches to problem restructuring, categorization, cognition, use of analogy, use of metaphor and perception of reality, as shown in Table 6.1 and Figure 6.5.

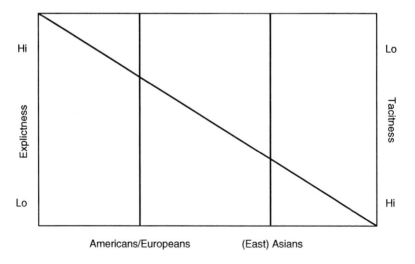

*Figure 6.4* The combination of tacitness and explicitness
*Source*: Authors.

A caveat to be made is that the 12 attributes we have identified are NOT systematically enumerated, nor are they exhaustive, and that analysts can use more or fewer categories, depending upon the purpose for which an analysis is to be conducted. These 12 attributes are simply those that we have identified as being relevant for analysing the cases we have presented. They are also, clearly, the categories that arose as relevant from the literature that we studied. We would clearly identify choosing these categories as an inductive process, although it is meant to provide both inductive and deductive thinkers with additional methods for subjectively evaluating how other people think.

Having asserted that there are good qualities to be gleaned from both inductive and deductive approaches, we now proceed to show how a combination of both inductive and deductive elements can be used to analyse people and cases.

We have already shown how each category can be polarized, such that it demonstrates how it is used to contribute to a more inductive or deductive thought process at one or other extreme of the category. In other words, the category 'predictability', for example, can be established to show how inductive thinkers expect the unpredictable at one end of this polarity, while deductive thinkers expect a high degree of predictability at the other.

While we assert that almost any category can be polarized, we also admit that this is a simplifying device that we have purposely established, in order

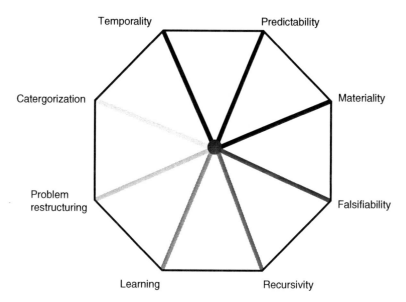

*Figure 6.5* Induction–deduction spider diagram analysis
*Source:* Authors.

to create a mechanism that permits both an inductive and deductive analysis of complex business situations and people. In other words, we are taking inductively identified categories, polarizing them on a line in a deductive way, and then showing how specific cases or people can be placed at some subjective or objective point on this line, in order to qualify just how inductive or deductive a person or situation is in that category.

We have also tried to take this method of analysis one step further, showing how a number of categories can be identified and polarized at the same time, to help illustrate the overall degree of inductiveness or deductiveness reached by a person or group in a given situation. This then allows analysts to group and compare categories in such a way, using what we earlier called an inductive perspective, that they can evaluate a whole that is no longer the sum of its parts.

We therefore present an analytical device that is based on a spider diagram, showing how each 'spoke' of the spider diagram can represent the 'poles' of either inductive or deductive thinking, and how individuals and situations can be pinpointed to fall at some point along each line between the poles and in each category. This is typically done in the field of Human Resources, for example, to establish what are known as '360 degree evaluations' (1998), serving thereby to define an individual in terms of a more holistic group of measurements.

Our proposed use of the spider diagram is presented in Figure 6.5. As stated in Chapter 3, the identified 12 items are the results of the literature review; we suggest that this list could be potentially extended or reduced contingent to the functionality of the usage of these items. Here, we have taken eight of these identified categories, and placed them in a circular manner, where the centre of the diagram can represent one extreme of the category (zero), while the outside of each line can represent the other extreme (5 or 10, for example). A point can then be drawn on the line to establish the degree to which a person who is being evaluated is, for example, highly focused on being in a predictable environment. In addition, this format allows us to darken some lines to differing degrees, in order to emphasize the evaluated importance of one category over another.

We then proceed to illustrate this with diagrams that could represent an 'inductive Asian' and a 'deductive Westerner', in Figures 6.6 and 6.7. The Westerner is high on predictability and falsifiability, but low on temporality, materiality, recursivity, learning, problem restructuring and categorization. The Asian, on the other hand, is high on temporality, materiality, recursivity, learning, problem restructuring and categorization and low on predictability and falsifiability. We assert that these diagrams can be used at virtually any level, for individuals, groups, cases, and entire cultures, to illustrate how the parts add up to the whole as well as how the whole is the sum of its parts. This method also allows a great deal of flexibility in choosing categories and degrees of measurement, thereby permitting students

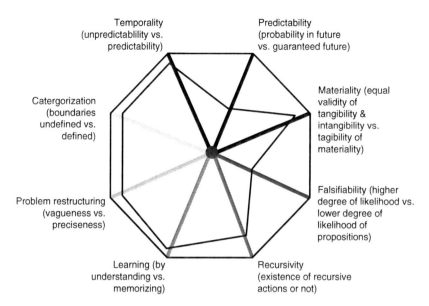

*Figure 6.6* Induction spider diagram analysis
*Source*: Authors.

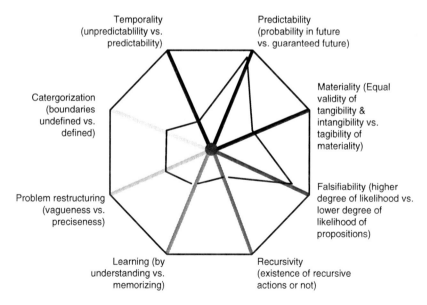

*Figure 6.7* Deduction spider diagram analysis
*Source*: Authors.

and analysts to use both deductive and inductive categories and methods in comparing the approaches taken by different individuals and groups.

## Theoretical frameworks for understanding induction and deduction, and tacit and explicit knowledge concepts

We now proceed to develop more detailed analyses of different theoretical frameworks that support our propositions related to inductive and deductive thinking.

In support of our proposition that Asians are inductive and Westerners are deductive, we will first proceed to avail ourselves of the tacit and explicit knowledge dimensions advanced by Polanyi (Polanyi, 1966, 2003). His argument runs as follows:

1. **Powers of thought:**
   The progress of science is determined by 'indefinable' powers of thought;
2. **Tacit powers of mind:**
   Scientific discovery is not achieved by explicit inference but by tacit powers of the mind;
3. **Coherence in nature:**
   These powers are conformed by perceptions because of the 'lasting shapes' they capture as *'gestalten* that indicate a true coherence in nature'.
4. **Tacit knowing:**
   Coherence is achieved by 'tacit knowing'.
5. **Proximal and distal terms:**
   Tacit knowing is composed of the proximal term and the distal term;
   The proximal term consists of things seen in isolation and the distal term, of the same things seen as a coherent entity. 'We always attend from the proximal to the distal term.'
6. **Indwelling:**
   '[w]hen we learn to use language ... a tool, and thus make ourselves aware of these things as we are of our body, we *interiorise* these things and *make ourselves dwell in them.'* Indwelling therefore bestows meaning.
7. **Comprehensive entity:**
   Tacit understanding takes place when the proximal and distal terms establish meaningful relationships. As a consequence 'comprehensive entity' is formed that is composed of these two terms. The proximal term is the entity's component elements. Comprehension occurs when these elements are perceived and captured as a coherent entity through the distal term.
8. **Four aspects of tacit understanding:**
   *Functional structure*: discoveries are made by steps we cannot specify. Intuition is a main mechanism.

*Phenomenological structure*: our focal awareness of observations is reduced to a subsidiary awareness of them (the proximal term) by shifting attention to their theoretical coherence (the distal term).

*Semantic aspect*: Interpretation converts meaningless perception into meaningful perception, just as the use of a probe converts sensual perception into a meaningful operation.

*Ontological aspect*: it teaches what understanding by tacit knowledge signifies.

Tacit and explicit understanding therefore may be graphically represented in Figure 6.8.

Starting from observations on scientific discoveries, Polanyi (1966) developed his theory on knowledge by focusing more on the tacit dimensions of knowledge, as explained above. Accordingly, for our purpose, Polanyi's exposition is limited to: (1) scientific discoveries and (2) tacit dimensions.

However, we consider Polanyi's exposition to provide a powerful explanation of the working of cognitive processes of both Asian and Western managers. It facilitates our understanding that there are four components in cognition: proximal term, distal term, indwelling and comprehensive entity. We can, for example, formulate a postulate that Asians and Westerners leverage them in different ways.

Figure 6.9 represents our postulation about how an Asian manager's mind works out a phenomenon perceived by him or her. The proximal and distal terms operate in the manner described by Polanyi to attain

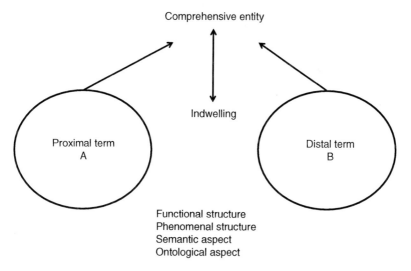

*Figure 6.8* Perception of phenomena: proximal and distal terms
*Source*: Polanyi (1966: pp. 1–25).

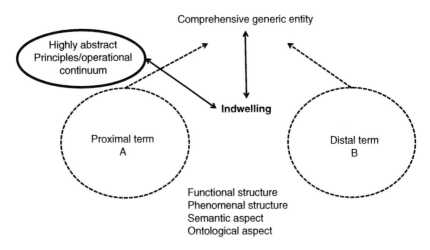

*Figure 6.9*   Inductive way: Asians
*Source*: Elaborated by Authors based on Polanyi (1966: pp. 1–25).

comprehensive entity, which becomes meaningful by means of the indwelling process. The particularity in this working of the cognition process
is that either (1) highly abstract principles or (2) 'operational continuums'
intervene actively in relation to indwelling. Highly abstract principles
may be tinged with moral or ethical nuances or totally devoid of them.
The operational continuum refers to implementation-oriented decision-
making. Mintzberg (1976, 1985) and Quinn (1980) named it 'emerging
strategy' and 'incrementalism', respectively. Prahalad and Hamel's strategic intent (1989) is an ex-post facto interpretation of past behaviours of the
firms displaying this type of cognition process. Their role is to reach the
comprehensive entity without going through individuation of each phenomenon and to help capture intuitively its 'substance'. Another particularity is that generalization from the observed phenomena tends not to be
practised, which may differentiate itself from what we usually understand
as inductive thinking.

Assuming that even model-based and deductive managers ultimately
depend to some extent on tacit knowledge, for example, intuition, then past
experience is assumed entirely and forms part of the basis of judgement.
Based on Chalmers (1999), Figure 6.10 sheds light on the working of the
deductive approach to thinking, and Figure 6.11 illustrates the relationship
between deduction and induction. (See also Figures 6.1b and 6.2b, which
follow and adapt the concept explained in these two figures.)

Deduction presupposes the existence of some premises that are established
through observations and induction. If the major and minor premises are
false, the conclusions reached by deduction are also false.

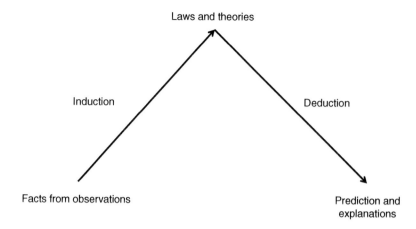

*Figure 6.10*   The working of the deductive approach
*Source*: Chalmers (1985: p. 6).

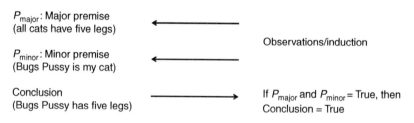

*Figure 6.11*   Induction/deduction
*Source*: Adapted from Chalmers (1985: pp. 5–8).

Nonaka, Toyama and Hirata (2008) caution that tacit and explicit understanding and knowledge are to be considered as a pair because they are two different faces of the same coin and they are positioned in a continuum. Behind explicit knowledge, there is tacit knowledge; in transmitting explicit knowledge, semantic interpretations intervene that presuppose the existence of tacit knowledge.

Nonaka and his co-workers (2003, 2000a, 2000b) propose a knowledge-creating model based on SECI – socialization, externalization, combination and internalization – that synthesizes tacit and explicit dimensions of knowledge and thus combines the inductive and deductive processes.

Unlike the Asians, Westerners have a strong penchant for using models to simplify what they perceive and endow it with some meaning. In our interpretation, this signifies that they conduct their cognition process in a deductive way, a penchant that may be inculcated even into Asian managers through education, as shown in our empirical survey in Annex 1 in which we observe that the higher the Asian respondents' educational level, the more individuated their observations are (more deductive).

The way the deductive process works ought to be different from the way tacit and intuitive induction conducts itself. The combination of proximal, distal terms and indwelling may not apply for its explanation. Figure 6.12 construes the functioning of a deductive way of thinking. Instead of an indwelling process, Weick's (1979, 1995) sense-making effort may provide a more explanatory interpretation.

In summary, we conclude that Asian managers usually handle and process the phenomena observed and experienced by them in an inductive way in contrast to their Western counterparts, who normally address and handle these phenomena in a deductive way. This thesis is further developed in the following section.

## Conclusion and discussion

This chapter has served to lay out and propose our theoretical framework, thereby providing an explanation of the perceived differences in cognition process (and, therefore, management approaches) between the West and Asia (specifically, East Asia).

The debate conducted on the nature of strategy, whether strategy is designed or it emerges in process, also largely relates to the topic we have analysed in this chapter. If a deductive mode is dominant, companies will opt for a more centrally designed strategy, while the inductive mode, if dominant, will direct companies towards operation-based, implementation-

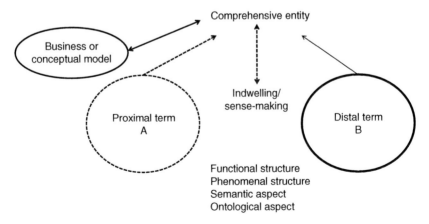

*Figure 6.12*   Deductive way: Westerners

*Source*: Elaborated by Authors based on Polanyi (1966: pp. 1–25).

biased strategy. Viewed ex post, the behaviour of such companies, if consistent over time, would suggest a set of continued actions that may be called strategic intent.

This proposition points to several implications, both theoretical and practical. First, the universal applicability of management theories may be called into question. Convergence and divergence theory was a precursor to this proposition. If the basic understanding and cognition of management phenomena goes different ways, the teaching of business models and theories will have to heed it more, if they are to be applicable.

Second, the view of the competitive environment must change. That competitors may think in the same or very much similar way, because they may be using the same analytical model and tools (that is to say, the same deductive method learnt, for example, in business schools) and may apply the same logic to the interpretation and explanation of a particular event is often true. Therefore the analytical and conceptual models must needs be modified and adapted, and management practices must be qualified accordingly. This would have an effect on competitor intelligence and analysis.

Third, therefore, the approach to training and coaching human resources will have to be changed, adapting it as required by different competitors. The relative weight of on-the-job training and theoretical education will change.

Fourth, there should be an increased awareness that the degree of competitor predictability varies depending on the individual's cognition process. It would be more difficult for deductive thinkers to predict their competitors' movements when the latter's cognition method is founded on an inductive approach. The inductive thinkers, on the contrary, may find it easier to understand their deductive competitors' behaviour, once they have learnt the business models their competitors are using.

The next chapter will develop further some of the debates opened in this chapter.

## Appendix

### Comparison between the induction/deduction paradigm and the PIF and PA models

From the viewpoint of cognition processes, Kase, Sáez and Riquelme (2005) study four transformational CEOs in Japanese companies and argue that excellent top executives are classified between long-term purported proto-image of the firm (PIF) and short-term biased Profit Arithmetic (PA) approaches.

For example, Sony's Ohga has a clear image of what the essence of Sony is, or should be, and Shin-Etsu's Kanagawa acts based on his extraordinary business acumen which allows him to discern what levers should be pulled

*Table 6.5*   Comparison of PIF and PA approaches

| | PIF | PA |
|---|---|---|
| Essential element | Image of the firm | Actions oriented to profit levers |
| Shaping or constituent factors | Professional background, environment, firm's business culture and institutionalization | Professional background, environment, knowledge of firm and industry and sense for business |
| Familiarity with the firm | Necessary | Not so essential |
| Time frame | Focus on mid- to long-term | Penchant for short-term |
| Domain | Wide, new competences and products are fostered | Narrow, existing portfolio |
| Cash flow position | Affluence required | At the time of crisis, the only option is to survive |
| Explicit or implicit instructions from the top | Implicit, second-guessed | Explicit |
| Applicable when changing firms? | Difficult | Possible |
| Succession | Relatively easy to find a person with a similar approach, if they share the belief | Imitability or replicability low |
| Combination with the other approach | PIF – top management PA – lower management | If PA at the top, PIF not possible at lower levels |

*Source*: Kase et al. (2005: p. 40).

if profit is sought. Both succeed despite the differences in their business approaches. Obviously, Ohga does not ignore profit levers entirely and neither does Kanagawa lack a corporate image against which he compares decision alternatives to check their fit.

If we call Ohga's way of basing his judgement on a specific image of a firm the proto-image of the firm (PIF) approach, by contrast, Kanagawa obviously operates on the basis of processing data and information through a mental model which enables him to discern which are profit levers and which are not. This we call the profit arithmetic (PA) approach.

Thus, factual phenomena are perceived to be complicated but their complexity is greatly reduced when the mental filter is applied to simplify and then to make sense of them by placing them in a meaningful context. Business leaders follow this thought process many times without realizing it.

Which of the approaches is applied depends on the leader's training, experience, character and business environment. The switch from one approach to the other cannot be made at will, since it is rooted deeply in the mindset of the person applying it. A change, either gradual or sudden, in the business environment, drastic restructuring, imminent demise of a firm due to near bankruptcy, may make the switch possible or even inescapable.

Table 6.5 compares the PIF and PA approaches.

The relationships between the induction/deduction paradigm and PIF and PA are summarized in Table 6.6.

We contend that both the PIF and PA approaches, combined with inductive thinking, as observed in Kase et al. (2005), except for PA-type Carlos Ghosn of Nissan who, educated in France, has a strong penchant for deductive thinking, reflect the two different modes of induction, namely, the one based on highly abstract principles and the other on an implementational continuum.

Lacking more empirical studies on the combination of the PIF and PA approaches with deductive thinking, apart from Carlos Ghosn as mentioned above, we may conjecture that PA may be more amenable than PIF to the combination with deduction. Process control as in the case of GE's Jack Welch, the cash flow maximization combined with corporate-level strategy pursued by Danone's Frank Riboud, the cash milking strategy from mature businesses championed by the now defunct Hanson Group, are some of the examples that confirm our conjecture.

*Table 6.6*  PIF and PA approaches in the light of induction and deduction

|      | **Inductive** | **Deductive** |
|------|---------------|---------------|
| PIF  | Creative Design Concept innovation Evolutionary Culture-bound Tacit knowledge | Balance between PIF and models |
| PA   | Operational efficiency Operation/process Pattern-based Continuity/routine Economic indicators Explicit knowledge | Some models that centre on cash flow generation |

# 7
# Conclusions and Discussions

As we have proposed and concluded in Chapter 6, there is probably more to say about further lines of research in management thinking than a normative theoretical conclusion. Writing this book, and the process the authors went through in doing so, brought out typical situations where 'West meets East'. For example: (1) the Westerners in our team (See Chapter 1 Appendix) sought a general framework and, if possible, a well worked-out plan, whereas the Asians felt comfortable with a general guideline directing their attention towards a specific final objective but sometimes ambiguous sub-objectives; and, (2) therefore, process-based Asian thinking was seen as chaotic or lacking in purposefulness by the Westerners, and precision and the emphasis on planning and following models by the Westerners were viewed as rigid and inflexible. Deduction and induction did, however, provide creative tensions that served as catalysts for further examination.

With the intention of understanding some of the differences between East and West, specifically regarding management phenomena, we identified the origin of such differences in the different philosophical backgrounds, giving rise to epistemological and cognitive thought processes which are eventually reflected as different cultures between these two cultural blocs in our living world. More concretely, we posit it as a penchant to tend either towards inductive or deductive thinking, which is the central theme of this book.

The literature was conscientiously reviewed in search of relevant information on philosophy in general and epistemology in particular, as well as on cognitive psychology and cross-cultural management studies to determine current knowledge about these differences and facilitate further understanding of the differences in approaching inductive or deductive decision-making processes by Westerners and Asians.

We also undertook a search for real-life examples, illustrating with eight cases written on entrepreneurs and 'actors' from both the West and Asia. The examples that we chose are not limited to specialists in management, but also include military and medical professionals in order to provide a wider set of exemplars. Industry-wise, they cover areas such as IT, banking, distribution, the military and health. Geographically, they are evenly divided between Asia and the West. In addition, we believe that they are also relatively evenly divided between what we would term 'inductive' vs. 'deductive' approaches to management. Essentially, the cases selected offer a richness of information and facilitate thought-provoking analyses by our readers.

To further strengthen our research, we approach the issue quantitatively by conducting a survey on the different cognition processes between Westerners and Asians, adopting and modifying several studies conducted by linguistic psychologists in the US and Japan (see Annex 1). We centred on the individuation of objects by respondents, based on the assumption that the individuation process is a method that can be used to distinguish between inductive and deductive thinkers.

## Induction and deduction

The central topic of this book addresses inductive and deductive thinking in management, based on a series of observed phenomena in diverse management decision-making situations. Our objective has been to highlight some patterns we find interesting through this research process, and encourage further reflection on the differences in epistemological thought processes in managerial decision-making by Westerners and Asians. Our aim was to improve understanding of different management practices based on different philosophies, epistemologies, cognitions and cultures. Hopefully, this improved understanding would foster better management theory development by integrating the best of both.

In relation to the philosophies underpinning the view of inductive and deductive management we have defined in Chapter 1, as well as the literature review chapters and the case analysis and theoretical frameworks proposed in Chapter 6, we can conclude that Asian managers have a tendency inductively to process information in such a way that they pursue a highly abstractive idea for their decision-making processes and to guide their actions. Meanwhile, Western managers tend to apply established patterns, approaches and categories to deliberate on their decisions and strategy implementation, as is typical of the deductive Western approach used to teach most MBA programmes.

As we will further discuss later in this chapter, we do not propose a generalized rule. On some occasions, decisions made by Asians do not fit the plausible rational behaviour outcome predicted by business models, business dicta and accepted wisdom. However, on other occasions, Asians do apply learning-from-Westerners business models to systematically approach certain managerial issues, such as in the case of Hua Wei, where Western consultants were invited to implement different systems in various areas. The success of MBA programmes in Asia is also changing this pattern. Neither are all Asians completely inductive thinkers, nor are all Westerners fully deductive thinkers, including those in our own team of authors. The case of Richard Branson illustrates this contrast, showing how a Westerner can demonstrate many of the attributes associated with what we view as a typical Asian inductive thinker.

Thus, even though we may agree that there is a general tendency for Asians to be associated with inductive thinking and for Westerners to be associated with deductive thinking, a number of additional questions arise:

1. Assuming that there are differences in the philosophical and epistemological background which are reflected in the cognitive processes, we may doubt to what extent this is due to a collective phenomenon or whether it can be put down to personal traits;
2. Accepting that the difference in cognitive processes can be captured on a collective basis, to what degree can such a trait provide an explanation for the behaviour of incumbent executives? Does it fully explain the most important phenomena shown by the executives analysed?
3. Is the division between induction and deduction a permanent one? Or can a person change his/her way of approaching management phenomena, for example, from induction to deduction, or vice-versa? And, related to point 2 above, is a person always inductive or does he/she sometimes veer in the direction of being on some occasions deductive?

### Personal traits vs. collective thinking

In this book, we have argued that Asians tend to be inductive thinkers and that Westerners tend to be deductive thinkers, and we have therefore generalized these groups into cohesive collectives for the sake of presenting our viewpoint in a simple and provocative, yet well-grounded form. Our review of the literature on cross-cultural management (CCM) demonstrates a similar approach. Empirical studies carried out by scholars such as Hofstede (2006) and Trompenaars (2006; Trompenaars & Hampden-Turner, 1997) as well as extensive research in cognitive psychology (including that which we have replicated ourselves in Annex 1), all point to the possibility that this viewpoint may be valid and useful for better understanding managers who cross national and cultural borders. The very idea that management approaches that originate from different cultural backgrounds can converge or diverge in a meaningful way presupposes that there indeed are differences in behaviour patterns on a collective scale.

This shift of traits and behaviour patterns from individual to collective levels raises some additional reflections, which can be further broken down into the following sub-issues:

1. In cases where both personal traits and collective patterns exist and can be shown to influence behaviours, how do they affect a person's individual behaviour and to what degree does this occur?
2. In the above case, how do they combine?

In response to the first sub-issue, our comment raises another question regarding whether, in the social sciences, there are situations that can be categorically classified in one direction or another by using unambiguous terms.

If so, the question will become one that can be phrased as follows: if both personal traits and collective behavioural patterns co-exist, which one will prevail over the other, in which context, and regardless of its relative weight?

Having so phrased the question, we may conclude that the two sub-issues merit further consideration by management scholars interested in differentiating between the two. We do not deny that there are many individual cases where managers might totally deviate from their culturally predicted epistemological and cognitive paths. This is like the normal distribution in the statistical data; there can always be outliers who diverge from the most probable profile. However, that such cases exist does not negate the usefulness of analyses that take into account collective, national or regional traits, which contribute subtle shades of meaning and understanding to their actions. Thus we think it is very likely that the analyses could be applied in 75–90 per cent of the situations studied.

## Executives under the influence of inductive or deductive thinking

As discussed above, we assert that many executives show basic behaviours that follow patterns set by their cultural background. This means that even if we cannot assert that a CEO is likely to approach a problem in a way that is fully inductive or deductive, we nevertheless argue that the probability is that his/her behaviour will tend to follow these patterns, based upon the learnt social, cultural, philosophical and epistemological approaches that underpin his/her actions.

In some cases, we argue, a combination of both inductive and deductive thinking is used to carry out actions within a firm. Exceptional CEOs, such as Toshiba's Atsutoshi Nishida, whose behaviour was governed by model-based deductive thinking, may tend towards discoursing and acting in a manner that is aligned with individual thought processes but ultimately is honed and refined by more inductively inclined staff. Virgin's Branson, whose inductive thinking is described in Annex 2.7, is supported by staff who tend to make use of deductive, model-based implementational measures. In the case of Hua Wei, even though the general course of development is very inductive, moving from being a local supplier to a global multinational in its own way, it has also learned a more deductive way of implementing Western business models in specific areas in order to adapt to global needs.

Therefore, even when referring to a basically heterogeneous environment (namely, inductive CEOs in deductive environments or deductive CEOs in inductive environments), we may propose that (1) a combination of inductive and deductive thought processes may work best under given conditions and (2) such combinations may even have positive synergistic effects. This balance and conciliation of an apparent contradiction or paradox have also been called 'paradoxical integration' by scholars such as Chen (2002), who also argues that a paradoxical cognitive process is critical in management.

### Shift from inductive to deductive thinking and vice-versa

As we have argued above, inductive and deductive thinking are combined. Assuming that one person is more inductive and another is more deductive, can we change our way of thinking from inductive to deductive or vice-versa over time? Regarding the first question of the two raised in the section on *Induction and Deduction*, the authors' personal experience, who acquired one way in their original culture and then developed another way of thinking in their later living and working environment, has shown that it is feasible.

While most of this above discussion is based to a considerable degree on individuals' cognition, our assumption of an inductive and deductive shift at organizational level is based on the changes in the organization's life cycle. Thus, when a firm is in the market entry phase, the organization as a whole probably needs to be more inductive in order to explore new business opportunities or new business models in order to differentiate itself from existing competitors. As the firm grows and the number of employees increases, the weight of deductive management increases. Similarly, previous experience may be extracted from practice and be formulated as a model to be followed in further development and expansion. When it reaches maturity, the organization in general follows a more deductive pattern in order to achieve greater efficiency.

However, induction is again necessary and regains weight when dynamic change requires the firm to be creative in order to survive in an excessively competitive environment. This is dependent not only on the firm's life cycle, but also on the life cycle of the industry in which it operates and other contingent environmental factors. For instance, in a mature industry, it is probably relatively easier to identify the business's operating pattern and a firm could deductively choose a follower strategy without needing to create a new business model. On the other hand, in an emerging market, where opportunities arise from different industries and different areas, a firm could probably diversify in very different businesses, without much interrelation between them, but with the common thread of financial controlling to maximize cash flow generation.

The second question referred to whether the same person or collective in a relatively short time frame may sometimes act inductively and on other occasions deductively. Some scholars (Ackermann, 1966; Carruthers, 2004; Locke, 2007; Stadler, 2004a, 2004b), studying research process and creativity, are in favour of combining induction and deduction. Smith and Tushman (2005) also propose a 'paradoxical cognition model', arguing that paradoxical cognition could contend with and coordinate two opposing forces. Moreover, by identifying the possible connection between the two, leaders are able to integrate them at a higher level, balancing strategic conflicts and achieving superior company performance. Thus, the locus of paradox in top management teams resides either with the senior leader or with the entire team (p. 522).

In this sense, Nisbett (2003) considers that holistic thinking combining two opposites is an important characteristic of Chinese and East Asian people compared with their Western counterparts. As Li (1994) argues, as is characteristic of holistic thinking, Chinese culture is open and adaptive in order to be able to include different visions. This 'pragmatic rationality' enables Chinese people to accept and internalize new concepts and methodologies. Within this frame, the paradoxical integration of Chinese culture has both the functionality to measure truth by its utility and results, and the emphasis on an ethical and aesthetic viewpoint.

We can observe from the above that the combination of two opposing managerial practices is not only feasible but also desirable in both Western and Asian contexts. The case of Logico sheds some light on this and also cautions us about its practices. Organizational coherence and creativity may lie in this trade-off.

## Implications for management

We now turn to the questions raised in the conclusions of Chapter 6 Theoretical Framework, which we can now analyse and answer.

First, the universal applicability of management theories may be called into question. In line with the precursor, convergence and divergence theory, if the basic understanding and cognition of management phenomena goes different ways, the teaching of business models and theories need to take this more into account, if they are to be applicable.

Second, the view of the competitive environment should be changed. If all competitors apply the same business model, think in the same way and apply the same logic to interpret and explain an event, then the same analyses and conclusions will be drawn with the consequence that no-one will achieve any real competitive advantages. Thus, at least some of the analytical and conceptual models need to be modified and adapted in order to qualify management practices. Accordingly, competitive intelligence and analysis would be influenced by inductive decision-making processes.

Third, the handling of human resources (HR) issues such as training and coaching will also need to be changed. HR management must be adapted to the competition and the environment. Thus, if a competitor is a more inductive-oriented thinker, a more inductive methodology probably needs to be applied to competitive intelligence and managers need to be trained to be able to do this. If the working context or the business environment in which the company is operating is full of inductive culture, inductive training will probably also need to be strengthened in order to better understand the decision-making processes of customers and other stakeholders, including competitors. The relative weight of induction and on-the-job training and other theoretical education will become very different, as the premises will have changed.

Fourth, an awareness needs to be developed that competitors' degree of predictability varies depending on one's cognitive process. It will be more difficult for deductive thinkers to predict their competitors' movements when the latter's cognition method is founded on inductive thinking. The inductive thinkers, on the contrary, may have easier access to their deductive competitors' behaviour, once they have learnt the business models that the competitors may be using. Since deduction from business models will have a higher degree of similarity in its result, inductive thinkers enjoy this advantage in predicting deductive thinkers while the latter will not find it easy to forecast the inductive thinkers.

Fifth, can there be situations or business environments in which one way of thinking prevails over the other and provides more chance of success? As argued above, each manner has its own advantages: deductive thinking is highly efficient in applying established methods while inductive thinking fosters creativity and innovation. Thus, a deductive decision-making process is probably advantageous in a company's growth and maturity phases when efficiency is critical for rapid development; and an inductive decision-making process is more beneficial in a company's and its industry's entry and decline phases since strategy innovation is needed for differentiation and survival. We have also argued that a possible paradoxical cognitive integration could be desirable to foster strategy innovation.

## 1. Convergence/divergence

Within the debate on convergence and divergence, convergence theorists seem to presume that divergent management styles in non-US companies or non-Anglo-Saxon countries, especially from Japan, would ultimately 'return to the fold', adopting management tools and concepts developed largely by American researchers or non-American researchers trained in a series of management paradigms developed in the US. Itami's (1987) invisible assets, Nonaka's (Nonaka, 1988, 1990, 1991; Nonaka & Takeuchi, 1995; Nonaka & Toyama, 2003; Nonaka, Toyama & Konno, 2000) middle-up-down management, knowledge management, the SECI model, provided some exceptions, though, 'in honour to the truth', we should also add concepts such as strategic intent (Hamel & Prahalad, 1989) or core competence (Prahalad & Hamel, 1990) that were found in research on Japanese management.

In the globalizing business world, while different management theories seem to show divergence, convergence appears to emerge again when both East and West learn from each other. As culture is not a simple static concept, it may absorb, merge, adapt and be modified when several cultures cross and interact. In this acculturation process, some elements may diffuse into the new culture set and these common cultural elements could be identified as convergent aspects. Thus, for instance, most Asian MBA graduates use certain business models to deductively analyse the business environment and identify opportunities and threats. Since it is generally easier to learn deductive thinking than the other way around, this convergence trend seems more obvious in applying deductive decision-making processes than the Westerners learning from the Asians and applying inductive decision-making processes.

In the aftermath of Japanese companies' turbulent entry into the world business arena in the 1960s through the 1980s, this trend was strengthened and business thinkers and leaders retracted their acknowledgement that other types of management could exist and even dominate. However, even though Korean managers graduated from well-known business schools use the same managerial terms invented by American scholars, they may still think and behave on the basis of their cultural values, despite the similarities with their American counterparts. Thus, even though convergence is foreseen, our business reality still tends towards divergence.

Hence, our thesis still holds in the light of the debate on convergence and divergence. If true, it highlights at least one problem: the difficulty in changing culture-based mindsets, especially at a collective level.

If coherence in actions is a hallmark of organization, the forced switch from one way of thinking to another may put organizational coherence, and consequently the firm's identity, in jeopardy. Thus, the forced convergence towards one specific management, concretely, US management anchored on a certain number of management models and tools that is taking place throughout the world may collide with the problem mentioned above. We are at the crossroads of convergence and divergence. It still seems unrealistic that a simplified universalistic management model such as the American model will be able to dominate the globalizing business world, even though it is still gaining market share. The Japanese management and the emerging Chinese management (Barney & Zhang, 2009; Tsui, 2009) demonstrate this divergent way of viewing the managerial world.

## 2. Competitive intelligence (CI)

One of the authors once heard a Western management consultant based in Tokyo express his opinion that it was not difficult to throw Japanese rivals into disarray. His reasoning was based on his observation that the Japanese, because of their inductive way of doing business, collect large quantities of data without too much order, which are sometimes enriched with two or three items of anecdotal evidence. Both groups of data (selected data in accordance with business models or disordered raw data with some basic assumptions) may carry the same weight. If the latter prevails, a Western competitor can disrupt its Japanese rival's intelligence gathering by sending it a couple of fictitious complaints. Complaints are seriously taken in many Japanese firms as a direct channel of communication with consumers and customers. The Japanese may extrapolate data from these complaints and come to a totally erroneous conclusion and strategy.

However, asymmetric relationships may be created in the combination of deductive to inductive CI, and inductive to deductive CI. In the first situation, in which a deductive Western company gathers information on an inductive Asian company in an attempt to pre-empt the latter's movements, what will happen?

The deductive company will first collect data and information, then it will analyse them using some well-known management tools such as the game theory, five-forces, value-chain analysis, PEST, scenario analysis and others. But the basic premise on which its analysis is based and which will decide the correctness of the analysis and strategy is that the competitor will go through the same steps and head in the direction predicted by the models, namely, it behaves 'rationally' (for the Westerners) and deductively. Even in the competitor's analysis, the same rationale is applied based on the assumption of certain premises of the competitors' view of the industry.

How will the Western rival fare if it its Asian competitor goes off on a tangent (from the Westerners' viewpoint)? An example is Honda's market entry in the US (Pascale, 1988, 1996; Pascale and Athos, 1981), in which any rational analysis using market forecasts, segmentation, key success factors and other sophisticated marketing tools would have predicted with certainty Honda's dismal failure. Honda, however, did not use any 'rational' (for the Westerners) tool. According to Pascale's (Pascale, 1988) narration, gut feeling, intuition and perseverance in lieu of abiding by cash-flow forecast techniques won the day.

Apart from the case of throwing Asian rivals into disorder by sending wrong data, what will happen if an inductive Asian company faces competition from a deductive Western firm? What will it do?

One common characteristic of management tools and models is that they can be bought from the market (namely, business schools, journals, magazines, consultancy firms and so on). This means that Asian companies can make CI by learning their Western rivals' tools. They can send their staff to US or European business schools. Management consultants are doing their utmost to sell their services to anybody who can afford to pay for them.

Therefore, there is an opacity in the Asian companies' behaviour that cannot be subjected to 'rational' deductive models, and there is easy access to sources of information in exchange for money.

Take the example of the arch-famous business portfolio planning (PPP) technique. Though dated, it may still be useful for a simplified view of strategic options for multi-business, multimarket corporations. Even if the businesses' financing is diversified and not wholly dependent on internally generated cash-flow and cost leadership based on the experience curve is not the only advantage, it still serves as a guide for measuring the sustainability of different businesses. A rival with businesses in the dog quadrant may move towards shedding these businesses, if no synergistic effects exist with other businesses in other quadrants. This can be easily forecast by Asian competitors with PPP knowledge.

### 3. Human resources management (HRM)

Traditionally, managers' training focus has been to learn business models and tools mainly developed in the West. In-company training courses, week-end management crash courses taught by consultants, executive programmes at management schools (and others) have been widely used, not only by companies but also by not-for-profit organizations and government entities. Porter's model comprising the value chain, the five forces analysis, generic strategies with differentiation and cost leadership, and strategic group concepts have been taught and followed throughout the world. Its basic premises, namely, the predetermination of the profit level by the industry and the pursuit of above-average profit in the industry, are accepted as the basis for the predominant paradigm.

Therefore, the deductive way of thinking has been at the forefront of management education, though in many companies, above all, in Asia, on-the-job training (OJT) was and is emphasized so that new hires can understand the way their companies operate, or simply put, the organizational culture. Tacit knowledge is thus valued. Induction is encouraged in this process as tacit knowledge is gained through working experience rather than by applying established models.

This has been the situation in many companies. In the light of what we described in the section regarding CI, the deduction-oriented Western companies will have to prepare their staff so that they can at least understand, if not follow, where their induction-oriented Asian competitors may be heading. Nonaka's (2000) SECI model may be useful. Likewise, increasing staff diversity and, therefore, the variety of ideas may help in generating new knowledge when competing with Asians.

Many induction-oriented Asian companies may need more disciplined discussions within the organization since induction can often become a synonym for chaotic and confused thinking. Even though it is termed 'vital chaos', training techniques such as critical thinking may be useful for generating better synergies between order and creativity.

As we said above regarding a possible combination of inductive and deductive management, Asians have probably succeeded more in learning deductive management through learning and training in Western-style business schools. Given the difficulty in explaining inductive thinking, since there is no clear model to follow as in deductive thinking, Westerners face greater difficulties in understanding it. The underlying knowledge is tacit, acquired by learning and training on a common knowledge base, probably starting from philosophy, epistemology, cognition and culture. A possible approach to this tacit knowledge could start with understanding its underlying philosophical, epistemological, cognitive and cultural basis. It could be desirable to incorporate these elements into modern management theory as Asian economies gain increasing weight in the world.

## 4. Prediction by deduction and general direction by induction

The ease of predicting Western deductive firms is amply described in the part on CI. It must be borne in mind, however, that even if a company's thinking discourses deductively, it is not always easy to fully predict its behaviour. There are areas which can hardly be made explicit. Grant (2007) cites the case of Intel which usually replicates existing plants in a new location because there are many aspects of its business that do not offer transparent cause-effect relationships and the only way to garner the success of existing plants is to replicate them. In such circumstances, there is no way to affirm that inductive Asian firms are better positioned, which proves that deduction cannot always provide a clear and rational explanation for everything.

In fact, as we have argued in earlier sections, a general deductive leader may be surrounded by inductive staff and vice-versa. At the organizational level, this inductive and deductive interaction between individual, group and organization is much more complex. Even though the representativeness of the leadership's style and cognitive process at organizational level can be generally accepted, as many scholars and we did, this weakens the predictability of organizational behaviours (even in a general deduction-oriented company), since many other contingent factors may vary. Specifically, as in the case of Intel, there exist unidentified elements or tacit knowledge within the complex organization which makes it difficult to fully forecast uncertain behaviours at organizational or even individual level.

While Western deductive management seeks to predict the success of certain management patterns (correlating certain best practices with performance), inductive management does not focus on predicting future success but instead moves ahead in a generic direction. In Eastern philosophy, if one wants to be the best archer, the first step is not to aim at the target, but to exercise oneself in the most appropriate way (Herrigel, 1984). In the classic story about training the mind, the highest level of archery is attained when one is no longer aware of the presence of the bow. This may sound ridiculous to the Western mind, but is understandable for an Eastern mind, even though most may not expect to reach this level in their lifetime (Herrigel, 1984).

By analogy, with this kind of training, background and philosophical influence, Asians tend to have a general idea of where they want to go, but do not necessarily have the specific method to get there. As in the case of Huawei, when Zhengfei Ren asked his officer to draft the Huawei's values, there is no certain procedure to follow but just a general idea for implementing the business.

## 5. Competitive environment: inductive vs. deductive thinking

As addressed in earlier sections, inductive or deductive management thinking may be contingent upon other external factors. They may also combine with each other in the organization. The question to address here is: can there be situations or business environments in which one way of thinking prevails over the other and provides a greater chance of success? In other words, can one way of thinking always be successful or should it be changed depending on the situation? If a change is needed, another question is: is change possible (which was analysed in the section on convergence and divergence)?

If we accept the prevailing assumptions that (1) business organizations pursue profit maximization, and (2) the profit level is configured and determined by their business environment, the market and the surrounding environment ought to be the determining force of companies' strategy. That is, the success of business organizations depends on how well they adapt themselves to the environment and find a new way to combine resources and build capabilities.

If so, the questions could be reduced to: To what extent can a company always be more adaptive and creative than its competitors? Can one way of thinking be more adaptive and creative than the other?

To complicate the matter further: Is the market and business environment always composed of the same actors and forces? Can some elements be more relevant than others in different markets and business environments?

The latter questions, at least, can be analysed from the perspective of an industry's or company's life cycle. In the inception stage, the key success factors are different from those in the growth, maturity and decline stages. Entrepreneurship, vision and foresight may play different roles in different stages. Financial skills, logistics, marketing knowledge, access to resources and technology, organizational routine, and many other organizational capabilities act differently at different stages. Thus, it appears evident that deduction- and induction-oriented decision-making processes carry different weights in different stages, which, probably, answers the first questions.

Thus, different weights and combinations of induction and deduction are required in different organization and industry phases to adapt to different market and business environment needs in each stage. Inductive thinking is probably more creative, given its open system that allows changes and dynamics to emerge with intuition and tacit knowledge.

However, deductive thinking can provide a systematic knowledge generation adds a certain efficiency to creativity and adds value to the profit-oriented nature of the firm. Thus, the adaptability of both ways of thinking also varies depending on the requirements of each stage in the life cycle. Inductive thinking is probably more useful at the entry and decline stages when we want to be more creative in order to differentiate ourselves, in the case of the former, and to renovate the industry to generate a new life cycle in the case of the latter. In the growth and maturity stages, deductive thinking helps the firm apply systematically the learned model that assured success in the earlier phases. Thus, it enables the firm to maximize efficiency, reduce cost and become more competitive.

## Limitations and future studies

### Limitations

Like all research in science and management, ours too has many limitations. Grosso modo, these limitations relate to two aspects: (1) definition of target areas and (2) methodology.

We initially defined our target areas as Asia and the West. Regarding the West, they comprise the US and Europe; regarding Asia, we mainly refer to three Asian countries, namely, Japan, Korea and China (and Taiwan) and exclude India as being closer to the West than to East Asian countries. The former have been influenced to a greater or less degree by Chinese or Sinicized ideologies.

In defence of our regional categorization, we reviewed the literature in different chapters on philosophy, epistemology, cognition and cross-cultural management, and concluded that countries in the same region adopt similar patterns.

However, it is also understandable that objections may be levelled against our categorization. China and Korea, in contrast to Japan, have had a stronger presence of Confucianism. Buddhism had a wider impact on Japan than, perhaps, on Korea. Autochthonous Shintoism set Japan apart from China and Korea.

As has been detailed in Chapter 5 on cross-cultural management, the optimal level of analysis for the study has been the subject of extensive debate. This debate has addressed not only whether the national or regional level is more effective for cultural comparison, but also whether organizational culture has been considered critical for organizational studies, together with industry culture and professional culture. To complicate matters more, we can continue adding to this list, with group level, ethnics and others.

In the general Western bloc, we can also find that Spaniards may raise a brow or two if informed that they are categorized in the same group as the British or North Americans. Germans may feel more comfortable with North American businesspeople than with Italian entrepreneurs. Continental Europe is an island apart for the UK. In fact, in the work of Filella (1991: p. 14) on studying European HRM, three clusters have been presented: 'A Latin cluster made up of Spain, Italy and France; a Central European cluster including the UK, the Netherlands, Germany (only the FRG) and Switzerland; and a Nordic cluster with Denmark, Norway and Sweden as its components.'

As stated in Chapter 5, despite the validity of this sub-categorization of regional cultural blocs, or even more specific national cultures, the purpose of this book lies in distinguishing the management thinking between these two large cultural blocs. As Nisbett (2003) laments in his Asian and Western comparison, we too do not have any intention to play down the importance, relevance and evident cultural differences at sub-regional or national levels. However, we find sufficient distinctions for differences in management thinking between these two cultural blocs.

We hope that we have gained a better insight into the working of Asian and Western minds regarding their cognition, to the detriment of more nuanced and subtle differences among countries in the same region. Likewise, we hope this initiative will be taken as a first step, and further studies are required along these lines to contribute more to our knowledge pool.

Second, we made ample use of the case method, supplemented with an empirical survey on cognition. By combining qualitative and quantitative studies, we hope that the triangulation of data will provide a greater explanatory power. However, there is no doubt that there is room for improvement and certain methodological limitations do exist.

The case method itself imposes constraints arising from the accessibility of useful corporate information. As we insisted in earlier chapters, the selection of cases studied is based on the corporations' soundness, their location and data accessibility. Thus, it has no means to represent the industry or the country in which they are located. Even though most of the case studies do not pretend to be as representative as the survey sample data, a better case selection with greater comparability certainly is more desirable and feasible. However, this may require surveying numerous firms in different regional locations and prior access to corporate information in order to know their comparability in advance. Thus, we employ these previously presented cases since they have already achieved our objective in writing this book by illustrating certain patterns and methods in management, namely, induction and deduction.

Regarding the survey used in the comparative cognition study (Annex 1), we have compiled different variables and questionnaire elements from several existing studies. Since previous studies have mainly compared the US and Japanese citizens, we have extended the comparison to more nationals in this quantitative study. However, we might have been able to contribute more if further theoretical development had been carried out before the survey design, in order to add more variables and elements. Since this is not the only focus of the book, we have based our survey design merely on existing work. Also, although the number of samples collected in the survey is sufficient to validate the statistical analyses, more samples are always desirable to make the final results more accurate. We hope that these limitations will be corrected in future studies.

## Future studies

The studies included in this book not only show the differences in management thinking (inductive and deductive), but also reveal several aspects for future studies. In addition to the above-mentioned limitations, future research may address, for example, the following issues:

1. To understand better the extent to which and how inductive and deductive management influences Western and Asian managers. Even though we have identified these two distinctions between Asian and Westerners and tentatively suggested how they influence managerial behaviour, further research is needed to identify more explicitly concrete variables, procedures and weights.
2. More specifically, further focus needs to be given to the possible combination of inductive and deductive management, within the framework of paradoxical integration in strategic management. As we addressed above on many occasions, a combination of induction and deduction is not only feasible but also desirable in both Western and Asian literature. The combination could be seen as transcendent for managing strategy constraints and balance conflicts. Future research may be able to focus on how the two could be combined.
3. The linkage of the cognition process with knowledge creation and management: the conversion of tacit knowledge for the benefit of the organization using explicit knowledge may or may not be possible if the basic cognition form conditions the entire knowledge creation and management system. Nonaka's SECI model presupposes that inductive tacit knowledge can be turned into deductive explicit knowledge. More work is required to shed more light on this.
4. The basic tenet on which management theories are based is that they can be shared and used universally, no matter where an organization may be and no matter when it may be applied. This assumption may need to be refined. More study is needed on how to carry out research on this.
5. In addition to exploring the convergence and divergence theory in relation with induction and deduction, it may be interesting to further develop application of these materials in qualitative and quantitative methods in relation to induction and deduction in order to explore methodological issues regarding knowledge generation and diffusion. Their application

in human resources management and training is important for the education of future managers.

6. Considering our earlier discussion of the limitations, it is also desirable and feasible to extend the research to regional and methodological issues. Much more research is needed along these lines to further our knowledge of our complex world and to manage it better.

# Annex 1

# Report: Survey on cognitive process differences between Westerners and Asians

In Chapter 4, Literature review: cognitive science perspective, we perused the literature on cognition and found that research conducted in the US and Japan by Imai and Gentner (1997) following the Whorfian tradition (Whorf, 1940, 1955a, 1955b, 1962, 1997) affirms the Westerners' predilection for individuating phenomena or objects – form preference – in contrast to the Asians' propensity not to do so but to subsume the phenomena under the coverage of substance – material preference.

In the same chapter we argued that the predilection for individuation is a pointer towards the deductive way of thinking when the individuation presupposes the existence of some kind of model, based on which observed characteristics of a new object are identified and compared before the object's cognition and identification.

We adapted Imai and Gentner's experiment to our purpose because:

1. These researchers' investigation addresses itself to the question of language learning and the capture of ontological meaning.
2. The sample used is a mixture of US/Japanese and children/adults.

Accordingly we (a) limited the age range (19 to 62) and (b) used a wider spread of nationalities (Spanish, Japanese, Korean, Chinese, US, Italian, French, German, Indian) and (c) centred exclusively on the individuation issue, as shown in Table A1.1.

## Summary of the findings[1]

• Asian (East Asians) and Western differences in shape/material distinction seem to exist, though no statistically significant differences were detected in this survey. As shown in Table A1.1 Tests of between-subjects effects, Sig. was .170.

- However, as also shown in Table A1.1, *Age by Mother Tongue* provides a statistically significant difference at p <.05, which means that age combined with language influences the shape/material distinction.
- As shown in Figure A1.1, Asians between 20 and 30 years old tend to recognize fewer shapes compared with their Western counterparts. Overall across ages, Asians have less shape bias.
- Asians recognize fewer shapes at different educational levels, but when better educated (that is with graduate degrees) they have more shape bias, as shown in Figure A1.2.

## Samples and method

### Preparation of the questionnaire

The text of the questionnaire was first written in Spanish and then translated into Japanese and English. Both the Spanish text and the graphics used were originally prepared by JA Ruiz and Nuria Villagra based on Imai and Gentner (1997).

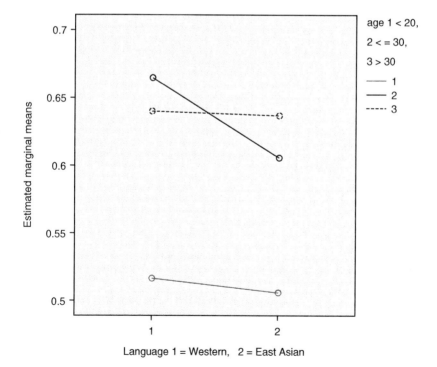

*Figure A1.1*   Age and form recognition frequency

*Table A1.1*    Samples

| Sex | Female | 77 |
|---|---|---|
| | Male | 74 |
| Age | Less than 20 | 28 |
| | <20 but >=30 | 69 |
| | Over 30 | 54 |
| Education | Vocational, etc | 10 |
| | Undergraduate | 84 |
| | Graduate | 57 |
| Mother tongue | Indo-Arian* | 89 |
| | East Asian | 62 |
| | | N = 151 |

* Includes 20 Indians with Indo-Arian languages as their mother tongue.

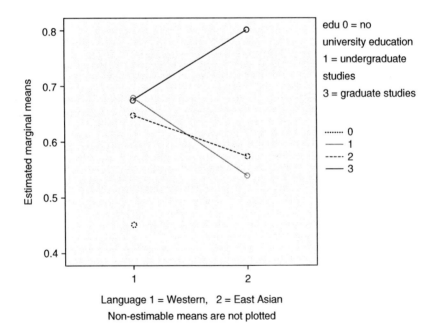

Language 1 = Western,   2 = East Asian
Non-estimable means are not plotted

*Figure A1.2*    Education levels and form recognition frequency

The questionnaire was tested in February 2010 with eight Spanish adults in Spanish and three Japanese executives in Japanese to improve the text and eliminate possible misunderstandings. English was corrected by an English native speaker.

Some minor corrections were made taking into account the suggestions by the test groups. Some shapes were disfigured, since they seemed to be too obviously linked to the original figures.

## Samples

The samples were collected as follows:

1. China, Japan and Korea: mainly through the personal contacts of one of the authors. Fifteen part-time MBA programme participants at Yonsei University (all of them are executives of Korean MNCs or international organizations), and 39 undergraduate university students from Japan took part. Eight Japanese respondents are former executives who volunteered to respond at the researchers' request.
2. Spain and the rest of Europe and the US: IESE Business School's network inserted the questionnaire in its alumni web site. There were 42 Spanish-speaking people and the rest were distributed among German, French, Italian and English-speaking respondents. Twenty Indian respondents were contacted by IESE network. Fifteen of them speak Gujarati as their mother tongue and five speak Sindhi.

## Method

The materials shown in slides to the respondents are given in Table A1.2. First, the respondents observe a slide in PowerPoint and they are told that this object is, for example, *nycko*; then they are shown a slide that comprises two objects or 'entities', one of which bears a certain resemblance in shape to the original entity, while the other shows an obviously non-discrete material of which the first was made, and are asked which one of the two is, for them, nycko.

Ten sets of slides are shown. To avoid orientation bias, some objects are placed horizontally while the original ones are shown placed vertically, and so on.

## Results

To examine the overall pattern 2 (Sex) × 3 (Age) × 3 (Education) × 2 (Mother tongue), a mixed ANOVA was conducted using the frequency of shape responses as the dependent variable. Age at $p < 0.004$, Age × Education at $p < 0.001$ and Sex × Education × language at $p < 0.1$ show statistically significant relationships. (See Table A1.3.)

Age has an impact on shape recognition both in the West and Asia (see Figure A1.1). The greater the age, the higher the shape recognition both in the West and Asia. The trend is greater in the respondents aged 30 or less.

The educational background is another factor that influences shape recognition. When Asian respondents' education is higher than undergraduate

*Table A1.2*   Slides shown to the respondents

| | Standard | Shape alternative | Material alternative |
|---|---|---|---|
| 1 | Metal clip | (Disfigured) metal clip | Metal piece |
| 2 | Porcelain rounded T-shape piece | Elongated T-shape piece | Porcelain piece |
| 3 | Coloured wood piece resembling a lemon juicer | Wood lemon juicer | Plastic pieces coloured in the same colour as the original piece |
| 4 | Wood piece resembling a whisk | Plastic whisk | Pile of wood |
| 5 | Wood pyramid viewed from top | Porcelain pyramid | Wood piece |
| 6 | UFO-like metal piece | Plastic saucer | Metal piece |
| 7 | Stone-like yellow object | Pebble | Amber piece |
| 8 | U-shaped luminescent piece | U-shaped piece (placed upside down) | Luminescent, amorphous scribbling |
| 9 | W-shaped wood piece | Disfigured W-shaped mould in dust | Wood |
| 10 | Brown disfigured S-shaped piece | Green round S | Heap of brown coloured earth |

degrees, Asians show a marked trend to opt for shape recognition, which is even better than their Western counterparts. Perhaps, the higher educational level exposes them more to Western-style, model-based deduction. When the educational level is undergraduate or lower, Westerners have a better shape recognition than Asians. (See Figure A1.2.)

## Conclusion and discussion

The Western respondents' stronger shape orientation cannot be seen independently of other factors in this survey. However, in the age and education cross-sections, a difference can be discerned compared with Asians.

Among both Westerners and Asians, younger people (under 30) show a greater shape preference than older respondents, while within the same age bracket, Westerners are more shape oriented. There can be several explanations for this. The younger age fosters more analytic and perhaps more rational thinking, which is reflected in this shape preference range across

*Table A1.3* Tests of between-subjects effects

**Dependent variable: freqform**

| Source | Type III sum of squares | df | Mean square | F | Sig. | Noncent. parameter | Observed power[b] |
|---|---|---|---|---|---|---|---|
| Corrected Model | 2.370[a] | 29 | .082 | 1.882 | .009 | 54.583 | .991 |
| Intercept | 13.747 | 1 | 13.747 | 316.581 | .000 | 316.581 | 1.000 |
| Sex | .031 | 1 | .031 | .703 | .403 | .703 | .132 |
| Age | .491 | 2 | .246 | 5.656 | .004 | 11.312 | .854 |
| Education | .202 | 3 | .067 | 1.552 | .205 | 4.657 | .401 |
| Language | .083 | 1 | .083 | 1.910 | .170 | 1.910 | .278 |
| Sex * Age | .374 | 2 | .187 | 4.304 | .016 | 8.607 | .740 |
| Sex * Education | .355 | 3 | .118 | 2.723 | .047 | 8.170 | .649 |
| Sex * Language | .005 | 1 | .005 | .123 | .726 | .123 | .064 |
| Age * Education | .952 | 4 | .238 | 5.481 | .000 | 21.926 | .972 |
| Age * Language | .340 | 2 | .170 | 3.918 | .022 | 7.837 | .697 |
| Education * Language | .067 | 2 | .034 | .775 | .463 | 1.549 | .179 |
| Sex * Age * Education | .312 | 3 | .104 | 2.393 | .072 | 7.179 | .586 |
| Sex * Age * Language | .269 | 2 | .134 | 3.092 | .049 | 6.184 | .587 |
| Sex * Education * Language | .412 | 2 | .206 | 4.743 | .010 | 9.487 | .783 |
| Age * Education * Language | .045 | 1 | .045 | 1.026 | .313 | 1.026 | .171 |
| Sex * Age * Education * Language | .000 | 0 | .000 | .000 | .000 | .000 | .000 |
| Error | 5.254 | 121 | .043 | | | | |
| Total | 60.910 | 151 | | | | | |
| Corrected Total | 7.625 | 150 | | | | | |

[a] R Squared = .311 (Adjusted R Squared = .146)
[b] Computed using alpha =

West and East. Or older age teaches people to reason more synthetically than analytically, which is reflected in a lesser shape predilection. Education may be a major driver for Asians to become deductive thinkers. In Western-style graduate education in management schools, where teachers stress model-based, rational, analytic thinking, Asians may rapidly turn themselves into strategic planners, with a high number-crunching capability. Their shape recognition, which is better than that of Western counterparts with a similar educational background, is thought-provoking at the very least.

# Annex 2.1

# Stan Shih: Acer's founder[1]

## Introduction

Paul Otellini, Intel's CEO, compares Acer's former chairman Stan Shih to the likes of Sony's Masaru Ibuka or Akio Morita for his contribution to Asian economy and analyses Shih's trajectory as follows:

> Thirty years ago, computer manufacturing had...a handful of companies building a small number of large and expensive machines a year, mostly using components made in-house. Stan Shih, a mild-mannered Taiwanese electrical engineer working on gadgets such as desktop calculators, saw a better way...Shih saw how marrying cheap chips with efficient manufacturing could spread computing power to the masses...By focusing on supply-chain optimization and cultivating a vibrant ecosystem of tightly clustered component suppliers, Acer was able to introduce new technology faster and at lower prices than competitors...Under his stewardship, Acer grew into a top-five PC brand. But Shih's innovations didn't stop there. Rather than competing head-on with low-cost Chinese manufacturers, he gradually moved Acer up the value chain to focus more on design and innovation. Acer...Instead of merely manufacturing cheap capacitors, radios and the like, Taiwan's PC industry grew far more ambitious under Shih's mentorship...his legacy of innovation-driven business will continue to power economic growth and inspire the next generation of Asian entrepreneurs.[2]

This case describes the history of the computer industry and of Acer, founded by Stan Shih, as background information, and follows with Stan Shih's personal history.

## The computer industry

### History[3]

The revolution in the computer industry started in the 1970s, with the development of the microprocessor, which would pave the way for the computer's popularity and accessibility to consumers. (See Table A2.1.1 Landmark events in the computer industry.)

In November 1971, Intel introduced its first microprocessor named Intel 4004 (a 4-bit processor with 108 KHz) which would be improved in April 1972 with the launch of an 8-bit 200 KHz Intel 8008 microprocessor.

In the same year, 1972, Bill Gates and Paul Allen founded the company Traf-O-Data to sell an operating system based on INTEL 8008 for traffic surveys. In 1975, the company's name, Traf-O-Data, was changed to Micro-Soft (the hyphen would be dropped later), and versions 4 KO and 8 KO of their BASIC 2.0 were released.

In March 1976, 21-year old Steve Jobs working for Atari and 26-year old Steve Wozniak working for Hewlett Packard developed a computer and set up Apple Computer on 1st April. Their computer was sold for $ 666.66 with 256 bytes of ROM, 8 KO memory and video output on TV. The computer was equipped with a small program called 'monitor' that allowed entry of the hexadecimal code directly from the keyboard. The machine was easy to use as it was programmed in BASIC, a computer language.

In June 1976, Texas Instruments sold the first 16-bit microprocessor, the TMS 9900. In July, Zilog introduced the 8-bit Z80 microprocessor with a frequency of 2.5 MHz.

*Table A2.1.1*   Landmark events in the computer industry

**Chronology of the computer industry**

| | |
|---|---|
| **1971** | Intel 4004 Microprocessor |
| **1972** | Intel 8008 Microprocessor |
| **1972** | Bill Gates and Paul Allen founded Trade-O-Data |
| **1972** | Trade-O-Data is renamed Micro-Soft and launches Basic 2.0 |
| **1976** | Apple was founded Apple Computer launches |
| **1976** | First 16-bit microprocessor from Texas Instruments |
| **1977** | Apple Computer II |
| **1981** | IBM Launches the IBM-PC |
| **1982** | Intel 80286 microprocessor |
| **1982** | Compaq Portable PC |
| **1984** | Apple Macintosh |
| **1985** | Intel 80386 microprocessor |
| **1985** | Microsoft Windows 1.0 |
| **1986** | Intel 80386SX microprocessor |
| **1987** | Microsoft Windows 2.0 |
| **1990** | Microsoft Windows 3.0 |
| **1994** | Apple PowerMac |
| **1998** | Apple iMac |
| **2006** | Apple uses Intel chips |

*Source*: Authors based on several sources.

In 1977, the Apple II[4] hit the markets and was the first computer to be a great public success, as a machine that allowed users to create their own application software.

In 1981, IBM launched its own computer named PC (Personal Computer), which did not provide any revolutionary ideas, and was viewed as the reaction of the world's number one computer maker to the emergence of microcomputers. It was built with a set of standard components and software subcontractors (e.g., Microsoft's operating system) in order to minimize the time needed for its development. PC would quickly become a 'standard', selling successfully from the first year of its existence.

In February 1982, Intel launched 80286, its new 16-bit processor at 6 MHz.

That same year, Compaq Computers was created, and in November, it introduced the Compaq Portable PC, the IBM PC clone, developed in such a way that it did not violate the IBM's copyrights. Compaq invested $1 million in entirely rebuilding a ROM BIOS.

In 1984, Apple's Macintosh computer broke into the market. It stood out for being 'user-friendly', thanks to the mouse and the quality of its graphics. It introduced the graphical interface (GUI) and had many features of a modern operating system: the use of icons and windows, the ability to move windows from one side to another, drag and drop icons from a source to a destination. It would become, over the years and versions, the other major standard competing with the IBM PC in the world of microcomputers.

In 1985, Intel launched the microprocessor 80386, and a year later would upgrade it with the 80386SX microprocessor.

The operating systems used by IBM and compatible computers, MS-DOS, were based on commands, which would display the type of indicator (A> or C>) on the screen, and the user would enter every character of the command that he wanted to run. Given the amount of complaints from users about the lack of friendly programs, software developers responded by adding menus and screen messages that improved the friendliness of the programs and reduced the number of commands needed.

Macintosh, as mentioned, succeeded in creating the first graphical interface, but it was Microsoft who would introduce the graphical interface for the operating systems used by IBM, in the form of Windows 1.0[5] in 1985, making its first GUI, graphic user interface, for a MS-DOS operating system. In 1987, Microsoft Windows 2.0 came out, which dramatically improved the management of windows that could be overlapped – one over another with several of them open – and resized. In 1990, Microsoft developed Windows 3.0, which made full use of the 386 processors, which could access more than 640 Kb, achieving better resolution (1024 × 768 pixels), and also improving the icons' design and appearance.

In 1994, Apple launched PowerMac, based on the Power-PC chip designed by Motorola in collaboration with IBM, presented as the successor to the chips used by PC and Mac. However, despite its good performance, it was slow to succeed.

In 1998, a straggling Apple launched iMac, boasting the most original computer design since the first Mac in 1984; the display and the central unit were integrated in a single colourful box, it contained USB ports and had no internal floppy drive.

In 2006, after 20 years of efforts to survive the competition by using non-Intel chips, Apple chose to stop using the Power-PC chips and use the same Intel processor as any PC.

## Industry Characteristics[6]

The introduction of the microprocessor (built with a single chip, a combination of transistors and semiconductor chips) by Intel in 1971 was crucial in shaping the industry, marking the beginning of the fourth generation of the computer industry. (See Appendix A2.1.1, Acer's Financial Statements and Appendix A2.1.2, the main players in the computer industry.)

In the last 30 years, the computer industry has shown a lot of dynamism, no doubt influenced by facts such as the rapid diffusion of technology and its relatively lower complexity in the case of the PC, compared with the information products produced earlier. Another noteworthy event was the invaluable opportunity provided by IBM to other producers when it waived the exclusivity of microprocessor supply from Intel, and of operating systems and major application programs from Microsoft.

The industry's dynamism is predicated on features such as:

– Technological advances in products.
– Acceleration of manufacturing productivity.
– More powerful and cheaper computers.
– Increasing penetration of personal computers for consumers and small and medium-sized enterprises.
– More frequent upgrades by consumers.

These features make it a highly competitive industry in prices, with very low margins and rapid price drop. Though this may be good for consumers, it may be bad for sellers, because their already low margins may be further squeezed if the product price falls between the time of purchase and sale to the consumer. This provides incentives for sellers to maintain low inventories.

On the other hand, the number of manufacturing countries has increased. At first, the industry was completely US, but later some developed countries joined such as Germany, UK, Netherlands and France, as well as Japan and some emerging countries where the State was active in promoting the industry.

Some of the reasons for the entry of new participants are:

– Reducing barriers to entry in segments where standard and 'open', not proprietary, technologies are used. Transformation of technology into a public good, as in the case of peripheral devices and the production of clones.
– Diversity and differentiation of products and applications. Introduction of new products with less expensive and less complicated production processes.
– Constant innovation. This opens up possibilities for participation in the segments from which developed countries are withdrawing.
– Persistent penetration of new markets. To export significant economies of scale and thus have the resources to finance the growing costs of R & D.
– The implementation of active industrial policies by States to promote this activity considered strategic.

Rapid technological change, where the equipment's improved performance and reliability, together with the reduction in size and price, are the main competitive strategic drivers for survival and prosperity.

Static and dynamic economies of scale and scope form the basis for competitive participants, but also the main entry barriers for potential entrants. In addition, constant improvements in hardware are showing its limits in continuing as the industry's driving force, which is why other aspects, especially software and services, stand out as the most promising lines.

The PC industry has become a commodity, with competition being fought mainly on price. The architecture[7] (the link between product design and the combination of components and production equipment) is *modular*, i.e., based on the combination and assembly of standard components using existing resources and standardized. Success, therefore, comes from sourcing the supply of price-competitive components and assembling them more cheaply than competitors.

There are two types of competitive strategy in hardware, cost leadership (Acer) or focused differentiation (Dell). However, the operating systems' competitive strategy is based on obtaining the highest market share; the acquisition of external economies (net work effect) is the most effective.

## Acer's history

### 1976–1986 Building the company

In 1976, in Taiwan, a group of five people founded Multitech, a marketing firm specialized in electronic devices, with a capital of $US 25,000 and eleven employees. That same year, Stan Shih, one of the founders, visited Silicon Valley and realized that the microprocessor would be the star of the second industrial revolution. He believed his country should not miss out on this opportunity. This was the reason for the birth of the firm with the mission of promoting the implementation of this new microprocessor technology and they put all their energy into bringing this technology from the United States to Taiwan.[8]

In its early days, it focused exclusively on supplying chips for other brands. It was not until 1981 that they launched their first commercial product of their own making, with a computer called Microprocessor[9] based on a simple and cheap system, using Zilog Z80 microprocessors.

Later, they released two new versions. The Microprocessor II,[10] one of the first Apple clones, whose main feature was Chinese BASIC, a version of BASIC Applesoft based on BASIC, which helped increase sales in the Chinese market. Multitech (Acer) had written some additional code, the text was drawn on the display through software instead of being generated by hardware. It was the only affordable way to generate the Chinese text on the screen at a time when generating Chinese characters based on hardware could cost hundreds of dollars. Due to these additional features, the MPF II was not fully compatible with Apple II.

In 1983, the Microprocessor III[11] was introduced on the market and, unlike the previous two, its design followed the IBM PC released in 1981 with considerable commercial success.

During these years, the company developed and improved its manufacturing operations, while popularizing the use of computers in Taiwan and introducing them in neighbouring markets such as Southeast Asia and the Middle East. By its tenth anniversary, it had consolidated its overseas expansion and its sales had doubled.

### 1987–1997 Multitech becomes Acer

In 1987, Multitech was rechristened as Acer, marking the beginning of the effort to become a brand with worldwide recognition.

From 1976–1988, Acer's average annual sales growth was 100 per cent, with $ 2.5 million in net earnings in 1988. That same year, Acer made its IPO (Initial Public Offering).

In 1989, Acer signed a joint venture with Texas Instruments and a Chinese investment bank to produce DRAM (dynamic random access memory) on which it spent $ 240 million. In 1990, it acquired Altos Computer Systems,[12] one of the leading manufacturers of multiuser and networked UNIX for business markets, for $ 94 million.

In 1989, Leonard Liu was hired as CEO,[13] with 20 years' experience at IBM. He tried to centralize the decision-making and rationalize Acer's operations, but the results of his management were not satisfactory. Sales increased from $ 530.9 million in 1988 to $ 977 million in 1990, but operating profit fell from $ 26.5 million to $ 3.6 million and in 1991, there were losses of $ 22.7 million.

The reasons are perhaps to be found in the industry's rapid maturing, which could affect performance, computers increasing commodity status, which shrank margins, and the strength of Taiwanese currency, the New Taiwan dollar, which meant that Taiwan-made products were considered expensive, losing competitiveness and therefore making it difficult to make a profit on the finished product.

In 1992, the company entered its first crisis, which led to Leonard Liu's resignation. Stan Shin[14] took over as CEO and began reengineering the company.

Stan Shih realized that the highest value-added, namely, research development, and innovation, and the marketing of a worldwide brand of PC product, design, and related services, was produced at the two ends of the value chain. Plotting this on a graph with 'value added' as the Y-axis and 'value chain' as the X-axis gives a curve that looks like a smile (See Figure A2.1.1 Stan's Smiling Curve).

Shih decided to transform Acer from an OEM (original equipment manufacturing) and ODM (original design manufacturing) manufacturer to one of the biggest brands worldwide. It would be necessary to undertake some 'revolutionary' strategies in order to re-engineer the organization.

The goal of becoming a brand entailed manufacturing to strict quality standards with high product reliability. At the same time, it was necessary to commit to innovation and design to create products with a higher value-added.

Shih's goal contrasts with the general situation of Taiwanese economy. Higher land prices and increasing labour costs had dented the strength of Taiwanese industry (Taiwan had of late the lowest export rate of the four 'Dragons of Asia,' namely, Singapore, South Korea, Hong Kong, and Taiwan, and the highest unemployment rate),[15] since Taiwan continued with a strategy dependent on cheap labour, low productivity, and low investment in research and development, doomed to failure unless modified.

In an article[16] published in *Financial World* in 1995, Shih compared Chinese computer manufacturers with Chinese restaurants, 'Chinese food is good, and is everywhere, but there is no uniform image quality.' The same applied to computers: they are made for different brands (mainly American or Japanese), with different levels of quality, but their manufacturers were not recognized by consumers. Shih wanted Acer to resemble McDonald's, with a strong brand image and quality standards, instead of Chinese restaurants.

This change or 'revolution' meant a complete revision of Acer's production and distribution system. A world-wide network of 32 independent subsidiaries was created, largely managed by local entrepreneurs who determined product configurations, pricing strategy and promotional programmes. This strategy gave each 'partner' the appearance of being a local company, and even helped it to become independent of the Taiwanese products' image, considered cheap and low quality in some countries.

The company began sending components to the 32 locations around the world for local assembly. Efforts were made to minimize shipping costs and storage. The vital components, subject to frequent change in technology and local taste, were procured from local suppliers. In addition to lower shipping costs, this strategy enabled real-time information to be obtained on consumers' needs and tastes. The strategy was named 'Global brand, local touch.'

Because of sales growth from $US 3.2 to 5.800 billion in 1994–1995, Acer advanced from 14th to 9th place in the world PC sales ranking.

Acer expanded globally to become a leading player in Southeast Asia, Middle East and even Latin America, making inroads into US in 1994 with the launch of Aspire model, the first computer in the world to combine a PC, monitor and speakers, all in one.

### 1998–2007 Towards global leadership in the market

In 1998, Acer was reorganized into five groups (Acer International Group, Sentek Service Acer Group, Acer Semiconductor Group, Acer Information Products Group and Acer Group Peripherals), but two years later the company concluded that this restructuring had no impact. The client companies for which it used to work as a contract manufacturer were wary of subcontracting Acer and preferred its rivals.

Therefore, in 2000 Acer proceeded to separate the contract manufacturers (OEM) business from branded sales by setting up Wistron Corporation[17] as an independent company. This separation was successful, above all in Europe where sales grew by 48 per cent within a year after the reorganization.

The strategy focused on the dealer channel (Channel Business Model),[18] eliminating direct sales and promoting more direct relationships with dealers and distributors, which, for example, would allow closer collaboration with its 'partners' in order to keep the inventory level in June (mid-fiscal year) to eight weeks of sales. Acer became more committed to the 'channel' and successfully developed multiple relationships, which improved results. In the PC market in EMEA (Europe, Middle East and Asia), its sales rose by 30.6 per cent in 2006 compared with the previous year, while the market only grew by 12 per cent.

The model offered flexibility in adapting to changing market trends, collaboration with partners and suppliers, reduced operating costs, and improved profitability. For example, logistics costs were incurred in finding the cheapest supplier. Other competitors, too, were reducing the inventory time, because excess inventory did not benefit anyone, neither the manufacturer nor the retail shops.

Having successfully improved Acer's performance in Europe, the channel-focused strategy was applied to the US market, which started to break even in late 2004. The Channel Business Model in the US and China fuelled sales growth above 100 per cent and doubled market share; it also achieved global growth.

In contrast, other manufacturers followed a different strategy that forced the sales channel to set high sales targets, resulting in a situation in which, more often than not, the sales channel, forced to even sell below cost to reach the sales targets and retain the franchise, became their competitors. During this period, Acer transformed itself from a manufacturer into a services company in the belief that the hardware itself provides little value, and a range of additional services are more profitable; and from a local manufacturer to a recognized worldwide brand.

Acer's global strategy, based on the combination of high global integration and a high national or regional responsibility and market responsiveness, brought good results. Global integration allowed for economies of scale and a tight cost control enabled it to remain profitable against constant price competition. The return on investment in manufacturing facilities increased thanks to the reduction of unit costs through economies of scale.

Devolution to national and regional operations allowed more aggressive pricing in search of market share, rapid adaptation to market changes due to its proximity, and more efficient management of inventory and manufacturing capacity.

### 2007 onwards Increasing global presence

In 2007, Acer reached No. 3 position in worldwide retail PC sales and began a multi-brand strategy to increase its global presence by tapping different customer needs. Thus, in recent years, a series of mergers have been carried out, for example, in October 2007 with Gateway Inc. and in March 2008 with Packard Bell Inc., which strengthened Acer's presence in the US and Europe. Today, the Acer Group (see Appendix A2.1.2) continues to be one of the top three companies in terms of total sales and is ranked number two in the category of PC laptop manufacturers. It employs more than 6,000 employees and its revenues stood at $US 16.65 billion in 2008. (See Table A2.1.2 for the global PC market.)

*Table A2.1.2*  Global PC market, last quarter of 2009

| Company | 4Q09 Sales | 4Q09 Market share | 4Q08 Sales | 4Q08 Market share | Growth |
|---------|-----------|-------------------|-----------|-------------------|--------|
| HP | 17.803 | 20.7% | 14.582 | 19.6% | 45.1% |
| Acer | 11.458 | 13.4% | 8.957 | 12.0% | 27.9% |
| Dell | 10.683 | 12.5% | 10.157 | 13.6% | 5.2% |
| Lenovo | 7.871 | 9.2% | 5.552 | 7.5% | 41.8% |
| Toshiba | 4.810 | 5.6% | 3.699 | 5.0% | 30.0% |
| Others | 33.176 | 38.7% | 31.540 | 42.3% | 5.2% |
| Total | 85.801 | 100.0% | 74.487 | 100.0% | 15.2% |

*Source*: IDC.[19]

According to its 2008 annual report, the company established five Acer Group keys (see Appendix A2.1.3) for a sustainable future:

1. Multi-brand strategy: given the enormous diversity of consumer tastes and to cover all market segments, other brands have been purchased (Gateway and Packard Bell), ensuring a multi-brand approach, and implemented differentiated product designs for effectively orienting all major market segments.
2. Sustainable and profitable business model: a business model involving collaboration with suppliers and distributors to leverage their resources, and ultimately, share the fruits of success.
3. Overall efficiency of operations: management of product development, marketing and regular communication from each region to discuss issues ensures good internal communication for effective decision-making, together with a flexible global logistics to guarantee product delivery.
4. Marketing strength: from knowing what customers want in order to satisfy their needs to building business skills to ensure the products' success.
5. Growth and Size: mergers have created substantial synergies, and revenue and market share growth worldwide.

## Stan Shih, Acer's founder

Stan Shih (Shi Zhenrong in Pinyin) was born on 8 December 1944 in Lukang Township, Changhua County, Taiwan in a poor family. However, while he helped his widowed mother to sell duck eggs and stationery,[20] he managed to study at the National Chiao Tung University for a B.Sc. and M.Sc. in electronic engineering.[21]

In an interview, Shih reminisced about his business training working for his mother, saying that 'the stationery business provided a hefty 50 per cent profit margin with inventory turning over every two to three months. The egg business...provided only a 10 per cent profit margin, but turned over every two or three days. Because of that rapid turn in inventory...his family actually made more money selling the eggs than the stationery.'[22] This realization lies behind the business model he later developed at Acer.

As mentioned before, Shih, together with his wife Carolyn Yeh and a group of five associations, founded Multitech in 1976, which would become later Acer. He headed the company as its CEO until he retired in 2004.

Asked by a journalist why he started the business, Shih referred to his visit to Silicon Valley where he conceived the idea.[23] He saw that the microprocessor would lead the second industrial revolution and thought that Chinese could not miss out on that opportunity, as it had in the first industrial revolution.

Around that time, Shih's company produced desktop calculators, but upon recognizing the market potential of microprocessors, he decided that the key to success was the combination of cheap chips with efficient manufacturing.[24]

Shih and his colleagues identified how to achieve this combination: the creation of an ecosystem of tightly clustered component suppliers, which ultimately allowed the Taiwanese firm to enjoy faster introduction of new technologies at lower prices than its competitors around the world.

Initially, possibly by sheer intuition but later grounded on experience, Shih and Acer progressively moved towards a trend to integrate whole manufacturing and marketing processes.

By coining the concept of the Smiling Curve, Shih gave expression to his idea that 'the smile curve hypothesis describes a phenomenon in the assembly-type manufacturing industry, in which the progression of global competition has caused the ratio of value added or profit ratios within the value chain to decline – where previously levels had been high – while both ends of the value chain, i.e. raw materials and parts on one side and services, etc. on the other, have increased.'[25] (See Figure A2.1.1, Smiling Curve and Table A2.1.3 and Figure A2.1.2, Smiling curve effects data.)

Thus, Acer was able to release the world's second Intel 386-based PC in 1986, one month after Compaq launched a similar PC. At the same time, Acer worked for IBM, Dell and Compaq as contract manufacturer.

Upon the emergence of cheap PCs in Continental China, Shih was insightful enough to move upmarket, based on design and innovation.

However, Acer continues to supply a wide range of PC components, in addition to its own PC. Shih was quoted as saying, 'I am looking for Acer to be inside every PC just like Intel.'[26]

That Shih was very analytical and liked a rational approach is shown in the following examples related to his retirement plan and his analysis of his company's business model.

In an interview in 2004, upon being asked[27] why he was retiring, Shih stated that the retirement had been planned for ten years. Shih admitted that four years ago, 2000, it was still too early since they had just split Acer into two units, Acer and Wistron, with the latter taking care of the ODM (original design manufacturing) business that was losing to Quanta and Compal, and the former, the brand-name business that was losing money in the US and not doing well in Europe. Consequently, he felt he had to wait until his group had become more competitive.

Shih's analysis of the failing business model they used until around 2002 pointed out that it was 'neither simple nor focused.'[28] The existing model focused alternately on small distributors and on education or vertical applications such as health care. Consequently, Shih decided to transfer Rudi Schmidleithner from Europe to the US on the grounds that Schmidleithner had successfully implemented a more focused two-tier distributor support system in Europe.

Apart from the pursuit of a simpler distribution system, the model centred its attention on the inventory minimization. Acer kept one week of

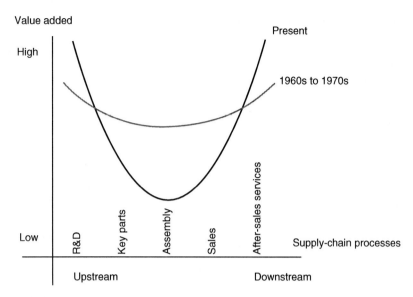

*Figure A2.1.1* Changes in the smiling curve over time
*Source*: RIETI (www.rieti.go.jp/en/china/04011601.html accessed on 28 March 2010).

*Table A2.1.3* Smiling curve effects data

| Item | Manufacturer | Place of production | Cost as % of retail price |
|------|--------------|---------------------|---------------------------|
| CPU | Intel | US | 10 |
| Motherboard | GIGA | Taiwan | 8 |
| Display | AOC | Taiwan | 10 |
| Hard disk | Quantum | US | 6 |
| Memory | KINGMAX | Taiwan | 5 |
| CD drive | Samsung | South Korea | 5 |
| Video card | CREATIVE | Singapore | 5 |
| Sound card | CREATIVE | Singapore | 4 |
| LAN board | 3 COM | US | 1 |
| Distribution margin | – | – | 10 |
| Others | – | – | 37 |
| Total | – | – | 100 |

*Note*: The data are based on a PC 'Made in China' by a major Chinese maker (as of April 2002).

*Source*: RIETI (www.rieti.go.jp/en/china/04011601.html, accessed on 28 March 2010).

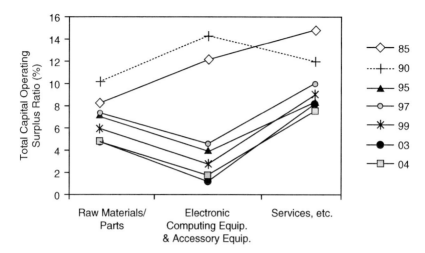

*Figure A2.1.2* Profit ratio curve for electronic computing equipment and accessory equipment

*Sources*: 'Ministry of Finance, Ministry of Finance Policy Research Institute, "Ministry of Finance Statistics Monthly"; Management and Coordination Agency, "1985–1990-1995 Linked Input-Output Tables"; Research and Statistics Department, Economic and Industry Policy Bureau, METI, "1997 Input-Output Tables", "1999 Input-Output Tables"; METI, "The Updated Input-Output Table 2003 (Quick Estimation)", "The Updated Input-Output Table 2004 (Quick Estimation)"' cited by Kimura 2006.

inventory, but it did not do this at the cost of distributors by pushing inventory onto them.

Shih entitled his autobiography 'Me Too Is Not My Style'.[29] He proposed a credo named reverse thinking to challenge difficulties and break through bottlenecks to create value.[30]

Shih learnt from his mother: 'Human nature is basically good and I try to run the company like a family. My children do not work for Acer.'[31]

While Shih centred his attention on the technology side, his wife Carolyn took care of the company's financial operations. Shih and his wife do not live in excessive luxury.

Asked about globalization and its impact on his business, Shih commented: 'When globalizing, you always have limited resources of talent and capital. The best way to globalize is therefore to localize, to integrate the local resources of talent and capital and integrate them with the parent company. We think in terms of "global brand, local touch"'.[32]

Shih's idea of managing the company is to control it 'by managing the common interest of the people inside it...which takes longer to establish...and then we can share the common vision and common goal and reach strategies that serve a mutual benefit.'[33]

# Appendix A2.1.1

Acer's financial statements

## Balance Sheet

As of March 31, 2009 Unit: NT$ Thousand

| Item | Period | Most Recent 5-Year Financial Information | | | | | Current Year as of 31 March 2009 |
|------|--------|---------|---------|---------|---------|---------|---------|
| | | 2004 | 2005 | 2006 | 2007 | 2008 | |
| Current Assets | | 85.029.907 | 139.242.560 | 161.267.661 | 191.626.201 | 186.390.592 | 201.740.858 |
| Fund and long-term equity investments | | 20.644.599 | 17.605.973 | 13.835.538 | 11.202.652 | 6.773.547 | 7.445.583 |
| Net property, plant and equipment | | 13.446.980 | 9.468.157 | 6.190.501 | 8.636.441 | 9.336.221 | 9.262.067 |
| Intangible assets | | 784.296 | 501.878 | 396.682 | 25.926.493 | 34.746.765 | 37.656.421 |
| Other assets | | 4.555.507 | 4.763.374 | 6.809.916 | 5.891.555 | 6.195.100 | 6.373.407 |
| **Total assets** | | **124.461.289** | **171.581.942** | **188.500.298** | **243.283.342** | **243.442.225** | **262.478.336** |
| Current | Before distribution | 59.989.759 | 102.158.601 | 109.970.460 | 142.842.574 | 149.315.158 | 164.687.935 |
| Liabilities | After distribution | 64.857.922 | 109.390.340 | 119.487.678 | 152.163.698 | unappropriated | unappropriated |
| Long-term liabilities | | 257.007 | 146.623 | 168.627 | 16.790.876 | 4.134.920 | 4.116.219 |
| Other liabilities | | 2.087.804 | 2.027.268 | 2.805.428 | 6.240.899 | 7.114.532 | 7.432.099 |
| **Total** | Before distribution | 62.334.570 | 104.332.492 | 112.944.515 | 165.874.349 | 160.564.610 | 176.236.253 |

| | | | | | | un-appropriated | un-appropriated |
|---|---|---|---|---|---|---|---|
| Liabilities | After distribution | 67.202.733 | 111.564.231 | 122.461.733 | 175.195.473 | un-appropriated | un-appropriated |
| Common stock | | 20.933.677 | 22.545.187 | 23.370.637 | 24.054.904 | 26.428.560 | 26.428.560 |
| Capital surplus | | 30.541.969 | 30.552.132 | 29.947.020 | 29.898.982 | 37.129.952 | 37.203.104 |
| Retained | Before distribution | 13.211.567 | 16.123.212 | 18.284.265 | 21.041.713 | 22.771.901 | 24.797.631 |
| Earnings | After distribution | 8.252.404 | 8.891.473 | 8.767.047 | 11.720.589 | un-appropriated | un-appropriated |
| Unrealized Gain (loss) on financial assets | | -731.426 | 65.608 | 4.361.608 | 2.524.500 | -1.729.631 | -1.085.579 |
| Transition adjustments | | 132.516 | -226.806 | 1.335.500 | 2.733.899 | 1.241.058 | 1.844.113 |
| Minimum pension liability adjustment | | 0 | 0 | 0 | -173.364 | -283 | -283 |
| Treasury stock | Before distribution | -3.411.280 | -3.270.920 | -3.270.920 | -3.270.920 | -3.522.598 | -3.522.598 |
| minority interest | | 1.540.696 | 1.461.038 | 1.527.674 | 599.280 | 558.656 | 577.134 |
| Stockholder' equity | | 62.217.719 | 67.249.451 | 75.555.783 | 77.408.994 | 82.877.615 | 86.242.082 |
| | After distribution | 57.258.556 | 60.017.712 | 66.038.565 | 68.087.869 | un-appropriated | un-appropriated |

## Consolidated Income Statement

Unit: NT$ Thousand

| Item | Most Recent 5-Year Financial Information | | | | | Current Year as of 31 March 2009 |
|---|---|---|---|---|---|---|
| | 2004 | 2005 | 2006 | 2007 | 2008 | |
| Operating revenue | 225.014.007 | 318.087.679 | 350.816.353 | 462.066.080 | 546.274.115 | 119.086.448 |
| Gross Profit | 27.219.303 | 34.121.461 | 38.171.313 | 47.418.310 | 57.285.660 | 11.918.367 |
| Operating (loss) income | 3.806.657 | 7.648.961 | 7.462.446 | 10.185.123 | 14.072.302 | 2.570.574 |
| Non-operating income and gain | 6.742.733 | 7.176.374 | 9.266.120 | 6.699.671 | 5.353.038 | 467.666 |
| Non-operating expense and loss | 1.908.790 | 4.172.803 | 3.180.259 | 1.776.157 | 4.618.613 | 282.903 |
| Continuing operating income before tax | 8.640.600 | 10.652.532 | 13.548.307 | 15.108.637 | 14.806.727 | 2.755.337 |
| Income (loss) from discontinued segment | 0 | 0 | 0 | 517.866 | 99.843 | 0 |
| Extraordinary items | 0 | 0 | 0 | 0 | 0 | 0 |
| Cumulative effect of changes in accounting principle | 0 | 0 | 0 | 0 | 0 | 0 |
| Income after income taxes | 7.011.661 | 8.477.502 | 10.218.242 | 12.958.933 | 11.742.135 | 2.025.730 |
| Eps | 2,86 | 3,48 | 4,20 | 5,33 | 4,72 | 0,78 |

## Segment Information

(1) Industry segment

The main business of the Consolidated is to sell 'Acer' brand-name desktop PCs, notebook PCs, and other related IT products, which represents a single industry

(2) Geographic information

Information by geographic area as of and the years ended 31 December, 2007 and 2008, was as follow

| | 2007 | | | | | |
|---|---|---|---|---|---|---|
| | Taiwan NT$ | North America NT$ | Europe NT$ | Asia NT$ | Eliminations NT$ | Consolidated NT$ |
| Area income: | | | | | | |
| Customers | 60.651.079 | 106.413.405 | 236.237.471 | 61.256.183 | 0 | 464.558.138 |
| Inter-company | 264.931.647 | 4.101 | 7.242.154 | 11.096 | −272.188.998 | 0 |
| | 325.582.726 | 106.417.506 | 243.479.625 | 61.267.279 | −272.188.998 | 464.558.138 |
| Area profit (loss) before income taxes | 264.812.614 | 926.347 | 15.381.028 | 2.194.840 | −272.187.926 | 11.126.903 |
| Next investment income | | | | | | 695.660 |
| Gain on disposal of investments, net | | | | | | 4.045.981 |
| Interest expense | | | | | | −759.907 |
| Consolidated income before income taxes | | | | | | 15.108.637 |
| Area indentifiable assets | 100.327.411 | 58.022.952 | 88.086.758 | 28.618.423 | −53.352.602 | 221.702.942 |
| equity method investments | | | | | | 4.689.684 |
| Goodwill | | | | | | 16.890.716 |
| Total assets | | | | | | 243.283.342 |
| Depreciation and amortization | 1.088.239 | 32.112 | 11.329 | 10.879 | 0 | 1.142.559 |
| Capital expenditures | 665.555 | 59.128 | 140.593 | 185.338 | 0 | 1.050.614 |

## Segment Information

| | 2008 | | | | | |
|---|---|---|---|---|---|---|
| | Taiwan NT$ | North America NT$ | Europe NT$ | Asia NT$ | Eliminations NT$ | Consolidated NT$ |
| *Area income:* | | | | | | |
| Customers | 25.879.015 | 152.469.649 | 279.790.219 | 90.925.741 | 0 | 549.064.624 |
| Inter-company | 341.107.152 | 3.203 | 6.057.224 | 13.642 | -347.181.221 | 0 |
| | 366.986.167 | 152.472.852 | 285.847.443 | 90.939.383 | -347.181.221 | 549.064.624 |
| Area profit (loss) before income taxes | 342.361.748 | -1.044.322 | 15.501.048 | 3.361.512 | -347.181.221 | 12.998.765 |
| Next investment income | | | | | | 404.184 |
| Gain on disposal of investments, net | | | | | | 2.709.524 |
| Interest expense | | | | | | -1.305.746 |
| Consolidated income before income taxes | | | | | | 14.806.727 |
| Area identifiable assets | 111.929.202 | 47.044.049 | 95.789.881 | 25.518.735 | -62.342.472 | 217.939.395 |
| equity method investments | | | | | | 2.928.790 |
| Goodwill | | | | | | 22.574.040 |
| **Total assets** | | | | | | 243.442.225 |
| Depreciation and amortization | 685.120 | 1.090.051 | 290.210 | 136.060 | 0 | 2.201.441 |
| Capital expenditures | 171.677 | 220.011 | 154.207 | 205.397 | 0 | 751.292 |

(3) Export sales

Export sales of the Company and its domestic subsidiaries do not exceed 10% of the consolidated revenues, hence no disclosure is required.

(2) Geographic information

2007 and 2008.

# Appendix A2.1.2: ACER Group[34] and its main competitors

**Acer's PC-centric** product offering includes desktop and laptop computers, servers and storage, LCD monitors and HDTVs, projectors, and handheld navigation devices. Sub-brands include the consumer-centric Aspire and TravelMate commercial sector, and series Veriton Altos.

**Gateway** was founded by Ted Waitt in 1985 on a farm in Iowa with a loan of US $ 10,000 guaranteed by his grandmother, a rental equipment and a business plan of three pages. Today, Gateway has become one of the top PC brands in the United States known.

The brand received national acclaim in 1991 when it introduced its distinctive cow spots in the boxes, a tribute to its heritage of agriculture. In early 2004, Gateway acquired eMachines, and then moved its headquarters to Irvine, California. In October 2007, Gateway was acquired by Taiwan-based Acer, and the combined entities now comprise the third largest PC company in the world.

Gateway has always been dedicated to treating customers with respect and decency while focusing on service, quality and value. As Gateway leads to new frontiers, remains committed to its original goal of helping people improve their lives through technology.

**eMachines**, one of the fastest growing in the world of PC brands, was acquired by Gateway Inc. in March 2004. Its market are families looking for reliable machines for everyday use, carries eMachines PC to any needy households. It remains an independent brand and sold through major retailers, e-tailers and channel partners in the US and selected international markets.

Since its launch in 1998, more than five million eMachines systems have been sold.

**Packard Bell**, very few brands can claim to have witnessed, let alone contributed, to the three major revolutions – radio, TV and PC – in the home entertainment of the past 80 years. Packard Bell is one of the rare exceptions. The brand was born in 1926. In the 1920s and 1930s, when radio was the rage, Packard Bell emerged as a popular brand of console radio with a reputation for stylish design. The first Packard Bell TV was launched in 1948, the same time as the TV revolution was sweeping the world.

Packard Bell entered the PC market in 1987. It pioneered the use of the PC at home, turning into an office tool, but useful in a friendly, indispensable feature of today's modern homes.

Stylish design (with several major awards) and customer-oriented features are the characteristics of all Packard Bell products. In 2008, Packard Bell keeps on developing design, innovation, ease of use and affordability that have been the hallmark of the brand for more than 80 years.

*Source*: www.acer-group.com accessed on 22 April 2010

## Appendix A2.1.3: The five keys to a sustainable future[35] according to Acer

### 1. Multi-brand strategy

The PC is becoming a commodity. Aware of the vast diversity among consumer tastes, a single brand cannot cover the preferences of all market segments. Acer saw the opportunity to adopt a multi-brand strategy by acquiring Gateway and Packard Bell. The results so far have assured us the multi-brand approach was and is the right response to an ever-changing market. In just over a year, Acer has set up a global multi-brand management framework, and launched differentiated product designs to precisely target all major market segments.

### 2. Sustainable and profitable business model

Acer adheres to a channel business model that involves collaboration with first-class suppliers and distributors, leveraging their resources and ultimately, sharing the fruits of success among all partners. Besides, our low capital and operating expense policy has been beneficial to the steady growth of our business operations.

### 3. Efficient global operations

Based upon the management philosophy of upholding a 'simple' and 'focused' approach, Acer spun off the manufacturing operations in 2000 to concentrate all resources on building its brand name business. Our top management from product development, marketing and the regions gather on a regular basis to discuss key issues.

This practice ensures clear understanding and smooth internal communication, which lead to efficient decision-making followed by accurate implementation. In addition, Acer has a flexible and dynamic global logistics network to ensure time-to-market delivery of our products.

### 4. End-to-end marketing strengths

To begin with, our products are designed around customer needs – that means understanding exactly what our customers want, and using our knowledge and skills to exceed their expectations by making technology simple to use, stylish to own and accessible to everyone. Combined with Acer's fast decision-making, call to action and timely release of products to market, to form an end-to-end marketing prowess that ensures continuing business success ahead.

### 5. Growth and scale

The recent mergers and combined scales have already created new synergies as predicted. With remarkable growths in revenue, operating income and market share worldwide, Acer is today more competitive than ever.

# Annex 2.2

# Imperial Japanese Army[1, 2]: The essence of failure[3]

## Introduction

Circumstantial evidence points to the possibility that the Imperial Japanese Army/Navy shared many common features – both positive and negative – with present-day Japanese companies and organizations.

Accordingly, the study of the Imperial Japanese Army/Navy will certainly shed light on the nature of organizations in Japan and may allow us to enjoy a certain level of insightful predictions regarding the way Japanese companies behave at any given time, and especially in moments of crisis.

First and foremost, the Imperial Japanese Army/Navy offers an example of an induction-based organization. Its inductive way of thinking during the Second World War resulted in an ambiguity of objectives by setting only a general direction, which sometimes allowed too much leeway for different units that ended up setting their own objectives. Learning by doing, making light of theory, lacking a mechanism for feeding the analysis of the causes of failure back into the planning system, were inductive elements that characterized the Imperial Japanese Army and led it to defeat in major battles as well as, ultimately, its surrender in 1945.

The overwhelming difference in economic and industrial capacity between the US and Japan may be an explanation for Japan's ultimate defeat[4] (see Appendix A2.2).

However, the strategic and organizational aspects also shed clarifying light on Japan's defeat, and are what will be specifically addressed in this paper. This analysis, therefore, is made from the viewpoints of strategy and organization. It is our contention that, by analogy, many of the merits and shortcomings of present-day Japanese companies can be detected by better understanding the inductive approach of the Imperial Japanese Army.

From the perspective of effectiveness and efficiency, we put forward that the effectiveness,[5] namely, the extent of the purpose being attained, and in this case the achievement of the war purpose (to win the war) was not abundantly clear from the beginning because of the immense difference in economic and industrial capacity between the US and Japan (see Appendix A2.2). In addition, the efficiency,[6] namely, the ratio between output and input, was impaired because of organizational and strategic blunders or missteps committed by the Imperial Japanese Army and Navy.

## Six operations

Japan suffered six successive defeats in its operations starting with the 1939 Battle of Khalkhin Gol (or Nomonhan Incident), the Battle of Midway (4 to 7 June, 1942), the Battle of Guadalcanal (11 October, 1942), the Battle of Imphal (March until July 1944), the Battle of Leyte Gulf (23 October to 26 October, 1944), and the Battle of Okinawa (late March through June 1945). (For a timeline of The Pacific War, see Table A2.2.1).

Though the failure may be explained partly by each independent circumstance, the sum of each operation, strategically designed by the Imperial Japanese Army, led in the long run to the final unconditional surrender, and each one was consequentially correlated through the cause and effect chain. Overall, these failures reflected some of the fundamental shortcomings of

*Table A2.2.1*   Timeline of the main events

|      | Year/month | Event |
|------|------------|-------|
| 1927 | May | The Japanese Army's First Shandong Expedition |
| 1931 | September | Manchurian Incident |
| 1932 | March | Foundation of Manchukuo |
| 1933 | March | Japan's withdrawal from the League of Nations |
| 1936 | January | Japan's withdrawal from London Naval Conference |
|      | November | Anti-Comintern Pact between Japan and Germany |
| 1937 | July | Sino-Japanese War |
| 1939 | May | Nomonhan Incident or the Battle of KhalkhinGol |
| 1941 | April | The Soviet-Japanese Neutrality Pact |
|      | December | Pearl Harbor attack, The Pacific War |
| 1942 | January to May | Japan's invasion of Manila, Rabaul, Singapore, Mandalay, etc. |
|      | June–July | The Battle of Midway |
|      | October | The Battle of Guadalcanal |
| 1944 | March–July | The Battle of Imphal |
|      | October–December | The Battle of Leyte |
| 1945 | February | The Battle of Iwo Jima |
|      | March–June | The Battle of Okinawa |
|      | August–September | Atomic bombs in Hiroshima and Nagasaki |
|      | August | The USSR's declaration of war against Japan |
|      |          | The Acceptance of Potsdam Declaration, the Unconditional Surrender of Japan |

*Source*: Kamei, Mikami, Hayashi and Horigome (2009: p. 81 and 83).

the Imperial Japanese Army (see Table A2.2.2), which was a serious problem in light of the fact that the direction of Japanese war policy was controlled by the military:

> Japan's governmental structure provided no effective civilian control of her Army and Navy. In the years between the 1931 invasion of Manchuria and the 1941 attack upon Pearl Harbor, the military cliques of Japan exerted a progressively tighter control over the foreign and domestic affairs of the nation. These cliques included groups within both the Army and Navy, but because of the repeated military successes of the Imperial Japanese Army in Manchuria and China and the prestige so acquired, and because of the more ambitious and aggressive nature of the Imperial Japanese Army leaders, the political position of the Army was ascendant to that of the Navy. The final decision to enter the war and to advance into the Philippines, the Dutch East Indies, Malaya, Burma and to the southeast was, however, made with the full concurrence and active consent of all-important Imperial Japanese Army and Navy leaders and of almost all her important civilian leaders. (United States Strategic Bombing Survey, 1946: p. 2)

The characteristics common to these six defeats are summarized as follows:

1. Involving multiple divisions and fleets, these operations required large-scale deployment of resources. Because of this, the central operational

*Table A2.2.2* Comparison of the Imperial Japanese Army and the US Army

| Category | Item | Japanese army | US army |
|---|---|---|---|
| Strategy | Objective | Ambiguous | Clear |
| | Strategy orientation | Short decisive battles | Long term |
| | Strategy options | Inductive (incremental) | Deductive (Grand Design) |
| | Technology | Focused on a small number of technology items | Standardization |
| Organization | Structure | Collectivism (personal network process) | Structuralism (systems) |
| | Integration | Personal principle (personal relations) | Integration by system (task force) |
| | Learning | Single loop | Double loop |
| | Appraisal | Motives, process | Results |

*Source*: Tobe, R., Teramoto, Y., Kamata, S., Sugino, Y., Murai, T., and Nonaka, I. (1991: p. 338).

units such as the Imperial General Headquarters of the Imperial Japanese Army and Navy intervened in determining the operational plans.

2. There was enormous remoteness between the general staff and the operational units, and even among operational units, in terms of time and physical distance.

3. These operations were undertaken by battle units with high technology and mechanization in addition to complicated logistics, communication and logistic support; as such, they were examples of modern battles comprising many aspects.

4. These operations were planned beforehand and fought based on these army plans, which means that they were organization-to-organization confrontations.

These issues indicate that the defeats were in the main not attributable to the misjudgement of commanding officers or to the deficiency in each individual operation; rather, they should be put down to the characteristics of the Imperial Japanese Army in systemic aspects. Given the fact that four of them (Midway, Guadalcanal, Leyte and Okinawa battles) were waged against the US Army, the Imperial Japanese Army was definitely inferior to the US Army as an organization.

We will carry out an analysis of the causes of the failures in the six operations from two points of view: (1) strategy and (2) organization (see Table A2.2.3).

## I. Reasons of defeat or failure from the strategic point of view

There are six causes for these Japanese failures, as set out below:[7]

1. Ambiguous objectives.
2. Lack of grand design.
3. Preference for short-term decisive battles.
4. Subjective and 'inductive' strategic planning – and dominance of mood.
5. Narrow and hard-fast strategic options.
6. Unbalanced battle technology system.[8]

### 1. Ambiguous objectives

Ambiguity in objectives[9] naturally leads to failure where military operations are concerned, since the absence of objectives forces a large-scale organization, the army in this case, into being directed and manoeuvred without a clear-cut course.

When the Battle of Khalkhin Gol or Nomonhan Incident was waged between the divisions of USSR and Japanese Army, the Imperial General Headquarters of Japan turned a blind eye to the situation and let Kanto

Army take the initiative.[10] The Imperial General Headquarters limited itself to indicating the allowance in the number of soldiers and military resources without dictating an explicit strategy regarding the battle. In other words, Kanto Army fought it without knowing its overall strategic significance or context.

*Table A2.2.3* Significance of the six battles in the Pacific War

| Battle | Significance |
| --- | --- |
| Battle of Khalkhin Gol (or Nomonhan Incident) | 'The decisive engagement of the undeclared Soviet-Japanese Border War, or Japanese-Soviet War, fought between the Soviet Union, Mongolia and the Empire of Japan in 1939.' http://en.wikipedia.org/wiki/Battle_of_Khalkhin_Gol accessed on 30 May 2009 |
| Battle of Midway (4 June to 7 June 1942) | 'Fought almost entirely with aircraft, in which the United States destroyed Japan's first-line carrier strength and most of its best trained naval pilots and ended the threat of further Japanese invasion in the Pacific.'* |
| Battle of Guadalcanal (11 October 1942) | 'The Guadalcanal campaign marked the first significant strategic combined arms victory by Allied forces over the Japanese in the Pacific theatre. For this reason, the Guadalcanal campaign is often referred to as a 'turning point' in the war. The campaign marked the beginning of the transition by the Allies from defensive operations to the strategic offensive, while Japan was thereafter forced to cease strategic offensive operations and instead concentrate on strategic defense.' (http://en.wikipedia.org/wiki/Guadalcanal_Campaign accessed on 30 May 2009) |
| Battle of Imphal (March until July 1944) | 'Japanese armies attempted to destroy the Allied forces at Imphal and invade India, but were driven back into Burma with heavy losses. Together with the simultaneous Battle of Kohima on the road by which the encircled Allied forces at Imphal were relieved, the battle was the turning point of the Burma Campaign, part of the South-East Asian Theatre of World War II. Many historians consider it to be the biggest Japanese defeat of the war.' (http://en.wikipedia.org/wiki/Battle_of_Imphal accessed on 30 May 2009) |
| Battle of Leyte Gulf (23 October to 26 October 1944) | 'Decisive air and sea battle of World War II, which crippled the Japanese Combined Fleet, permitted US invasion of the Philippines and gave the Allies control of the Pacific.' (*) |

Continued

*Table A2.2.3*   Continued

| Battle | Significance |
|--------|--------------|
| Battle of Okinawa (late March through June 1945) | 'The Battle of Okinawa, also known as Operation Iceberg, was ... the largest amphibious assault in the Pacific Theatre of World War II as well as the last pitched battle of the entire war ... The battle has been referred to as the "Typhoon of Steel" ... The nicknames refer to the ferocity of the fighting ... Approximately one-fourth of the civilian population died due to the invasion.' (http://en.wikipedia.org/wiki/Battle_of_okinawa accessed on 30 May 2009) |

\* Encyclopaedia Britannica 2004 Standard Edition CD.

In the battles of Midway and Leyte the ambiguity of objectives wreaked havoc. Simplification of several objectives into one allows concentration of military resources; on the contrary, the dispersion of resources to pursue multiple objectives per se constitutes failure.

The objective for the battle was phrased as 'to block the enemy's mobile operations to attack Japan from Hawaii by conquering Midway Islands, and to annihilate the enemy's fleet that may turn up at the time of attack.'

The objectives were, therefore, twofold (with dual purposes): 1) the conquest of Midway and 2) annihilation of the US fleet. The duplicity influenced Commander Nagumo's decision not to send attack planes immediately when a reconnaissance plane sighted the US aircraft carrier and instead a) wait for the return of the first group of attack planes and b) at the same time continue preparations to attack the islands, which went counter to the accepted wisdom[11] Churchill (2002: p. 546) qualifies Nagumo's judgment as being 'clouded.' The victory of the US Army was, instead, an example of objective simplification. Commander Nimitz issued a strict order to concentrate on the attack on aircraft carriers.

In the Battle of Leyte, the Japanese Navy attempted a last-ditch defence of the logistic route to and from the resource-rich (for example, rubber) south front and the suppression of the US intent to attack the Philippines even at the cost of Japan's Combined Fleet. If the US Army were to land on the islands, the Imperial Japanese Army would confront it with the First Division, which meant that the intention of the Imperial Japanese Army was to deploy a large-scale integral operation from land, sea and air. Differing from this was the idea cherished by staff officer Koyanagi from Kurita Fleet, the main defence force, consisting of an all-out confrontation between the main battleships.[12]

Therefore there was no uniform objective between the Imperial General Headquarters and the force in situ. This was an outcome resulting from the typical way in which the Imperial Japanese Army mapped out its strategy. It used to work out only the general outline, leaving the elaboration of its details to be carried out on the basis of communication and decisions taken between the general staff and the force in situ, as the situation developed.

As regards the Battle of Imphal, differing objectives also existed between the Burma Area Army and the Fifteenth Army. The former attempted to focus on the defence of Burma and therefore limit the deployment to Imphal, whereas the latter wanted to invade India. This contrasted with the fact that Lieutenant-General Geoffrey Scoones spent time sharing the same objective by discussing lengthily with his staff members and, in the process, building up a relationship of trust, typically taking a walk on board the aircraft carrier *Enterprise* with them.

In the Battle of Okinawa, the Imperial General Headquarters was in favour of fighting by air in contrast to using the Thirty-Second Army located in Okinawa, which insisted on a protracted warfare mainly based on ground battles. In a conference held between the two parties, no discussion was made to settle the difference.

## 2. Lack of grand design

The differences between the Imperial Japanese Army and Navy and resultant multiplicity in objectives and their ambiguity are to be sought in the lack of a *grand design* that would have helped to combine individual operations in an organized way and to win the war.

Without any knowledge of where Japan was heading or without an orientation based on an overall grand design, Sakamoto (1989) contends that before the War, the Japanese Navy reckoned that Japan would be able to live on the stock of resources for a year, and refers to the bloating of the national budget (general account) from ¥130 million in 1941 to ¥21.49 billion in 1945 with the special military budget increasing from ¥9.48 billion to ¥73.49 billion in the same period. Citing Jerome Cohen's book[13] on the wartime Japanese economy, Sakamoto (1989: p. 619) reports that in early 1945, Japanese aluminum and steel producers lacked iron ore and coke and by then the Japanese war economy was at its lowest.

The US War Plan Orange,[14] on the other hand, was clear in its definition of the war: to attack Japan proper and to conclude the war by landing in Japan itself. Its grand strategy consisted of conquering the Mid-Pacific Ocean islands and, once its stronghold was secured, in destroying Japan's power to resist by air-raiding Japan.

Japan, in contrast, emphasized the logic that by destroying the bases of the UK, the US and the Netherlands in East Asia, by accelerating Chiang

Kai-Shek's surrender through 'positive' measures and by allying with Germany and Italy and by impairing, as a consequence, the war motivation of the US, it would be able to consolidate its position – which was obviously predicated on very ambiguous wishful thinking, resulting in ambiguous objectives for each battle and operation waged.

### 3. Preference for short-term decisive battles

The Imperial Japanese Army/Navy tended to stress the short term. In starting war with the US, Japan thought that the war would end shortly thanks to its victory in the initial battles and the securing of resource-rich Southeast Asia and the South Pacific area, which would dissuade the US from continuing the war.

Japan's Combined Fleet aimed at improving its skills and capabilities to challenge the US fleet in the Pacific Ocean; even if it defeated the enemy's fleet, no discussion was held about how it would bring peace, not to mention the contingency of defeat at the hands of the US and its consequences.

The preference for short-duration battles was evident in Yamamoto Isoroku's answer to Premier Konoye's question about the resources and capabilities of Japan's Navy in case of war with the US: 'If we were to comply with our obligations, we would be able to wreak a lot of havoc in the US fleet for the first six months or for a year; but should the war last more than that, I don't feel sure at all.'

### 4. Subjective, inductive strategy making – dominance of mood

In simple terms, the way the Imperial Japanese Army prepared its strategy may be classified as inductive, whereas the US Army's was deductive, if we define induction as a way to draw a generalizable law from a series of experienced facts, and deduction as a way to resolve each individual question from a known generalizable law. However, it may be conjectured that the Imperial Japanese Army did not even have a conceptual apparatus to generalize the findings from the facts into a law, and stayed at the level of facts as such.

The absence of a conceptual apparatus for analysis may have been made up for by the use of a certain way of viewing phenomena. Tobe et al. (1991: p. 350) call it 'strategic paradigm'. The paradigm's rigidity precluded any possibility of thinking differently. The Army held that hand-to-hand combat was the key to victory and the Navy was convinced that ultimate victory in naval battle was decided by artillery between main battleships. The Army's belief was grounded on its experience in the Satsuma Rebellion against Satsuma ex-samurai in 1877, and in the attack on 203 Hill during the Siege of Port Arthur in 1914–15 in the Russo–Japanese War. The Navy's conviction was derived from the Sea of Japan Naval Battle in the Russo–Japanese War in which the Japanese Fleet inflicted a severe blow to Russia's Baltic Fleet. On account of the Japanese artillery fire turned against the

Russians, their Baltic Fleet lost six battleships out of eight (two of them captured), five out of nine cruisers sunk (one sunk by the Russians themselves, three unharmed), one patrol boat out of three (two surrendered) with 4,524 casualties and 6,168 prisoners, whereas Japan only lost three torpedo boats with 115 casualties.

The balance-tipping power of mood also characterized the decision-making process in the Imperial Japanese Army. Higher staff member Yahara lamented the lack of rigour in the planning before the Battle of Okinawa on account of the preference for guts, the Japanese spirit, bargaining and so on In the Taipei conference, held to deliberate the plan for the Battle of Okinawa, Colonel Yahara presented his highly logical 'Opinion from the commander of Thirty-Second Army,' which went counter to the general mood and as a consequence, made the conference mood 'unbearable'. Another attendee at the conference, Colonel Hattori, in charge of operations at the Imperial Japanese Army, noted that his contrarian opinion put a damper on the mood. Serious debate was ultimately avoided and the decision was made on the basis of the dominant mood.

When the Fifteenth Army worked out the plan for the Battle of Imphal, staff officers were at a loss for how to refute it, in view of the 'conviction to win' expressed by Lieutenant General Mutaguchi. When asked about the logistic plan for the Battle, Mutaguchi is reported to have joked: 'No problem. When faced with the enemy, all that we must do is to shoot in the air three times, which is an agreed sign with the enemy for its surrender.' The General Headquarters preferred harmony in the organization to the detriment of military logic. Sugiyama, the chief of the general headquarters, persuaded the chief of Operations, Sanada, who was against the general opinion, to accept it on the grounds that Terauchi, the chief commander of the South Army, desired a harmonized opinion.

The fatal flaw in the thought process and methodology of the Imperial Japanese Army consisted of: (1) learning by doing without theoretical support (2) having no contingency plan in case the experience-based decision-making went wrong (3) therefore, lacking the capability to map out drastically different strategies in case of failure. Lieutenant General William Slim, in charge of the UK's Fourteenth Army in the Battle of Imphal, pointed out that the Imperial Japanese Army's fault was its incapacity to rectify the strategy immediately in case it failed.

## 5. Narrow and hard-fast strategic option

The Imperial Japanese Army's strategic options tended to be narrow. One preferred option was surprise attack. In contrast to the Army, which focused on the USSR as its enemy, the Navy had traditionally considered the US as its hypothetical enemy and had prepared for years for a confrontation. However, its strategy concept was narrow and based on tactics and operations for pre-emptive and intensive attacks. Importance was not given to technology. For torpedo attacks on enemy fleets by its destroyers, the Imperial Japanese Navy relied on sentinels capable of discerning the movement of the enemy fleet from a distance of 8,000 metres at night. The US Army, on the other hand, developed a radar technology that did not depend on the unique capability of individual soldiers, which enabled it to bring total destruction to the fleet commanded by Nishimura heading for the Battle of Leyte.

The basic ability of the Imperial Japanese Army related to the conversion of tactics and operations into strategy and its utilization. It was effective in warfare in which the movement of the enemy was visible and for which a high integration of component parts' manoeuvres was not needed. However, once the balance of equipment and combat resources tilted in favour of the US Army, the operations turned into strategy were not effective any more.

In the sea battle fought off the Mariana Islands on 19 June 1944, Japan's elite First Manoeuvring Fleet suffered irreparable damage because the US Army captured its movement from a distance of 150 miles and sent nearly 450 combat planes. It also attacked it with the newly-developed VT fuses (that exploded near the target even if they did not hit it). The innovation in technology did not allow for operational-level skills to be effective.

The narrow strategy options were observed in the case of the Navy because of its success in the Sea of Japan Naval Battle against Russia in 1915. The success fostered the belief in large battleships with large cannons and fleet battles, which was reflected in the Rules of Sea Battles (kaisen yomurei) as (1) the essence of battle being the rapid destruction of the enemy with preemption and intensity in which battleships and fleets are the main force (2) the submarines focused on attacks to enemy fleets in collaboration with other ships.

For example, the last point regarding the use of submarines bucks the trend in the world. Europe and the US considered the use of submarines as effective against merchant fleets. Japan stuck to submarine attacks on enemy fleets and did not use them for the protection of merchant ships.

The defeat in the Battle of Khalkhin Gol[15] (or Nomonhan Incident) was partly due to Japanese success in the surprise attack in the Battle of Lake Khasan (29 July, 1938–11 August 1938), also known as the Changkufeng Incident. The Japanese became convinced of the usefulness of surprise attacks by night, whereas the Russians learnt how to defend against them. In Khalkhin Gol, the Imperial Japanese Army pinned its hope on success in the initial surprise attack but the Russians preempted its usefulness.

The US Navy was more versatile in adapting its strategy to the requirements of the situation and in improving it. For example, the Battle of the Coral Sea fought on 8 May 1942, one month before the Battle of Midway, dealt a severe blow to the US Navy. Two aircraft carriers, *Lexington* and *York Town*, forming a circular layout, were attacked by Zero fighters and they moved apart too much, which was taken advantage of by the Japanese Navy to further intensify their attack. As a result, even though Japan lost two aircraft carriers, the US suffered a bigger loss due to the loss of its main aircraft carrier *Lexington*, an oil tanker and a destroyer as well as severe damage inflicted on *York Town*. The US Navy, however, learnt a lesson from this defeat and it placed each of its three aircraft carriers with respective convoys in a separate circular layout, with each convoy separated by 10 to 20 km to prevent the Japanese scout airplanes from capturing the entire panorama. It is a well-known fact that the delay in sighting the enemy's fleet was a main cause of the defeat suffered by the Japanese Navy in the Battle of Midway.

The narrowness of strategic option was reflected in the disregard for contingency plans. The Battle of Imphal was mainly designed around strategic surprise attacks. But no contingency plan was worked out in preparation for the cases in which surprise attacks did not succeed. Commander Mutaguchi expressed his disagreement with designing any contingency plan in a way that would mean calling into question the possibility of victory and go against their *wish to win*.

## II. Reasons of failure from the organizational point of view

### Organizational structure heavily dependent on personal networks

The Imperial Japanese Army, especially its ground force, tended to emphasize the importance of the General Staff or Headquarters, as evidenced by the Battle of Khalkhin Gol.

In the preparation and execution of the battle, the de facto decisions were driven by Kanto Army to the detriment of control by the Imperial General Headquarters. Kanto Army Lieutenant Colonel Takushiro Hattori, the chief of planning at the First Section, and Major Masanobu Tsuji in charge of the battle, were in control.

The key question is why the general staff at the Kanto Army and the Imperial General Headquarters could not hold back their overbearing presence and influence. This may be chronologically analysed.

In the aftermath of the first battle, the Imperial General Headquarters hardly issued any official instructions, only expressing that appropriate actions be taken.

By the end of May, the Imperial General Headquarters prepared a basic plan which meant to put an end to the conflict, but it was not shown to the Kanto Army. Tsuji and his staff prepared their own plan for the operation, but for fear that if the Imperial General Headquarters was shown the plan and would most probably veto it, the plan was not submitted for consideration and approval until just before the operation was to be executed. The Army Minister decided that operations executed at the division level ought to be decided by the division.

On 23 June, the Kanto Army decided to carry out an attack by air but did not inform the Imperial General Headquarters. The plans, however, were leaked. The HQ in Tokyo, through its deputy chief, asked the Kanto Army to refrain from the air attack until the right moment, but did not explicitly given them orders to that effect. The Kanto Army accordingly carried out the operation on 27 June.

On 20 July, the Imperial General Headquarters informed the Kanto Army of its late May plan, stopping short of a clear instruction to lay down arms. On 30 August, the Imperial General Headquarters finally issued an imperial order to stop the conflict, phrased so ambiguously that the Kanto Army did not interpret it as such. The Imperial General Headquarters sent its deputy chief to explain its decision but was not listened to. In view of a renewed belligerent operation, the Imperial General Headquarters at long last issued an imperial order in unambiguous terms, ordering them to cease the battle on 3 September.

A similar situation was repeated in the Battle of Imphal. One month after the battle had started, General Hikosaburo Hata, the deputy chief of staff, visited the battleground from late April to late May and suggested that the operation be suspended in light of the manifest defeat. Hata thought that his suggestion would be understood by the commanders of South Army and Burma Area Army. In early June, Commander Kawabe in charge of the Burma Area Army visited Commander Mutaguchi of the Fifteenth Army, but despite both of them being convinced of the need to stop the battle, neither of them expressed their idea clearly, both men reportedly expecting that the other would guess his opinion.

These two instances of miscommunication point to the fact that in the Imperial Japanese Army, although on the surface it had a highly hierarchical system, communication depended on guesswork, reading thoughts, non-verbal conveying of opinions and so on. Personal networking played an essential role.

In the Imperial Japanese Army (land force) the chosen few went to the Army College which operated as an institution to educate future public servants in the army. Its graduates and their promotions were the responsibility of the general staff, not of the Army Minister. The graduates formed a close network and wielded strong influence through their positions as general staff. More often than not, leadership was displayed by staff members, not by the heads of line. Soon, there were double layers in the Army: on the one hand, a steep hierarchy and, on the other, a system dominated by personal networking in which strong emotional ties had a remarkable presence.

The Navy was slightly different in that the Navy College only admitted officers with first-line commanding experience and its graduates were controlled by the Navy Minister, which avoided the creation of elite and non-elite officer groups. However, as WWII progressed, young officers tended to overrule the decisions of their seniors. Tobe et al. (1991: p. 315) classify the behavioural pattern of the Imperial Japanese Army as 'collectivism':

> The collectivism we mention here does not mean that it ignores the existence of individuals or reifies the service and immersion in the cause held by the group. It does not demand the choice between the individual and the group as mutually exclusive options. In pursuance of the co-existence both of member individuals and the group, it considers the human relations among its members as of the most important value. We may call it the 'Japanese collectivism.' In this regard, the ultimate consideration concerns the 'relationship' among the members instead of the logical and systematic formation and selection of the group's objectives and their achievement.

## The person principle[16]

The organizational structure or system did not serve for the integration of plans and strategies elaborated by different units of the Imperial Japanese Army or Navy. Given the fact that the objectives were ambiguous and the strategic planning was conducted based on the inductive method and *incrementalism* (in other words, the decisions were the accumulation and set of small incremental decisions), the resolution of differences was based on the fine-tuning of intentions in the place of operation, thus avoiding ambiguity in judgment. The officers in charge of resolving differences liaised with their personal friends from the same graduating class in the academy and Army College; because of the collectivism referred to above, such a personal network and the exertion of influence by specific individuals was of paramount importance.[17]

In October 1941, Hideki Tojo held concurrently the posts of Premier and Army Minister in order to coordinate the nation's basic policy and steer the war effort. Three years later, he added that of chief of the general staff in an effort to homogenize control of the military forces and implementation of the government's orders by the army.

Such coordination through individuals and officers was a reflection of organizational deficiency. Imperial General Headquarters allowed the Army and the Navy to have their own independent and separate organizations and staff. The only person with the authorization to decide in the event of discrepant opinions between the Army and the Navy was the Emperor who, however, refrained from micromanaging concrete details. His basic stance was to wait for the differences to be overcome by the consensus between the two forces, which translated into difficulties in collaboration and integration between them in practice.

After the defeat in the Battle of Saipan as a part of the World War II Pacific campaign, fought on the island of Saipan in the Mariana Islands from 15 June 1944 to 9 July 1944, the Japanese government agonized about it and proposed six ideas:

1. To abolish the two positions of chiefs of staff and to place a chief supervising the mixed general staff from the Army and the Navy;
2. To place a chief of staff on top of the two chiefs from the Army and the Navy;
3. To keep the two chiefs but to create the position of a coordinating chief of staff;
4. To place a coordinating office between the Army and the Navy under the two chiefs;
5. To include several Army officers in the Navy's general staff;
6. To physically place the offices of the two chiefs within close proximity to each other.

However, no alternative was adopted and implemented because of resistance from both forces.

### An organization that does not attach importance to learning

One of the causes of the defeat at the hands of the Russians in the Battle of Khalkhin Gol was the inferiority of the equipment for modern warfare. Tanks and heavy artillery emerged as the basic decisive weapons. However, the Imperial Japanese Army would not learn the lesson. Instead of improving its equipment and artillery, the Army increased the number of recruits. Basically, the Army and the Navy operated in keeping with Admiral Togo's famous saying just after the Sea of Japan Naval Battle on 27 and 28 May, 1905, that 'a cannon hitting the mark ten out of ten conquers another hitting once out of ten.' For the Imperial Japanese Army, a will to hit the mark and its conviction had greater weight than the modernization of equipment.

The all-out frontal charge in the Battle of Guadalcanal was an example of the operational vestige from the time of the Russo–Japanese War (1914–1915). Its ineffectiveness was proven time and again, but the Imperial Japanese Army stuck to this dogmatic credence. What happened was that the Imperial Japanese Army did not have a mechanism to analyse the failed battles and wars from the strategic and tactical viewpoints and to draw lessons from them to apply in the organization.

Another shortcoming was the lack of a system to facilitate information sharing within the organization. Owing to the stultified atmosphere inhibiting free discussions, information tended to be focused on a small number of circles or individuals. It was impossible for the organization to leverage knowledge garnered from the failures. Elite staff members were far removed from battlegrounds both mentally and physically. To make up for the dearth of information and experience, they had no other choice but to resort to dogmatic tactics and repeat them time and again. The all-out frontal charge in Guadalcanal, the belief in battleships as the key factor in Leyte, are but some of the examples.

The US Army acted differently. It paid maximum attention to theory, theorization and learning. Based on its experience in the Battle of Guadalcanal, the US Army had conducted a thorough analysis of what measures could be effective against the Imperial Japanese Army by the end of 1942. In other words, it used Guadalcanal as an experimental ground to probe into useful strategy in land and sea battles.

The educational system at the military academy, the Naval academy, Army College and Naval College of Japan was excellent at the beginning. However, they ended up placing more emphasis on the selection and learning of existing measures that were considered efficient in achieving given objectives to the detriment of creative thinking about calling into question objectives and redefining them. Objectives and targets were givens. Only rote learning of methods and measures was important. The organizational learning at the Imperial Japanese Army was the single-loop learning process, that is it 'assumes that problems and their solutions are close to each other in time and space (though they often are not). In this form of learning, we are primarily considering our actions. Small changes are made to specific practices or behaviour, based on what has or has not worked in the past. This involves doing things better without necessarily examining or challenging our underlying beliefs and assumptions. The goal is improvements and fixes that often take the form of procedures or rules. Single-loop learning leads to making minor fixes or adjustments, like using a thermostat to regulate temperature.'[18] In other words, the process targets the search and selection of the optimum solution with the objectives and problem structure considered to be givens.

For an organization to survive by adapting to its environment in the long run, double-loop learning is indispensable. It allows behaviour to be modified in the light of changing realities or even to recreate the organization itself.

### Appraisal based on process and motivation/intention

The Imperial Japanese Army's personal evaluation system shied away from assessing officers' performance in black and white, and preferred to leave the evaluation rather ambiguous. 'Sincerity' in the intention, rather than the results, was considered important.[19] Such a system resulted in giving preference to officers 'playing to the gallery' and at the same time tended to thwart organizational learning, as neither good nor bad performance was set apart for evaluation.

The ambiguous evaluation was patent in the aftermath of the catastrophic Battle of Khalkhin Gol (or Nomonhan Incident) when an organizational renewal was made in the Kanto Army. In the Army itself, the deputy chief of staff, the first director, and at the Kanto Army, the commander, the chief of staff as well as the commander of the Sixth Army and the divisional commander of the 23rd Division were sent to the reserve. However, Colonel Hattori, the chief of operational planning at the Kanto Army and Major Tsuji, who were materially responsible for the incident, were not punished with being sent to the reserve. Instead, they were only relocated to other posts. The commander of the Sixth Army advocated Tsuji's inclusion in the reserve on the grounds that Tsuji had acted against the internal rule by going to the front and directing the troops from there, an opinion shared by the head of the personnel department at the Army Ministry. It was overruled by the director general at the Imperial General Headquarters to whose jurisdiction Tsuji belonged. As a matter of fact, both Hattori and Tsuji fared rather well, since in later years they managed to occupy positions of power as the chief of operation planning at the Imperial General Headquarters and deputy chief of the same unit, respectively.

It is well known that 'Col. Masanobu Tsuji [was] a fanatic repeatedly wounded in action and repeatedly transferred by generals exasperated by his insubordination. Tsuji once burned down a geisha house to highlight his disgust at the moral frailty of the officers inside it. His excesses were responsible for some of the worst Japanese blunders on Guadalcanal. He was directly responsible for brutalities to prisoners and civilians in every part of the Japanese empire in which he served. In northern Burma, he dined off the liver of a dead Allied pilot, castigating as cowards those who refused to share his meal: "The more we eat, the brighter will burn the fire of our hatred for the enemy" '.[20]

Another blatant example of the lack of punishment in the face of failure was Lieutenant General Mutaguchi. His destination after the Battle of Imphal illustrates this. 'After the failure of the Imphal offensive in late 1944, Mutaguchi refused to allow his divisional commanders to retreat, and instead dismissed all three of them. Some 50,000 of Mutaguchi's 65,000-man force died, most from starvation or disease. With the complete collapse of the offensive, Mutaguchi was himself relieved of command and recalled to Tokyo. He was forced into retirement in December 1944. Mutaguchi was recalled briefly to active service in 1945, to resume his former post as Commandant of the Military Preparatory School.'[21]

### Conclusion and discussion

Many of the traits and characteristics analysed about the Imperial Japanese Army still apply to Japanese companies. Their similar characteristics in terms of handling of ambiguity, inductive thought processes and the narrowness of strategic options are conspicuous.

Pascale and Athos (1981) hold that US management is very similar to Japan on all the hard S's of strategy, structure, and system, but that Japan has advantages in the soft S's of staff, skills, and style, and conjecture that the advantages stem largely from the Japanese culture, which differs in its approach to ambiguity, uncertainty, imperfection, and interdependence. The authors maintain that when communicating with others, the Japanese manager is good at making the most of ambiguity, hints, subtle cues, trust, interdependence, uncertainty, implicit messages, and process management.

Mintzberg (1973, 1990, 1994, 1996, 1976) questioned the very concept of strategy in its planned version by watching how the Japanese were gaining ground on their competitors in the 1970s and 1980s and proposed the idea of emerging strategy.

Quinn's (1978, 1980a, 1980b) idea of incrementalism in strategy-making is another side of the coin of how Japanese companies deploy their strategy, namely, one at a time and step by step without a grand design.

At the root of the way the Japanese behave is their inductive way of thinking. They pass judgment on the phenomena they face separately and individually, without paying too much attention to the context in which they ought to be analysed.

This raises two questions:

1. Why were Japanese companies successful when the Imperial Japanese Army, based on a similar pattern of behaviour, was ultimately defeated?
2. Why aren't they (at least some of them) successful at present?

In the first place, there must be basic differences between warfare in actual, physical battles and in the business arena. One of them could be the fact that war is a zero sum game, and if somebody wins, someone else loses. In business competition, there can be win-win situations. Situations such as complementary relationships (Brandenburger and Nalebuff, 1995) may be hard to find in actual warfare.

A second explanation can be that the members of companies in Japan (employees and their families in particular) can identify more easily with the cause pursued by their employers, namely, the company's survival, than that offered by the army, namely, the survival of the country and its population in general.

Third, advances in management studies offer better management techniques such as internal control, budget and planning systems, different responsibility centres, corporate governance, not accessible to the army in the last century, which compensate for the ambiguity in stated objectives.

Fourth, military power is hard to regain once destroyed, whereas business setbacks, though impaired by competition, may allow for more space to recover and more time for planning and thinking.

Fifth, there is a difference in the way the units in an organization are linked, which relates to 'the degree to which means are tied to ends, actions are controlled by intentions, solutions are guided by imitation of one's neighbour, feedback controls search, prior acts determine subsequent acts, past experience constrains present activity, logic dominates exploration and wisdom and intelligence affect coping behaviour' (Weick, 2001: p. 382). Tobe et al. (1991: p. 380) characterize a loosely coupled organization as having units (1) with high autonomy capable of adapting rapidly to small changes in the environment, and (2) capable of keeping their own idiosyncratic creativity, and therefore (3) with a high degree of resilience vis-à-vis unexpected changes in the environment, thanks to its lower dependency on other units.

Tobe et al. (1991) argue that the Imperial Japanese Army was, like almost all other military organizations though more so than others, a tightly knit organization, compared with enterprise organizations. And it did not equip its units with flexibility. For example, the frontline commanders did not have authority over their subordinates regarding demotion, relocation, and had to accept the decisions taken in Tokyo, which often hampered their operations.

Sixth, unlike present-day Japanese companies, the Imperial Japanese Army was not a self-renewing organization in the sense that innovations following Schumpeterian creative destruction (Schumpeter, 1962) were not linked to strategy rethinking (Tobe et al., 1991: p. 384).

Seventh, related to the second reason, there can be such things as strategic intent (Hamel and Prahalad, 1989) and core competence (Prahalad and Hamel, 1990) that may facilitate the success of business entities. Likewise, the shared value system and the belief system such as the proto-image of the firm (Kase, Sáez, and Riquelme, 2005) may help a firm's personnel to understand the basic goal towards which it heads and may accordingly lessen the need to have explicitly and precisely phrased objectives.

Nonaka and Takeuchi (1995) stress the capability of some Japanese companies in leveraging knowledge creation. Grant (2007: pp. 159–165) even advocates a knowledge-based view of the firm that 'considers the firm as a set of knowledge assets with the purpose of deploying these assets to create value.'

The excellence of middle management at Japanese companies and 'resource redundancy' may also serve as an explanation (Nonaka, 1988, 1990).[22]

As to the second question, it should be emphasized that it may not be right to paint all Japanese companies with the same brush (for example, because of a wide panorama of business environments) and the inductive way of thinking may actually work quite well in many situations. However, with these caveats in mind, it may be answered by pointing out the rigidity into which social or corporate systems in Japan may 'degenerate', as in the case of the Imperial Japanese Army. Incremental improvement is excellent when the direction is right, but if it is not, companies lacking the leadership capable of reorienting the entire organization may head for disaster. Homogeneity in the way of thinking, empiricism based on past learning and on-the-job training may enhance this trend. Lifetime employment coupled with the low-point method of scoring in the personnel evaluation system may also foster a trend to copy what others do so as not to stand out too much.

Our guess is that much depends on who the leader is, what business system – the entire set of strategic and behavioural patterns – is in place, what kind of business environment the firm faces, etc. As to the role played by business leaders in the turnaround of Japanese companies, see Kase et al. (2007; 2005), Niihara (2002).

## Appendix A2.2: Industry capacity statistics of WWII nations

Steel production (in thousands of tons)

|      | Japan | US     | UK     | Germany |
|------|-------|--------|--------|---------|
| 1870 |       | 70     | 230    | 170     |
| 1880 | 2     | 1,267  | 1,316  | 733     |
| 1890 | 2     | 4,346  | 3,636  | 2,232   |
| 1900 | 1     | 10,351 | 4,979  | 6,646   |
| 1910 | 252   | 26,512 | 6,476  | 13,699  |
| 1920 | 811   | 42,807 | 9,212  | 8,538   |
| 1930 | 2,289 | 41,351 | 7,443  | 11,511  |
| 1940 | 6,850 | 60,755 | 13,183 | 19,141  |

Automobile production (in thousands of cars)

|      | Japan | US     | UK    | Germany | Canada |
|------|-------|--------|-------|---------|--------|
| 1930 | 5     | 33,560 | 2,460 | 960     | 1,530  |
| 1935 | 51    | 39,470 | 4,240 | 2,470   | 1,730  |
| 1940 | 361   | 44,720 |       |         |        |
| 1945 | 255   | 7,260  |       |         |        |

Oil production (in thousands of tons)

|           | 1930    | 1935    | 1940    | 1945    |
|-----------|---------|---------|---------|---------|
| Japan     | 283     | 314     | 300     | 1,22    |
| US        | 123,117 | 134,615 | 182,867 | 231,575 |
| Venezuela | 20,109  | 22,039  | 27,497  | 46,341  |
| Iran      | 6,036   | 7,608   | 8,765   | 17,108  |
| Indonesia | 5,532   | 6,082   | 7,939   | 976     |
| Mexico    | 5,662   | 5,807   | 6,271   | 6,187   |

Reserve of oil in Japan (in thousands of barrels)

|      | Crude oil | Refined oil | Total  |
|------|-----------|-------------|--------|
| 1937 | 10,470    | 32,600      | 43,070 |
| 1938 | 12,470    | 31,890      | 44,360 |
| 1939 | 20,240    | 31,160      | 51,400 |
| 1940 | 19,900    | 29,680      | 49,580 |
| 1941 | 20,860    | 28,040      | 48,900 |
| 1942 | 12,350    | 25,880      | 38,230 |
| 1943 | 6,840     | 18,490      | 25,330 |
| 1944 | 2,350     | 11,460      | 13,810 |

*Source*: http://www.luzinde.com/database/nation_industry.
(accessed 1 June 2009).

# Annex 2.3

# Liu Chuanzhi: Lenovo's founder

## Introduction[1, 2]

On 8 December, 2004, Lenovo's Liu Chuanzhi held a press conference at a hotel in Beijing to make public their decision to acquire IBM's Personal Computer Division for US$1.75 billion, of which US$650 million in cash and US$600 million in new shares would be paid to IBM, with the remaining $500 million corresponding to the assumption of the division's debts.[3]

In exchange for this payment, Lenovo would gain access to the expertise of IBM's personal computer business and to the use of the 'ThinkPad' and other IBM brands for five years. The deal would allow IBM to concentrate on its core IT service business and other B2B businesses. The 18.5 per cent stake in Lenovo would enable it to keep tabs on the computer business.

The agreement foresaw the moving of Lenovo's headquarters to New York. Yang Yuanqing, Lenovo's president, would become the new company's chairman, while his former position would be assumed by Stephen Ward, IBM's former senior vice-president and managing director in charge of PCs. IBM's 10,000 and Lenovo's 9,200 employees would be secure in their jobs.

The reaction on the stock markets was mixed. IBM's share price shot up from US$96.65 to US$97.51 on the following day, whereas Lenovo's dropped from HK$ (Hong Kong dollars) 2.675 to HK$ 2.575, that is a 3.7 per cent fall. The caution was due to the fact that Lenovo's turnover in 2003 was only US$3 billion, a third of IBM PC Division's US$9 billion. The Chinese company's debt to equity ratio worsened to 42.1 per cent.

Thanks to this acquisition, Lenovo's world market share increased to 8.2 per cent in 2004, lifting the company to the number three position in the world ranking. (See Table A2.3.1.)

Why and how did this 22-year-old Chinese start-up business manage to arrive on the world stage? Where was it headed? What was its strategy? And, most of all, what was its underlying management philosophy? (See Appendix A2.3.1 regarding Lenovo's financial statements.)

*Table A2.3.1* World market share (%) of PC makers in terms of units sold in 2004, prior to the acquisition

| | |
|---|---|
| Dell | 16.4 |
| HP | 13.9 |
| IBM | 6.2 |
| Fujitsu | 3.8 |
| ACER | 3.2 |
| Toshiba | 3.2 |
| NEC | 2.6 |
| Gateway | 2.2 |
| Lenovo | 2.0 |
| Apple | 1.9 |

*Source*: Xu (2007: p. 67).

## History

Liu Chuanzhi and a colleague of his at the Chinese Academy of Sciences' Institute of Computer Science requested an interview with the head of the Institute in October 1984 and expressed their wish to start up a new business.[4] They asked for financial support and were assigned 200,000 yuan from the Institute's non-operational income. Even though the financial support was not taken from the state budget, the new start-up business was designated as a state-owned enterprise (SOE).

Liu and his colleague managed to reserve rights to intellectual property, human resource management and managerial independence from the Institute for the new company. The Institute offered the new business other advantages: (1) the new business's staff would continue to belong to it and would be paid their salaries, and (2) the staff might make use of their research facilities and results at the Institute, without having to pay royalties. These generous conditions derived from the fact that the Institute's budget, if not fully spent, would be cut back the following year. It was therefore in the Institute's interest to encourage the new business, which it did not view as distinct from the Institute in management terms.

On 1 November 1984, the Chinese Academy of Sciences authorized the Institute's application to set up a business. Despite the initial reticence shown by the Institute's staff approached by Liu and his colleague, eight research staff joined the new business start-up. The start-up was named the New Technology Development Company (NTDC) of the Chinese Academy of Sciences' Computer Science Institute, in a clear demonstration of the company's need to show its link with the academic world. Thanks to the hierarchical position the academy enjoys in China, the new business was classified as having the same administrative importance as a prefecture.

The company's road to success was not an easy one. It could not expect special assistance from the state because, having developed as a private initiative within the Chinese Academy of Sciences, it did not fall within the category of businesses fostered by the State.[5] In the 1980s, the NTDC attempted to make money by selling colour TVs. The company made a 140,000 yuan deal with a TV distributor in Jiangxi Province, but the seller disappeared as soon as he got the money.

The company later lost money selling colour TVs because it forgot to allow for tax. When the tax collector demanded the payment, the firm had to chalk up the losses. Eleven staff members tried to make up the losses by selling electronic watches, roller skates, vegetables, etc., at the entrance of the Institute. The Institute continued to pay salaries and the company rode out the storm.

Around this time, the academy decided to import 500 PCs for its research centres, but needed somebody who could install them and train end users. For Liu this was a windfall. The Institute had a number of researchers who were knowledgeable about computers, although they had never used PCs. The NTDC won the bid to carry out the installation and training services, charging a 7 per cent commission on the price of the computers.

The contract was successfully fulfilled and the academy praised the NTDC and raised its commissions from 7 to 9 per cent, which generated a 700,000 yuan profit for the company.

## Hangzi Card

As far back as 1974, the Computer Science Institute (CIS) started several parallel projects to develop a computer system that would allow the use of Chinese characters (Hangzi). By 1983, Ni Guangnan, one of the team leaders, had managed to create a computer application named LX-80 Lianxiang type Hangzi System or Hangzi Card with LX standing for Lianxiang – the association of ideas. Ni graduated from Nanjing Technology University (currently Dongnan University) in 1961 and entered CIS at a time when computer research and development was just beginning in China.

Liu learned about the Hangzi application and approached Ni and convinced him to join his company as chief engineer. Ni accepted on condition that he would not be forced to accept a managerial position, attend meetings or deal with journalists.

Liu borrowed 600,000 yuan from the CIS to develop the systems, in addition to the 700,000 yuan the company had earned.

In June 1985, LX-80 Lianxiang type Hangzi System overcame implementation problems and went into production. Whatever is entered via the keyboard is translated and displayed on the screen as the corresponding Chinese character.

That same year, at the Beijing Computer Exhibition, the NTDC received orders worth 550,000 yuan. In 1985, the company's turnover amounted to 3.5 million yuan with operating profits amounting to 2.5 million yuan. Hangzi Card contributed profits of 400,000 yuan, 16 per cent of the total figure. The remaining profit was broken down into 600,000 yuan for service fees charged to the CIS for outsourced research projects, US$ 70,000 from IBM for sales commissions, and 700,000 yuan for the aforementioned work for the Academy of Sciences.

Hangzi Card's sales peaked in 1991 when 22,000 units were sold. Its demise came with the introduction of the Chinese version of Microsoft Windows. In 1995 Liu decided to suspend its production.

## The PC business

Liu set up a new company on 23 June 1988 in Hong Kong, with an initial capital of HK$900,000.[6] The company was named Hong Kong Lianxiang Company Ltd. The NTDC's partners were a Hong Kong company and a Chinese company. (As to the company's organization chart see Appendix A2.3.2.)

The new company bought PCs from AST, a US start-up business owned by two Hong Kong residents and a Pakistani. It largely sold PCs in mainland China. The four months of operations brought in profits of HK$550,000 on monthly revenues of HK$9 million.

Liu decided to plough these profits into the development of a motherboard for computers. Though a main component for PCs, the labour-intensive motherboard, comprising 200 parts and 400 welding points did not offer high profitability.

According to the Smile Curve theory advanced by Acer's founder, the motherboard was positioned at the lowest point in terms of profitability. (See Figure A2.3.1.)

Liu asked Ni and his staff to develop the motherboard. The Lianxiang Q286 PC based on the motherboard developed by these researchers was launched in March 1989 at a fair held at Hannover where it was favourably received. During the fair, orders for 2,483 motherboards and 2,073 PCs were received. By 1994, the Hong Kong Lianxiang Company's world market share in terms of units sold in the motherboard market reached 10 per cent.

In November 1989, Liu decided to change the company's name to Lianxiang Group. In the following year, the Chinese government granted Lianxiang permission to manufacture 5,000 PCs per year, which corresponded to 5 per cent of the demand in China.

Except for motherboards, the components would be purchased from abroad: central processing units (CPUs) from the US, memories from Japan, hard disks from Singapore, displays from Korea, casing and keyboards from Taiwan.

Liu disagreed with his colleagues' view that Lianxiang ought to develop and manufacture some of these components in-house, and stuck to the outsourcing decision.

Liu took the view that to take on world-class competitors, the Chinese product would have to be on a par with the competitors in terms of technology, research and development, manufacturing, and operating system, which was not the case in China. Therefore, for him, the strategy needed to focus on how to compete using all-outsourced components except for the motherboards.

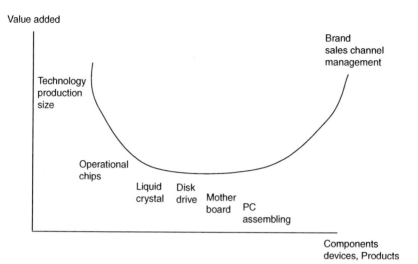

*Figure A2.3.1* Smile curve

*Source*: Lianxiang material cited in Xu (2007: p. 41).

The answer to the strategic focus was what Liu would call 'product technology'. It consisted of finding a gap in the value proposition prevalent in the market and filling it with a new proposition. Market surveys of potential customer needs were essential. Liu would cite an example: in the 1980s, the electronic appliance market in China was dominated by Japanese brands, which would be ultimately replaced by Chinese products. One reason was that Japanese products were designed to run on stable current, whereas the reality in China was that the voltage went up and down. Chinese manufacturers designed products that could tolerate voltage fluctuations, reducing the number of failures caused by power surges.

In line with this thinking Lianxiang, in launching its PCs in China, differentiated its products from its competitors by ease of use and low price. With a Lianxiang PC, customers did not have to sign up with an ISP to get Internet access nor ask for permission from the authority that controlled Internet-related issues, and only had to push a button on the PC.

By 1995, Lianxiang was China's top PC manufacturer and in 1997, it became the largest, including Chinese and foreign computer makers.[7] Marketing strategy was a key factor behind this success.

## Marketing strategy

Four stages mark the marketing history of Lianxiang: (1) 1990–1993 (2) 1994–1997 (3) 1998–1999 and (4) 2000–2004.

## 1990–1993

Lianxiang switched from IBM computers to ASTs in 1987. ASTs PC sales contributed a 24 per cent margin even after paying commissions and expenses to the importing agent.

Problems arose in 1990 when Lianxiang decided to manufacture and sell its own PCs. Keen for customers to decide for themselves, it exhibited both ASTs and its own, lower-priced PCs side by side. For example, Lianxiang's 286-type model cost 10 per cent less than AST's. The consumers, however, preferred foreign-made products. While AST's brand sold 80,000 units, Lianxiang's sold 13,874 units, falling short of the firm's target to sell 25,000 units.

The reduction of import duty in 1993 had a negative effect on Lianxiang. The firm's 486–type model was priced at 6,800 yuan higher than AST's product. Twenty-two Chinese PC manufacturers lost their price competitiveness to foreign rivals who gained almost 80 per cent of the market share that year. The company, nonetheless, fared better and managed to sell 25,669 units with a net profit of 7 million yuan.

## 1994–1997

The PC Division was created in March 1994 and Yang Yuanqing was appointed to head it. Yang faced two issues, one of which was to review the product concept or value proposition. He concluded that their products needed more differentiation. The minimum functional offer to enhance ease of use was one answer. At the time, a 386-type PC cost 30,000 yuan, which was way beyond the purchasing power of an ordinary worker whose annual income was less than 20,000 yuan. Yang's target was to produce a PC at half the price of a foreign model. To achieve this, the entire production process was reviewed from the design down to the packaging. If the price target was not met, even Hong Kong Lianxiang's motherboards would be returned. The E Series PCs were the outcome.

The other issue was related to the distribution system. The direct sale system was dropped and a distributor network was set up. Yang learned about this system from Hewlett-Packard when he had been the head of another business unit at Lianxiang. Yang and his staff travelled extensively in China and persuaded electric appliance shops to handle their PCs.

Thanks to the low-cost E Series (priced from 9,999 to 16,000 yuan), sales in 1994 soared to 45,000 units, bringing 8 per cent of market share and positioning the company as the number one manufacturer in China. The year also marked a turning point since the market share of foreign makes plateaued and would start to decline after 1994.

Yang and his team also began to develop a sales campaign named '1995 Lianxiang PC Express' focused on the Chinese interior where people's knowledge of PCs was all but non-existent. Between May and August 1995, Lianxiang visited more than 300 cities throughout the country in a large bus loaded with PCs, posters and pamphlets. At the same time, ads were placed in the *Economic Daily, Guang Ming Daily*, CCTV. The effort bore fruit as the company broke through the 100,000 units barrier, making Lianxiang China's top PC manufacturer.

In the belief that, following Moore's law,[8] the price could fall still further, Lianxiang launched a PC with Pentium 75MHz at 9,999 yuan in March 1996 and then another with Pentium 120MHz at 9,888 yuan in May. Foreign makers sold Pentium PCs at over 20,000 yuan. Lianxiang's market share in 1997 reached 10.8 per cent, with 435,860 units sold that year.

## 1998–1999

This period was characterized by the sale of the one millionth unit on 6 May 1998. It took eight and a half years: 763,365 units were sold that year.

PCs that were easy to connect to the Internet were developed and launched. On-line sales of PCs also began. On its first day alone, 28 June 1999, 85 million yuan worth of orders were received from 10,000 customers.

## 2000–2004

Competition became fiercer with the entry of new competitors such as TCL, a manufacturer of colour TVs, and Haier, an electric appliances manufacturer. Above all, Haier was strong in terms of research and development, quality and cost control. These competitors had strong, extensive distribution networks. Haier had 8,000 agents in its distribution network, which compared favourably with Lianxiang's 4,000. Beijing University's and Tsinghua University's business start-ups waged a cut-throat price war. The US company Dell opened its own plant in November 2000.[9] (See Table A2.3.2.)

Lianxiang adopted three measures to compete against these rivals. First it established a parallel Internet network in addition to the distributor network. Dell's inroad made this necessary for survival.

Second, management decided to establish a suggestion system for cost and productivity from the personnel.

Third, partial outsourcing from Taiwan was implemented, since the demand was in excess of its own four million PC units production capacity.

*Table A2.3.2* Market shares of the top five PC manufacturers in China (in per cent)

|  | 2000 | 2001 | 2002 | 2003 | 2004 |
|---|---|---|---|---|---|
| IBM | 4.8 | 4.2 | 4.6 | 4.7 | 5.3 |
| Dell | 2.9 | 3.9 | 5.0 | 6.9 | 7.5 |
| Tongfang (Tsinghua Univ.) | 1.5 | 3.8 | 4.9 | 7.1 | 7.5 |
| Fangzheng (Beijing Univ.) | 8.4 | 8.9 | 9.1 | 10.7 | 11.5 |
| Lenovo (Lianxiang) | 26.4 | 27.5 | 27.3 | 27.0 | 26.3 |

*Source*: Adapted from Xu (2007: p. 56).

## Change of name: Lenovo

Lianxiang decided to change its name on 28 April 2003 to Lenovo, of which Le stands for the initial of the original name and Novo from Latin *novum*. The need for the change derived from the fact that Legend, Lianxiang's brand in English, was too commonplace and could hamper its entry in foreign markets. The force behind the growth of Lenovo is its founder, Liu Chuanzhi, so it is important to examine his background and management philosophy in order to see in what direction he was taking the firm.

## Liu Chuanzhi, the founder

Liu was born in Shanghai in 1944. His father was a banker with the Bank of China. After the bank's headquarters moved to Beijing when the Communist Party came to power in 1949, his family established itself in the capital.

Liu originally wanted to become an Air Force pilot and applied for the academy. Though he passed the physical test, he was denied the position because of the rule banning admission to people with a family member (including grandparents, parents, first cousins and brothers and sisters) with an anti-Communist background. Liu's mother's younger brother was anti-communist. This was his first setback in life.

In September 1961, Liu joined what is now the Xi'an Electronic Science and Technology University. It then belonged to the Army. He specialized in radar technology, but as it was an Army university he also underwent military training, which has reputedly influenced his outlook.

In May 1966, when Liu was finishing his five-year academic curriculum, the Cultural Revolution broke out. He was popular among his fellow students, but managed to shy away from getting involved too actively in the student movement. Nonetheless, academic activities were suspended.

In 1968 the government authorized the graduation of his class. Liu was assigned to a post at a research institute in Chengdu to develop radar technology. However, the Cultural Revolution caught up with him and he was sent to a farm near Macao as the government believed that intellectuals ought to learn the reality of the countryside.

Two years later, due to tension with the outside world, the government decided to relocate military engineers and Liu was assigned to the Chinese Academy of Sciences Computer Institute in April 1970. Liu, however, felt that too much time had been lost for him to be a good engineer and in 1983, applied for a position in the academy's personnel department.

Some time before Liu joined the academy, China began reforms to open its economy towards the end of the 1970s. Special Economic Zones were created and, as the results were positive, the opening up was extended to the 14 cities along the coastal line. Further reforms came with 'The Decision on the Reformation of the Economic System' and 'The Decision on the Reformation of the Scientific and Technological System' passed on 20 October 1984 and 13 March 1985, respectively.

The former emphasized the importance of the mercantile economy for the development of the socialist economy. The concept of the mercantile economy was later replaced with that of 'the socialist market economy' as the reform took root.

The latter reflected the same spirit regarding the fields of science and technology. Criteria were established regarding research centre budgets, freedom to participate in state-promoted projects, co-operation between industry and university, permission for researchers to work both for the university and industry.

These initiatives coincided with the move to start venture businesses in Beijing's Zhongguan-cun area where the Chinese Academy of Sciences was located. The elite Beijing University and Tsinghua University were nearby. Many researchers who had worked in the United States in Silicon Valley or the Route 128 area were involved in the movement.

Influenced by the new spirit of entrepreneurship, Liu Chuangzhi and Wang Shuhe, a colleague, applied for financing from their organization to start a business of their own and were granted 200,000 yuan. And that was the beginning of what would later become Lenovo.

## Liu Chuanzhi's management philosophy[10]

### 1. Two laws for the development of a high-tech enterprise

Two laws are to be abided by if a high-technology is to succeed. One is the Law of the Industry's Development and the other, the Law of the Firm's Development.

The first law relates to the market's needs and the technology. Studying this law will allow you to predict trends in the industry through analysis of the industry's past and present.

The second lays the basis for the firm's strategy. The fit with the environment, organization structure, mapping out rules and regulations, personnel assessment, establishing the firm's corporate culture, training the personnel, all fall within the categories set out by the second law.

### 2. Biased views

In the planned economy system, everybody, from government officials to the masses, have biased views or concepts regarding many aspects of life.

Take the example of innovation[11] in technology. Government officials consider that industrialization through high technology is a question of technology. Liu, in common with other entrepreneurs in the private sector, thinks differently. Innovation for them consists of turning the technology into merchandise and then into money and from there back into technology. The entire process is innovation and leads to industrialization through high technology.[12] The key to industrialization does not lie in technology or production, but in marketing and sales.

High-level technology does not necessarily lead to the possibility of commercialization. Marketing development and sales channels carry more weight in commercialization.

For example, in 1992 and 1993, there were two devices for PCs. One was Intel's CPU, and the other, the PowerPC developed by IBM, Motorola, and Apple. The latter was better in functions and price. But the combination of Intel's chips and Microsoft's operating system, popularly known as Wintel, won the day. This was a logical consequence of the marketing prowess shown by the former. Compatibility and externality exploited by Wintel resulted from better marketing capability. Technological specifications are not everything. Marketing is the key word.

The 'product technology' concept referred to earlier is of vital importance in Lenovo's strategy. This concept may be illustrated as follows: until the mid-1990s, the Chinese market was flooded with TVs from Japan until Chinese manufacturers invested in developing devices to cope with voltage changes, thus ending Japanese dominance.

Product technology, as understood by Liu, means the ability to adapt products to the market's requirements. It depends more on marketing than on sophisticated R&D, which may result in technological 'overkill'.

For Liu, in addition to the use of the product technology concept, Lenovo's success is attributable to cost reduction (without sacrificing quality) and sales. Liu believes that, compared to Lenovo, Japanese companies make little effort to keep total costs under control. The overheads at Japanese companies are very high, which, according to Liu, leads to low profitability, which, in turn, means high overall costs.

Liu argues that cost reduction policies differ depending on the industry. In the software industry, it derives from increased personnel productivity and decreased personnel costs, whereas in hi-tech manufacture such as the PC industry, reducing the time finished and semi-finished products spend in stock is the key, and managing this is in itself an innovation.

## 3. Clear and explicit ownership

Without a clear sense of ownership, no enterprise can develop. Lenovo did not worry about ownership between 1984 and 1988, because the Chinese Academy of Sciences gave them freedom in the fields of finance, personnel and general management. Uncertainty remained, though. Freedom of operation in these three fields still left it unclear as to where the final responsibility lay: with the state or the enterprise?

Uncertainty about ownership may result in four phenomena.

First, people may behave as Chu Shijian, the president of a large tobacco company, did. He received a life sentence for embezzling funds because he felt he was underpaid.

Second, the transfer of power and responsibility may shift from a state-owned company to a private sector company. Lenovo would not otherwise have survived.

Third, the appointment of the CEO's successor will be based on whether the CEO will benefit personally from the successor. In other words, the company will turn into a personal fiefdom of the president if there is a conflict of interest between ownership and management.

Fourth, if they are not under pressure from the owners and poor work goes unpunished, managers tend to be concerned only with maintaining their personal positions.

Overall, the ownership mechanism may not be a sufficient condition for a company's development but it is a necessary one.

*4. Managerial competence*

There are many stages in the process of turning research products into saleable products and producing profits. The questions to be addressed include: How to develop the market? How to manage sales channels? How to maintain the production system? How to make the feedback loop between the R&D system and the market system? How to optimize logistics and use of finance?

Lenovo's experience points to the importance of management competence, understood as the systematic handling of various aspects of management. The firm twice suffered large losses, which were not attributable to R&D but to inventory problems. Excessive inventory was generated as a consequence of bad feedback regarding market needs and component supply, which lowered logistics efficiency.[13]

Drawing on its experience as well as on the lessons learned from management books, Lenovo stresses three elements of management: (1) teamwork (2) strategy preparation and (3) personnel motivation.

First, team-building includes the way management teams act, make decisions, seek self-discipline, enlist support from their staff. A split management team spells disaster for a company.

Lenovo has adopted four ways of building management teams: (1) workshops are organized every year to emphasize the management team's importance – boosting the management team's authority will facilitate strategy implementation; (2) the decision-making procedure is defined in such a way that the team leaders can have the decisions implemented in a smooth manner; (3) great importance is attached to the relationships between the team leaders and their teams – conflicts between team members and their leader, if repeated, will result in their replacement; (4) the elimination of power cliques and nepotism – recruitment of staff's children is prohibited.

Second, strategy mapping is prioritized. External factors such as the industry's development, the market situation and competitors, as well as internal factors such as finance, human resources, management competence, the technology level and the firm's strengths and weaknesses are analysed and used to draw up medium- and long-term strategic plans and objectives. It ought to be possible to quickly amend the strategy, if it is considered wrong.

Lenovo's strategy making has five steps: (1) the vision – to become a century-old enterprise, the economies of scale and high-technology; (2) the medium- and long-term strategic plans – designing a road map is important; (3) the short-term objectives; (4) the breakdown in detail of the short-term objectives; and (5) defining the strategy and the objectives and implementing them. The management resources ought to be developed within the company. Coinciding with the thinking of Collins and Porras, the authors of *Visionary Company*, Liu is convinced that his successors must be instilled with a business spirit, which can only be achieved by having lived and been nurtured in the company's culture. People instilled with the business spirit will shy away from decision options alien to the company's culture.

Regarding the above-mentioned road map, five points are stressed: (1) the diversification debate – Lenovo brings a multi-faceted outlook to the discussion, as seen in the avoidance of the real estate business during the real estate boom in 1993 and 1994; (2) the focus on the domestic market – unlike Taiwanese PC component manufacturers, Lenovo enjoys a large domestic market where it will consolidate its brand and accumulate financial strengths and other management competencies to succeed in overseas markets; (3) 'mao-gong-ji' (commerce–industry-technology) principles[14] – to learn PC sales and business to understand the market and its needs, to build up its own manufacturing base, then to develop its own technology; (4) the development of product technology (or applied technology) which will become the core technology; (5) reduction of the capital costs by capturing funds on the stock market – for which it is important to gain and maintain the investors' confidence.

Third and last, it is important to keep the personnel motivated. Strategy mapped out by the management teams will be implemented if the personnel are motivated. Maintaining staff motivation relates to the organization structure, management system, ways to 'pep them up', corporate culture and staff training.

At Lenovo, the organization continually adapts to the demands of the situation. The group used to be organized on the convoy model, controlled from above, but, after adopting the divisional form, it switched to the company system, with each business unit being organized as a company.

The management system sticks to its original policy that any malpractice, when uncovered, will be severely punished. Embezzlement leads to dismissal. There is also a strict policy on punctuality at meetings.

The three most obvious means Lenovo uses to motivate its staff are: salary, bonus and stock options.

## 5. Rigidity and flexibility

Having been trained in an Army-owned university, Liu's management follows the command and order style and he tends to be unyielding and insistent in what he wants.

Shortly after Lianxiang was set up, the company received an enquiry from the State Commission for Sports for 12 units of IBM PCs. But the Commission's financial director did not authorize the purchase. So Liu did everything to persuade him, but then learnt that the State Commission entrusted all the import transactions-related matters to China Electronic Devices Export Import Company (CEDEIC), which meant that unless this company issued an import permit, Lianxiang would not be able to carry out the transaction. Liu was even ordered by CEDEIC not to enter its building on account of his being an agent for a foreign company. Liu swallowed this affront and finally obtained the permit.

Another example of Liu's perseverance was when a business correspondent in Shenzhen disappeared with 30 million yuan, which Liu had borrowed with much difficulty from the Chinese Academy of Sciences to buy PCs. Liu flew to Shenzhen and kept watch outside the man's home for several days. The fugitive, when he finally appeared, was so scared of Liu that he immediately dispatched the PCs. Around that time there were many cases of fraud and embezzlement in China. Years later, Liu confessed that he would have done anything to save his company.

An example of Liu's flexibility or soft approach is seen in a troubled transaction Lianxiang had with Hong Kong China Bank. Due to his lack of business experience, Liu deluded himself that a verbal agreement with the bank was enough. However, once everything was settled and calculated, he realized that US$ 20,000 were missing, an amount almost equal to the company's entire salary bill. The bank refused to honour the verbal agreement. Liu spent a whole day in a hotel writing a letter to the bank, narrating the entire history of the company's struggle and survival and the threat to its continuity that the missing amount represented. The bank official in charge of the affair was deeply touched by Liu's entrepreneurial enthusiasm, and decided to settle the disputed amount.

*6. Severity and at the same time a human touch*

For the efficient use of the company's resources, Liu built up a command and order system as mentioned before. When faced with a problem, Liu's stance is simple: follow the rules. For example, when Hangzi Card was being developed, it was decided that anyone who caused a conflict would be dismissed in order to facilitate the development process.

Another case in point is punctuality. Punctuality is not a great virtue in China. Therefore, Liu decided to punish anyone who turned up late for a meeting by making them stay standing for a minute. The first victim of this policy was a former superior of Liu's, which caused considerable embarrassment both to the punished person and to Liu himself. Later that night, Liu visited his former superior's house and told him that he would stand for a minute outside it to atone for the affront. Liu, however, stuck to his rule.

*7. Thinking and actions harmonized*

Liu prefers well thought-out decisions to rushed decision-making, which the industry watchers tend to mistake for conservatism. Liu justifies his way of acting on the basis of his conviction that, before taking any decisions, he has to understand the necessity and rationality of each situation. The shared belief among his staff is that once Liu expresses his opinion, he sticks to it and gets it implemented.

**8. *The middle-way (Zhongyong), magnanimity (Hongyi), and perfect virtue (Ren) and belief or trust (Xin)***

The middle-way philosophy is phrased in the company's mission statement: 'To owe responsibility to society, to the shareholders and to the employees.' In other words, to strike a balance between extremes.

Hongyi, or magnanimity, is another important rule for Liu. This is illustrated by his handling of his relations with the developer of the Hangzi Card who, after developing the card, created his own clique and accused Liu of malpractice before the government commissions. As a consequence, Liu faced the possibility of being expelled from the firm, which fortunately did not happen. The accuser's employment contract was rescinded. Liu, however, offered to pay him a five million yuan settlement, which ultimately was not accepted.

Renxin (virtue and belief) is another guiding principle. Liu's effort is centred on trying to show that the Chinese proverb ('there is no merchant who does not commit frauds') is groundless.

When Lianxiang was formed, it represented a foreign manufacturer but it received some claims against it. Liu negotiated with the represented firm but could not obtain any compensation for the claims. Lianxiang did not have enough financial resources to pay for them, but the first thing Liu did, when the company was large enough, was to settle the claimed amount.

Another illustration of Renxin took place at the time of the yuan's depreciation in 1988 and 1989 from six to nine yuan to the US dollar, a 50 per cent fall in value. Lianxiang absorbed this difference by paying the import company in dollars and the financing banks in yuan, as a consequence of which it chalked up a one million yuan loss. However, it enabled the company to consolidate its relations with the importer and the banks, laying the foundations for its future growth.

**9. *Future diversification***

Lianxiang Holding (See Appendix A2.3.2) comprises five diversified businesses: PCs, software, venture capital, investment funds, real estate.

There is talk of Lianxiang Holding diversifying into automobiles, insurance businesses, management consultancy, publishing, the film industry, sport businesses and bio-technology.[15]

Liu's dream is to strengthen weak industries and establish new ones in China, all of which are becoming as competitive as Lenovo.

In line with the Chinese proverb ('one mountain does not accommodate two heroes'), Liu set up a new business (Digital China) independent from Lenovo to avoid unnecessary rivalry between Yang Yuanqing, Lenovo's current president, and Guo Wei, Digital China's president. Developing and retaining capable executives is an essential resource for the future of Lianxiang Holding companies.

# Appendix A2.3.1: Lenovo's Financial Statements[16]

## Consolidated Income Statement

### For the year ended 31 March 2006

| | Note | 2006 HK$'000 | 2005 HK$'000 |
|---|---|---|---|
| Turnover | 5 | 103,550,857 | 22,554,678 |
| Earnings before interest, taxation, depreciation, amortization, impairment charge, gain/loss on disposal of available-for-sale financial assets and restructuring costs | 1(b) | 2,978,519 | 1,173,616 |
| Depreciation expenses and amortization of prepaid lease payments | | (492,469) | (184,490) |
| Restructuring costs | 6 | (542,756) | – |
| Amortization of intangible assets | 7 | (779,664) | (58,078) |
| Amortization of share-based compensation | 7 | (232,013) | – |
| Impairment of assets | 7 | (22,785) | (51,364) |
| (Loss)/gain on disposal of investments and available-for-sale financial assets | 7 | (4,913) | 156,958 |
| Finance income | 7 | 188,986 | 105,677 |
| Profit from operations | 7 | 1,092,905 | 1,142,319 |
| Finance costs | 9 | (438,126) | (6,667) |
| | | 654,779 | 1,135,652 |
| Share of profits/(losses) of jointly controlled entities | | 1,073 | (12,327) |
| Share of profits of associated companies | | 3,627 | 4,182 |
| Profit before taxation | 8 | 659,479 | 1,127,507 |
| Taxation | 10 | (443,667) | (35,184) |
| Profit for the year | | 215,812 | 1,092,323 |
| Profit attributable to: | | | |
| Shareholders of the Company | 13 | 173,236 | 1,120,146 |
| Minority interests | | 42,576 | (27,823) |
| | | 215,812 | 1,092,323 |
| Dividends | 14 | 461,741 | 388,806 |
| Earnings per share | | | |
| – Basic | 15(a) | 1.97 HK cents | 14.99 HK cents |
| – Diluted | 15(b) | 1.93 HK cents | 14.97 HK cents |

## Balance Sheets

|  | | At 31 March 2006 | | | |
|---|---|---|---|---|---|
|  | | Group | | Company | |
|  | | 2006 | 2005 | 2006 | 2005 |
|  | Note | HK$'000 | As restated *(Note 1(a))* HK$'000 | HK$'000 | HK$'000 |
| *Non-current assets* | | | | | |
| Property, plant and equipment | 16 | 1,734,440 | 827,876 | 12,733 | 25,130 |
| Prepaid lease payments | 17 | 50,018 | 50,268 | – | – |
| Construction-in-progress | 18 | 218,127 | 257,159 | 141,180 | – |
| Intangible assets | 19 | 14,896,476 | 513,078 | – | – |
| Investments in subsidiaries | 20(a) | – | – | 8,071,501 | 2,327,875 |
| Investments in jointly controlled entities | 21 | – | 191,523 | – | – |
| Investments in associated companies | 22 | 70,672 | 52,067 | – | – |
| Deferred tax assets | 23 | 486,290 | 53,498 | – | – |
| Available-for-sale financial assets | 24 | 235,949 | – | 3,661 | – |
| Investment securities | 25 | – | 62,970 | – | 4,413 |
| Other non-current assets | | 287,163 | 569,673 | – | 565,340 |
| | | 17,979,135 | 2,578,112 | 8,229,075 | 2,922,758 |
| *Current assets* | | | | | |
| Amounts due from subsidiaries | 20(b) | – | – | 8,750,366 | 3,965,624 |
| Inventories | 26 | 2,832,454 | 878,900 | – | – |
| Trade receivables | 27(a) | 3,781,230 | 851,337 | – | – |
| Notes receivable | 27(b) | 721,668 | 1,137,174 | – | – |
| Deposits, prepayments and other receivables | | 6,163,015 | 567,046 | 104,497 | 19,595 |
| Cash and cash equivalents | 28 | 7,838,854 | 3,019,385 | 814,291 | 401,939 |
| | | 21,337,221 | 6,453,842 | 9,669,154 | 4,387,158 |

Continued

Continued

| | Note | Group 2006 HK$'000 | Group 2005 As restated (Note 1(a)) HK$'000 | Company 2006 HK$'000 | Company 2005 HK$'000 |
|---|---|---|---|---|---|
| *Current liabilities* | | | | | |
| Amounts due to subsidiaries | 20(b) | – | – | 2,029,357 | 115,494 |
| Amounts due to jointly controlled entities | 21 | – | 108,446 | – | – |
| Trade payables | 29(a) | 13,128,737 | 2,276,070 | – | – |
| Notes payable | 29(b) | 385,576 | 195,032 | – | – |
| Accruals and other payables | 30 | 9,827,844 | 716,906 | 181,880 | 163,643 |
| Tax payable | | 308,914 | 493 | – | – |
| Short-term bank loans | 35 | 1,001,196 | – | 936,000 | – |
| Current portion of non-current liabilities | 31 | 169,880 | 175,866 | – | – |
| | | 24,822,147 | 3,472,813 | 3,147,237 | 279,137 |
| Net current (liabilities)/assets | | (3,484,926) | 2,981,029 | 6,521,917 | 4,108,021 |
| Total assets less current liabilities | | 14,494,209 | 5,559,141 | 14,750,992 | 7,030,779 |
| Share capital | 32 | 222,330 | 186,870 | 222,330 | 186,870 |
| Reserves | 33 | 7,920,109 | 5,017,528 | 10,933,967 | 6,843,909 |
| Shareholders' funds | | 8,142,439 | 5,204,398 | 11,156,297 | 7,030,779 |
| Minority interests | | 5,803 | 23,609 | – | – |
| Total equity | | 8,148,242 | 5,228,007 | 11,156,297 | 7,030,779 |
| Non-current liabilities | 31 | 6,345,967 | 331,134 | 3,594,695 | – |
| | | 14,494,209 | 5,559,141 | 14,750,992 | 7,030,779 |

## Consolidated Cash Flow Statement

| For the year ended 31 March 2006 | | | |
|---|---|---|---|
| | | 2006 | 2005 |
| | Note | HK$'000 | HK$'000 |
| **Cash flows from operating activities** | | | |
| Net cash generated from operations | 38(a) | **8,832,287** | 1,214,223 |
| Finance income | | **188,986** | 105,677 |
| Tax paid | | **(575,312)** | (53,688) |
| Net cash generated from operating activities | | **8,445,961** | 1,266,212 |
| *Cash flows from investing activities* | | | |
| Purchase of tangible fixed assets | 16 | **(574,731)** | (74,611) |
| Sale of tangible fixed assets | | **23,542** | 20,352 |
| Payment for construction-in-progress | 18 | **(201,556)** | (102,159) |
| Payment for internal use software | 19 | **(177,189)** | – |
| Purchase of investment securities | | – | (80,500) |
| (Payments)/net proceeds from disposal of investments | | **(3,278)** | 91,075 |
| Payment for acquisition of a business | | **(5,082,572)** | (411,022) |
| Capital contribution to an associated company | | **(11,538)** | (6,399) |
| Dividends received from an associated company | | – | 3,813 |
| Settlement of loan from a jointly controlled entity | | **10,000** | 10,000 |
| Payment for acquiring minority shareholder's interests in a subsidiary | | **(69,231)** | – |
| Proceeds from disposal of an associated company | | **79,936** | 63,669 |
| Net cash used in investing activities | | **(6,006,617)** | (485,782) |
| *Cash flows from financing activities* | | | |
| Issue of convertible preferred shares and warrants | 31(c) | **2,730,000** | – |
| Exercise of share options and issue of new shares | | **271,724** | 15,233 |
| Repurchase of shares | 38(b) | **(1,195,729)** | (16,093) |
| Contributions to employee share trust | | **(398,132)** | – |
| Dividends paid | | **(457,897)** | (403,570) |
| Bank loans | 38(b) | **1,781,196** | – |
| Finance costs paid | | **(350,322)** | (6,667) |
| Net cash generated from/(used in) financing activities | | **2,380,840** | (411,097) |
| Increase in cash and cash equivalents | | **4,820,184** | 369,333 |

Continued

Continued

| | Note | 2006 HK$'000 | 2005 HK$'000 |
|---|---|---|---|
| Effect of foreign exchange rate changes | | (715) | (19) |
| Cash and cash equivalents at the beginning of the year | | 3,019,385 | 2,650,071 |
| Cash and cash equivalents at the end of the year | | 7,838,854 | 3,019,385 |

## Corporate Information

### Board of Directors
*Executive directors*
Mr. Yang Yuanqing
Mr. William J. Amelio
Ms. Ma Xuezheng

*Non-executive directors*
Mr. Liu Chuanzhi
Mr. Zhu Linan
Mr. James G. Coulterw
Mr. William O. Grabe
Mr. Shan Weijian
Mr. Justin T. Chang
(Alternate director to Mr. James G. Coulter)
Mr. Vince Feng
(Alternate director to Mr. William O. Grabe)
Mr. Daniel A. Carroll
(Alternate director to Mr. Shan Weijian)

*Independent non-executive directors*
Mr. Wong Wai Ming
Professor Woo Chia-Wei
Mr. Ting Lee Sen
Mr. John W. Barter III

### Qualified Accountant
Mr. Damian Glendinning
### Company Secretary
Mr. Mok Chung Fu

### Registered Office
23rd Floor, Lincoln House,
Taikoo Place,
979 King's Road, Quarry Bay,
Hong Kong

### Principal Bankers
BNP Paribas
Standard Chartered Bank (Hong Kong) Limited
ABN AMRO Bank N.V.
Industrial and Commercial Bank of China (Asia) Limited
China Merchants Bank
Citibank, N.A.

### Auditors
PricewaterhouseCoopers
*Certified Public Accountants*
22nd Floor, Prince's Building,
Central, Hong Kong

### Share Registrar
Abacus Share Registrars Limited
26th Floor, Tesbury Centre,
28 Queen's Road East, Hong Kong

### American Depositary Receipts
(Depositary and Registrar)
Citibank, N.A.
14th Floor, 388 Greenwich Street,
New York, NY 10013, USA

**Stock Codes**
Hong Kong Stock Exchange: 992
American Depositary Receipts:
LNVGY

**Website**
www.lenovo.com

## Appendix A2.3.2: Lianxiang Holding Organization Chart

**Lenovo:**

- Composed of Lenovo China and Lenovo International (located in Purchase, NY). Management is based in Lenovo International except for Liu Jun, COO, based in Lenovo China.
- It has 14 divisions (PCs, servers, mobiles and note PCs, printers and so on), one research centre, 33 staff units (planning, HRM, Government procurements, corporate client service, international business development and so on), and four plants with 19 subsidiaries and five affiliated companies.

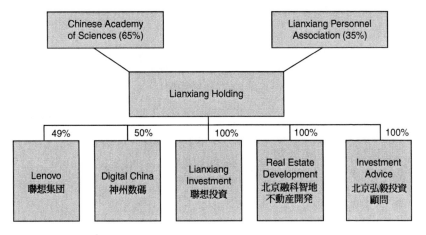

*Source*: Adapted from Xu (2007: p. 56).

# Annex 2.4

# Huawei's Zhengfei Ren[1]

In 2009, *R&D Magazine* announced its widely recognized R&D 100 awards, popularly known in fields of technology and innovation as the 'Oscars of Invention'. Among other winners, Huawei was awarded the prize for its advanced Optix OSN 6800/OSN 3800 wavelength division multiplexer. While many may recognize Lenovo (another Chinese technology company that acquired IBM's PC unit in 2004), Huawei keeps a low profile within the industry and most Western popular media. Nevertheless, we can still find financial journals such as *The Economist* (2009) classifying the growth of this Chinese company as 'astonishingly fast'. In fact, Huawei was already the world's fourth-largest manufacturer of network equipment ranked by sales, after Ericsson, Nokia Siemens Networks and Alcatel-Lucent. It also ranked second in optical networking and third in mobile-network gear in 2008 (see Appendix A2.4.3, Consolidated Financial Statements).

What was the driving force behind its rapid growth and emergence in the world market? Can it continue to grow at its current pace?

We will explore the history and background of this IT giant in China in order to analyse the firm, its culture, its management system, cost competitiveness and customer relationships. We will also attempt to answer the question of whether or not the firm will outlive its founder (Zhengfei Ren) when he retires or relinquishes his position.

## What is Huawei?

Huawei is one of the leading global telecommunications solution providers with revenues of US$18.33 billion and a net income of US$1.15 billion in 2008. Contrary to the typical image of Chinese companies that depicts them as basing their competitive advantage on low labour costs, Huawei's principal growth strategy focuses on research and development (R&D). Its 14 global R&D centres are located around the world, in the Silicon Valley and Dallas in the United States, Stockholm in Sweden, Moscow in Russia and Bangalore in India, as well as major cities in China such as Beijing, Shanghai and Shenzhen.

Huawei's products and solutions include wireless products, core network products, network products, software applications and terminals. Most of these products are designed based on its own ASIC (Application-Specific Integrated Circuit) chipset-shared platforms. By 2009 these were sold in over 100 countries around the world, serving 36 of the world's top 50 operators and more than one billion users.

Huawei's marketing materials state that they employ a customer-focus strategy with long-term partnerships with operators around the world. This is clearly reflected in their mission statement: *'To focus on our customers' market challenges by providing excellent communications network solutions and services in order to consistently create maximum value for customers.'*[2] Through their vision *'to enrich life through communication,'*[3] Huawei has managed to successfully bid on international projects, with 75 per cent of their contract sales coming from international markets in 2008.

With more than 86,000 employees, 100 international branches and 29 worldwide training centres supporting customers and local staff, how did this 20-something-year-old Chinese company transform itself into a global telecom solutions provider?

## Huawei: a history of growth through constant innovations

Founded in October 1987 by 43-year-old Zhengfei Ren (Ren Zhengfei in Chinese – 任正非) in Shenzhen, China, Huawei was converted into a limited corporation in 1988 with 14 employees. The initial registered capital was only 24,000 Yuan.[4] After reaching revenues of 100 million Yuan in 1992, with more than 100 employees, Huawei just seemed to never stop growing until it achieved a turnover of 125 billion Yuan in 2008 with a year-on-year increase of 46 per cent (see Figure A2.4.1).

While maintaining low costs was important in order to offer an affordable price and provide a reasonable margin, Huawei's competitive advantage to sustain this fast-paced growth lay in its high innovative capability focused on customer needs. According to Huawei's policy, at least 10 per cent of annual revenues were ploughed back into R&D. Of this sum, 10 per cent was allocated for research into new technologies and breakthroughs to stay ahead of the competition. Since 2009, Huawei has successfully provided solutions to its clients in areas including Fixed and Mobile Convergence (FMC), IP Multimedia Subsystem (IMS), Worldwide Interoperability for Microwave Access (WiMAX) and Internet Protocol Television (IPTV).

After his first entrepreneurial venture creating Huawei and establishing the brand in the Chinese market, Zhengfei Ren, Huawei's CEO, reckoned that the second entrepreneurial project was to benchmark the company's R&D on world-class Western multinationals in a strategic collaboration effort with another Chinese enterprise in 1996. To be more specific, his

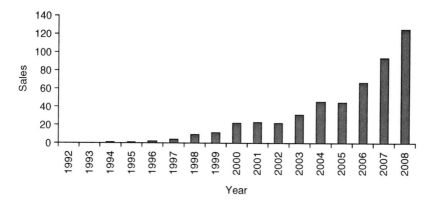

*Figure A2.4.1* Sales evolution of Huawei technologies (in billion RMB)
*Source*: Authors based on Huawei's annual reports.

objective was to be on a par with international standards within 10 years, as he explained in a speech on Huawei's international development vision. He foresaw three years to catch up in operations and management, five years in marketing and ten years in research and technology. For a more detailed description of Huawei's growth path, see Appendix A2.4.1.

## The internationalization of Huawei

The successful internationalization of Huawei was based on the constant effort made by its teams on each project. As of 2010, project-based sales accounted for over 75 per cent of the company's total. Their products are widely deployed by leading operators in developed markets such as Europe and Japan, with steady progress in North America. Their products have been gaining an increasingly wider acceptance in emerging markets.

Despite the fast expansion of its business, Huawei's internationalization process was not at all similar to that of Western multinationals that had already established themselves in the most advanced markets with high technology and strong financial positions, as claimed by Cheng & Liu (2007) in *'an internationalization of Huawei's characteristics: a combination of Western and Chinese wisdom'*.

For Huawei, as a telecommunication equipment supplier, globalization was a given. Indeed, Zhengfei Ren considered globalization to be part of the company's core values: *'if we close the door and survive by protecting ourselves, we will collapse at the first encounter once it is opened...we need to work hard to support the globalization of our products'* (Cheng & Liu, 2007). When Huawei successfully positioned itself as the 26th among the 100 top electronic enterprises in China in 1995, Ren foresaw the future scenario of Chinese and international telecommunication markets, and decided that it was the right moment to launch into the international market.

The internationalization of management teams in Huawei was the base for the company's rapid international expansion. Despite the already surprising growth rate, it was not a great achievement in the eyes of Zhengfei Ren. He considered it in fact a low growth rate, and thought that it could have been three to five times faster in light of the pace of other American IT companies that started at the same time and in terms of the turnover of other American companies having a similar size.

Ren concluded that this discrepancy was a result of internal managerial issues, as opposed to external factors. In contrast to America's mature market, it was not easy for Huawei to recruit experienced managers and employees from China's local market. At the initial growth phase, none of Huawei's employees had worked previously in large hi-tech companies, or had experience in R&D, marketing, production or finance.

Consequently, Huawei has invested a significant amount of time and resources in training its own employees for international expansion. Rather than focusing on studying the company's internationalization strategy, senior managers at Huawei have concentrated on training its employees in the internationalization process.

The employees' learning process developed as they progressed in an extremely slow process of international expansion. After three years of international learning, without any spending on large-scale marketing or promotion, Huawei started to see some results. For one reason or another, the advantage of lower cost for extra software replication could not be leveraged, resulting in less capability and less re-innovation opportunities for the company. To make up for it, Huawei's employees sacrificed their personal time by working overtime, which illustrated the enthusiasm and identification they felt with the firm in its initial stage, despite the primitive level of management.

Even though the thoughts and words of Zhengfei Ren envisaged internationalization – 'the official language of the board of directors will be English in the future' (Wu & Ji, 2006) – the diversity of its management team in terms of nationalities was limited. Huawei's strategy to foster the internationalization of its human capital consisted of sending senior managers overseas to enable them to gain more international exposure and learn good practices. Top managers in charge of Huawei's domestic market were sent to international markets and were appointed overseas regional directors.

By 2006, there were about 5,000 non-Chinese employees of whom more than 200 occupied managerial positions (Cheng & Liu, 2007). The external recruitment of senior managers was not an easy task for Huawei given its strong organizational culture. There were, however, successful new hires: the chief purchasing officer joined Huawei after working for IBM as procurement officer for the Asia Pacific area; and the vice president (VP) for finance was a Chinese native with more than ten years of overseas international investment management experience. Nonetheless, as mentioned earlier, not all the new efforts to hire international-profile managers were satisfactory. Some attempts to recruit Harvard doctoral graduates failed because the systems these graduates planned to develop and implement would not adapt to Huawei's existing managerial system. As a result, Huawei could not benefit from their capabilities and they could not play a leading role in Huawei, either. This was due in part to the strong indigenous management system and culture that Huawei had built over the years through its own experience and growth path. Consequently, Huawei's autochthonous and internally developed Chinese management system encountered difficulties in implementing a Western management system in the corporation.

## Huawei's management culture

Huawei's strong corporate culture was seen as a strength in its impressive growth path. Moreover, because Ren had worked in the Chinese army as an engineer in the years before founding Huawei, the management culture and strategy were often compared with those of the army, and Huawei's marketing system was often described as a 'war machine' of a 'modern army' (Zhang, 2007).

The analogy of a 'wolf' culture is often used by many Chinese popular media outlets to describe Huawei's culture. Wolves live a collective life. Normally a wolf pack will divide into groups of seven and individually carry out part of the tasks required for the group's prosperity and development. Thus, tacit understanding and collaboration between wolves is the decisive factor for their success as a pack. Regardless of the circumstances, they would always manage to achieve their objective with the strength of their collective power. They are also very patient, waiting for long periods of time without losing sight of any objective. Wolves are effective due to their keen powers of observation, their specific objectives, their tacit understanding, curiosity, patience, attention to detail and perseverance. Implementing the 'wolf culture' in management at Huawei Technologies gave the company a more sensitive 'sense' of market trends and opportunities, a more enhanced role of teamwork, greater strength against stronger competitors and the ultimate ability to overcome them.

The wolf culture was described by *IT Manager's World*, a Chinese magazine, as an indigenous Chinese company's way of doing business. It was compared with the lion culture (Western multinationals) and the leopard culture (Western-Chinese joint ventures in China).

During the period of economic development in China, indigenous Chinese companies were not as strong as Western multinationals and Western-Chinese joint ventures when competing in the local market. It might be compared with the battle between a wolf and a lion or a leopard in the forest. However, in the fierce market competition to get their ration of food, both the lion and the leopard might feel threatened by the wolf, even though the first two are supposedly physically stronger.

Zhengfei Ren pointed out that a wolf pack possesses a terrific capacity for survival, a strong desire to win and dedication in pursuing its target. With their aim always at the forefront, they could launch an all-out attack at any cost, using any means and investing all efforts to fight in a collective manner, until the lion and the leopard are exhausted (Chinese Entrepreneurs, 2008). Because of this, Huawei's CEO used the expression wolf culture, which became well known and served as a guideline for behaviour in different areas.

The only time Zhengfei Ren systematically talked about the wolf culture, however, was in the early 1990s when he had a conversation with a senior manager of a well-known American consultancy. According to Chunbo Wu, the senior consultant of Huawei and a professor at Renmin University, in an interview with *Business Week*, 'Ren hasn't spoken much about the wolf culture; [in fact], Huawei is kind of against the theory of the wolf culture' *(World Business Report, 2006)*. Even though the metaphor could be applied to Huawei's business practice in sales and their particular approach to international expansion, Tang (2004) argued that Huawei was not only about wolf culture, but also about the message of learning the wolf's fighting spirit and attack methods. However, it would be difficult to summarize Huawei's corporate culture in a single phrase such as 'wolf culture'. Huawei could be evolving increasingly towards a lion culture in its process of becoming a world-class multinational.

As a former senior export manager pointed out, the most important of all Huawei strategies might be the lack of a specific pattern in the firm's strategic and marketing practice. It became a formidable competitor whose managers had a higher education, many with an MBA from internationally recognized business schools (Zhang, 2007). While no specific pattern could be seen in Huawei's market strategy, it was its invincible spirit and cultural resilience that helped build its track record in the creation of a telecom equipment empire.

In the words of Zhenfei Ren:

> Resources could be exhausted; only culture could be renewed. All industrial products are created by the intelligence of human beings. Huawei has no natural resources to rely on for survival; hence we could only cultivate, in the human mind, large mining fields, large forests and large coal mines ... The spirit could be transformed into materials, and help consolidate the material and spiritual civilization. We adhere to the principle of the spiritual promoting the material. In this culture, it not only contains knowledge, technology, management, sentiment ... but also includes all the intangible factors that promote the development of productivity. (Zhang, 2007)

## Huawei's basic law

The essence of the management and spirit of Huawei's culture is explained in its Basic Law (see HR.com.cn, 2007). This summarizes the company's core values, which all employees and managers must abide by. The final draft of Huawei's Basic Law with 103 articles was completed on 27 March, 1997, after three years and eight drafts.

At that time, Huawei's CEO, Zhengfei Ren, needed to reinvent his strategy, fully aware that the initial entrepreneurial stage he and the company had come through was coming to an end. Inspired by the Hong Kong Basic Law, Hong Kong's constitutional document after its integration into China, Ren felt that Huawei also needed something similar for its reorientation. But how this document should be drafted was not clear. This vague idea was conveyed to the CEO's office with the instruction to develop it further.

After some time, the office came up with a draft and its representative handed it over in a folder with the label: Huawei Basic Law. Inside the folder were key documents such as the salary system. Zhengfei Ren responded by saying, 'This is not the basic law that I wanted'. When the associate asked him what type of basic law he wanted, Ren replied,

'If I knew that, why would I need your assistance? I would do it myself.'
(*World Business Report*, 2006)

Professor Chunbo Wu and his colleagues from Renmin University happened to be doing an assessment of Huawei's marketing department. So Zhengfei decided to ask them for help. Wu had no idea what Ren wanted either. After a whole day of discussions, they had only agreed on two points: (1) the Basic Law would not be a law and could not be drafted as such; and (2) Wu and his colleagues did not have any idea about how to draft the Basic Law.

Based on these two points, both parties agreed on the need for further discussion on the topic. To this end, Ren Zhengfei for the first time opened his heart, and shared his personal experience with the academics for three full days. Finally, it dawned on them that Huawei had to free itself of the chaos which its growth was causing.

To do so, three issues had to be clarified. First, why did Huawei achieve success? Second, what were the factors sustaining Huawei's success? And third, what factors did Huawei need for greater success in the future?

These three questions, addressing 'who I am', 'where I am' and 'where I am going', became the thread for drafting the Basic Law. The drafting process lasted three years, but as Wu said, '[we] cannot fail at the important thing. These three years of drafting have been an indoctrination process of identity and faith. Through the constant agonizing during these three years, each item has been thoroughly chewed over and agreed on by each member of staff. If it had been out in three months, I am afraid that the result would have been the opposite' (*World Business Report*, 2006).

The majority of Huawei Basic Law's clauses start with 'we want...' which would influence many market strategies with its survival-targeted proposition. Some examples from the competition were 'Tactics of 100:1 human waves', "Regardless of cost – not daring to spend money is not a good cadre', 'Shock our customers, give the contract to me', 'Price offensive – kill opponents', and 'Quitting brave win'. These were not merely some written words, but offered guidance for day-to-day behaviours, decisions and strategic decisions for Huawei's on-going growth.

## Managing people at Huawei

After the 'wolf' period, when Huawei concentrated on fighting against multinationals in order to succeed in the Chinese market, Huawei Basic Law helped to unify the corporation's value, based principally on Zhengfei Ren's cause-effect logic and value proposition/orientation. The alignment of the value orientation among the top executives, management teams and employees achieved a tacit agreement among all of them in terms of how they should construct their reasoning and ought to behave, and helped the organization to become much more efficient and effective. This common cultural ground laid the foundations for incorporating the Western managerial style and methods needed for its international expansion.

For its globalization process to succeed, Huawei sensed the need to assimilate the management system of multinational corporations (MNCs) in 1996. Reforming human resource management (HRM) at Huawei was considered key for a modern and comprehensive system focused on manager training and selection. Starting in 1997, Hay Group collaborated with Huawei in this aspect of HRM transformation. With its help, Huawei established the basic models for job design, reward system, assessment and appraisal, performance management and employee qualification, which enabled Huawei to develop its systems for manager and employee selection, training, deployment and retention. Since 1998, Hay Group has monitored HRM improvement on an annual basis, and identified problems for their solution by Huawei.

By using Hay Group's appraisal and reward system, Huawei intended to benchmark its management team with international standards. In 1998, when this system was introduced, many middle managers could not even reach an evaluation standard two levels lower than other MNCs.

Therefore, Zhengfei Ren made it clear that managers must reach international standards within three years, or otherwise Huawei would not be able to systematize its management practice.

As a result of the appointment of a HR vice president (VP) in Huawei, the company would not see higher turnover for two years, due to Ren's idea that the company needed a larger number of managers who could only be trained on the job. Ren argued that if managers were not trained by experience, the company might be guided incorrectly.

One criterion at Huawei for selecting and promoting managers stressed that the candidate had to have experience in basic and low-level management or as an operator, secretary or seller if he or she wanted to be promoted to the higher-level management team, regardless of his or her academic background. In 2005, Huawei collaborated with Hay Group to establish the model for training, development and characterization of leadership, in order to satisfy the company's needs for global expansion.

The essence of Huawei's HRM system was to train its personnel with a focus on customers and their needs. Customer satisfaction was one of the key performance indicators for all management levels, including the CEO, Zhengfei Ren. This focus was strongly integrated into the HRM system, which highly valued external customer satisfaction. The pattern of interviews, training, promotion, was therefore designed accordingly.

For training new employees, the case study *Who Killed the Contract*, was often used in order to explain all the potentially disruptive factors. In the selection of talent; one of the norms was to not consider the top three students from the best universities, in the belief that outstanding students in the Chinese educational context were very self-interested and they might have difficulty in adapting to the customer focus principle.

Chinese companies were often concerned with new recruits' technical skills. Huawei, in contrast, emphasized that perseverance was more important than skills, and morality was more important than perseverance, and mind was more important than morality, in terms of connecting with customers.

The company's current management team can be grouped under three headings: 30 per cent have the potential of entering Huawei University, the company's corporate university, to receive training opportunities for further development; 20 per cent belong to the backward cadres, as the priority group for downsizing; and the remaining 50 per cent are somewhere in-between. Thus, the backward cadres are encouraged to move towards the group in-between. The group in the middle senses the pressure and has to move forward. Practice is the benchmark in Huawei; managers are promoted on the basis of practice. Academic degrees are important but are not the only parameter. In fact, it is the only one not listed on the assessment sheet, which evaluates performance based on previous work (Shi, 2005).

Three priority principles are applied for promoting associates: (1) priority is given to excellent teams; (2) priority is given to associates who have achieved good results, worked hard in the front line and in difficult areas overseas; and (3) priority is given to those who are self-analytical and leadership-minded.

Similarly, there are three managerial incentives in Huawei: (1) the incentive encouraging managers to work in the front line, especially overseas and in difficult areas; (2) the incentive encouraging professional talents to develop their careers as technology and business professionals; and (3) the incentive encouraging managers to transform internationally and professionally. One of the most appreciated of the promotion criteria is to work hard in the most difficult countries and achieve excellent results. Consequently, the Huawei University's first training programme was held in Nigeria. All Huawei managers are required to voluntarily apply to work in the most difficult areas. Otherwise, there is no possibility of advancing in the company no matter how good you may be.

The HRM reform, integrating Western managerial instruments to the firm's Chinese indigenous culture, has given Huawei's HRM a unique structure. Defined by the HR Committee, administration, business and HR working with business knowledge are three separate units but work together.

The HR committee assigns five levels for the organizational structure. The first level is the presidential level for general management. The second level is the level of key managerial decision makers in the functional department. The levels proceed sequentially until the fifth level, which consists of sales managers and departmental managers. The HR committee is the institution designated for collective decisions and evaluation to ensure justice and fairness within the organization.

HR managers separate their administration and business function at each departmental level. Departmental HR associates' performance assessment, pay and bonus are directly linked to their department, while their professional work is directed by corporate HR at headquarters.

HR working with business knowledge means that the HR director in each business unit is the number two in the business, while the number one focuses on the business unit. Only when HR professionals are very familiar with the business can they really become strategic partners for the corporation (ICXO, 2008).

### Zhengfei Ren: leadership and management team

As the company's founder, Zhengfei Ren's way of being and doing inevitably influenced and determined Huawei's growth. He won the Lifetime Excellence Award among the 25 most influential enterprise leaders in 2008, awarded by *Chinese Entrepreneurs*.[5] Even though Ren keeps a low profile in the popular media, he is influencing the company, influencing Chinese enterprises and their entrepreneurs, and influencing the worldwide communication industry.

The silent strengths of Zhengfei Ren relate to his unwillingness to collaborate with the Chinese media in general. He would turn down interviews with the popular media, and refused to socialize with government officers and attend award ceremonies.

According to Wu (2008a), the internal speech given by Zhengfei Ren after being ranked as one of the 100 most influential people in the world by *Time*

*Magazine* in 2005 reflected best his thoughts in this sense: 'Don't take what the outside world and the media say too seriously, and just keep working hard. Me too, I will not carry a heavy load for that. I will be like you, lively, relaxed, with bad memories, and still work hard for the future of the company.'

Born in a poor village of Guizhou in 1944, Zhengfei Ren entered Chongqing Architecture Engineering Institute (today integrated in Chongqing University) at the age of 19. He lived up to his parents' expectations. After graduation he was employed by the Chinese Army as a technician in different posts before changing jobs to become a manager in a private enterprise in Shenzhen. Later on, he went on to found Huawei Technology. Because of his experience in the Army, he was often criticized for his authoritative military management style. Such military-style management may tend to have the image of order and strict discipline. Nonetheless, the level of success that Huawei enjoys today would have been impossible with a bureaucratic style, since Huawei's key strategy is innovation.

The work that Zhengfei Ren carried out was closely related to technology and inventions. The military style may better reflect the well-designed collaboration between market and administrative departments. One works hard at the frontline to gain market experience while another provides all the necessary services and logistics to enable marketing people to work as effectively as possible.

As the CEO and a true leader, Zhengfei Ren evaluated himself as follows:

I am basically a person who only half understands technology, management and finance. I am constantly in the process of learning and practicing at the same time. Therefore, only by modestly uniting a group of people can we drive the company's development by collective management. I am a common person. If I do actually have any influence, it is confined to within Huawei (Wu, 2008b)

Zhengfei Ren made a point of publishing a speech of his in almost every edition of Huawei's newsletter, *Huawei Ren* (People of Huawei). In each speech, Zhengfei Ren focused on some topic that was strategically important for the company, either in terms of vision, encouragement or issues for employees to remember. One of his famous articles, *The Winter of Huawei*,[6] was recommended by many Chinese CEOs within or outside the IT industry, including the Lenovo Group's CEO, Yuanqing Yang. On other occasions, Ren has also repeatedly suggested that 'when Huawei was a small company an individual "hero" could create history. However, over time it was transformed into a professional company of a substantial size. During this process, toning down the role of the hero, especially that of the leader and the founding entrepreneur, is the path Huawei has to go down. Thus, professionalization and systematization are what a big company needs to improve operational efficiency and reduce management cost.'

In order to maintain and improve the competitiveness of its employees, the marketing department was restructured through a collective resignation of staff in 1997, as part of its 'wolf' culture approach. In this collective event, all marketing employees resigned and then participated in the new recruitment process in order to re-align themselves with the new competencies that the organization demanded. Certainly, Huawei significantly improved its organizational structure and capability after this collective resignation and other similar events.

During the last decades, the company has constantly brought Western management experience into its management, structure and system, such as the implementation of IBM's integrative logistics management in 1998 and the centralization structure model in 2004, besides the above-mentioned HRM system from Hay Group. The restructuring makes the organization procedure-based instead of the previous functional structure. At the same time, it enables an internationalized marketing system to adapt to customers' needs in international markets, which in turn also benefits customers in the local market.

Huawei's growth rate not only presents a learning opportunity for managers and employees in the company but also an opportunity for them to grow along with the company. According to Huawei Basic Law article 102, whoever takes the baton from Zhengfei Ren at Huawei must be a leader naturally generated from employees and managers after experiencing hard work as part of the group and immersed in its spirit. Even though saying this sounds mechanical, it conveys the message that the leader will come from the ranks, and thus could be culturally well connected. Therefore, he will overlap with the current leader, Zhengfei Ren, to form a collective management. Creating a new leader for the future is the succession challenge that Huawei needs to face.

## The way ahead: what is Huawei's competitive advantage?

When Huawei stated that globalization is its core value, Zhengfei Ren summoned and told his collaborators: 'We need to dare to open ourselves up. Don't close yourselves. Compete positively with Westerners, and learn to manage the competition.'

Huawei is in a constant process of management reform in order to catch up with industry leaders. According to Ren, 'we can only survive by targeting the best in the world'. Often he reminds the Huawei team that the team is too young and has grown in an easy time. This means that they are weak in the areas of risk awareness and crisis management. Therefore, Huawei takes the current opportunity of competitive advantage to increase market share, and invest in consolidating and extending their innovation differentiation. Otherwise, this temporary competitive advantage may disappear immediately in the fierce competition prevailing in the technology and knowledge sector. If no strong international team is built soon, Huawei could easily fail when the Chinese market reaches the maturity and saturation stage, according to Zhengfei Ren (Zhang, 2007).

The telecommunications industry is very dependent on economies of scale (Bourdeau de Fontenay & Liebenau, 2006). In order to reach higher marginal benefits, it was extremely important for Huawei to go international and take full advantage of their already invested research and production capability. Huawei's internationalization process is in fact a process of catching up with Western multinationals, which used to directly compete in the Chinese market. At the beginning, Huawei had comparative cost advantages in labour, research and other areas compared with its 'lion' competitor: Western multinationals. Through the internationalization process, its globalized research activities with its international R&D centres implied an equal R&D cost. Its cost advantage could still stem from manufacturing, marketing and services. However, from Huawei's perspective, these costs will gradually increase as a result of the globalization process it is carrying out. By then, the current cost advantage will also decrease and they will only be able to compete by strong innovation.

Innovation is considered as so crucial for Huawei's survival that 38 per cent of the employees work in this field. Even though today, Huawei's technologies are among the best in the world (*The Economist*, 2009), this was not the case years ago when the internationalization process had just started.

Customers in international markets did not trust Huawei's high-tech products and did not even give them a chance to enter the list of suppliers. Although there were no sales in international markets, they had to invest constantly in exploring overseas markets. It was a hard period. Meanwhile, they kept the promise to constantly invest more than 10 per cent of turnover in R&D, as stated in Huawei's Basic Law.

Zhang (2007) argued that the company's success has been partly based on the strong customer relationship in the Huawei team. Huawei has been described as having a 'top level of marketing, second standard of services, and third tier of products.'

When Huawei was not so competitive in terms of international technology standards, this weakness was offset by a high level of attention to detail and to customer needs and a great capacity to react to those needs in building different types of interest groups among them. This marketing strength helped Huawei's management team constantly to take advantage of market opportunities, which sequentially accumulate important financial capital to be able to invest more in research and development, improve their own products, technologies, quality, and value for money. This same cycle is a catalyst for continuous improvement.

Would this advantage be the key and continue to contribute to Huawei's further success, of even when their production and research costs reach the same level as other multinational competitors? How do they maintain such customer relationship management while investing as little as possible in advertising, with no advertising at all most of the time? Does their learning culture continue once they reach the top? How will the next generation's management team perform in comparison with Zhengfei Ren's influence on Huawei (see Appendix A2.4.2)?

## Appendix A2.4.1: Huawei technologies timeline

1987   Ren Zhengfei founded Huawei at the age of 43 in Shenzhen (China). The registered capital was 24,000 Yuan.

1988   Huawei Ltd. Co. was founded with 14 employees. The business included engineering consultancy projects, and a sales agent for a Hong Kong company resulted in Private Branch Exchange (PBX) switches.

1990   Huawei started independent research and commercialization of PBX technologies, targeting hotels and small enterprises.

1992   Sales reached 100 million Yuan with own production line and more than 100 employees. R&D on rural digital switching solution was launched.

1993   Sales increased to 400 million Yuan. Successfully designed own products of digital switching equipment. Became number one in the Chinese telecommunication market in the rural area. Huawei entered a period of accelerated growth. It built the first microchip research institute in Silicon Valley.

1994   Sales reached 800 million Yuan. Huawei established a research institute in Beijing for researching digital telecommunication. Borrowed money at high interest rates to invest in R&D; at a certain point, employees were paid half in cash and half in hand-written notes.

1995   Sales reached 1.5 billion Yuan, with a capital increase to 7 billion Yuan and 800 employees; 'Huawei Basic Law' drafted; the first HR reform after the collective resignation of managers in the marketing department; intellectual property department created; transformation from leadership in the rural market to urban market leadership and internationalization.

1996   Sales reached 2.6 billion Yuan; first international project with a Hong Kong company; changes in management style, including structural reform, strengthening manager training and management performance appraisal. In terms of research, it established a research centre in Shanghai and broke down the process into various phases: strategic planning, product research and middle test. The successfully designed product C& C08 allowed Huawei to become part of a small group of corporations that could provide this technology in the world.

1997   Huawei employed 5,600 persons, reached a turnover of 4.1 billion Yuan with R&D investment of 400 million Yuan. It created joint research labs with Texas Instruments, Motorola, IBM, Intel, Agere Systems, Sun Microsystems, Altera, Qualcomm, Infineon and Microsoft. With the collaboration of international consultancies such as IBM, Towers Perrin, Hay Group, PriceWaterhouseCoopers (PWC) and Fraunhofer-Gesellschaft (FhG), Huawei transformed its managerial procedure, human resource management, financial system and quality control. Made persistent inroads into the Russian market. Launched wireless GSM-based solutions.

1998    With a turnover of 8.9 billion Yuan and 8,000 employees, Huawei started its internationalization process on a large scale, especially to European and US markets. It created a software institute in India. 'Huawei Basic Law' was formally launched. It invested 500 million Yuan to contract an international consultancy to transform its operational system. It donated 40 million Yuan to people in need after the floods. Employees were encouraged to think in terms of collective benefits as well as their own private interests, to develop critical thinking and self-assessment skills, and the enhancement of private, collective and organizational objectives. Leading position in the metropolitan areas of China.

1999    Sales hit 12 billion Yuan, including international sales of 53 million USD, with 15,000 employees. It invested 1.39 billion Yuan in R&D, opened a research centre in Bangalore, India and another in the US. Huawei started to develop the African market, and established large-scale distribution channels and service networks in overseas markets.

2000    Sales reached 22 billion Yuan, including international contracts worth 128 million USD. Its profits were the highest of Chinese electronic companies. Forbes ranked Ren Zhengfei as the third-richest Chinese businessman, with a fortune of 540 billion USD. Negotiations with Lucent on OEM collaboration failed. Established R&D centre in Stockholm, Sweden.

2001    Divested non-core subsidiary Avansys to Emerson for 750 million USD. Established four R&D centres in the US. Joined the International Telecommunications Union (ITU). The Indian R&D centre achieved CMM level-4 accreditation.

2002    International market sales reached USD 552 million.

2003    Established joint venture with 3Com focusing on enterprise data networking solutions. The Indian R&D centre achieved CMM level-5 accreditation.

2004    Established joint venture with Siemens to develop TD-SCDMA solutions. Achieved first significant contract win in Europe valued at over 25 million USD with Dutch operator Telfort.

2005    International contract orders exceeded domestic sales for the first time. Selected as a preferred telecom equipment supplier and signed a Global Framework Agreement with Vodafone. Selected as a preferred 21st Century Network (21CN) supplier by British Telecom (BT) to provide multi-service network access (MSAN) components and optical transmission equipment.

2006    Divested 49 per cent of stake in H3C for 880 million USD. Established Shanghai-based joint R&D Centre with Motorola to develop UMTS technologies. Introduced new visual identity (VI), which reflected the principles of customer focus, innovation, steady and sustainable growth, and harmony.

2007    Established joint venture with Symantec to develop storage and security appliances. Established joint venture with Global Marine, to provide end-to-end submarine network solutions. Partner to all the top operators in Europe at the end of the year. Won the 2007 Global Supplier Award by Vodafone as the only network equipment supplier to be awarded this specific accolade. Unveiled its ALL IP FMC solutions strategy designed to leverage distinct benefits for telecom carriers, from TCO savings to reduced energy consumption.

2008    Recognized by *Business Week* as one of the world's most influential companies. Ranked No. 3 by Informa in terms of worldwide market share in mobile network equipment. First large-scale commercial deployment of UMTS/HSPA in North America, for TELUS and Bell Canada. Ranked No. 1 by ABI in mobile broadband devices having shipped over 20 million units. Ranked as the largest applicant under WIPO's Patent Cooperation Treaty (PCT), with 1,737 applications published in 2008; accounted for 10 per cent of LTE patents worldwide.

*Source*: Adapted from Cheng & Liu (2007)
and www.huawei.com accessed 24 March 2008.

## Appendix A2.4.2: Message from the Huawei executive management team

Over the years, Huawei has grown into a true market leader, gaining recognition and trust from an increasing number of leading operators. Credit for this success is due to our customers, partners and our dedicated employees and we thank them for their support and confidence in Huawei.

In the current global economic situation, the telecom sector is facing many uncertainties. However, we believe that the global telecom industry will continue to experience dynamic growth over the longer term because communication is a basic human need and telecommunications have become integrated into the daily life of billions of people. New growth in this sector will be driven by the continued demand for mobile broadband in mature markets, together with the fast-growing user requirements for easy access to telecommunication services in emerging markets.

Driven by rapid technological evolution and emerging user demands, the boundary between telecom, the Internet, software solutions, digital bid and consumers is becoming blurred, resulting in the advent of a new era – a 'networked world'. In the next few years, the number of mobile users is projected to exceed five billion, while over two billion fixed and mobile broadband users will be tapping into new services that are being enabled by the ubiquitous broadband technology. These billions of users, and the content that they develop and consume, will have a huge impact on the current networks of operators around the world.

In the future, the availability of networks with low Total Cost of Ownership (TCO) and innovative services that increase revenue will be the key to addressing the rapidly changing challenges of operators. Our commitment to our customers and our position as a trusted partner will enable operators to break bottlenecks in broadband and offer users ubiquitous, consistent broadband experiences. Our All-IP-based Fixed-Mobile Convergence (FMC) solutions will enable operators to substantially reduce TCO while protecting their initial investments. In emerging markets, operators will be able to get a head-start advantage from our targeted solutions and service models. We are already working with our customers to assist them in strengthening their competitiveness and reducing their energy costs, while enhancing end-user experiences and generating increased revenue through the use of innovative services.

Our customers' success will continue to drive Huawei's growth as a leading global supplier. In 2009, we believe that Huawei will maintain a pace of steady growth and this will be driven mainly by 3G network deployments in emerging markets, including the Asia-Pacific region, and particularly in China. In North America and Europe, our consolidated partnership with leading operators will also generate new growth opportunities. Overall, the increasing recognition of Huawei's unique values will strengthen our strategic partnerships with leading operators and it will be a foundation for our future success.

Huawei's development over the past 20 years has taught us that only through the success of our customers can we succeed. It is for this reason that we will continue to optimize our organization and processes and promote management efficiency. By promoting a value of 'customers first', we will continue to strive to meet customer needs with premium products and services. In partnership with our customers, every Huawei employee is dedicated to constructing a truly networked world, one that enriches people's lives through communication.

Huawei Executive Management Team (Huawei EMT).

*Source*: www.huawei.com (accessed 1 February 2010).

## Appendix A2.4.3: Consolidated Financial Statements

Consolidated balance sheet

|  | Note | 2009 CNY' million | 2008 CNY' million |
|---|---|---|---|
| **Assets** | | | |
| Property, plant and equipment | 6 | 8,317 | 7,285 |
| Intangible assets | 7 | 553 | 127 |
| Investments in associates and jointly controlled entities | 8 | 311 | 490 |
| Other non-current financial assets | | 108 | 225 |
| Deferred tax assets | 9 | 5,147 | 3,742 |
| Other non-current assets | | 611 | 643 |
| **Total non-current assets** | | **15,047** | **12,512** |
| Inventories | 10 | 24,947 | 23,044 |
| Trade and other receivables | 11 | 63,282 | 52,854 |
| Other financial assets | | 7,145 | 8,813 |
| Cash and cash equivalents | 12 | 29,232 | 21,017 |
| **Total current assets** | | **124,606** | **105,728** |
| **Total assets** | | **139,653** | **118,24** |
| **Equity** | | | |
| Equity attributable to equity holders of the company | | 43,253 | 37,421 |
| Minority interests | | 63 | 33 |
| **Total equity** | | **43,316** | **37,454** |
| **Liabilities** | | | |
| Borrowings | 13 | 8,490 | 1,026 |
| Defined benefit post-employment obligations | | 3,512 | 2,791 |
| Deferred government grants | | 933 | 626 |
| Deferred tax liabilities | 9 | 631 | 203 |
| **Total non-current liabilities** | | **13,566** | **4,646** |
| Borrowings | 13 | 7,887 | 12,983 |
| Income tax payable | | 3,696 | 1,355 |
| Trade and other payables | 14 | 70,013 | 60,528 |
| Provisions for warranties | 15 | 1,175 | 1,274 |
| **Total current liabilities** | | **82,771** | **76,140** |
| **Total liabilities** | | **96,337** | **80,786** |
| **Total equity and liabilities** | | **139,653** | **118,240** |

Consolidated statement of cash flow

|  | Note | 2009 CNY' million | 2008 CNY' million |
|---|---|---|---|
| **Cash flows from operating activities** | | | |
| Cash receipts from customers | | 165,802 | 114,612 |
| Cash paid to suppliers and employees | | −141,411 | −105,745 |
| Other operating cash flows | | −2,650 | −2,412 |
| **Net cash from operating activities** | | **21,741** | **6,455** |
| **Net cash used in investing activities** | | **−5,219** | **−12,477** |
| **Net cash (used in)/from financing activities** | | **−8,384** | **13,992** |
| **Net increase in cash and cash equivalents** | | **8,138** | **7,970** |
| Cash and cash equivalents at 1 January | | 21,013 | 13,822 |
| Effect of foreign exchange rate changes | | 81 | −779 |
| **Cash and cash equivalents at 31 December** | 12 | **29,232** | **21,013** |

*Source*: Huawei's 2008 Annual Report.

# Annex 2.5

# Kantha Bopha Children's Hospitals: Dr Beat Richner's lifework[1]

## Beatocello

On a sultry Saturday evening in mid-August 2009, a weekly concert to collect donations was taking place in a freezingly air-conditioned lecture room at a children's hospital in Siem Reap, a town in northern Cambodia, not far from the world-famous Angkor ruins. Dr Beat Richner (aka Beatocello), a Swiss paediatrician who ran the hospital, played Pau Casal's *El Cant dels Ocells*. The 100-strong audience was mostly composed of European tourists. After the applause, 62-year-old Dr Richner greeted the audience and started to describe with bitterness the situation of public health in the country: 'Without our hospitals, 90,000 children a year would die in a passive genocide. The creed of the World Health Organization and UNICEF is that medical treatment must correspond to the economic reality of each country – but the economic reality of most Cambodians is zero.'[2]

His concerts bring in nearly US$6 million every year. In total, US$22 million are raised annually, of which only 8 per cent and 7 per cent are paid by the Swiss and Cambodian governments, respectively, with the balance coming from private donations obtained thanks to Dr Richner's personal effort.[3]

That evening, Dr Richner seemed especially irate and dissatisfied with the health system in Cambodia, and concerned about the future of this and other hospitals financed mainly by private donations and managed by him.

## Beat Richner: a short biography

Beat Richner was born in Zurich on 13 March, 1947. He graduated in medicine in 1973 and specialized at the Zurich Children's Hospital. In 1974, he joined the Swiss Red Cross and was sent to work at the Kantha Bopha Children's Hospital,[4] in Cambodia. Dr Richner was forced to go back to Switzerland when the Khmer Rouge gained sway over the country. Initially, he returned to his former work at the Zurich Children's Hospital. In 1980, he opened his own practice. During these years in Europe, Beat Richner developed the character of Beatocello, an entertainer, giving numerous performances both in Switzerland and abroad.

In December 1991, Cambodia's King Norodom Sihanouk asked him to rebuild and manage the Kantha Bopha Hospital. Richner moved to Cambodia, and has ever since managed, expanded and built Kantha Bopha children's hospitals in different locations in Cambodia.

## The Kingdom of Cambodia: politics, society and economics

### Basic data

With an area of 181,035 sq km, and a population of 14.8 million (2005 estimation), Cambodia has three border countries – Laos, Thailand and Vietnam – and a coastline of 443 km on the Gulf of Thailand, connecting with the South China Sea (see the map in Appendix A2.5.1 and Appendix A2.5.2 regarding macroeconomic data). The main religion is Theravada Buddhism and the language, Khmer, a member of the Mon-Khmer subfamily of the Austro-Asiatic language group. However, English is widely spoken and taught in the major cities, and even in rural areas most young people speak some, due to the number of tourists from English-speaking countries.

The capital is Phnom Penh with an estimated population of 1.3 million (data from the 2008 census); the major cities are: Phnom Penh, Siem Reap and Sihanoukville.

### Recent history[5, 6]

In 1863, King Norodom, enthroned with the support of Thailand, sought the protection of France from Thailand and Vietnam, after tensions between them grew. In 1867, the Thai king signed a treaty with France, renouncing suzerainty over Cambodia.

Cambodia was a French protectorate from 1863 to 1953, administered as part of French Indochina, though occupied by the Japanese empire from 1941 to 1945. After King Norodom's death, in 1941, 18-year-old Norodom Sihanouk was enthroned. Under his reign, Cambodia gained independence from France on 9 November, 1953, and Cambodia became a constitutional monarchy.

Sihanouk adopted neutrality in the Cold War (1945–1991). However, Cambodia began to take sides, and the king was ousted in 1970 by a military coup with the support of the United States, while travelling abroad. Settling in Beijing, China, Sihanouk had to realign himself with the Chinese communists. The pro-China Khmer Rouge rebels used him to gain territory in the regions. The king urged his followers to overthrow the pro-United States government of Lon Nol, which led to the civil war.

Between 1969 and 1973, after bombardments, South Vietnam and US forces briefly invaded Cambodia to disrupt the Viet Cong and Khmer Rouge. Some two million Cambodians fled to Phnom Penh. Estimates as to how many Cambodians were killed during the bombing campaigns vary widely, as do opinions about the effects of the bombing. Some authors[7] argued that the bombing drove peasants to join the Khmer Rouge.

As the war ended, the country faced famine in 1975, with 75 per cent of its draft animals destroyed, meaning that rice planting for the next harvest would have to be done 'by the hard labour of seriously malnourished people'.

The Khmer Rouge reached Phnom Penh and took power in 1975. The regime, led by the notorious Pol Pot, changed the country's official name to Democratic Kampuchea (DK), and was heavily influenced and backed by China. They immediately evacuated the cities and sent the entire population on forced marches to rural work projects. The constitution promulgated in January 1976 abolished private property and organized family-oriented agricultural production on the model of the 11th century, discarded Western medicine, and destroyed anything considered Western. Over one million Cambodians, out of a total population of eight million, died from executions, overwork, starvation and disease.

The number of people killed by the Khmer Rouge regime is estimated to lie between one and three million. Hundreds of thousands fled across the border into Thailand. Minority ethnic groups were targeted by the regime. The Cham Muslims suffered serious purges with as much as half of their population exterminated. In the late 1960s, an estimated 425,000 ethnic Chinese lived in Cambodia, but by 1984, as a result of Khmer Rouge genocide and emigration, only about 61,400 Chinese remained in the country. The professions, such as doctors, lawyers and teachers, were also targeted.

On Christmas Day 1978, over 100,000 Vietnamese troops mounted a major offensive to stop Khmer Rouge incursions across the border and the genocide in Cambodia. Violent occupation and warfare between the Vietnamese and Khmer Rouge holdouts continued throughout the 1980s. Peace efforts began in Paris in 1989, culminating two years later in October 1991 in a comprehensive peace settlement. The United Nations was given a mandate to enforce a ceasefire, and deal with refugees and disarmament.

In recent years, reconstruction efforts have progressed and led to some political stability in the form of a constitutional, multi-party, democratic monarchy.

### Government and politics[8]

The political system is based on the nation's constitution of 1993. Today, the system consists of a constitutional monarchy operated as a parliamentary representative democracy. The Prime Minister is head of government based on a multi-party system, and the King is head of state. The Prime Minister is appointed with the approval of the National Assembly; the Prime Minister and his ministers exercise executive power. Legislative power is the responsibility of the executive, the Senate and the National Assembly of Cambodia. On 14 October, 2004, King Samdech Preah Baromneath Norodom Sihamoni was chosen by the Throne Council, following the selection process that had been quickly put in place after the surprise abdication of King Norodom Sihanouk a week earlier. He was enthroned in Phnom Penh on 29 October, 2004.

While the violent political turbulences of the 1970s and 80s have passed, several border disputes between Cambodia and its neighbours persist. There are disagreements over some offshore islands and sections of the boundary with Vietnam, and undefined maritime boundaries and border areas with Thailand.

## Basic macroeconomic data[9]

From 2004 to 2008, the economy grew about 10 per cent per year, driven largely by an expansion in the garment sector, construction, agriculture and tourism. With the January 2005 expiration of the WTO Agreement on Textiles and Clothing, Cambodian textile producers were forced to compete directly with lower-priced countries such as China, India, Vietnam and Bangladesh. (See Table A2.5.1, Macroeconomic Data Summarizing Cambodia's Economic Situation.)

The garment industry currently employs more than 320,000 people and contributes more than 85 per cent of Cambodia's exports. In 2005, exploitable oil and natural gas deposits were found beneath Cambodia's territorial waters, representing a new revenue stream for the government if commercial extraction begins. Mining is also attracting significant investor interest, particularly in the northern parts of the country, and the government has said opportunities exist for mining bauxite, gold, iron and gems. In 2006, a US-Cambodia bilateral Trade and Investment Framework Agreement (TIFA) was signed and several rounds of discussions have been held since 2007.

*Table A2.5.1*  Macroeconomic data

| Subject description | Units | 2006 | 2007 | 2008 | 2009 |
|---|---|---|---|---|---|
| GDP, current price | $US billions | 7.26 | 8.69 | 11.25 | 10.90 |
| GDP per capita, current price | $US | 513 | 649 | 823 | 782 |
| GDP, purchasing power parity | $US billions | 23.04 | 26.11 | 28.46 | 28.137 |
| GDP per capita, purchasing power parity | $US | 1,627 | 1,949 | 2,082 | 2,018 |
| Population | Millions of people | 14.16 | 13.4 | 13.66 | 13.94 |

\* 2008 and 2009 are estimated by the IMF.

*Source*: The International Monetary Fund, World Economic Outlook Database, October 2009.

The tourism industry has continued to grow rapidly, with foreign arrivals exceeding two million per year in 2007–08; however, economic troubles abroad will dampen growth in 2009. Rubber exports declined by more than 15 per cent in 2008 due to falling world market prices. The global financial crisis is weakening demand for Cambodian exports, and construction is declining due to a shortage of credit.

The major economic challenge for Cambodia over the next decade will be fashioning an economic environment in which the private sector can create enough jobs to handle Cambodia's demographic imbalance. More than 50 per cent of the population is less than 21 years old.

In order to qualify the GDP per capita data with the distribution of wealth and poverty, we should add that one in three Cambodians earns less than one dollar a day.

The population lacks education and productive skills, particularly in the poverty-ridden countryside, which suffers from an almost total lack of basic infrastructure. Fear of renewed political instability and corruption within the government discourage foreign investment and delay foreign aid, although there has been significant assistance from bilateral and multilateral donors. Donors pledged US$504 million to the country in 2004, while the Asian Development Bank alone has provided US$850 million in loans, grants and technical assistance.

### Kantha Bopha hospitals[10]

Dr Richner, a Swiss Red Cross envoy, worked as a paediatrician at the Kantha Bopha Children's hospital in Phnom Penh in 1974–75 until he was forced to leave the country by the Khmer Rouge regime.

When he returned to Cambodia in 1991, he found the hospital had been destroyed and was asked by the King to reopen it to attend to the needs of children.

In March 1992, Dr Richner created a foundation (Kantha Bopha) in Zurich to run future hospitals and raise funds.[11] He himself moved to Phnom Penh and began the reconstruction work.

By 1995, Kantha Bopha I had more than 1,000 outpatients and over 350 hospitalizations per day. During that year, King Norodom Sihanouk offered some land to build a new hospital. One year later, Kantha Bopha II, the second children's hospital was inaugurated in the presence of the King and Jean-Pascal Delamuraz, President of the Swiss Federal Council. (See Annex 3 for the health situation in Cambodia.)

In March 1999, Dr Richner's third children's hospital was opened, as well as an annexe to existing Kantha Bopha hospitals. One year earlier, the Prime Minister, Hun Sen, had granted a plot of land in Siem Reap for the new hospital. In the new hospital, the facilities included a prevention and health education centre, an outpatient station and additional facilities for hospitalizations and adequate medical treatment of children.

By 2004, Kantha Bopha I had again become too small and two of its three buildings were in a bad and even dangerous condition. A new construction was required to avoid closing the hospital. This time, a plot giving on the Wat Phnom was bought. The work started in August 2004, and the new children's hospital Kantha Bopha IV was inaugurated in December 2005. Next, two of the three buildings of Kantha Bopha I were evacuated and restored. Kantha Bopha IV is now connected with Kantha Bopha I.

Kantha Bopha IV has 555 beds. The facilities include four operating theatres, two intensive care units, a complete laboratory with a blood bank, an imaging department with X-ray, four US scanners and a CT scanner, a huge pharmacy, an outpatient station and a prevention centre. The total cost of this hospital was US$15 million.

Just to give an example of the growth in demand for hospitalization: by 2006, the number of hospitalized patients in Phnom Penh had increased by 50 per cent. Even at the moment of the inauguration, Kantha Bopha IV was overcrowded.

Kantha Bopha V was inaugurated in December 2007, attended by Cambodia's highest political authorities. The new hospital had 300 beds, a prevention station, X-ray, fluoroscopy, ultrasound, laboratories and nine units with 34 beds. In addition to this, they had a conference room and a medical library.

Furthermore, in December 2008, an extension at the Jayavarman VII hospital was inaugurated by Dr. Beat Richner with the attendance of King Norodom Sihamoni and Prime Minister Samdech Hun Sen. It had 200 beds, laboratory, pharmacy and radiology.

The Kantha Bopha hospitals had become a highly respected model in terms of efficiency and transparency all over Southeast Asia, both in curative and preventive medicine and in research.[12] At the Kantha Bopha hospitals, medical attention is free of charge for all children and their mothers.

According to Dr Beat Richner, from 1993 until 2008, the Kantha Bopha hospitals treated 8.2 million outpatients and 650,000 inpatients, and performed 90,000 chirurgical operations. 550,000 children would not otherwise have survived.

Dr Richner has also created the Kantha Bopha Academy of Paediatrics (KBAP), a teaching hospital system.

'The KBAP offers a six-month intensive postgraduate course for young physicians from the ASEAN countries and Africa as well as from other parts of the world. The course will include the following components:
   Review of the spectrum of regular paediatrics specialities given in weekly modules of five morning and five afternoon sessions by eminent visiting professors mainly from Swiss university children's hospitals.
   Lectures on paediatric diseases characteristic of the poor Cambodian population. These pathological features are similar for all children

living under poor and tropical conditions. The lectures will be scheduled daily and will be given by Cambodian professors attending the Kantha Bopha hospitals.

Introduction to the philosophy of the Kantha Bopha project, with its material and economical aspects and requirements, will be part of the programme. Special sessions will be arranged to show how to design the infrastructure, logistics and management of a paediatric facility in an underprivileged country, including personnel and equipment. This will include discussion of hygiene, safety and salary. The teaching sessions will be given by medics and technicians from the Kantha Bopha hospitals.

Daily medical inpatient and outpatient practice will be tutored by Cambodian doctors affiliated to the Kantha Bopha hospitals. Course participants in small groups will be able to take turns in the various divisions and gain personal experience of the medical activity.

In addition, practical introduction to ultrasonography, CT and MRI may be arranged.'[13]

## Management and operations[14]

In Jayavarman VII Hospital, a 12-year-old girl sat on a bed, did not smile and looked gravely at the man in white. After studying her lungs, Dr Richner explained: 'without proper treatment, she would die in three to four months. The mother told us that she had paid US$12 to a private doctor but he had not been of much help. When her neighbour spoke about our hospital, they drove 90 kilometers. Without money. But they knew they would be helped. At night, the parents are allowed to stay in the hospital because it improves the chances of the children's recovery. If they have no money, they will get it from us.'[15]

'In the five hospitals, Kantha Bopha I, II, IV and V in Phnom Penh and Jayavarman VII in Siem Reap Angkor, 82,354 children have been hospitalized in 2008 (the average hospitalization period is five days), 671,682 ill children receive treatment in the outpatients department, 400,000 healthy children get vaccinated, 14,778 operations are performed, there are 15,138 births in the maternity wards (designed to prevent mother-to-child AIDS and TB transmission) and 3,000 families receive healthcare education every day.'[16]

Between two and three thousand children came daily to the hospital in Siem Reap alone, brought by their parents from the surrounding villages in the early morning to take a place on the list.

The structure in 2009, as described by the institution, was: total personnel of 2,100, with 180 doctors running the hospitals, together with Dr Richner, on a salary of US$1,000 per month (US$40 in state hospitals), low administration expenses (5 per cent of the budget). Dr Richner raises the funds required, governs the hospitals' management, manages relations with public institutions and expansion activities in terms of new hospital developments

and new treatments for the children, such as successfully cutting the rate of transmission between HIV-infected mothers and their newborn children (from 40 per cent to 5 per cent).
The Swiss doctor emphasizes:

> All treatment in the Kantha Bopha hospitals is free. There is justice for all. There is no corruption. We pay adequate salaries ... There are facilities and medicines and drugs of the same standard being used in Europe or the US. That's why the hospitals are a huge success. They are recognized by the international evaluations as centers of excellence.[17]

Dr Richner imports all his drugs and medical supplies directly from Thailand to avoid the counterfeit pharmaceutical products flooding Cambodia. The head nurses personally distribute the medicines every day, to avoid theft. This vigilance goes for patients as well as staff. The example was given of a young girl being treated for TB with a nine-month course of drugs.[18] Like every other patient, she returned to the hospital for her check-up carrying the empty blister packets to prove that she had taken her medication rather than sold it to a back-street pharmacist.

Dr Richner says: 'Hospitals are provided with the highest quality equipment available, even in the first world and, as seen, salaries are higher than the average in the sector in the country.'

Up to 2008, 8.8 million sick children were treated, of which more than 850,000 had serious diseases.

The Dengue fever severely affected Cambodia and its neighbouring countries in 2007. From January to 15 August, 19,950 severe cases were reported. 181 Dengue cases died in the Kantha Bopha Hospital that year up to 15 August. 95 per cent of the patients died because of liver failure and kidney failure – namely, by drug intoxication. They were treated outside Dr Richner's hospitals with wrong and too many drugs. Dr Richner believed that, after the WHO's recommendation that the patient should pay, 80 per cent of hospitalized severe Dengue cases would have stayed at home and would have died.[19] (See Appendices A2.5.3 and A2.5.4 regarding Cambodia's sanitary situation and the WHO's country policy, respectively.)

'In 2008, 85% of the children hospitalized in Cambodia were received at Kantha Bopha hospitals.'

### Finances[20]

The annual budget of the operational costs currently runs at US$24 million. Kantha Bopha's costs/healing ratio is the best worldwide, as proved by international evaluations.[21]

Between 1991 and 2009, the Kantha Bopha Foundation has raised and spent more than US$370 million, with the vast majority of funding coming from private donors, many of whom live in Switzerland.[22]

The sources of funding for the project have been (interannual average):

| | |
|---|---|
| Government of Cambodia | 7% |
| Swiss government | 8% |
| Donations from individuals* | 85% |
| Total income | US$ 22 million |

*Most of them Swiss, but also includes tourists in Cambodia; 25% of total funds are from individuals, due to Beatocello's performances in Switzerland and Cambodia.

Source: Elaborated from Kantha Bopha Foundation's 2008 annual report

The 2008 Annual Report approved by the Foundation Board on 12 May 2009 showed a surplus of CHF[23] 2,525,175.96 (down from CHF 3,989,796.28 in the previous year).

Due to new regulations, from 1 January 2008, PricewaterhouseCoopers AG carried out its audit according to Art. 728 ff. OR. Apart from the usual attestation of conformity for the annual financial statement, the auditing company also confirmed the existence of an internal control system. In addition, the Foundation Board was presented with a detailed report according to Art. 728 b OR.

Cambodian laws excluded the acquisition of land by a Swiss foundation. Accordingly, the two plots of land were held in trust for the Foundation by Dr Denis Lawrence, a member of the management of the hospital with dual Cambodian and French citizenship. Written agreements have been concluded on the relevant fiduciary relationship.

In 2006, the contribution of the Swiss Confederation of CHF 2.75 million, together with that of the Cambodian government of approximately CHF 2 million, corresponded to only 15 per cent of total revenue. 85 per cent of overall revenues were from individuals and non-state institutions. Legacies brought in around CHF 3 million (8 per cent).

In 2008, total donations reached CHF 34.5 million, the highest in the Foundation's history. This sum was influenced by a particularly high private individual donation, specifically intended for the new building and the extension of Kantha Bopha III.

In the 16 years up to 2008, approximately CHF 330 million in donations have been made.

The cash donations were saved and invested in securities, real estate or other investments.

The construction cost of Kantha Bopha IV amounted to US$15 million. In order to finance Kantha Bopha IV, Beat Richner asked the Swiss people to each contribute a 20 CHF bill. This action raised enough money to finalize the undertaking. Even school children helped, and Swiss citizens all over Switzerland contributed a 20 CHF bill.[24] The total costs of the Kantha Bopha

V hospital were US$9 million. Between 2006 and 2008, expenditure on new construction projects was US$34 million.[25]

In 2008, management costs were around US$17 million and annual average total costs (investment costs included) were around US$25 million. Only 5 per cent of the total funds are earmarked to run the Foundation's infrastructure in Switzerland.

According to the data provided by Dr Richner, he has just five months for fundraising but, unlike many charitable foundations, the only endowment he has is the commitment from the Swiss and Cambodian governments to cover 15 per cent of his annual budget. 'The hospitals are working well and everything can continue without me, but the ongoing nightmare is the money,' he discloses as he puffs on a Davidoff mini cigarillo, well away from the main hospital buildings. 'I can only start to think of my [succession] plan when I get the money – this US$200m I need to save Kantha Bopha for 20 years. Then I will be a free man.'[26]

## The Foundation's governance structure[27]

The Foundation Board (that is the Board of Trustees) regularly meets twice a year in January and May. The Board of Trustees is kept continually informed by e-mail, and Dr med. Peter Studer presents the Board of Trustees with precise information on the continuing work in Cambodia. (See Table A2.5.2.)

Statutory business could be dealt with in collaboration with all of the Foundation Board's members.

Unanimous approval of the annual report and annual accounts and approval of the budget takes place in the presence of the auditor, PricewaterhouseCoopers SA.

In 2006, the claims and review commission (President: Dr F. von Meiss, other members: Dr C. Steinmann, Dr A. Lohrer) met in March. It studied indemnities, accounting and review expenses and advertising costs. The work of the law firms of Dr F. von Meiss (BLUM Rechtsanwälte) and Dr C. Steinmann (Bär & Karrer) was provided free of charge.

The Foundation's equity capital was CHF 19.5 million in 2006. The funds were immediately available in cash. They covered current expenses for eight to nine months. The equity capital was reduced in 2008 because of operating losses of CHF 2.5 million. The capital resources were in liquid form and can secure running costs for only five to six months without additional donations.

Avoidance of corruption is a major concern of Dr Richner's. In principle, the money is handled in Switzerland by the Foundation. No medical doctor in Cambodia is involved. The donation from the Cambodian Government goes directly to the Foundation's account in Switzerland. The hospital staff's payroll is also handled in Switzerland and paid directly to the Foundation's Swiss account at the Thai Commercial Bank from which the staff withdraw their payroll through their passbooks. No-one in Cambodia touches the money.

Table A2.5.2   Governance structure of the foundation

| |
|---|
| **President** |
| Dr. med. Alfred Löhrer, Zürich |
| **Vice-President** |
| Dr. med. Peter Studer, Reinach |
| **Finances** |
| Arthur Müller, Winterthur |
| **Office Switzerland** |
| StiftungKinderspitalDr. Beat Richner |
| Susanna Cohen Straka |
| **Members of the Board** |
| Susi Eppenberger, Wildhaus |
| Prof.Dr. med. Andreas Fanconi, Zürich |
| Peter Rothenbühler, Lausanne |
| Dr.iur. Christian Steinmann, Zollikon |
| Dr.iur. Florian von Meiss, Zumikon |
| SerainaPrader, Ärztin, Zürich |
| **Board of the Hospitals** |
| Dr. med. Beat Richner, Head of Hospitals |
| Dr. med. Peter Studer, Deputy |
| Dr. Biologiste Denis Laurent, Deputy in Cambodia |

*Source*: http://www.beat-richner.ch/Assets/richner_
foundation.html (accessed 1 November 2009).

Medicines are inventoried, which is daily checked by a person in charge and approved by a doctor and a head nurse. These medicines are procured from Diethelm Keller's Thai office, because Dr Richner believes that the price of medicines is lowest in Thailand and Philippines. Parents of infant patients are not given a whole packet of medicine. Instead, the medicine is unpacked and given in smaller batches with instructions.

Dr Richner takes part in each interview with all the doctors and staff. The turnover rate is low as the staff tend to stay once their probationary period is over. He is informed of the situation at each hospital by 6:00am, no matter where he may be.

## Dr Richner's public statements

### On justice and poverty

'Initially an excellent student, I felt, during the third school year, that I was undergoing a crisis. I was afraid that my soul would become crippled due to the excessive...studying of natural science...I was afraid of spiritual emptiness.

I was ready to leave school and take up musical studies instead...More and more I came to think that music and art were just luxuries and of little real use...Towards the end of secondary education, the idea of studying medicine grew within me. I thought this might be more useful, more humane...

This stage of development of my psyche and the described ambivalence both reached at the time of graduation remained unchanged ...

Tolstoy's world and thinking, *his political and consistent activities* fascinated ... Tolstoy was inspired by Heinrich Pestalozzi, especially with regard to Pestalozzi's social and political writings ... Gandhi and Tolstoy ... exchanged numerous letters ... Gandhi's thoughts were crucial to Martin Luther King, Jr., and Mandela and many others ... Pestalozzi's thinking does not persist as ideas and words, but becomes relevant in its realization. The most difficult, as Gandhi told, is the way that leads from the idea to the doing (realization).

There is no peace without justice! ...

Thirty years of war with three and half years of genocide under the terror of the Khmer Rouge devastated Cambodia. Today there is no war in Cambodia. However, there is no justice, either ...

Over the years, millions of children have been treated free of charge and 850,000 have been hospitalized free of charge within our five Kantha Bopha hospitals. These are places of justice. There is no corruption. The poor, that is to say, 80 per cent of the people, and the rich are both entitled to be cured ... Without these infrastructures of justice, there would be 90,000 deaths per year[28] ...

In health matters, it is my daily experience that the wealthy world, indeed, does not use measures of justice in dealing with the politics of health and the question of the survival of the poor in poor countries. The international community, including official Switzerland, promotes the creed that medical facilities, medical procedures and treatment resources must conform to the economical reality of a given country. For 80 per cent of Cambodia's population, the economical 'reality' is zero. If we were to follow that creed, we would be unable to cure any child with Dengue fever nor any child with tuberculosis ...

The other creed of the international community is that the patient or the patient's parent should pay for treatment. 80 per cent of Cambodians, however, have no money.

Over the past years, the attitude of the health sector of the Swiss Department for Development and Cooperation in Bern, of the WHO in Geneva and of various NGOs has been disappointing. They all monopolize the pity felt for the poor of this world. However, the mandate is not pity, but to fight for and implement justice ...

Our activity is not aid, but restoration of justice ... '[29]

## Kantha Bopha's strategy versus international aid agencies

Dr Richner was very critical of international aid agencies such as the WHO and other international health organizations in Cambodia. These organizations believed that they had seen countless unorthodox humanitarian agencies fall by the wayside, when the funding for their donor-heavy projects ran out. 'I can think of at least three or four other great individual initiatives in Cambodia that have atrophied when donor funding has dropped off,' says one long-standing NGO worker in Phnom Penh. 'It would be nice to think that someone else would come in to the fill the gap if funding drops off, but you can't just assume that.'

Ben Bland, a *Financial Times* journalist, pointed out that NGO workers in Cambodia were reluctant to speak against Dr Richner, so as not to escalate the tension, as well as to avoid adverse publicity at a time when the Cambodian government was planning to legislate a law on NGOs that might restrict their ability to operate in the country.[30]

The tension even led to death threats and a situation as extreme as that in 1995 when the Health Ministry tried to close Dr Richner's hospital on the grounds that it was undermining the attempts to build a national health system, and the King had to intervene personally to prevent this from happening.[31]

Dr Richner let off 'steam' by expressing his frank opinion on the aid agencies:

'In (UNICEF's) Child Survival Report Card... Cambodia is reported to be a country where the under-5 mortality rate has increased since 1990.

... let me explain why this information on increasing child mortality by UNICEF is wrong, why UNICEF's strategy in the health sector in Cambodia is not only inefficient but dangerous...

... who can tell you the figures for child mortality in Cambodia in 1990 or 1980 or 1975? At this time, access to many regions was not possible for different reasons... nobody can compare any actual figures with figures from 1990.

... these very figures were reported to the media in Phnom Penh on 2 June 2004. But this so-called report is based on mere estimates for the years 1998/1999.

In 1999, we opened our third hospital in Angkor, in the north of Cambodia, the Jayavarman VII Hospital. In the last 12 months, 25,000 severely sick children were hospitalized there. 80 per cent of these children would have died without this hospital...

Since 1998, the hospitalization rate in Phnom Penh (Kantha Bopha I and II) has increased by 35 per cent every year. During the past 12 months, we hospitalized 45,000 severely sick children in Phnom Penh. 80 per cent of these children could not have survived without hospitalization.

So the child mortality rate in Cambodia has not increased.

Excellency, in 1998, UNICEF's representative in Siem Reap province told people on Swiss Television (the Swiss are the main donors for the Kantha Bopha hospitals) that the Jayavarman VII Hospital, then under construction, was not necessary. The needs were covered by 10 health centres managed by UNICEF, so the Swiss people were told... In the last 12 months, 22,000 children more would have died in Cambodia without this hospital that opened in 1999 in Siem Reap, and UNICEF thought this hospital was not necessary. This error was never corrected or excused by UNICEF... UNICEF thinks that the way we are doing our job together with 1,500 well-trained Cambodian employees is wrong – not adequate for the economical reality of the country. Most childhood deaths occur for simple reasons, they are telling you. That is why you have to perform simple medicine, which is not expensive. This philosophy of UNICEF and the WHO is wrong, and that is the reason why the health situation in Cambodia is still so bad ...

Frequent and fatal stories about pregnant mothers not being operated on because of no electricity, because the money for diesel for the generator had been stolen, about mothers or sick children not being transferred to our centre until there was money for diesel for the ambulance that the families had to borrow ...

On June 2 UNICEF told the media in Phnom Penh that you must 'refocus on simple, low tech and doable interventions.' This is exactly what UNICEF has been doing for 13 years without any effectiveness ...

And this strategy is dangerous. They use cheap and dangerous drugs and medicines forbidden for children in the so-called civilized world, where they are still produced for the poor world countries and stocked in the central pharmacy of UNICEF in Copenhagen ... They implement simplified medical protocols ignoring the main killers of Cambodia's children: tuberculosis and others.

The success of Kantha Bopha hospitals with their low mortality rate of 1.2 per cent is first explained by the transfer of technology and by the transfer of correct drugs and medicines, allowing correct diagnosis and treatment, and second by excluding deadly corruption ... All is free of charge. We give money to the families for their travel costs, too ...

... Wrong figures are distributed and blindly accepted ... (80 per cent of the international organizations' money is for their employees' salaries). This spirit of intellectual corruption with its severe consequences ... must be changed ...'[32]

### Appeal to the President of the International Court of Justice and Human Rights

'... the passive genocide of Cambodia's children called for a change in the WHO's and other organizations' policy and strategy – poor medicine for poor people in poor countries.

Up to now nothing has changed.

Even worse: representatives of the UN and other organizations try to ... undermine activities for carrying out correct diagnosis and correct treatment of suffering children. The WHO told ... the media that Kantha Bopha was wrong; its conception was wrong, too expensive in relation to the health budget in Cambodia.

In 2008, Kantha Bopha I and II have hospitalized 28,000 very sick children. In 2007 there was an epidemic of Dengue fever. In Cambodia, 12,400 cases were registered. Among these, 10,000 cases were hospitalized in Kantha

Bopha. 60 per cent arrived in shock. So, 60 per cent would have died without Kantha Bopha; only 1.5 per cent actually died...

...what would have happened without the facilities of Kantha Bopha hospitals? You cannot manage it in a cheaper way...a haemorrhagic shock has to be treated by blood transfusion. If you do not spend money for the tests (US$500,000 per year, US$50 per blood bottle...), you contaminate the children with HIV and hepatitis...

On 31 March 1999, we opened a third children's hospital in Siem Reap. Representatives of UNICEF and the Swiss Red Cross told the media several times not to build this hospital...Representatives of the DEZA (Direktion für Entwicklung und Zusammenarbeit, a section of the Swiss Foreign Ministry) were opposed to this hospital. They call it subversion of the current health system (created and managed by the WHO).

Since 31 March 1999, we have hospitalized 3,800 very sick children there. 80 per cent would have died without the hospital. 80 per cent would have died if the policy and statements of these representatives had been followed...Children as thin as those seen in concentration camps. Malnourished not because of lack of food but because of chronic tuberculosis, some suffering from the severest forms of tuberculosis: meningitis, pott, miliaris...

At times the representatives of the WHO and UNICEF defend themselves by denying their own responsibility: 'the responsibility lies in the hands of the Ministry of Health. We are consultants.' But by these public statements...it becomes obvious: they are culprits.

It is a crime to continue this system. A crime against humanity.

...according to Article 34, paragraph 1, of the Statute of the Court of Justice and Human Rights, only states may be the parties in cases before the Court.

In a letter from the Ministry of Health (April 1995) addressed to Cambodia's two Prime Ministers, the Ministers of Domestic and Foreign Affairs, in a letter engineered by the WHO, Kantha Bopha was declared a state in the state not following the protocols...So the UN Organization of Health considers Kantha Bopha a state.

...So please accept the following statement of claim...'[33]

## Kantha Bopha in the battle against poverty

'Farmers need to borrow money to pay for the healer, private doctors or those in pitiful official hospitals and for medicines. Eventually they are forced to sell their herds and the land...for growing rice crops. Their livelihoods are in tatters, the land is no longer tilled and becomes desolate...and all without having helped the sick relative: 80 per cent of the medicines available in Cambodia are imitations and therefore ineffective, 20 per cent are even toxic...

Kantha Bopha treats all children free of charge. All medicines used meet correct, Western standards...Kantha Bopha also saves these people's children – the next generations in a country that suffered atrocious genocide under the Khmer Rouge...'[34]

## Not for help but for reparation

'While in 1969, Cambodia's health system was superior to that of Singapore and Kuala Lumpur, its subsequent annihilation, along with its elite, mentality and infrastructure, has been orchestrated by the ignominious intervention of 1970. This so-called secret war led by Mr Kissinger and Mr Nixon provoked the civil war with the terrifying dominance of the Khmer Rouge. The Khmer Rouge was supported by numerous foreign governments. And, from 1979 until 1992, immediately after the Vietnamese occupation of the major part of Cambodia to liberate them from the Khmer Rouge terror, the Reagan Administration conceded an annual support of US$100 million.

The humanitarian and moral request, therefore, is not for help but for reparation.

Until the international support is realized, it will be exclusively your contribution to the Kantha Bopha Foundation that allows for annually preventing 80,000 children from avoidable suffering and death or from lifelong disability.'[35]

## Personal Life

A German paper[36] judged that Dr. Richner had never been integrated into the local way of life and did not speak the local language. According to them, Dr. Richner often spent his evenings alone practicing the cello. 'In such a chaotic country you either become an alcoholic or a reader and I became a reader,' Dr. Richner told the paper. He also emphasized that 'he was not a good person but was just a prisoner of his conscience.' He also had bodyguards.

## Succession Plan

Dr. Richner jokingly told a British journalist that he would only start to think of his succession plan when he had managed to raise funds estimated by him at around $200 million to support Kantha Bopha's activities for 20 years.[37]

A German newspaper[38] opined that the hospitals would stand or fall with Dr. Richner himself, and cited Burkhard Wilke of the German Central Institute for Social Issues: 'The charity can quickly end up in a dead end when the main actor disappears.' The paper also revealed the WHO's scepticism for the same reason.

## Wrapping up

On the night of the concert Richner looked tired. He had been burdened with an obviously never-ending struggle to find money, and this weighed heavily on him. After a few cursory bows before appreciative applause, Dr. Richner quickly disappeared backstage.

Half an hour later he appeared in the corridor leading to the exit to greet lingering supporters, donors and medical students. But he appeared uncomfortable. His timidity made him feel very awkward when talking to his audience. Despite it Dr. Richner had to go to Switzerland two or three times a year for concerts. He had not had a holiday in 17 years and never really had a day off.[39]

Dr. Richner felt anguished, wondering how, if he were to be no longer there for any natural cause, the hospitals would be maintained, and who would take charge of collecting donations and managing the hospitals so that sick and poor Cambodian children were not left unprotected.

## Appendix A2.5.1: Cambodia and her neighbouring countries

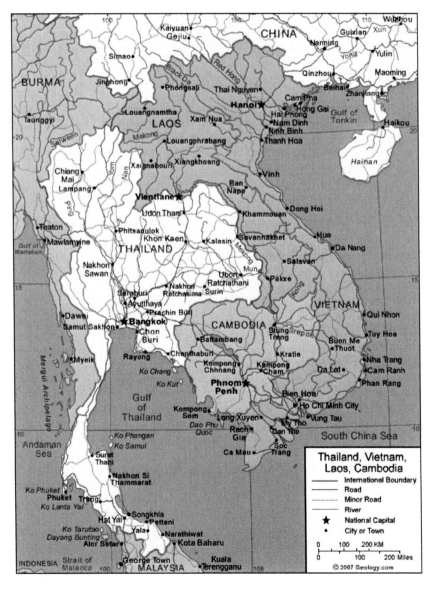

## Appendix A2.5.2: Main macroeconomic data (as known at the third quarter, 2009)

GDP (purchasing power parity):
$27.95 billion (2008 est.)
$26.62 billion (2007)
$24.15 billion (2006)
*Note*: Data are in 2008 US dollars.

GDP (official exchange rate):
$10.3 billion (2008 est.)

GDP – real growth rate:
6.8% (2008 est.)
10.2% (2007 est.)
10.8% (2006 est.)

GDP – per capita:
$2,000 (2008 est.)
$1,900 (2007 est.)
$1,800 (2006 est.)
*Note*: Data are in 2008 US dollars.

GDP – composition by sector:
Agriculture: 29%
Industry: 30%
Services: 41% (2007 est.)

Labour force:
8.6 million (2008 est.)

Labour force – by occupation:
Agriculture: 75%
Industry: NA%
Services: NA% (2004 est.)

Unemployment rate:
3.5% (2007 est.)

Household income or consumption by percentage share:
Lowest 10%: 2.9%
Highest 10%: 34.8% (2004)

Inflation rate (consumer prices):
20.2% (2008 est.)

Agriculture – products:
Rice, rubber, corn, vegetables, cashews, tapioca, silk

Industries:
Tourism, garments, construction, rice milling, fishing, wood and wood products, rubber, cement, gem mining, textiles

Industrial production growth rate:
8.4% (2008 est.)

Current account balance:
–$1.27 billion (2008 est.)

Exports:
$4.616 billion f.o.b. (2008 est.)

Exports – commodities:
Clothing, timber, rubber, rice, fish, tobacco, footwear

Exports – partners:
US 58.1%, Germany 7.3%, UK 5.2%, Canada 4.6%, Vietnam 4.5% (2007)

Imports:
$6.424 billion f.o.b. (2008 est.)

Imports – commodities:
Petroleum products, cigarettes, gold, construction materials, machinery, motor vehicles, pharmaceutical products

Imports – partners:
Thailand 23.1%, Vietnam 16.9%, China 15%, Hong Kong 10.4%, Singapore 7.5%, Taiwan 7.2%, South Korea 4.8% (2007)

Reserves of foreign exchange and gold:
$2.375 billion (31 December 2008 est.)

Debt – external:
$4.317 billion (31 December 2008 est.)

Exchange rates:
Riels (KHR) per US dollar – 4,070.94 (2008 est.), 4,006 (2007), 4,103 (2006), 4,092.5 (2005), 4,016.25 (2004)

*Note*: The information regarding Cambodia on this page is re-published from the 2009 World Fact Book of the United States Central Intelligence Agency. No claims are made regarding the accuracy of Cambodia Economy 2009 information contained here. All suggestions for corrections of any errors about Cambodia Economy 2009 should be addressed to the CIA.

### Appendix A2.5.3: Cambodia's sanitary situation

More than one third of Cambodians live below the poverty line, struggling to survive on less than $1 a day. Poverty is especially pervasive in rural areas and among children, who constitute more than half of the country's population.

### Issues facing children in Cambodia

- Cambodia has the highest infant and under-five mortality rates in the region, at 97 and 141 per 1,000 live births, respectively. Vaccine-preventable diseases, diarrhoea, and respiratory infections are among the leading causes of childhood death. Maternal mortality is also high.
- Malnutrition affects most Cambodian children: 45% show moderate or severe stunting.
- Primary school enrolment rates are high, with a declining gender gap. But so many children repeat grades that it takes on average more than 10

years to complete primary school. Less than half of all students make it that far.

* Accidental death, for example as a result of traffic accidents or drowning, is a serious threat to children in Cambodia.
* Landmines pose a grave hazard for internally migrating children and youths who attempt to salvage unexploded ordnance and sell it as valuable scrap metal.

## Activities and results for children

* Even though immunization rates declined slightly in 2005, vaccination campaigns have significantly reduced incidence of tetanus and measles. Coverage against hepatitis B was expanded nationally. Cambodia has been polio-free since 2000.
* The spread of HIV/AIDS may be coming under control, thanks to a dramatic increase in HIV counselling, testing and education programs focusing on prevention. Life-saving antiretroviral therapy is being provided to 10,000 people (including 1,000 children) who have AIDS.
* UNICEF provided de-worming tablets to 95% of children in primary school.
* Production of iodized salt has ramped up in the past two years. Nearly three quarters of households now use iodized salt.
* Many UNICEF pilot projects are scaling up to serve additional communities. A child rights training program serving 130 locales has been adopted by the Ministry of the Interior. UNICEF's Child-Friendly Schools initiative, which improves learning outcomes, has been extended to more than 500 schools. And the national education agenda has incorporated UNICEF's 'school readiness' model.
* Community preschool classes benefited 12,000 children under age five in nearly 100 communities.
* UNICEF and its partners built latrines, dug wells and tested drinking water for arsenic, improving access to safe water and sanitation for thousands of families.
* Cambodia's legislature passed the Prevention of Domestic Violence and Protection of Victims Law in 2005.
* After four people died from H5N1 avian influenza (bird flu), UNICEF helped to coordinate strategies for vaccinations and public education to prevent an epidemic.
* UNICEF and its partners destroyed 6,000 mines and 17,000 pieces of unexploded ordnance, and educated 400,000 children (both in and out of school) about avoiding landmines.

**Basic indicators**

| | |
|---|---:|
| Under-5 mortality rank | 40 |
| Under-5 mortality rate, 1990 | 119 |
| Under-5 mortality rate, 2007 | 91 |
| Infant mortality rate (under 1), 1990 | 87 |
| Infant mortality rate (under 1), 2007 | 70 |
| Neonatal mortality rate, 2004 | 48 |
| Total population (thousands), 2007 | 14444 |
| Annual no. of births (thousands), 2007 | 382 |
| Annual no. of under-5 deaths (thousands), 2007 | 35 |
| GNI per capita (US$), 2007 | 540 |
| Life expectancy at birth (years), 2007 | 59 |
| Total adult literacy rate (%), 2000–2007* | 76 |
| Primary school net enrolment/ attendance (%), 2000–2007* | 90 |
| % share of household income 1995–2005*, lowest 40% | 17 |
| % share of household income 1995–2005*, highest 20% | 50 |

*Source*: Unicef (http://www.unicef.org/infobycountry/cambodia_2190.html, accessed on 29th October 2009).

## Appendix A2.5.4: The WHO in Cambodia

Cooperation between the World Health Organization and Cambodia began in 1953, focusing on such projects as malaria control and maternal and child health. The programme expanded but was suspended from 1975 until 1980, when periodic technical consultation and other forms of support for some programmes (rehabilitation of the water and sanitation works in Phnom Penh; prevention and control of diseases such as malaria, diarrhoea, tuberculosis; development of human resources with specific focus on medical education and nursing) were extended by the WHO to the country under the auspices of UNICEF or the International Committee for the Red Cross (ICRC). In March 1991 a WHO office was re-established in Phnom Penh and a new programme of support was initiated. In May 2000 the WHO team consisted of 70 people, including 20 internationally recruited professional staff members and 10 volunteers. In 2000/01 the country budget was US$6.7 million, including an estimated US$3.7 million in extra-budgetary funds. About 60 per cent of the budget is for technical assistance and other personnel.

### Key programme areas

Key areas where the WHO provides support include:

- *Health Sector Reform*: a team, funded jointly by DFID, NORAD, UNDP and the WHO, works to strengthen the capacity of the national health administration to manage existing health services, improve the national health system and plan for future health system development; to support prioritization of healthcare needs; and to establish effective coordination mechanisms at national and provincial level, (including a sector-wide approach), in order to make better use of external resources to the health sector. One aim is to achieve a strengthened rural health infrastructure, capable of providing quality basic health services to the majority of the population.

- *Human Resources for Health*: to increase Ministry of Health (MoH) capacity in health workforce planning, production and utilization; to improve coordination, relevance, effectiveness and efficiency of basic training programmes for all professionals, especially physicians and nurses/midwives; and to strengthen the coordinated system for continuing education of all health professionals.
- *Malaria and Dengue Haemorrhagic Fever Control*: support is given to the National Malaria Programme, through the Roll Back Malaria initiative, to reduce mortality and morbidity associated with malaria in Cambodia, and to increase institutional capacity to control mosquito-borne diseases.
- *Essential Drugs*: to assist the MoH in developing a long-term drug policy, and ensuring the availability of vaccines and the rational use of essential drugs, at all levels of the health care system. The intended outcome is to assure the quality, safety and efficacy of locally produced and imported drugs and vaccines.
- The planning and implementation of *a National Integrated Management of Childhood Illness* strategy: this will build government capacity to reduce mortality and morbidity from the main causes of disease in children below five years of age, including acute respiratory infections particularly pneumonia, diarrhoeal diseases, measles, dengue haemorrhagic fever, malaria and malnutrition in young children.
- *The National Immunization Programme,* in close partnership with UNICEF: to reduce morbidity and mortality from diphtheria, pertussis, tetanus, measles, poliomyelitis and tuberculosis by providing immunization against these diseases for every child in Cambodia, with the introduction of Hepatitis B immunization and injection safety. The eradication of poliomyelitis was certified in 2000.
- Capacity strengthening of the Ministry of Health and a national *AIDS programme*: to reduce HIV transmission and the morbidity and mortality associated with HIV infection, and to introduce a syndromic approach to the management of sexually transmitted diseases.
- *Environmental Health:* the WHO is promoting healthy settings, helping the Government to monitor water quality and strengthening capacity for training and management in water and sanitation.
- *Nutrition, Maternal and Child Health, Prevention of Blindness, Mental Health, Leprosy, and Blood Transfusion Service:* the WHO provides substantial support to the Government through consultants and staff.

- *A variety of coordinating mechanisms,* sub committees and working groups.
- Members of the WHO team have actively contributed to Common Country Assessment and UNDAF activities, to the Programme of Administrative Reform, and to working groups set up to monitor activities following the Consultative Group meetings. They are active in UN system theme groups, especially that on HIV/AIDS. They also participate in joint reviews and planning missions of other external partners. They are supporting the Government's response to the need to develop a Poverty Reduction Strategy paper. All members of the team have a responsibility to share information, particularly technical information available through the WHO, and all play a role in advocacy.

*Source*: WHO Country Policy: Cambodia, April 2001.

# Annex 2.6

# Banco Santander
## CEOs as leaders and strategy designers[1]

### The global financial crisis in September 2008

In keeping with its mission statement to consolidate as a large international financial group providing an increasingly high return to its shareholders, Spain's Banco Santander (with a market value of €92.5bn at end-2007) was busy acquiring other banks in September 2008 amid the turmoil in the world's financial markets. It all began when the Federal Housing Finance Agency (FHFA) announced, on 7 September 2008, it was to place two US Government-sponsored enterprises (GSEs), Fannie Mae (Federal National Mortgage Association) and Freddie Mac (Federal Home Loan Mortgage Corporation) into conservatorship run by the FHFA, and was aggravated when Lehman Brothers, an investment bank, filed for bankruptcy on 14 September after the Federal Reserve Bank declined to participate in creating a financial support facility for it. (See Appendix A2.6.1, for Banco Santander's financial statements.)

The *New York Times* pointed out on 26 October 2008 that 'the banks that are surviving the best today, the ones that are buying others and not being bought – like JPMorgan Chase or Banco Santander, based in Spain – are not surviving because they were better regulated than the banks across the street but because they were better run. Their leaders were more vigilant about their risk exposure than any regulator required them to be.'

On 14 October, 2008 Spain's top newspaper *El País* published an article about Santander's intention to acquire Philadelphia's Sovereign Bank in which the Spanish bank already had a 24.35 per cent stake.[2]

The acquisition would be carried out by the exchange of shares at the rate of one Santander share for 3.42 of Sovereign's, which meant the US bank would be valued at US$ 2.53bn. Santander's payment would amount to US$ 1.90bn, equivalent to 2 per cent of the Spanish bank's shares, a much lower amount than the US$ 2.39bn paid for 19.8 per cent of the shares in 2006.

At about the same time, Emilio Botín, the bank's chairman and a major shareholder, launched a diatribe against the attempt by several European governments to nationalize banks in the light of the financial crisis. In Botín's view, the 'excesses' of different economic players in the market are to blame.[3] In his speech at the bank group's First Conference of International Banking organized in Madrid on 16 October 2008, Botín emphasized the need to assess clients and their products, not to accept a disproportionate level of indebtedness, and to carry out an adequate evaluation of risks and the economic and financial cycles. It was obvious that his bank was prepared to buck the prevailing pessimistic trend in the market.

How could the Spanish bank allow itself such a contrarian movement when world investors were for selling instead of buying, and many major banks were hoping for government money as a godsend? Could Santander be an exception to the dismal outlook in the financial world's panorama?

## Spanish banking industry: historical background[4]

The Spanish banking industry had to undergo a drastic deregulation process during two decades which ended in 1987.[5]

The regulations imposed in 1941 to ban the opening of new branches and banks and to thwart competition in interest rates were lifted in 1971. Until then, banks were also forced to freeze a substantial part of their assets in illiquid investments, mostly in the public sector.

Overall, these restraints led to a fairly inefficient financial system. Public investments at very low interest rates made by the banks had a crowding-out effect on credit to the private sector. Holders of savings and demand deposits earned virtually no interest on their accounts. Under such conditions, no money or debt market could exist.

By the late 1970s, the Spanish banking industry had 120 private banks even without counting savings banks (*cajas de ahorros*) and state-owned banks, though the seven largest commercial banks accounted for more than half of the total bank deposits.

In those years, SMEs (small and medium-sized enterprises) had no easy access to long-term loans, which led to the creation of official credit institutions aimed at filling this gap.

The savings banks were non-profit institutions lending to farmers, small businesses and household savers. With the establishment of democracy in Spain in 1976, Spain opted for a federal regime leading to the empowerment of the savings banks because they converted themselves into an auxiliary of the regional executive powers.

The liberalization of the rules on the opening of new branches in 1971 was a fundamental move because the Spanish banks were retail banks, and it was nearly impossible to attract new customers without amendments to the regulations. The move was followed by the liberalization of the opening of new banks and some of the interest rates in 1974, and the entry of foreign banks in 1977.

After some drawbacks in this liberalization and deregulation process in 1982 due to the increase in government-imposed, obligatory investment coefficients from 27 per cent to 52 per cent to make up for soaring public deficits, all interest rates and commission were liberalized and a programme to gradually eliminate the investment coefficients was put forward in 1987. Two important measures to protect the customer were introduced: first, a service to process the complaints filed with the Bank of Spain by the bank's customers, and second, banks were obliged to inform their clients about the true interest rates of all their products.

Parallel to the liberalization process, institutional and market structures were improved.

In 1988, the *Comisión Nacional del Mercado de Valores* (CNMV – National Commission of Market Values, the stock market regulator) was created to supervise stock market institutions, intermediaries and issuers with the aim of ensuring transparency, safety and efficiency.

The money market barely existed in the late 1970s, with just a few commercial banks borrowing from the cash-rich savings banks, rather like a network of personal relationships between bank treasuries.

The money market began to take off when a group of four banks joined forces, followed by some other banks a few years later. In 1985, commercial papers were sold on the wholesale market for the first time.

Public debt soared from 12 per cent of GNP in 1976 to 60 per cent in 1994. During these years, the Government forced the banks to finance its deficit at very low costs but in the late 1980s, it turned to the Bank of Spain to fulfil its needs at zero cost. This crowded out private credit. The Government attempted to create the public debt market. After a substantial increase in commissions to the banks, it managed to achieve this.

In 1989, unlike the Government-initiated creation of the monetary and public debt markets, the derivative market was set up, thanks to the initiative of a group of banks.

The development of all these markets brought Spain's financial system on a par with the best in continental Europe in terms of scope and efficiency.

The impact of the deregulation process took place in three waves. First, competition induced a crisis among the Spanish financial institutions. Second, financial restructuring led to mergers and modernization. Third, as a consequence, the banks developed the international market in Latin America.

In the first wave, the banking crisis broke in 1978 (and lasted until 1985) with the failure of a small local bank, Banco de Navarra. The Government set up the FGD (*Fondo de Garantía de Depósitos*) to insure deposits up to a certain level, similar to the FDI in the US.

The majority of banks refrained from participating in the FGD rescue scheme, though larger banks had to acquire smaller banks as in the case of Banesto (Banco Español de Crédito), the largest bank, which took over three banks between 1977 and 1982. The botched restructuring of the three banks led the governor of the Bank of Spain to force the resignation of Banesto's CEO, replacing him with a former governor of the central bank in 1986.

The second wave took the shape of mergers and acquisitions of banks between 1987 and 1999. Out of it emerged two world-class banks: Santander and BBVA (Banco de Bilbao Vizcaya Argentaria). The wave was triggered by Santander launching a highly-remunerated current account in 1989. The offer of over 20 per cent per annum interest yield on demand deposits caught its competitors by surprise, some of which were forced by the troubled and ill-prepared Banesto to seek shelter through mergers with other banks.

The third wave landed the Spanish banks in Latin America. This internationalization process started in 1995 when Spain's banking industry became increasingly aware that its home market was mature and competitive, and its prospects for growth were fading.

According to a study, deregulation contributed to the improvement of productivity on the whole. Between 1991 and 1994, deregulation contributed to the growth of TFP (Total Factor Productivity),[6] a variable that accounts for effects in total output not caused by inputs or economies of scale, by 0.56 per cent every year in the case of commercial banks out of its total yearly growth of 2.24 per cent, and by 0.11 per cent in the case of savings banks out of its total yearly growth of 1.75 per cent.[7]

By 2000, Santander had become the largest banking group in Latin America with total assets of over US$86 bn, and BBVA the second largest with around US$68 bn, surpassing Citibank's US$60 bn.

Investment in Latin America offered four main advantages for Spanish banks:

1. higher profit margin than in Spain;
2. substantial growth potential;
3. feasible amount of required investment for the Spanish banks;
4. ease of working in the same language and a similar culture.

## Banco Santander: its background, structure, business model, and top executives

### Background

When in 1986 Emilio Botín was appointed Chairman of the then Banco de Santander, established by one of his ancestors in 1857, his bank was ranked sixth in the elite-club Spanish banking industry and 152nd in the world. The focus among banks was on profitability rather than size. See Table A2.6.1A and Table A2.6.1B.

In 1989, the bank launched the highly remunerated demand deposit account named '*Supercuenta Santander*', which opened up the financial sector to competition and changed the status quo of the Spanish banking map.

*Table A2.6.1A* Market share change of the seven largest banks in Spain, 1985–2005 (percentage)

| 1985* | | 2005* | |
|---|---|---|---|
| Central | 9.57 | Santander | 40.25 |
| Banesto | 8.88 | BBVA | 29.72 |
| Bilbao | 7.51 | Popular | 8.34 |
| Hispanoamericano | 7.51 | Sabadell | 5.61 |
| Vizcaya | 6.30 | Bankinter | 3.98 |
| Santander | 5.35 | Barclays | 1.99 |
| Popular | 3.55 | Pastor | 1.87 |
| Total | 48.68 | Total | 91.72 |

* The market share of the total assets in Spain's financial system.
*Source*: Kase and Jacopin (2007: p. 51).

The previous year, 1988, Santander had established a strategic alliance with the Royal Bank of Scotland and together they took over ABN-Amro in consortium with Fortis, a Dutch and Belgian enterprise, in 2007.

In 1994, Santander acquired Banesto which made it one of the leading players in the Spanish financial system.

In 1995, the bank unleashed an aggressive inroad into the Latin American market by developing business in Argentina, Brazil, Colombia, Mexico, Peru and Venezuela in addition to Chile, Puerto Rico and Uruguay.

The first inroad between 1996 and 1998 in the wake of privatizations of state-controlled entities began with the acquisition of Banco de Venezuela and Banco Río in Argentina in 1997. The same year, Santander also bought a stake in a Mexican bank. This first foray ended with the purchase of Banco General de Comercio y Noroeste in Brazil.

In 1999, Banco Santander and BCH (Banco Central Hispano) merged to become Banco Santander Central Hispano (BSCH) and subsequently bought Totta y Açores and Crédito Predial Portugués, financial groups in Portugal. After some post-merger squabbling was settled, agreement was reached with two BCH top executives about their severance payments and Botín assumed the helm.[8]

The bank's buying binge was followed by the acquisition of Banespa in Brazil for €8.23 bn, Grupo Serafín in Mexico for €2.32 bn and Banco Santiago in Chile for €2.18 bn.

It should be pointed out that the bank's expansion in Latin America was not made on the spur of the moment to take advantage of speculative movements, but rather in the expectation that the region would offer great opportunities on account of its high economic growth potential.

The expansion in Europe was undertaken at two levels: first with Santander Consumer, a group company specializing in consumer finance especially

*Table A2.6.1B*  The Spanish banking sector: major items in the profit and loss account

| | 2006 | | 2007 | | 2008* | | ROA | On the total national net result |
|---|---|---|---|---|---|---|---|---|
| *Savings banks* | | | | | | | | |
| Intermediation margin | 7,854 | 73% | 11,601 | 76% | 10,395 | 73% | | |
| Financial operations results | 565 | 5% | 1,020 | 7% | 1,328 | 9% | | |
| Ordinary margin | 10,751 | 100% | 15,220 | 100% | 14,321 | 100% | | |
| Operational margin | 5,257 | 49% | 9,221 | 61% | 7,773 | 54% | | |
| Loss due to asset impairment | 1,443 | 13% | 1,951 | 13% | 3,287 | 23% | | |
| Provisions | 243 | 2% | 242 | 2% | 108 | 1% | | |
| Net result | 3,183 | 30% | 6,558 | 43% | 4,268 | 30% | 0.34% | 36.87% |
| *Banks* | | | | | | | | |
| Intermediation margin | 8,014 | 63% | 10,331 | 64% | 11,497 | 66% | | |
| Financial operations results | 1,063 | 8% | 1,505 | 9% | 1,863 | 11% | | |
| Ordinary margin | 12,893 | 100% | 16,127 | 100% | 17,547 | 100% | | |
| Operational margin | 7,274 | 56% | 9,955 | 62% | 10,958 | 62% | | |
| Loss due to asset impairment | 1,055 | 8% | 1,113 | 7% | 2,228 | 13% | | |
| Provisions | 373 | 3% | 119 | 1% | 632 | 4% | | |
| Net result | 5,611 | 44% | 7,684 | 48% | 7,398 | 42% | 0.52% | 63.13% |

*Source*: *Dinero*, No. 984, Nov. 2008, p. 20.
* January–October 2008.

for car purchases, and second by Santander itself developing its retail bank network.

Santander Group set up Santander Consumer in 2003 with the merger of the German CC-Bank, the Italian Finconsumo, Hispamer in Spain and others. By 2008, the consumer banking franchise had a presence in Spain, the

UK, Portugal, Italy, Germany, the Netherlands, Poland, the Czech Republic, Austria, Hungary, Norway, Sweden, the USA and Chile.

On 26 July, 2004, BSCH and Abbey National, the sixth largest bank in the UK announced the latter's acquisition by the former for which BSCH would pay £9.5 bn (or £6.50 per share). The UK bank was delisted and removed from the FTSE 100 Index on 12 November 2004 at close of trading, but BSCH was subsequently added as a secondary listing in 2005. Abbey National shareholders swapped one share in Abbey National for one of the Spanish bank's shares, and received a special cash dividend of 31 pence per share on 14 December 2004. BSCH took over 19.8 per cent of Sovereign Bancorp, the 18th biggest bank in the US in 2005. The following year, the bank made a record profit of €7.60 bn, the largest corporate profit ever gained by a Spanish company.

On 13 August, 2007, BSCH changed its legal name to Banco Santander.[9] The bank had 131,819 employees, 65.1 million customers, 11,178 branches and 2.27 million shareholders. Retail banking generated 82 per cent of the group's profit in 2007. The group was among the top ten banking organizations in the world and is the biggest bank in the Eurozone by market capitalization in 2007.[10]

## Organizational structure

Emilio Botín joined Banco de Santander in 1958 after graduating from the University of Deusto with a degree in law and economics. In 1964, aged 30, he was appointed Director General. In 1986, he followed his grandfather's and father's footsteps into the chairmanship of the bank. And the transformation of the entire banking industry in Spain ensued.

The other key leading figure at the bank is Alfredo Sáenz, CEO and Second Vice-Chairman. Born in 1942, he obtained a degree in economics from the University of Deusto. From 1958 to 1980 he worked for Tubacex, a steel pipe producer. Sáenz was hired by Pedro Toledo, Banco Vizcaya's top executive, as director of planning in 1980. Toledo sent him to rescue the failing Banca Catalana, which, thanks to Sáenz and his management team, soon became Spain's most profitable bank. After the merger of Banco Vizcaya with Banco de Bilbao to become Banco Bilbao Vizcaya (BBV, which was to merge with Argentaria in 1999), Toledo died. In December 1993, Sáenz was named president of Banco Español de Crédito (Banesto) which had failed and was under governmental supervision. Sáenz recruited many former Banco Vizcaya executives for his new task. By 1995, he had rescued Banesto which was turning in a profit and had halved the amount of bad loans. After the acquisition of Banesto by BCH, Sáenz joined BCH as its CEO in March 2002.

Appendix A2.6.2 on the Santander Group companies shows the bank's territorial and functional coverage, while Appendix A2.6.3 lists the key data for each principal segment.

The board is organized into six committees – Executive Committee, Risk Committee, Audit & Compliance Committee, Appointment and

Remuneration Committee, International Committee, and Technology, Productivity & Quality Committee.

The bank's top two executives, Emilio Botín and Alfredo Sáenz, only participate in three committees, but coincide in each of them: the Technology, Productivity, & Quality Committee, the Executive Committee and the International Committee. The Executive Committee is the most important of all, since all the powers of the Board of Directors have been permanently delegated to it except for some issues such as the approval of general strategies.

## Business model

According to the bank's annual report,[11]

1. '[Santander's] model is based on retail banking, backed by extensive distribution networks (branches, telephone, Internet, agents and so on).
2. Vertical strategy in retail banking: I believe that in the current scenario, the model of universal, transactional banking has been vindicated yet again, given its stability and cross-selling possibilities. This model was questioned in recent years, when lending was the 'star product.'
3. The importance of the universal banking model and of deposit franchises. That is, strong and competitive operations in attractive markets, rather than an alternative model of being in a very large number of countries but with little critical mass in each market. Being a significant force in retail banking also means having a significant presence in each local market.
4. Focus on commercial efficiency: our retail banking model enables us to generate revenue growth (based on boosting customer business) while, at the same time, keeping costs flat. This continuous improvement in productivity and efficiency is based, on one hand, on the advantages of our technological platform and, on the other, on our culture of continuously restructuring the operating areas. This enables us to achieve a good balance between investments in the long term and surpassing our targets (and the market's expectations) in the short term.
5. Exploit the advantages of size: We believe our global size must represent a source of competitive advantage which all our local units must exploit.'

Sáenz was quoted by *The Economist* magazine as asserting that 'excellent execution' (including its computer systems and good management of costs, people and risks), its decision to stick to commercial banking, and the fact that 'we haven't made big mistakes' are three things that have led to the bank's success.[12]

In an interview Sáenz spoke of his belief that the bank's operations were similar to the production process in factories and expressed his admiration for the Toyota Production System.[13]

The concentration on commercial banking does not preclude, nonetheless, the possession of a large investment portfolio in the manufacturing industries. The 30 per cent stake in Cepsa, a petroleum company, worth €5.22 bn at the market price of July 2007, is a case in point.[14]

## Growth strategy

In perfect harmony, Botín and Sáenz expressed their similar points of view regarding the management orientation centred on growth. Botín explained their growth orientation:

> You are never 100 per cent happy with what you have done, but obviously you have achieved certain targets. One piece of data: in 1987 our bank was in sixth position in the ranking of Spanish banks...The sky's the limit.... we are not going to stop growing. I think what's happening now worldwide, not only in Spain, Europe or the US, is the trend towards consolidation: we increasingly see larger, more important banks compared with the panorama twenty years ago. Globalization is accompanied by the banks playing a major role both nationally and internationally.[15]

while Sáenz emphasized the operational aspect of its implementation:

> Basically, the most important task of a manager is to establish a broad-based series of objectives in order to set the company on the right course with specific, quantifiable targets...based on knowledge of the market. Secondly, you have to align the organization and the team so they are focussing on this direction...Thirdly, you have to ensure excellent execution.[16]

As a matter of fact, in the bank's 2007 Annual Report, the word or concept most referred to by Botín and Sáenz was 'growth' (52 times) after 'the banking industry' (55 times). See Figure A2.6.1.

Before Botín took over the management, the bank had grown in a traditional way, both organically and through mergers and acquisitions (M&A). Uncertainties surrounding the banking business, the relative weakness of Spanish banks in terms of expertise and financial health compared to their foreign competitors, and the country's joining the EEC, clearly indicated it was time to focus on short to medium-term financial health. Some authors identified its strategic approach as a short-term, cash flow-based, operation-oriented profit-arithmetic (PA) approach:[17]

Short-term feasibility analysis is more important in the PA approach than in PIF.[18] However, this does not mean that a large amount of information is needed to make a decision. A PA manager knows what kind of information is relevant for every case and will demand that information.

Therefore, the factors shaping this approach are the CEO's professional and personal background, knowledge of the firm and its industry, business sense and the environmental situation.

PA business leaders make sense of the situation they face by looking for similar previous situations. Patterns learnt in the course of their business career have taught them how to endow meaning. The experience of prior success or failure guides them in their analysis, leading to feasible alternative solutions. The selected solution's goodness of fit is a function of the richness and variety of their experience.

However, when uncertainty is high or when the situation is completely new, PA managers make a decision based on their business sense.

Business sense is an important component of the PA approach. Kanagawa, a Japanese entrepreneur, consistent with existing literature on the resource-based view of the firm...holds that there are things one cannot do anything about – will and effort cannot change them.

Inspiration and luck are two of those things. A manager with a business sense is the one who has been lucky and inspired in key moments and has been able to take advantage of this.

The CEO's internal and external knowledge is key in a PA approach. A CEO must be aware of profit levers, that is, where there is waste that should be cut, where value is created and which areas need prioritizing. This knowledge allows them to take the right decisions. (See Appendix A2.6.4 on different business approaches and Appendix A2.6.5 on comparison with other business models).

Santander stressed the growth opportunities in Spain, the European and Latin American consumer sector, but also emphasized that its core competence centred on managing retail banking networks, their improvement through restructuring in which IT expertise plays a key role, and the entry into new markets to which its business model could be adapted. See Figure A2.6.2.

Typically, in the acquisition of Abbey National, Santander identified the opportunity to create value and benefit from two main aspects. First, by improving its efficiency ratio (expenses divided by income) difference – Abbey's 63 per cent compared to Santander's 52 per cent – and, in this, the use of IT systems was essential. Second, by creating new product silos in which Santander is already a main player and where the experience can be transferred easily to Abbey thanks to its current business sphere.

Alfredo Sáenz also stressed three aspects: the bank's wish to become a global player, customer orientation and continuous renewal. According to him, growth was in Santander's blood.

Regarding the first aspect, the globalization of competition and growth will strongly affect both the cost and income of the bank's Profit & Loss

Iterations = 8000

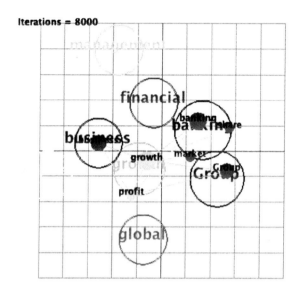

*Figure A2.6.1*   Content analysis of Botín's and Sáenz' messages in the 2007 annual report

*Source:* Authors.

account. For example, a data processing centre covering various national markets will be more efficient in terms of cost than one owned by a single national or local bank. Similarly, a global business unit handling bank cards for the whole world will accumulate strong know-how on the card business and the use of IT systems thanks to a steeper learning curve effect.

Second, focusing on customers comprises five 'principles' according to Sáenz. Quality of service recognizes the importance of long-term relations with the customer, since they are prioritized to 'maximize the present and future profit of the bank'. In retail banking, financial services are open to easy replication, whereas innovations are strictly controlled and channelled by regulatory bodies. Accordingly, only quality of service and a higher rate of product innovations can stabilize long-term relations with customers. Examples of the bank's innovation are the '*supercuenta*' (1989), the '*superdepósitos*' and '*superfondos*' (1991), the '*supercrédito vivienda*' (1992), the '*superhipoteca*' and '*superlibretas*' (1993), the '*superseguridad*' pension funds (2001), the '*depósito supersatisfacción*', the '*hipoteca superoportunidad*' and '*fondo superelección*' (2003), the '*supergestión*' fund and '*superoportunidad*' mortgage plan, (2004), and so on.

As to the third aspect, Sáenz considered technology as a necessary condition but not sufficient in itself, and advocates continuous 're-engineering' of the bank, showing a lot of interest in Toyota's production system, as he views the banking process as being similar to production in factories.

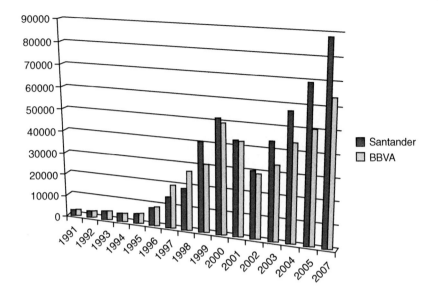

*Figure A2.6.2*    Market capitalization: Santander and BBVA (in million euros)

*Source*: Fernández and Carabias (2007). Creación de valor para los accionistas de bancos españoles (1991–2006), Working Paper (DI–680), IESE.

IT merits special attention in the development and growth of Santander, since it provided a competitive advantage, mainly due to the absence of legacy problems and its relatively early modernization at the end of the 1980s and early 1990s.

## Technology policy/IT systems

Sáenz had overseen Banesto's progress towards becoming a technologically highly advanced bank and Santander took advantage of at least some major elements of its IT strategy.

Three phases were envisaged. First, Sáenz aimed to control expense by the application of partial technology solutions.

Second, as cost savings were hampered by limits imposed by the official regulations and by differences in the national credit management system, the implementation of common IT systems was needed to simplify the business's technological architecture. Santander implemented IT systems in its branches in Latin America (called 'Altair') and in Europe (called 'Partenón'). Table A2.6.2 shows this development.

Through automatic handling of transactions, Partenón allowed access to resources for administrative purposes, flattened the back office structure and reduced the maintenance costs of obsolete information 'silo systems'.

*Table A2.6.2*   Evolution of IT systems at Grupo Santander

| Year | Concept |
| --- | --- |
| 2002 | • Partenón project initiated to modernize the group's IT systems in Spain and Europe and to reduce technology costs. |
| | • Altair project (a platform for Latin American operations) continued |
| 2003 | • Approval of Technology and Systems project to "increase the efficiency and improve service, making the IT system the core of it." |
| 2004 | • Appointment of CIO (Chief Information Technology officer) and Technology Strategy Committee chaired by the CEO. |
| | • Launch of Alhambra project to develop the future technology strategy of the group, based on Partenón and Altair platforms. |
| 2005 | • Partenón project completed in Spain. |
| | • Implementation of Alhambra project at Banesto. |
| | • Development of technology. |

*Source*: Elaborated from Banco Santander's annual reports.

'All of a customer's relationships with the bank, be it mortgages, deposits, cash management, cards, brokerage services, or insurance products, are automatically linked and immediately visible to bank employees. This leads to higher cross-sell ratios, higher levels of customer satisfaction and better operational performance'[19] and integrated customer management, short-time-to-market product development and information consistency and quality.[20]

Implementation of the Partenón project required moving its main banking systems onto the Banesto platform. Santander uses IBM mainframe architectures and IBM's DB2 database technology. It uses a single customer database, from Banesto, for all applications across the bank.

The Altair system was implemented in Banco Santander Chile, Banco Río de la Plata, Banco Venezuela, Banco Santander Colombia, Banco Santiago and Banco Santander Puerto Rico and Mexico. In 2001, US$925 m were spent on its development in contrast to US$610 m and US$500 m in 2005 and 2006, respectively.

The third phase introduced a new operational process architecture for cost saving and the enhancement of commercial activities. Three affiliated companies took care of information systems, production and support systems, and business process outsourcing, respectively.

A specialist at Accenture, a consultancy firm, held that 60 per cent of the top executives of European banks considered the Spanish banks to be the best equipped in terms of IT systems. Santander was considered the forerunner.[21] In stark contrast, 'the UK's banks, for example, still find it difficult to trace whether their current account customers also have savings products or mortgages in some other division of the same organization'.[22]

It should be noted, first, that Spanish banks made use of IT systems fundamentally to improve their back-office operations, rather than to differentiate their products and services. Clients benefit from IT systems by way of better service quality and not so much by external or apparent advantage of differentiated products and services. Between 1991 and 1994, 26 per cent of the productivity growth of commercial banks was explained by technological change, mainly by IT systems.[23]

Second, Santander, like BBVA, its rival bank, tended to take on proven technology in lieu of adopting a ground-breaking revolutionary technology. Immediate yield of advantage was their criterion for decision-making.

## Growth strategy and IT systems[24]

Integrating the business of one bank into the existing IT systems of the acquired bank is a daunting task because of their complex nature and the fact that the systems are business critical 24 hours a day. IT is one of the major fixed-cost items. Santander invested in a standardized IT platform, which enabled it to acquire banks and rationalize their IT systems.

Santander's growth strategy is predicated on the acquisition and integration of the acquired banks' IT operations into its in-house middleware (Banksphere).

This rationalizes IT and also leads to possible cross-selling opportunities, such that customer satisfaction and operational performances improve. For example, at Santander Consumer Finance in continental Europe, revenues from net fees increased 37 per cent in 2007 compared year-on-year, because of cross-selling.

The cross-selling was put into practice independently within each of Santander's business units, whereby the number of available products was increased, based on the experience gained in other markets and by applying the same strategies adopted in other markets for their sales. Sharing the customer database in other markets was avoided. Usually payroll accounts served as the starting point. Their account holders were provided with credit cards, consumer's credit, funds, mortgages and insurances. In Chile, for instance, between December 2006 and 2007, current account clients increased by 13.8 per cent, from 496,000 to 565,000. The number of current account clients subject to cross-selling increased from 339,000 in 2006 to 394,000 in 2007, a 16.2 per cent increase. In the same Chilean market, 40,000 SMEs were offered cross-selling in 2007, up 22 per cent from 2006.

Santander's platform uses a single database, which allows customer relationships with the bank to be automatically connected through a single view of customers (the information on corporate customers was shared, but not that of private individual customers). Unlike many other banks, compartmentalized silo IT systems and databases were shunned.

In the event of a takeover, a strong IT system will ease the acquisition of a target bank with a less developed system. A banker in Spain claimed that

6 to 15 points difference in the efficiency ratio could offset the acquisition cost. Moreover, cost could be cut in software licensing, software maintenance, data centre and communications.

At the time of Santander's takeover of Abbey in 2004, cost savings of £300 m were estimated as a result of performance improvements provided by the new IT systems, since 'Abbey was a creaking mass of IT platforms. In the Glasgow headquarters of its life assurance subsidiaries, for example, there were 18 different computer systems in operation at the time Santander took control'.[25] During the integration of the British bank, Santander consolidated all customer records into a single database and replaced obsolete legacy systems.

An analyst at Towergroup, a firm of IT consultants, suggested that 'it was highly likely that Santander would continue to spend on its IT systems ... (since) because of its previous investment in Partenón, it had the ability to grow very quickly because it was easier to integrate other banks' IT.'

## Operational efficiency and IT systems

Operational efficiency is a distinguishing feature of Santander as well as BBVA, its rival in Spain. Commoditization and securitization processes in the financial sector take heavy tolls on the financial institution's coffers.

As shown in Table A2.6.3, Spain has positioned itself as the top runner. Santander has shown constant improvement – from 62.1 in 1998 to 44.22 in 2007. See Tables A2.6.4 and A2.6.5 for financial and operating ratios.

*Table A2.6.3*  Efficiency ratio in Europe

|    |         | 1997  |    |         | 2004  |
|----|---------|-------|----|---------|-------|
| 1  | Sweden  | 51.14 | 1  | Spain   | 53.87 |
| 2  | Denmark | 51.92 | 2  | UK      | 54.98 |
| 3  | UK      | 59.86 | 3  | Ireland | 55.12 |
| 4  | Finland | 60.07 | 4  | Portugal| 58.23 |
| 5  | Portugal| 60.64 | 5  | Denmark | 58.82 |
| 6  | Ireland | 61.59 | 6  | Sweden  | 60.91 |
| 7  | Belgium | 64.35 | 7  | Greece  | 60.93 |
| 8  | Spain   | 64.69 | 8  | Finland | 61.61 |
| 9  | Greece  | 66.84 | 9  | Belgium | 64.02 |
| 10 | Austria | 68.26 | 10 | Italy   | 65.31 |
| 11 | Germany | 68.72 | 11 | Austria | 66.67 |
| 12 | Holland | 68.77 | 12 | France  | 66.81 |
| 13 | Italy   | 72.03 | 13 | Holland | 67.89 |
| 14 | France  | 72.28 | 14 | Germany | 75.47 |

*Source*: Kase & Jacopin, 2007: p. 72.

*Table A2.6.4*   Santander's financial and operational ratios

|  | 2007 | 2006 | 2005 |
|---|---|---|---|
| Efficiency | 44.22 | 48.56 | 52.94 |
| ROA | 1.09 | 1 | 0.91 |
| RoRWA | 1.95 | 1.83 | 1.78 |
| ROE without capital gains | 19.61 | 18.54 | 16.64 |
| ROE | 21.91 | 21.39 | 19.86 |
| BIS ratio | 12.66 | 12.49 | 12.94 |
| Tier 1 | 7.71 | 7.42 | 7.88 |
| Non-performing loans (NPLs) | 0.95 | 0.78 | 0.89 |
| NPL coverage | 150.55 | 187.23 | 182.02 |

*Source*: Elaborated from Banco Santander's annual reports

*Table A2.6.5*   Operating expenses

| Million euros | 2007 | (%) | 2006 | (%) | Amount | (%) | 2005 | (%) |
|---|---|---|---|---|---|---|---|---|
| Personnel expenses | 6.510 | 53 | 5.926 | 54 | 584 | 10 | 5.555 | 54 |
| General expenses | 4.430 | 36 | 3.973 | 36 | 457 | 12 | 3.719 | 36 |
| Information technology | 487 | 4 | 417 | 4 | 70 | 17 | 418 | 4 |
| Communications | 417 | 3 | 346 | 3 | 70 | 20 | 390 | 4 |
| Advertising | 561 | 5 | 472 | 4 | 89 | 19 | 387 | 4 |
| Buildings and premises | 846 | 7 | 845 | 8 | 1 | 0 | 758 | 7 |
| Printed and office material | 138 | 1 | 122 | 1 | 16 | 13 | 117 | 1 |
| Taxes (other than income tax) | 277 | 2 | 226 | 2 | 51 | 22 | 178 | 2 |
| Other expenses | 1.705 | 14 | 1.545 | 14 | 160 | 10 | 1.472 | 14 |
| Personnel and general expenses | 10.940 | 90 | 9.899 | 90 | 1.041 | 11 | 9.274 | 90 |
| Depreciation and amortization | 1.268 | 10 | 1.147 | 10 | 121 | 11 | 1.014 | 10 |
| Total operating expenses | 12.208 | 100 | 11.045 | 100 | 1.162 | 11 | 10.288 | 100 |

*Source*: Santander Annual Report 2007.

The efficiency gain was attributable mainly to IT systems and product architecture. First, IT systems, due to facilitating better access to information across different geographical areas and time zones, the reduction in dissemination time, and a larger capacity to store and process information, essential for a retail bank's competitiveness.

Second, in the light of the fact that banking fundamentally concerns the handling and management of risk, IT systems bring about better customer relations, and at the same time improve operational efficiency and decision-making processes.

The other aspect of this efficiency is a high net operating income per employee. In a bank that draws over 80 per cent of its income from the retail banking businesses, this carries a considerable weight.

## Product architecture and IT systems

The way in which the core components forming a product are combined is called the product architecture. The modular-type architecture is based on the combination and assembly of standard parts and components using standard production facilities.

Perhaps owing to a concept similar to the modular-type architecture, Spanish banks, especially Santander, pursue their cost leadership advantage by commercializing similar products and services throughout their geographic spread, homogenizing their offering. Substantial savings in product developments are achieved by applying skills and knowledge already learnt in one area, with the comfort of offering quality-assured products and services. IT systems are essential for this. See Figure A2.6.3.

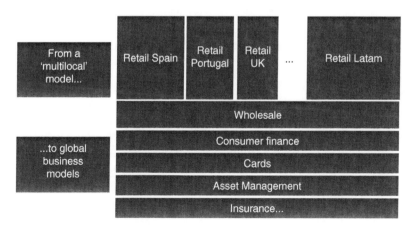

*Figure A2.6.3*   Global synergies

*Note*: The case for *global synergies*: Global organizations such as Santander are in a unique position to create value by developing *global business units* in areas such as credit cards, asset management or insurance.

*Source*: Kase and Jacopin (2007: p. 98).

## What will the future have in store for Santander?

On 10 November 2008, in the wake, or rather, in the middle of the world's financial tsunami, Santander issued a press release announcing its €7.2 bn capital increase by rights issue. For every four existing shares, a new share would be issued. New shares would be priced at €4.5 with Merrill Lynch, Bank of America Securities and Santander Investment being joint global co-ordinators and joint book runners. The period of subscription was to be between 13–27 November, 2008.

The rationale for this rights issue was fourfold according to José Antonio Alvarez, the group's CFO. Firstly, a drastic change was taking place in the banking sector, which demanded higher capital ratios to face an environment of greater uncertainty.

Second, it was not related to any acquisition plans. Third, it was not to cover hidden losses. The bank stressed it had €6.3 bn as generic provisions on its balance sheet. Lastly, it did not reflect a deterioration of business. The bank had suffered a fall in business volume but it had higher spreads than had been envisaged at the beginning of the year. Overall, therefore, the capital increase was to strengthen its solvency, aimed at 7 per cent in line with the general feeling in Europe that 6 per cent core capital would not be enough as had been the belief before the summer.

The market did not welcome it, however, and punished its share price with a 5 per cent drop on the following day.

On 12 November 2008, the bank's market capitalization stood at €46.62bn. Compared with the peak period in May, the price showed a 45.63 per cent loss. PER,[26] EpS[27] and BPR[28] stood at 5.15, 1.42, and 0.89, respectively.

Does this mean that the market is wary of Santander's future? Has its business model and strategy outlived their usefulness and is it time to change in the light of the fact that of the Spanish banks' outstanding loans to clients (amounting to €1.83 trillion), 60 per cent corresponded to housing-related clients in the second quarter of 2008 according to the Bank of Spain?[29] Will the so-called 'balance-sheet' problems in the enterprise sector not end up by affecting Santander's business model?[30] Can the current management cope with the new situation or do they have to seek a generational transition? Is Santander running the risk of acquiring banks faster than it can assimilate them, which happened with banks such as UBS? Can or should the Spanish bank enter more high-risk, high-return businesses?

# Appendix A2.6.1: Financial Statements

| Income statement (Million euros) | 2007 | | 2006 | Variation amount | (%) | 2005 |
|---|---|---|---|---|---|---|
| Net interest income (o/w dividends) | 14.882 | | 12.076 | 2.806 | 23.2 | 10.324 |
| Dividends | 413 | | 404 | 9 | 2.3 | 336 |
| Net interest income | 15.295 | | 12.480 | 2.815 | 22.6 | 10.659 |
| Income from companies accounted for by the equity method | 441 | | 427 | 15 | 3.4 | 619 |
| Net fees | 8.040 | | 7.024 | 1.016 | 14.5 | 6.061 |
| Insurance activity | 319 | | 253 | 66 | 26.2 | 201 |
| Commercial revenue | 24.096 | | 20.184 | 3.912 | 19.4 | 17.541 |
| Gains (losses) on financial transactions | 2.998 | | 2.149 | 849 | 39.5 | 1.534 |
| Gross operating income | 27.095 | 100% | 22.333 | 4.761 | 21.3 | 19.076 |
| Income from non-financial services | 152 | | 119 | 33 | 27.9 | 156 |
| Non-financial expenses | −78 | | −70 | −8 | 11.7 | −91 |
| Other operating income | −119 | | −119 | 0 | 0 | −89 |
| Operating expenses | −12.208 | | −11.045 | −1.162 | 10.5 | −10.288 |
| General administrative expenses | −10.940 | | −9.899 | −1.041 | 10.5 | −9.274 |
| Personnel | −6.510 | | −5.926 | −584 | 9.9 | −5.555 |
| Other administrative expenses | −4.430 | | −3.973 | −457 | 11.5 | −3.719 |
| Depreciation and amortization | −1.268 | | −1.147 | −121 | 10.6 | −1.014 |
| Net operating income | 14.842 | | 11.218 | 3.624 | 32.3 | 8.765 |
| Impairment loss on assets | −3.549 | | −2.551 | −998 | 39.1 | −1.802 |
| Loans | −3.470 | | −2.467 | −1.002 | 40.6 | −1.615 |
| Goodwill | −14 | | −13 | −2 | 13.1 | |
| Other assets | −65 | | −70 | 6 | −8.3 | −187 |
| Other income | −383 | | −45 | −337 | | −265 |
| Profit before taxes (o/w capital gains) | 10.910 | | 8.622 | 2.288 | 26.5 | 6.698 |
| Tax on profit | −2.392 | | −1.947 | −444 | 22.8 | −1.287 |
| Net profit from ordinary activity | 8.518 | | 6.674 | 1.844 | 27.6 | 5.411 |

Continued

*Appendix A2.6.1* Continued

| Income statement (Million euros) | 2007 | 2006 | Variation amount | (%) | 2005 |
|---|---|---|---|---|---|
| Net profit from discontinued operations | 112 | 470 | −357 | −76.1 | 331 |
| Net consolidated profit (o/w capital gains) | 8.631 | 7.144 | 1.487 | 20.8 | 5.742 |
| Minority interests | 520 | 562 | −41 | −7.4 | 530 |
| Attributable profit to the Group (o/w capital gains) | 8.111 | 6.582 | 1.528 | 23.2 | 5.212 |
| Net extraordinary capital gains and allowances | 950 | 1.014 | −64 | −6.3 | 1.008 |
| Attributable profit to the Group | 9.060 | 7.596 | 1.464 | 19.3 | 6.220 |
| *Pro memoria:* | | | | | |
| Average total assets | 877.682 | 814.235 | 63.447 | 7.8 | 740.225 |
| Average shareholders' equity | 41.352 | 35.505 | 5.847 | 16.5 | 31.326 |

Source: Santander Annual Report, 2007.

| Balance sheet (Million euros) | 2007 | 2006 | Variation amount | (%) | 2005 |
|---|---|---|---|---|---|
| **Assets** | | | | | |
| Cash on hand and deposits at central banks | 31,063 | 13,835 | 17,228 | 124,50 | 16,086 |
| Trading portfolio | 158,800 | 170,423 | −11,622 | −6,80 | 154,208 |
| *Debt securities* | 66,331 | 76,737 | −10,406 | −136,00 | 81,742 |
| *Customer loans* | 23,704 | 30,583 | −6,879 | −22,50 | 26,480 |
| *Equities* | 9,744 | 13,491 | −3,746 | −278,00 | 8,078 |
| *Other* | 59,021 | 49,612 | 9,409 | 19,00 | 37,908 |
| Other financial assets at fair value | 24,830 | 15,371 | 9,459 | 61,50 | 48,862 |
| *Customer loans* | 8,022 | 7,973 | 49 | 0,60 | 6,431 |
| *Other* | 16,808 | 7,398 | 9,410 | 127,20 | 42,431 |
| Available-for-sale financial assets | 44,349 | 38,698 | 5,651 | 14,60 | 73,945 |
| *Debt securities* | 34,187 | 32,727 | 1,460 | 4,50 | 68,054 |
| *Equities* | 10,162 | 5,971 | 4,191 | 70,20 | 5,891 |
| Loans | 579,530 | 544,048 | 35,481 | 6,50 | 459,784 |
| *Deposits at credit institutions* | 31,760 | 45,361 | −13,601 | −300,00 | 47,066 |

Continued

*Appendix A2.6.1*   Contiued

| Balance sheet (Million euros) | 2007 | 2006 | Variation amount | (%) | 2005 |
|---|---|---|---|---|---|
| *Customer loans* | 53,3751 | 484,790 | 48,961 | 10,10 | 402,918 |
| *Other* | 14,019 | 13,897 | 122 | 0,90 | 9,801 |
| Investments | 15,689 | 5,006 | 10,683 | 213,40 | 3,031 |
| Intangible assets and property and equipment | 11,661 | 12,555 | -894 | -7,10 | 12,204 |
| Goodwill | 13,831 | 14,513 | -682 | -4,70 | 14,018 |
| Other | 33,162 | 19,423 | 13,739 | 70,70 | 26,968 |
| Total assets | 912,915 | 833,873 | 79,042 | 9,50 | 809,107 |
| **Liabilities and shareholders equity** | | | | | |
| Trading portfolio | 122,754 | 123,996 | -1242 | -1,00 | 112,466 |
| *Customer deposits* | 27,992 | 16,572 | 11,420 | 68,90 | 14,039 |
| *MarkeTable A2.6. debt securities* | 17,091 | 17,522 | -431 | -2,50 | 19,821 |
| *Other* | 77,671 | 89,902 | -12,231 | -136,00 | 78,607 |
| Other financial liabilities at fair value | 33,156 | 12,411 | 20,744 | 167,10 | 11,810 |
| *Customer deposits* | 10,669 | 273 | 10,396 | | |
| *MarkeTable A2.6. debt securities* | 10,279 | 12,138 | -1,859 | -153,00 | 11,810 |
| *Other* | 12,208 | | 12,208 | | |
| Financial liabilities at amortized cost | 652,952 | 605,303 | 47,649 | 7,90 | 565,652 |
| *Due to central banks and credit institutions* | 77,434 | 73,345 | 4,089 | 5,60 | 116,659 |
| *Customer deposits* | 317,043 | 314,377 | 2,666 | 0,80 | 291,727 |
| *MarkeTable A2.6. debt securities* | 206,265 | 174,409 | 31,855 | 183,00 | 117,209 |
| *Subordinated debt* | 35,670 | 30,423 | 5,247 | 17,20 | 28,763 |
| *Other financial liabilities* | 16,540 | 12,749 | 3,792 | 29,70 | 11,293 |
| Insurance liabilities | 13,034 | 10,704 | 2,329 | 21,80 | 44,672 |
| Provisions | 16,571 | 19,227 | -2,656 | -13,80 | 19,823 |
| Other liability accounts | 16,368 | 14,491 | 1,877 | 13,00 | 10,748 |
| Preferred securities | 523 | 668 | -146 | -21,80 | 1,309 |
| Minority interests | 2,358 | 2,221 | 138 | 6,20 | 2,848 |
| Equity adlustments by valuation | 722 | 2,871 | -2,149 | -74,80 | 3,077 |
| Capital stock | 3,127 | 3,127 | | | 3,127 |
| Reserves | 43,828 | 32,595 | 11,233 | 34,50 | 29,098 |
| Attributable profit to the Group | 9,060 | 7,596 | 1,464 | 19,30 | 6,220 |
| Less: dividends | -1,538 | -1,337 | -201 | 15,00 | -1,744 |
| Total liabilities and shareholders equity | 912,915 | 833,873 | 79,042 | 9,50 | 809,107 |

*Source*: Santander Annual Report, 2007

## Appendix A2.6.2: Santander Group Companies

### European operations

| | |
|---|---|
| Austria | • Santander Consumer Bank Austria AG |
| Belgium | • Santander Consumer Finance Benelux B.V. |
| Bosnia and Herzegovina | • Nova Santander Banka d.o.o. Trebinje |
| Czech Republic | • Santander Consumer Finance a.s. |
| Finland | • Santander Consumer Finance Oy |
| Germany | • Santander Consumer Bank AG |
| | • Santander Consumer Debit GmbH |
| | • Santander Consumer Leasing GmbH |
| Hungary | • Santander Consumer Finance Zrt. |
| Italy | • Santander Consumer |
| | • Santander Private Banking |
| Jersey | • Abbey International |
| Netherlands | • Santander Consumer Finance B.V. (Abfin) |
| | • Santander Consumer Finance Benelux B.V. |
| Norway | • Santander Consumer Bank AS |
| Poland | • Santander Consumer Bank S.A. |
| Portugal | • Crédito Predial |
| | • Português |
| | • Hispamer |
| | • Banco Santander Totta S.A. |
| Spain | • Banco Santander |
| | • Banesto |
| | • Santander Consumer Finance, formerly Hispamer |
| | • Openbank |
| | • Banco BANIF |
| Switzerland | • Santander Private Banking |
| United Kingdom | • Abbey |
| | • Alliance & Leicester Bradford & Bingley |
| | • Cahoot |
| | • Cater Allen |

### Latin American operations

| | |
|---|---|
| Argentina | • Banco Santander Río (formerly Banco Río) |
| Brazil | • Banco Santander – formerly Santander Banespa, resultant of the merger of the following Santander- owned banks: |
| | • Banespa |
| | • Banco Santander Meridional (formerly Banco Meridional) |
| | • Banco Santander do Brasil (formerly Banco Noroeste) |
| | • Banco Real |
| Chile | • Banco Santander (formerly Banco Santander Santiago) |
| | • Banco Santander Banefe |
| Colombia | • Banco Santander Colombia |
| Mexico | • Banco Santander Mexicano (formerly Banco Santander Serfín) |
| Peru | • Banco Santander Perú S.A. |

Continued

*Appendix A2.6.2* Continued

| | |
|---|---|
| Puerto Rico | • Banco Santander Puerto Rico Santander Overseas Bank |
| Uruguay | • Banco Santander Uruguay |
| Asian Operations | |
| | • Banco Santander, S.A. – Hong Kong Branch |
| | • Banco Santander, S.A. – Shanghai Branch |
| African Operations | |
| | • Attijariwafa Bank |
| North American | |
| Operations | |
| USA | • Santander Private Banking |
| | • Sovereign Bank |
| | • Santander Consumer USA |

*Source*: Santander Annual Report, 2007.

## Appendix A2.6.3: Key data for the principal segments

| Income statement (Million euros) | Net operating income | | | | Attributable profit to the Group | | | |
|---|---|---|---|---|---|---|---|---|
| | 2007 | 2006 | Variation amount | (%) | 2007 | 2006 | Variation amount | (%) |
| Continental Europe* | 7,786 | 6,270 | 1,516 | 24.2 | 4,423 | 3,471 | 952 | 27.4 |
| o/w: Santander Branch Network | 2,863 | 2,429 | 435 | 17.9 | 1,806 | 1,505 | 300 | 19.9 |
| Banesto* | 1,312 | 1,060 | 252 | 23.7 | 668 | 585 | 83 | 14.2 |
| Santander Consumer Finance | 1,867 | 1,201 | 666 | 55.5 | 719 | 565 | 153 | 27.1 |
| Portugal | 672 | 570 | 102 | 17.8 | 511 | 423 | 88 | 20.8 |
| United Kingdom (Abbey) | 1,913 | 1,620 | 293 | 18.1 | 1,201 | 1,003 | 198 | 19.8 |
| Latin America | 5,808 | 4,236 | 1,572 | 37.1 | 2,666 | 2,287 | 379 | 16.6 |
| w/o: Brazil | 2,533 | 1,727 | 806 | 46.7 | 905 | 751 | 154 | 20.5 |
| Mexico | 1,506 | 1,066 | 440 | 41.3 | 654 | 528 | 126 | 23.8 |
| Chile | 894 | 769 | 125 | 16.3 | 543 | 489 | 54 | 11 |
| Operating areas* | 15,507 | 12,125 | 3,381 | 27.9 | 8,290 | 6,760 | 1,530 | 22.6 |
| Financial management and equity stakes* | −665 | −908 | 243 | −26.8 | −180 | −178 | −1 | 0.8 |
| Total Group* | 14,842 | 11,218 | 3,624 | 32.3 | 8,111 | 6,582 | 1,528 | 23.2 |

Continued

*Appendix A2.6.3*   Continued

| Income statement (Million euros) | Net operating income | | | | Attributable profit to the Group | | | |
|---|---|---|---|---|---|---|---|---|
| | 2007 | 2006 | Variation amount | (%) | 2007 | 2006 | Variation amount | (%) |
| Net extraordinary capital gains and allowances | | | | | 950 | 1,014 | −64 | −6.3 |
| Total Group | 14,842 | 11,218 | 3,624 | 32.3 | 9,060 | 7,596 | 1,464 | 19.3 |

\* O/w: extraordinary capital gains and allowances.
*Source*: Santander Annual Report 2007.

## Appendix A2.6.4: Different business approaches: comparison of PIF * and PA **

| | PIF | PA |
|---|---|---|
| Essential element | Image of the firm | Actions oriented to profit levers |
| Shaping or constituent factors | Professional background, environment, firm's business culture and institutionalization | Professional background, environment, knowledge of firm and industry and sense for business |
| Familiarity with the firm | Necessary | Not so essential |
| Time frame | Focus on mid to long term | Penchant for short term |
| Domain | Wide, new competences and products are fostered | Narrow, existing portfolio |
| Cash flow position | Affluence required | At the time of crisis, the only option is to survive |
| Explicit or implicit instructions from the top | Implicit, second-guessed | Explicit |
| Applicable when changing firms? | Difficult | Possible |
| Succession | Relatively easy to find persons with a similar approach, if they share the belief | Imitability or replicability low |
| Combination with the other approach | PIF – top management PA – lower management | If PA at the top, PIF not possible at lower levels |

*Source*: Kase and Jacopin (2007: p. 67).
\* Proto-image of the firm.
\*\* Profit arithmetic.

## Appendix A2.6.5: Comparison with UBS's universal bank/'One Bank' business model[31]

One of the frequent business models, adopted especially within German-speaking countries, is the universal bank model that is composed of retail, commercial and investment banking activities.

The logic behind it is (i) that it reduces overall risk as a diverse set of businesses would shield from economic volatility in that risks come from a wide variety of activities; (ii) that it generates synergies among businesses regarding both cost and revenue, which makes the value of a universal bank higher than the sum of its stand-alone individual businesses units, and finally (iii) that this business model facilitates the development of a stronger brand.

Before the credit crunch of 2007, one of the most successful universal banks worldwide was the 'one bank integrated approach' of UBS, a Swiss bank, which was predicated on investment banking, assets management and private banking working together through important cross-selling activities.

This integrated model was designed to maximize profit by sharing clients and their assets across the bank. Historically, UBS argued that 10–15 per cent of its market capitalization was obtained from one-group synergies estimated at CHF 2.5 billion in revenues and CHF 1.5 billion in cost savings.

ABS AG, UBS's parent organization, was born from the merger of the Union Bank of Switzerland (UBS) and the Swiss Bank Corporation (SBS) in 1988. Two years later, it was organized into three businesses under the 'one Bank model': UBS Switzerland (private and corporate client business), Assets Management, and UBS Warburg (investment banking).

The bank carried out a series of acquisitions – one of the most critical was the takeover of PaineWebber, an American stock brokerage. Marcel Ospel, UBS's CEO, contended that 'the combination of UBS's international reach and product range with PaineWebber's leading position in the US market for affluent and high net worth individuals will create a premier global investment services firm.'[32]

In 2002, UBS became the largest private bank in the world with more than CHF 430 billion in assets under management. In 2003, the bank's brand was merged into a single UBS brand. It would reflect the UBS integrated business model, as it would move through co-operation between business groups towards UBS as a single firm.

In 2003, UBS was named Best Private Banking, Best Assets Management and Best Bank in Switzerland by *Global Finance* magazine, in 2004, UBS won *Euromoney* magazine's inaugural 'Best Global Private Bank award', and was named the world's 45th most valuable brand, and in 2005, *Business Week* named UBS as one of the five biggest winners, as the firm's brand moved up to the 44th place in the annual ranking of the world's top 100 brands.

During the same year, *Euromoney* again nominated UBS as 'best private bank worldwide' with CHF 2,895 billion of assets under management. Everything seemed to be going smoothly. UBS's ambitions were growth, reputation and ranking among the top-tier players. Its 5-year strategic plan launched around this time targeted double-digit top line increases. The Board of Directors and senior management approved the growth of certain businesses that involved the investment or the increase of UBS's exposure to the US Subprime sector,[33] in particular the investment in Dillon Read Capital Management (DRCM) and Investment Banking (IB) Fixed Income.

The development of the new business unit (DRCM) reflected the intention to establish a new business in alternative investment. The IB Fixed Income business commissioned an 'external consultant' to undertake a review of IB strategic initiatives presented to the IB Management Committee, who recommended that the IB must grow significantly to avoid falling behind competition and emphasized that, in particular, the biggest competitive gap was in Fixed Income had been declining vis-à-vis the competition since 2002.

The consultant suggested certain strategic initiatives to address this competitive gap that included developing certain areas of the business like Credit, Rate, MBS Subprime (Mortgage-backed security, a bond backed by mortgage payments) or other related products in which the underlying assets had a subprime nature.

However, as mentioned in the Shareholder Report on UBS's Write-Downs, 'the consultant's review did not consider the risk capacity (stress risk[34] and market risk) associated with the recommended product expansion'.

The same report indicated, among the 'overarching' causes of the losses related to Subprime with the IB Business (responsible for almost 2/3 of the losses related to subprime) that:

> IB (growth strategy) was focused on the maximisation of revenue. There appears to have been a lack of challenge on the risk and reward of the business area plans within the IB at a senior level. UBS's review suggest an asymmetric focus in IB Senior Management meetings on revenues and P&L, especially when compared to discussion of risk issues... Fixed Income growth strategies submitted to the IB Management Committee and the Group Executive Board, were intent on closing perceived gaps with competitors, but apparently were not sufficiently challenged internally. In particular, it seemed to be assumed that there were no infrastructure constraints that might affect implementation, or that there was no balance sheet utilization limit or other natural market barriers.

Thus, the commitment to growth to close the gap with top-tier competitors, coupled with inadequate risk methodologies and risk management practice, led to a debacle at UBS.

The Shareholder Report on UBS's Write-Downs pointed out the failure in risk control and indicated that '...Market Risk Control provided support to the business that requested more favourable treatment in relation to the application of the Stress Loss methodology to the CDO warehouse. While this may have been an opportunity to rethink the rationale for the business model as a whole, Market Risk Control accepted these proposals from the business and thus enabled it to grow further.'

As a consequence, UBS was dethroned from its privileged position as one of the best brands in Wealth Management and Investment Banking and became the most affected European Bank by the Subprime crisis with a write-off of more than $US 40 billion in the Investment Banking Fixed Income business.

In addition to the huge destruction of shareholder value, this damaged UBS's entire business model as well. In the second quarter of 2008, the bank had a net money outflow of almost CHF 44 billion ($ US 41 billion) in contrast to the inflow of CHF 34 billion a year earlier. To cap this, customers had withdrawn CHF 50 billion ($US 45 billion) by the time the Swiss Government came to its aid with a capital injection in October 2008.

With the benefit of hindsight, analysts now call into question UBS's integrated business model, since they conjecture that the integrated model added an 'unnecessary layer of complexities' and specific risk. (See Table A2.6.6, Credit loss write-downs carried out by the world's banks.)

Table A2.6.6 lists credit loss write-downs carried out by the world's banks in the wake of the financial tsunami from January 2007 until November 2008.

*Table A2.6.6*   Credit loss write-downs

| Banks | Amount in $US billion |
|-------|----------------------|
| Wachovia | 96.6 |
| Citigroup | 68.1 |
| Merrill Lynch | 55.9 |
| Washington Mutual | 45.5 |
| UBS | 44.2 |
| HSBC | 33.1 |
| Bank of America | 27.4 |
| National City | 26.2 |
| JP Morgan | 20.5 |
| Wells Fargo | 17.1 |

*Source*: Bloomberg cited by *Financial Times* dated 13 November 2008.

# Annex 2.7

# Virgin Finance: Sir Richard Branson's pursuit of a significant presence in retail financial services[1]

## Introduction

In the 40 years to 2010, Virgin Group's Sir Richard Branson (b. 1950) turned from a 'high school dropout' to a billionaire and global legend. The creation of over 300 business interests in parts as far afield as the UK, South Africa, Australia and the USA resulted from a unique management style. One he described as 'creative', 'fun' and ultimately, for him:

> ...like painting. You start with a blank canvas. You can paint anything – anything – and there, right there, is your first problem. For every good painting you might turn out, there are a zillion bad paintings just aching to drip off your brush. (Branson, 2008: p. 3)

His style has been given labels such as mercurial, maverick and many other positive and not so positive qualifiers. But the fact remains that Branson is the 'role model' for many actual and would-be entrepreneurs across the globe.

Branson and the Virgin brand are often associated with music (such as records and music stores) and travel (airlines, trains and booked holidays) but between September 2007 and February 2008, they were involved in a failed takeover of Northern Rock, a collapsed British bank.

As this case study will detail, Virgin Group was keen on entering the finance industry. The Northern Rock affair was one of a long series of steps dating to the mid-1990s through which Branson and Virgin had been developing capabilities and brand awareness to create a significant presence in retail finance. By the end of 2009, Virgin Money provided services such as credit cards, savings and mortgages, as part of a partnership or joint venture with other organizations such as Bank of America and the Royal Bank of

Scotland (RBS).[2] A further step was taken in January 2010, with the purchase of Church House Trust, a small regional bank based in Somerset (Southwest England), for £12.3m while expecting to invest £37.3m in the business. 'The Church House Trust business offers us a strong platform for growth,' stressed Sir Richard at the time. At the same time, Jayne-Anne Gadhia, chief executive of Virgin Money, stated that her company would now be in a position to provide consumers with a different type of banking experience: 'The financial crisis has tarnished the reputation of many UK banks', she said. Virgin was clearly moving relentlessly to expanding its repertoire of products and customers while building upon the 'core values of quality and fun'.

Brand overstretching, opacity of the control system, management heterodoxy, and so on, were some of the words used to describe Richard Branson's management style and his far-flung business empire.

In order to open discussion on these doubts felt by financial analysts and management researchers, the case will first describe the historical development of what is now Virgin Group, followed by an overview of Sir Richard's business philosophy and management style.

## Baby steps: the making of Sir Richard as an entrepreneur

The genesis of Richard Branson as a business leader is perhaps one of the most often contested areas of the distinctive traits of his entrepreneurial style. The official version of events (Branson, 1999, 2008) has found both supporters (Dick, 2007; Grant, 2005) and detractors (Armstrong, 2005; Bower, 2008b; Jackson, 1998). Differences in interpretation have led to some lengthy (and costly) legal action. Our general approach to avoid dispute here is to start with Branson's autobiography and then present alternative readings using clearly identified sources. For instance, we rely on Bower (2008b) only for direct quotations from the people he interviewed. As to Sir Richard Branson's management thought, see Appendix A2.7.1, Virgin Group's management statement.

The first steps that led to the creation of the 300+ business empire date back to the late 1960s when he was still at Stowe, a respected boarding school. He was 'a 16-year [old] student who needed to borrow £4 off [his] mother to launch [his] first business venture' (Branson, 2003: p. 1). Together with school friend Johnny Gems, Branson set up a magazine called *Student*. First published in 1968, it was aimed at Sixth Formers (seniors at high-school) and undergraduates, that is, 16 to 25 year olds. Branson dropped out of school about a year after founding the magazine (for reasons that remain contested, see Bower, 2008b: pp. 12–16).

The magazine's eclectic style reflected its founder's ability to commission articles by celebrities and to identify subjects not touched by many well-established magazines (Grant, 2005, p. 310). Norman Mailer, Vanessa

Redgrave and Jean-Paul Sartre contributed pieces which appeared among articles on sex, rock music, interviews with terrorists, and proposals for educational reform. Though the magazine never made money and ultimately foundered, the loosely-defined group which gathered around it proved to be a crucial resource in Branson's take-off into entrepreneurship. The magazine's staff was made up of a closely-knit, cooperative group of friends, acquaintances and hangers-on which were recruited to help with production, distribution and, on several occasions, fend off creditors. The group that built around *Student* served as the nucleus and prototype of a workforce willing to work for low wages in exchange for a lifestyle centred on sexual freedom, drugs and music (Armstrong, 2005). It was the culture of this group which generated the ideas for new businesses on which Branson was able to capitalize (ibid.).

But *Student*'s circulation remained low and static. In an attempt to boost sales, he tried to tap into the potential he saw in the sale of records. The idea to form the mail-order record business that would become Virgin Records came from John Varnom and Tony Mellor, Branson's business partners, not Branson himself (Bower, 2008b: p. 1 and 9). Initially they sought to distribute an unreleased single by John Lennon through *Student*. The song never materialized and *Student* went out of business soon after, but in the last issue and to test the market, an ad was printed listing only records likely to appeal to young people and offering discounts of up to 15 per cent on store prices. The price difference was enough for a large number of orders and payments to start coming in, since records were still 'overpriced', despite the formal abolition of regulation that allowed manufacturers and suppliers in certain industries to 'recommend' prices to retailers.

In thinking of a name for the new venture, Varnom came up with 'Virgin' as a combination of sex and subversion (Bower, 2008b: p. 2), reflecting values typical of the youth culture of the time, in which authority was challenged, fashion changed rapidly and rock stars were idolized. The name appealed to everyone else and was adopted. Lacking capital for a retail outlet, Virgin Records started trading as a mail-order supplier of pop records in April 1970.

To the dismay of everyone at Virgin, strike action by British postal workers over their pay started in January 1971. Although it proved short lived and only lasted a couple of months,[3] it clearly threatened the viability of the new venture. Undeterred, Branson immediately rented retail space while transferring the stock of records to a small store in Notting Hill (central London).[4] Virgin Retail was thus born. True to the emergent management style, the shop's decor was a mix of outrageous and shabby, attracting customers interested in enjoying the experience and in spending money (Dick, 2007: p. 3).

At the time, records were manufactured close to the recording studios and there were a large number of tariffs and quotas to international trade.

As the mail-order business started to attract foreign orders, Branson and colleagues woke up to the possibility of buying records wholesale for export (tax-free), drive them to France and resell them in London while pocketing unpaid duties (33 per cent purchase tax on sales)(Bower, 2008b: p. 3). It seems that the records never actually left London and Branson and company were eventually found out by the H. M. Inland Revenue and Customs (the tax authority). Branson was released from jail after his parents put their own home as collateral for a £30,000 bail. Formal charges were dropped in return for an out-of-court financial settlement.

The venture, however, had generated enough cash flow to finance the purchase for £30,000 of a seventeenth-century manor house in Shipton in March 1971, a town located about five miles from Oxford (Bower, 2008b: p. 24). A room within it was fitted out as a recording studio and, by 1973, they had developed a polished composition of Tubular Bells by a then unknown author named Mike Oldfield. It was Simon Drapper's rapport with 'alternative' tastes in music which enabled him to pick up the potential of Oldfield's composition (Bower, 2008b: p. 29; Branson, 1999: p. 105). But it was Branson's persuasive style that managed to convince several DJs to play the record and these included the very influential John Peel at BBC's Radio One, who devoted a whole programme to the record. Tubular Bells was a hit and rose to be the best-selling album of 1973. Atlantic Records bought the US rights and re-sold the music as sound track for *The Exorcist*, a Hollywood blockbuster.[5] The result was that at twenty three, Branson was a millionaire.

Success in the record business (notably with the signing of the punk rock group Sex Pistols in 1976) was accompanied with the expansion of the record shops and the creation of a host of new successful and unsuccessful ventures such as Virgin Rags, a nationwide clothing chain, a sandwich delivery service, a health-food mega store, Virgin pubs and the sale of a hi-fi systems outlet (Bower, 2008b: pp. 33–34). This rationale of unbridled diversification was quite simple:

...I can be quite persuasive in getting people to accept my point of view. I never do this lightly – but, as I've said, usually go with my gut instinct, disregarding volumes of painstaking research. I would love to be able to tell you that every ace I've played has turned out to be a Virgin Blue or Virgin Mobile. But I can't – which is why I make my senior colleagues at Virgin very, very nervous! (Branson, 2008: p. 9)

In 1984, age 34, the business empire of the 'hippie millionaire' was estimated at £150m (Fishlock, 1984: p. 10). That same year, Sir Richard started an airline with a single old Boeing 747 purchased from Aereolíneas Argentinas. Backed by the Thatcher government's market-oriented reforms and the apparent success of US-based People Express,[6] what was to become Virgin Atlantic began with a phone call from Randolph Fields, a Californian lawyer, who proposed founding a transatlantic, cut-price airline. To the horror of executives at Virgin Records, Branson joined the drive for cheap-fare air travel to show '... how much better they can satisfy consumers by growing at breathtaking speed' (Branson, 1985: p. 14). Unlike Branson's other activities, not only was the airline business highly capital-intensive, it also required a completely new set of business skills, in particular the need to negotiate with governments, regulatory bodies, banks and aircraft manufacturers (Grant, 2005: p. 311).

But as his group and his profits grew, the stage of going for public funding through a stock market flotation in the London Stock Exchange rapidly approached. This was 'regrettable', he said, as 'it's one thing to worry about staff and yourself, another to worry about shareholders' (Fishlock, 1984: p. 10). By 1985, it was evident that Branson's drive for expansion was mired in a transatlantic airfares price war and the investment needs of Virgin Atlantic had created a cash squeeze for Virgin (Grant, 2005: p. 312). Flotation came on 13 November 1986. In this move, Virgin's music, retail and media businesses were combined into Virgin Group plc, a public corporation with 35 per cent of its equity listed in London.[7] Virgin favoured the small investor in deciding share allocations after its offer for sale, which was three times oversubscribed at the 140p per share price (Milner, 1986). The price valued the group at £242m and although it compared favourably with the minimum tender price of 120p, it was a little lower than the City[8] had been expecting, with many estimates being pitched at around the 150p mark (Milner, 1986).

But under the influence of Branson, Virgin was unable to keep within the rigour and discipline required of a company quoted on a major international stock market. A year later, the shares had not had a good ride and stood at 115p per share. There had been notable defections from the board, including the surprised departure of Sir Phil Harris, chairman of Harris Queensway.[9] It was widely believed that Harris was not happy with some aspects of the management of Virgin, and stock market sources speculated that Cob Stenham, the highly respected head of Bankers Trust's European operations, was also considering resigning his non-executive directorship (Jay, 1987).

True to his disinclination for a corseted and rigid management discipline, Branson's dislike of 'the onerous demands' from the City was undisguised (Bower, 2008b: p. 82; Grant, 2005: p. 312). Sir Richard grumbled,

> 'My dream of taking over EMI Music came to an end there and then. The City of London has misunderstood our business – we would now go off and become one of the largest groups of private companies in the world with several quoted investments to boot. (Branson, 2008: p. 190)'.

Meaning that stock market analysts failed to see his vision and recognize the potential of his plans. There were clear signs that the market undervalued his company. A conflict thus existed between the financial community's expectations of the chairman of a public corporation and Branson's 'laid-back' personal style. Within a year of the October 1987 stock market crash, in 1988, Branson raised £248m (£182m in debt) to buy out the Virgin Group's 40,000 small external shareholders. The deal was struck at 140p a share – the same price at which Virgin came to the market two years before. But it ensured that none of Virgin's shareholders – which included the company's staff and pop stars such as Peter Gabriel and Phil Collins – would lose on their original investment. (John, 1988)

At the time, Branson stated that his decision was 'not meant to be a snub to the City' and had been taken purely for business reasons (John, 1988). He revealed that they had been planning a further issue of £50m but since Virgin's profits had not matched City expectations and he did not anticipate any dramatic improvement in either its results or the stock market, there were no incentives which might make him stay public (idem). Branson then ended up owning 80 per cent of the revamped Virgin. As a private group of companies once again, the Virgin Group continued to expand both its range of business and the regions where they were active.

## The Virgin empire: developing checks and balances

There are claims that early on in the development of Branson as an entrepreneur, there was a realization that his organization (then still seen as a cooperative venture of like-minded friends and acquaintances) required proper control and systems. It is for this reason that he turns to '... Nik Powell, to help him manage [the buying and selling of music records in bulk], offering in return a 40 per cent stake in the company. Methodical where Branson was erratic, cautious where Branson tended to overextend himself, Nik Powell was the ideal counterbalance of the fledging business' (Dick, 2007: p. 2). This claim is inconsistent with Branson's own recollection, which places Powell as part of the community around *Student* in 1968 and then being ousted when a 'secret' memorandum from Powell to others in 1970 proposed to relieve Branson of his position as editor and publisher (Armstrong, 2005; Branson, 1999: pp. 75–75).

The accuracy of the Powell incident aside, it is clear that Richard Branson increasingly needed to attract and retain talent and skills to help run an increasingly diversified and transnational operation. It should be emphasized at this point that the Virgin Group is not a single corporate entity.[10] The Virgin empire comprises several holding companies and over 300 stand-alone operating businesses, including those which are wholly or majority-owned by Sir Richard and others in which he holds a minority equity stake. The equity owned by Branson, both individually and through a series of family trusts, is held by Virgin Group Investments Ltd (Grant, 2005: p. 314). The linkages between the companies include: the

*Table A2.7.1*  Selected list of Virgin Group companies, 2010

| Sector | Name | Homebase | Description in website | NAICS (*) |
|---|---|---|---|---|
| **Travel** | | | | |
| | Virgin Atlantic Airways | UK | Airline (premier) | 481111 Scheduled Passenger Air Transportation |
| | Virgin Blue | Australia | Airline (discount) | 481111 Scheduled Passenger Air Transportation |
| | Virgin America | USA | Airline (discount) | 481111 Scheduled Passenger Air Transportation |
| | Virgin Australia | Australia | Airline (premier) | 481111 Scheduled Passenger Air Transportation |
| | Virgin Trains | UK | Train and coach | 48211 Rail Transportation |
| | Virgin Holidays | | Booked holidays | 453998 All Other Miscellaneous Store Retailers (except Tobacco Stores) |
| | Virgin Holidays Cruises | | Cruises | 487210 Scenic and Sightseeing Transportation, Water |
| | Virgin Holidays+HIP Hotels | | Booked holidays (Premier) | 487110 Scenic and Sightseeing Transportation, Land |
| | Virgin Limited Edition | | Hotels | 453998 All Other Miscellaneous Store Retailers (except Tobacco Stores) |
| | Virgin Vacations | | Booked holidays | 487110 Scenic and Sightseeing Transportation, Land |
| | Blue Holidays | | Reward program | 453998 All Other Miscellaneous Store Retailers (except Tobacco Stores) |
| **Lifestyle** | | | | |
| | Virgin Active | UK, Spain, Australia Portugal, Italy, South Africa | Fitness centre | 451110 Sporting Goods Stores |
| | Virgin Digital Help | | IT Support | 517911 Telecommunications Resellers |
| | Virgin HealthMiles | | Reward program | |
| | Virgin Books | | | 511130 Book Publishers |
| | Virgin Games | | On-line games | 454111 Electronic Shopping |

| Category | Company | Countries | Type | NAICS* code |
|---|---|---|---|---|
| **Media & Mobile** | Virgin Mobile | UK, Canada, USA, Australia, France, India, South Africa | Telephone | 517911 Telecommunications Resellers |
| | Virgin Media, Virgin 1, Virgin Connect | | Cable TV, TV Channel, Internet broadband service | 515210 Cable and Other Subscription Programming, 515120 Television Broadcasting, 517911 Telecommunications Resellers |
| **Money** | Virgin Money | US, UK, Australia, South Africa | Retail finance | 52229 Other Nondepository Credit Intermediation |
| | Virgin Unite | Australia, Canada, Keynia, Nigeria, South Africa, UK, USA | Microfinance | 81331 Social Advocacy Organizations |
| **People & Planet** | Virgin Earth Challenge, Virgin Green Fund | | | 541620 Environmental Consulting Services, 813312 Environment, Conservation and Wildlife Organizations |
| **Music** | Virgin Megastore | France (others under licence) | Music and games retailer | 451220, Prerecorded Tape, Compact Disc, and Record Stores. |
| | Virgin Radio International | | Radio | 515111 Radio Networks |
| | Virgin Festivals | | | 487110 Scenic and Sightseeing Transportation, Land |

* NAICS - North American Industry Classification System (US Census Bureau).

*Source*: http://www.virgin.com/company/ (Accessed 7 April, 2010).

common use of the Virgin trademark, Branson's role as shareholder (both directly and indirectly through the trusts), Branson's role as chairman of the companies (whose board meetings he does not attend regularly, see Dick, 2007: p. 8), and Branson's management role, which is primarily in publicity, public and government relations, and appointing senior executives. Appendix A2.7.2 gives a historical view of Richard Branson's business ventures.

The summary in Table A2.7.1 above is not a fully comprehensive listing. This would be nearly impossible given the private nature of most of the Virgin companies. Limited and fragmented public information as well as different financial years for those companies which do offer some details also hamper external efforts to estimate consolidated financial statements. However, there is an overall impression that the financial performance of the Virgin companies as a whole was poor during the 1990s and more recent evidence suggests this was still the case for many individual companies in the 2000s (Bower, 2005; Grant, 2005: p. 312).

As can be seen from Table A2.7.1, most of these businesses have operations within Britain, Australia, South Africa and the USA. The priorities for this group are 'transport and tourism, communications and media, financial services, entertainment and music, health and wellbeing, and renewable energy and the environment'. Branson, 2008: p. 82). Consistency in brand delivery is seen as key to Virgin's success (Branson, 2008: p. 6). Sir Richard's business model is based, firstly, on the concept of 'developing discrete businesses with their own investors' whenever these businesses 'should fulfil or have the potential to fulfil both the emerging public perception of the Virgin brand and provide the shareholders with a good return on their equity investment' (Grant, 2005). Second, convergence marketing. This is predicated on the concurrent convergence of e-commerce and mobile telephone technologies and it aims to bundle Virgin's businesses into a one-stop consumer operation – 'UK consumers ... use their mobile phone to bank, buy or book virtually any service ... Travel ... financial services and content businesses will be ... beneficiaries'. (Grant, 2005).

But the entrepreneurial spirit that enabled Sir Richard to build an estimated £4 billion personal fortune, one of the most recognized brands in the world and which took pride in its 'win some, lose some' attitude, took a new direction in 2007 (Robertson, 2007). That year, Sir Richard handed day-to-day control of the group to an investment committee of accountants, lawyers and consultants whose aim is to improve the win-loss ratio. Sir Richard adopted the title of 'founder' and would continue to promote the brand and develop business ventures for the group, but he effectively gave up executive control (ibid.).

Virgin calls its pioneering concept 'branded venture capitalism' (Robertson, 2007), that is, as a large private equity concern which not only invests but has a 'hands-on' approach and shares a common brand and values (Branson, 2008: pp. 82–86).[11] The 'new' Virgin aspires to operate as a professional manager of assets and sees itself as a consumer-focused private equity group with the financial discipline of a big City or Wall Street firm. The seven-strong investment committee is led by Stephen Murphy, an accountant, who joined the Virgin Group in 1993. Gordon McCallum is Virgin's strategy director and the man responsible for developing new ventures.

In their first media interview, Murphy and McCallum explained Virgin's new direction (Robertson, 2007). Mr McCallum said: 'A brand of our size can take the hits if a business fails because we are famous for being entrepreneurial. But if we keep getting it wrong, we undermine the whole thing, so we think pretty carefully about what we do.' (ibid.). Murphy added: 'Because of the publicity that Richard generates, the cost of failure probably is higher, and that is one of the questions we ask before we start.' (ibid.)

This idea of 'branded venture capitalism' is strengthened by the flurry of hundreds of business ideas that are pitched to Branson every month (Branson, 2008: pp. 6–9). Many come directly through Virgin's website while others come internally, through managers and employees. These are then recorded, catalogued and some of them, researched a bit further. A 'tiny number' of them are passed on to investment professionals (working in London, Switzerland, New York, Shanghai and Sydney). The most promising ones are invited for a face-to-face presentation at one of the weekly meetings of Virgin's Investment Advisory Committee. None of the committee members has day-to-day responsibilities for running a company of the group but they do work closely with top people (as a type of internal management consultant). The meetings usually take place in London, New York and Geneva (but sometimes in Japan or China). The meetings can also be attended by up to six managers with direct responsibilities in companies within the Virgin Group and related to the project being presented, with the aim of helping to evaluate the proposal.

As is the case for any other venture capital firm, it takes several meetings before a final decision is made. Spending plans, marketing budgets, income forecasts, procurement (including identifying potential joint ventures) and the exit strategy for Virgin (flotation or sale) must be reviewed. But more importantly, Branson rarely attends the meetings. 'The team doesn't like [his] interruptions and interference' and if Branson likes 'your idea, but the investment committee have concerns, then [he] usually asks them to go find solutions to the problem they've identified'. (Branson, 2008: p. 9). Indeed, according to Sir Richard, it was the result of his 'persuasion' and constant prodding fuelled by his 'gut instinct' and disregard of 'whole volumes of painstaking research' that Virgin went into mobile phones and the Australian low-cost airline (Virgin Blue) (Branson, 2008: p. 9).

## Virgin Money: diversification into retail financial services

### Virgin Freeway: from air miles to credit cards

There is another strand to Virgin's intermediating activities and these refer to entry into the provision of retail financial services. Virgin's move to this sector 'astonished many, and still raises incredulous eyebrows among some politicians and heads of industry'. (Branson, 2008: p. 159).

Speculation about Branson's ambitious drive into branded consumer goods and services, and expanding into retail finance first emerged in October 1994, after Virgin signed a tie-up with American Express through its frequent flyer programme, Virgin Freeway (See Table A2.7.2). Like many other airlines across the world, Virgin was expanding its Freeway programme to embrace other airlines (namely British Midland, Scandinavian Airlines and Air New Zealand), plus petrol stations and Holiday Inns. American Express's Membership Miles (launched in November 1993 by the charge card group), gave customers one point for every £1 they charged on their cards whether they were paying for an airline ticket or a restaurant bill. By linking with American Express, Virgin was promised access to its 'select group of cardholders' at the same time that cardholders booking with their American Express cards could earn double points, one lot from the card company and another from the airline or hotel booking (Webster, 1993).[12]

Entering the credit card business was seen as the next logical step if the group's brand diversification into products such as vodka, cola and computers were to continue generating the revenues that Branson anticipated. At the time, a Virgin spokesman said: 'It is a project that we have looked at and continue to look at but we haven't pushed the button yet' (Harrison, 1994).

Set for a debut in 1999, talks for a partnership with the Royal Bank of Scotland (RBS) broke down and the card failed to materialize (Prestridge, 1999). After searching for alternatives, the card was launched in 2002 in the UK and the USA, 2003 in Australia[13] and 2006 in South Africa. As in many other ventures, Virgin aimed to focus on finding new avenues to retain existing customers. Indeed, Branson saw it as a 'loyalty card', that is, a way of 'keeping in touch' with the myriad of different customers across the sprawling Virgin empire (Hunt, 2002). At the same time, partnerships were formed with the credit card specialist MBNA in the USA and UK, Westpac in Australia (until 2007) and London-based Standard Chartered in South Africa.

As such, the launch of yet another card slugging it out with 1,500 other cards in Britain for a slice of the £84 bn market in 2002 would have been unremarkable (Hunt, 2002). However, Virgin credit cards in the UK offered a flexible credit programme and allowed customers to choose interest rates, annual fees and rewards from a range of options (Condie, 2003). Card users earned points to spend on Virgin products and were offered discounts on Virgin Atlantic flights.

Table A2.7.2 List of some of Virgin's financial companies

| Year of establishment | Name | Activities | Location | Partner | Source |
|---|---|---|---|---|---|
| 1993 | Virgin Freeway | Frequent flyer miles expanded to credit card purchases | | American Express | Evening Standard (23 November, 1993) |
| 1995 | Virgin Direct Financial Services (UK) | Mortgages, pensions, PEPs, share tracker funds | UK | Norwich Union (NU) | Dick (2007), Bower (2008: 205) |
| 1996 | Virgin One | Personal insurance (?), flexible mortgage account | Australia (?) | AMP replaces NU | Bower (2008: 206) |
| 1997 | | | UK | Royal Bank of Scotland | Bower (2008: 280) |
| 1999 | (negotiations for a credit card are on the way) | | UK | RBS | |
| 1999 | Virgin-money.com | on-line broker | UK(?) | | Bower (2008: 344) |
| 2001 | | | | Virgin One's 50% stake sold for £45m to RBS | Bower (2008: 360) |
| 2002 | Virgin credit card | credit card | US, UK (Australia, 2003; South Africa, 2006) | MBNA (Westpac until 2007 in Australia; Standard Chartered in South Africa) | |
| | | | | AMP in trouble. Might sell stake | Sydney Morning Herald (Australia), April 16, 2002 |
| 2007 | (failed bid for Northern Rock) | | UK | RBS(?) | |
| 2008 | Virgin Money USA | | US | | Bower (2008: 390) |
| 2009 | (purchase of Chatham House) | retail finance specialist | UK | | Bower (2008: 389) |
| | micro-finance? | | | | |

Source: Author's own compilation based on Dick (2007), Grant (2004), Bower (2008), Branson (2008), The Guardian and The Times.

### Virgin Direct: selling pensions, insurance and investment funds

The financial services group was launched in December 1994. On that date a joint venture with an insurance company called Norwich Union was signed, with the latter and Virgin putting in £2m each (Branson, 2008: p. 161). The company became operational in March 1995 in the UK as Virgin Direct Financial Services. At the time, Branson said

> I have identified a sector that was arrogant, complacent and fleecing the customer. I saw an opportunity to shake it up. So I set up Virgin Direct to offer people straightforward financial products that are easy to understand. (Bower, 2008b: p. 205)

Branson thus saw an industry 'ripe for reform', characterized by poor service, high charges, disreputable practices and dissatisfied customers; but, at the same time, he seems to have been influenced by forecasts that the personal finance market was bound to grow as more and more people took a greater responsibility for their financial security in their old age (Dick, 2007: p. 21). Virgin Direct employed 60 people and sold directly to consumers over the telephone, offering retirement plans called 'PEPs' (personal equity plans), income protection insurance and life insurance.

Less than a year later, the joint venture was dissolved. According to Branson, 'Norwich Union didn't have the appetite for building a bigger business, but Virgin Direct needed the capital to grow' (Branson, 2008: p. 162). So in 1997, Norwich Union sold its 50 per cent stake to Australian Mutual Provident (AMP), another insurance company, with Virgin owning 49.9 per cent.

By 1997, Virgin Direct had attracted some 220,000 customers and its mutual funds had £1.5 billion under management (German, 1997; Grant, 2005: p. 319). Around this time, a joint venture with RBS created a subsidiary of Virgin Direct called Virgin One (Treanor and Cassy, 2000). This new company enabled Branson's Virgin to launch a deposit (current/cheque) account called One on 1 November 1997 (German, 1997). According to Branson, the idea originated at RBS as they wanted to bring something to Britain that was becoming quite popular in Australia, namely

> ... putting all of a customer's products together. At the end of each evening, your net balance is charged interest. Most people have a separate mortgage, current account and savings, and you're paying interest on the whole mortgage. If you roll everything together, you'd have a lower negative balance and you could pay off your home loan more quickly. (Branson: 2008: p. 162).

Unlike most traditional banks there were no high-street branches to be seen. Like Virgin Direct, Virgin One was also a telephone operation based in Norwich (East Anglia), open 24 hours a day throughout the year. About staffing, Branson opined

[we] recruited people who wanted to help the customer and make a difference – it was a huge part of the training. There were no stifling scripts to follow, or average talk-times to listen to. We just answered questions. We hired people who believed – like we did – that Virgin was one revolutionary crusade to change banking in the UK. (Branson, 2008: p. 163)

Virgin cash cards were usable at all but two of the 22,000 cash dispensers in the UK (the exceptions being those operated by the United Bank of Kuwait) (German, 1997). Credits were to be paid in by post but Virgin customers also had access to RBS's retail bank branch system in the UK.[14]

Initially the account was available only to Virgin's existing customers (through Virgin Direct) but was to open up to the general public as soon as practical.[15] At the time, a spokesmen for Sir Richard said that the venture aimed to operate profitably from the start and was not be used as a 'loss leader' to siphon off business from existing banks and building societies (mortgage specialists that also accepted retail deposits) to later rack up charges when the business had been built up (German, 1997). By October 1998, there were 2000 accounts, increasing to 9000 in 1999 and 15000 the year after that (Branson, 2008: p. 163). While reflecting on this success, Branson said:

I admit it was difficult to start because the UK public weren't used to the idea of putting all their eggs in one basket, however safe it may be…. [But the] dinner-party brigade became our best promoters. Doctors, lawyers and professional people were converting to its merits; they told their friends, and the idea began to spread through recommendation. We heard that people would take their Virgin One cards out at meals with friends and sell the idea. In business terms, this is pure gold. You can't buy this kind of advocacy. (Branson, 2008: p. 162)

Shortly after, AMP and Virgin decided to rename Virgin Direct as Virgin Money. The change of name took place in 2001 (Dick, 2007: p. 18). This move coincided with the amalgamation of Virgin Direct with Virgin-money. com. The latter was an independent, online stock trading website launched in 1999. Virgin Money was to be the single brand name and umbrella company for all of Virgin's financial services. Accordingly, it was reorganized into three main units, namely: Virgin Direct Life (life insurance and retirement plans), Virgin Unit Trusts Manager (managed mutual funds); Virgin One; and Virgin Credit Card (Grant, 2005: p. 319).

Virgin Money's financial services were characterized by three features. First, they were low cost (Grant, 2005: p. 319). Virgin's credit card interest rates, fund management charges and other fees tended to be below those of the major financial institutions. Second, Virgin's products offered several ease-of-use features (Grant, 2005: p. 319). For example, the Virgin One account allowed a number of products – home loans (mortgages), savings account, checking account, credit card debt – to be pooled into a single account offering significant administrative and interest cost conveniences.[16] Third, they are all joint ventures in which Virgin outsources critical capabilities. For instance, risk management which results in, ultimately, most debts sitting in someone else's balance sheet. Says Branson:

'Virgin Money undertakes the marketing and designs the products – credit cards, savings and investments, life and general insurance – while partners provide the rest. (Bank of America operate [sic] our credit cards,[17] which means the cards are on Bank of America's Balance sheets, not Virgin's!)' (Branson, 2008: p. 165)

In spite of apparently having broken new ground in personal finance through an innovative and simple offering, Virgin Money continued to lose money. Indeed, the amalgamation of Virgin Direct with Virgin-money.com had been an attempt to strengthen the asset base of the joint venture with AMP (Treanor and Cassy, 2000). In July 2001, Virgin sold its 25 per cent stake in Virgin One to RBS for £45 million (Bower, 2008b: p. 360; Dick, 2007: p. 18; Grant, 2005: p. 319). Continuing poor performance in Virgin Money together with losses elsewhere prompted AMP to dismantle its banking operation and to divest non-core businesses (Condie, 2003). Not surprisingly, in April 2003 AMP announced its intention to divest its 50 per cent stake. In April 2004, Branson purchased AMP's 50 per cent equity of Virgin Money for £90m (Grant, 2005), after AMP sources reckoned to have invested £144m in the venture (Condie, 2003).

But in spite of the financial travails, Virgin Money pressed ahead and unveiled operations in the USA in 2008. Virgin Money USA was based in Boston, MA and powered by 30 employees. The rationale for this new outlet was familiar: 'We can give American mortgage companies, banks and credit card companies a run for their money', said Sir Richard (Bower, 2008b, pp. 389–380).

### Virgin Queen: attempt to take over Northern Rock

On 14 September, 2007, the news broke that Britain's fifth largest bank (in terms of total assets), Newcastle-based Northern Rock, had appealed to the government in desperate need of greater liquidity. The days that followed saw Armageddon. The media were full of images of long queues of ordinary people outside its retail branches, all of them waiting to withdraw their deposits. This was the first run on a British bank in over a century.

The idea to take over 'the Rock' came from Jayne-Anne Gadhia (b.1961), chief executive (CEO) of Virgin Money. She graduated in history from Royal

Holloway (one of the colleges of the University of London) and then pursued an accounting qualification while working at Ernst & Young, from where she moved to Norwich Union. She was introduced to Branson in 1994 by Rowan Gormley, her colleague at Norwich Union who had just become head of Virgin Direct (Branson, 2008: p. 160).[18] She then moved to the joint venture but left as part of the purchase of Virgin One by RBS in 2001. At RBS, she rose to become the head of consumer finance in charge of a mortgage book worth £67 bn (Armitstead, 2007). Branson then asked her back as CEO in February 2007.

She returned with a mandate to re-launch the mortgage portfolio 'and propel the [Virgin Money] brand into the big league'. (Farndon, 2007). Ramping up sales of financial products by organic growth would take years. But when it was evident that Northern Rock was to lose its independence, she saw a chance to shortcut the process and transform the business overnight. Initially she called Gordon McCallum, strategy director, who politely turned her down. Undeterred, she then blasted off a follow-up email that same evening to McCallum and Stephen Murphy, head of the Investment Committee,

Hi there.

Call me insane, but I have been thinking hard about how we might take some advantage from the current situation at Northern Rock – and help out at the same time. I think there are a number of opportunities – ranging from the possible to the outrageous:

Accept that the big balance sheet providers will take the assets and look to take the systems, etc. for a decent price.

Do a deal with a Citi [Citi Group] or BOA [Bank of America] where they buy the company but we put in the brand so they get a Virgin-branded retail presence in the UK.

Talk to Northern Rock and the Bank of England direct. Richard could be used as frontman to make some sense of the crisis. Northern Rock could be rebranded Virgin and the Bank of England stand behind the current loan facility. We could withdraw from mortgages for the time being and focus on savings to rebalance the balance sheet – and with Richard fronting a saving campaign – Branson making sense of the current crisis – it's all about increasing savings and reducing debts, etc.

Whatever happens, I think we should do some research into who people would trust with financial services now. I bet the answer will be – Richard Branson.

On the one hand, I know that this all sounds batty, but on the other hand – discontinuities in the system make it right for change – and I think we could do something. If Richard was able to speak to [Alistair Darling, Chancellor of the Exchequer] or [Gordon Brown, Prime Minister] to ask how we could help.

What do you think? I've restrained myself from copying this to Richard until I got your views.

J-A. (Branson, 2008: pp. 196–197)

McCallum's reply was still not very enthusiastic and asked for a discussion the following morning. But Gadhia pressed on and called Sir Richard directly, who after hearing her out embraced the idea wholeheartedly.

When the idea became public, the popular press awarded Gadhia the nickname of 'Virgin Queen' in remembrance of the capture of the Rock of Gibraltar and the marital status of Queen Elizabeth I (Farndon, 2007; Watson, 2007).[19] Publicly, she would admit to have long admired Northern Rock's efficient business model and innovative approach to mortgages: 'when I was at RBS, we always looked with interest at Northern Rock', she said (Farndon, 2007). But the point the financial press really wanted to make with the nickname was whether she was up to the job as she had little experience running a 'blue chip' company (Farndon, 2007).

The differences in size and scope between the two were substantial: before its collapse, Northern Rock was a FTSE 100 business with 6000 staff.[20] Virgin Money employed 240 staff and had a £200m annual turnover. Gadhia argued that as head of consumer finance at RBS she was in charge of a mortgage book worth £67 bn, roughly the same size as Northern Rock's, which was valued at £90 bn in 2007. She explained

The problem was that 75 per cent of [Northern Rock's] balance sheet relied on external funding. The fact that this dried up could be seen as unlucky. But what can't be down to luck but a point of management is the acquisitions that Northern Rock made in the first half [of 2007]. During that time the bank took vast market share which then got into trouble with the credit crunch. Growth at all costs will go wrong. (Armitstead, 2007)

A credible bid for Northern Rock had to raise at least £26 bn, in order to pay £16 bn for the loan from the Bank of England plus another £10 bn or so to keep funding levers up. Although Branson was to invest a significant amount of cash and assets into the venture (that is, £1.25 bn in new cash plus Virgin Money), the bulk of Virgin's bid was backed by insurance giant AIG; buyout firm WL Ross; private investment firm Toscafund, led by Martin Hughes and Sir George Mathewson (the former CEO of RBS); and Hong Kong investor First Eastern Investment; with debt finance from RBS; and Sir Brian Pitman, former CEO and chairman of Lloyds-TSB (the third banking group in the UK in terms of assets) as non-executive chairman. There were, of course, competitors such as that put together by buyout firms JC Flowers and Cerberus.

But while others planned to break up Northern Rock, lay off several hundred employees and sell its assets, Sir Richard and Gadhia insisted in trying to keep things together by not only avoiding any sale of the assets but also not having any lay-offs (at least not until the recession was over). They also promised to allow existing shareholders to take part in any rights issue on preferential terms and to pay all debts to the government by 2010 (Bower, 2008a: pp. 202–203). Said Gadhia,

'We want to rebalance Northern Rock into a building society, diversify the products and put the Virgin brand on top. We are confident this can work out.' (Farndon, 2007)

But in spite of everything, Virgin's bid was seen as a poor offer. It never got the full backing of the financial press. It was criticized in Parliament by David Cameron (at the time, leader of the opposition and to become Prime Minister in May 2010) and Vince Cable (at the time, deputy leader of the Liberal Democrats and to become Business Secretary with responsibilities for banks in May 2010) (Bower, 2008a: pp. 207–208). For Sir Richard, the final 'nail in the coffin' came in February 2008 when bad publicity in the media following his trip to China with Gordon Brown, the then Prime Minister, made the sale to Virgin, at that point the sole bidder, unsustainable and Brown nationalized Northern Rock (Bower, 2008a: pp. 208–209). However, we must also consider that as the credit crisis progressed, the cost of funding the operation was becoming increasingly expensive for everyone (Bower, 2008a: p. 204). Indeed, the rising cost of external funding and accumulated losses would ultimately lead to the collapse of AIG (September 2008) and RBS had to receive financial support from the British government (October 2008) and was virtually nationalized (January 2009).

But as the purchase of Church House Trust in January 2010 suggested, the Northern Rock affair was not going to dampen the enthusiasm for a greater presence in retail banking. The newly elected Conservative-Liberal Democrat coalition government had yet to decide what to do with their large equity stakes in Northern Rock, RBS, and the enlarged Lloyds Group (resulting from the amalgamation of Lloyds–TSB and Halifax-Bank of Scotland). So it looked very much that it was only a question of time before Virgin Money became a significant presence in the British retail financial sector.

## Appendix A2.7.1: Virgin Group's management thought[21]

Virgin is a leading branded venture capital organization and is one of the world's most recognized and respected brands. Conceived in 1970 by Sir Richard Branson, the Virgin Group has gone on to grow very successful businesses in sectors ranging from mobile telephony to transportation, travel, financial services, media, music and fitness.

Virgin has created more than 200 branded companies worldwide, employing approximately 50,000 people, in 29 countries. Global branded revenues in 2008 exceeded £11 billion (approx. US$17 billion).

We believe in making a difference. Virgin stands for value for money, quality, innovation, fun and a sense of competitive challenge. We deliver a quality service by empowering our employees and we facilitate and monitor customer feedback to continually improve the customer's experience through innovation.

When we start a new venture, we base it on hard research and analysis. Typically, we review the industry and put ourselves in the customer's shoes to see what could make it better. We ask fundamental questions: is this an opportunity for restructuring a market and creating competitive advantage? What are the competitors doing? Is the customer confused or badly served? Is this an opportunity for building the Virgin brand? Can we add value? Will it interact with our other businesses? Is there an appropriate trade-off between risk and reward?

We are also able to draw on talented people from throughout the Group. New ventures are often steered by people seconded from other parts of Virgin, who bring with them their trademark management style, skills and experience. We frequently create partnerships with others to combine industry-specific skills, knowledge and operational expertise.

Contrary to what some people may think, our constantly expanding and eclectic empire is neither random nor reckless. Each successive venture demonstrates our devotion to picking the right market and the right opportunity.

Once a Virgin company is up and running, several factors contribute to making it a success. The power of the Virgin name; Richard Branson's personal reputation; our unrivalled network of friends, contacts and partners; the Virgin management style; the way talent is empowered to flourish within the group. To some traditionalists, these may not seem hard-headed enough. To them, the fact that Virgin has minimal management layers, no bureaucracy, a tiny board and no massive global HQ is an anathema. But it works for us! The proof of our success is real and tangible.

Our companies are part of a family rather than a hierarchy. They are empowered to run their own affairs, yet the companies help one another, and solutions to problems often come from within the Group somewhere. In a sense we are a commonwealth, with shared ideas, values, interests and goals.

Hopefully exploring the activities of our companies through this site demonstrates these ideals well, but if you have any comments or feedback, feel free to post them.

Managing the Virgin group is a pretty full-time job and we have developed a canny way of doing it that keeps it fresh and lively whatever the company does and wherever it is based.

At the centre, Virgin Management Ltd (VML) provides advisory and managerial support to all of the different Virgin companies and our specialist Sector teams around the world. Our people in London, New York and Sydney offer regional support and between us and the Sector teams we manage Virgin's interests across the whole of the Virgin Group.

VML's fastidious number-crunchers get to manage Virgin's financial assets in the group, our cheeky marketeers and spin doctors get to protect and maximize the value of the Virgin brand and our touchy-feely people teams ensure Virgin is an employer of choice.

Seeing as the Virgin businesses are all so diverse and independent, we pretty much practice a collaborative and supportive style of custodianship. Some of us would like to wear special uniforms.

We give birth to new Virgin companies, encourage them to walk, hold their hands and then watch them on their way as they become fully-fledged members of the Virgin family. It can sometimes get quite emotional.

To help manage the growth and development of our Virgin family, we have set up sector teams, each run by a Managing Partner. These bigwigs look after interests in aviation, media & telecom, financial services, health & wellness, leisure, and Green (clean technology) investments. The specialists keep our companies on their toes and ensure we keep developing better experiences and world-beating products.

### Appendix A2.7.2: Richard Branson's business ventures

**1960s**

1966    After failed attempts to grow and sell both Christmas trees and budgerigars, Branson launches his first successful business, a magazine named Student.

**1970s**

1970    Starts selling records by mail order

1971    Opens his first record shop on Oxford Street

1972    Opens a Virgin Recording Studio

1973    Launches Virgin Records record label

1979    Buys the gay nightclub Heaven, located under Charing Cross railway station. It is subsequently sold in 2003 to a private speculator.

**1980s**

1980    Virgin Records goes international

1983    Virgin Vision, later to become Virgin Communications, is formed to distribute films and videos in the television and broadcasting sector.

1983    Virgin Games is launched.

1984    Virgin Atlantic Airways and Virgin cargo are launched.

1984    Virgin Vision (launched the previous year) launches "Music Box", a 24-hour satellite music station.

1985   Virgin Group now includes record labels, retail outlets, exported music publishing, broadcasting, satellite television, and film and video distribution.

1985   Branson starts Virgin Holidays

1987   Branson takes Virgin Records to the United States

1987   The Virgin Group, along with Granada, Anglia and Pearson, founds BSB (British Satellite Broadcasting) and receives a UK license to broadcast five new TV channels by satellite in the UK.

1987   Virgin sets up 525, a post-production facility in Los Angeles, to work on high-end commercials and pop videos.

1987   Virgin sets up "Music Box" as an independent producer of music programmes.

1987   Virgin buys a 45 per cent stake in Mastertronic Group. Later, Virgin Mastertronic becomes a wholly-owned subsidiary of Virgin Group, creating, marketing and distributing computer games software and Sega consoles in several European countries.

1987   Virgin buys Rushes Postproduction in London.

1987   Virgin launches Virgin Airship & Balloon Company.

1988   Virgin re-opens the recently acquired and re-modelled Olympic Studios in Barnes, London.

1988   Virgin launches Virgin Classics, another Virgin international record label specializing in high-quality classical music.

1988   Virgin sells some of its smaller UK retail stores and puts more money into Virgin Megastores, opening new stores both in the UK and abroad.

1988   Virgin sets up Virgin Broadcasting.

1988   Virgin Hotels is created, combining three properties: the Norton House Hotel in Edinburgh, the Crathorn Hall hotel in North Yorkshire, and the Rhinefield House Hotel in Hampshire.

1988   Virgin sells its shareholding in BSB.

1990s

1990   Virgin Megastores arrives in Japan

1991   Virgin Publishing (Virgin Books) is formed

1992   Virgin Records is sold to Thorn EMI

1993   Virgin Radio hits the airwaves with Virgin 1215AM

1994   Launch of Virgin Vodka and Virgin Cola

1995   Virgin Direct Personal Financial Services opens for business

1995   Virgin Express, a European low-cost airline, is launched in Brussels after the purchase and rebranding of EBA Express

1996   V2 Music is created

1996   Virgin.Net launches

1996   Virgin Brides launches

1996   Virgin Trains is launched

1996   Virgin Group becomes controlling shareholder in London Broncos rugby league team

| | |
|---|---|
| 1997 | Virgin Radio is acquired by Chris Evans |
| 1997 | Virgin Cosmetics launches |
| 1998 | Virgin Mobile launches Virgin's first telecom venture |
| 1999 | Virgin Active launches in South Africa, UK and Italy |
| 1999 | The controlling shareholding in London Broncos is sold to David Hughes |

**2000s**

| | |
|---|---|
| 2000 | Virgin launches Virgin Blue |
| 2000 | Virgin sells Rushes Postproduction to Ascent Media – then Liberty Livewire |
| 2000 | Virgin launches Virgin Energy |
| 2000 | Virgin launches Virgin Cars |
| 2004 | Virgin launches Virgin Galactic |
| 2005 | Virgin Express merges with Sn Brussels Airlines to form Brussels Airlines. Virgin retains minority share. |
| 2005 | Virgin Active UK acquires Holmes Place |
| 2006 | Virgin announces Virgin Fuel, a new company to produce a clean fuel in the future |
| 2006 | Virgin Active Spain is launched |
| 2007 | Virgin Active Portugal is launched |
| 2007 | Virgin launches Virgin Health Bank |
| 2007 | Virgin launches Virgin Media |
| 2007 | Virgin launches Virgin America |
| 2007 | Buys 20 per cent stake in AirAsia X |
| 2007 | Sells Virgin Megastore in the UK and Ireland |
| 2007 | Virgin Media Television launches Virgin 1 |
| 2007 | Closes Virgin Digital in the UK (Virgin now sells music downloads though Virgin Media's website) |
| 2007 | Virgin Fuel US$400 million in Virgin Atlantic jet flight on biofuels and in renewable energy. |
| 2007 | Virgin Money becomes preferred bidder for acquisition of Northern Rock (but is ultimately unsuccessful). |
| 2007 | Virgin Radio Italia launches in Italy a joint venture with Gruppo Finelco S.p.A. |
| 2008 | Virgin Australia Airlines offers competitive prices between Australia and Los Angeles. Known as V Australia due to naming rights. |
| 2008 | Virgin launches Virgin Healthcare |
| 2009 | Virgin launches Virgin Money Giving |

**2010s**

| | |
|---|---|
| 2010 | Virgin launches Virgin Racing, a Formula One team previously known as Manor Grand Prix |

*Source*: http://en.wikipedia.org/wiki/List_of_Richard_Branson's_business_ventures (accessed 16 May 2010).

# Annex 2.8

# Logico[1]

## Introduction

'It's almost as if each department is speaking a different language', Jane Doe, European Strategy Director for Freight Management in Logico,[2] thought to herself as she shook her head. 'How in the world are we going to be able to automate the Sales Force if our IT department can't even begin to understand how the Sales department works and thinks?'

Jane, in late 2003, worked for Logico, a global leader in supply chain management that provided customer-focused logistics solutions to a wide range of manufacturing, high technology and retail industries. As a UK listed company, it had a worldwide turnover of over GBP 7 billion, and was generally considered to have the kind of vast stores of knowledge and superior resources that would permit it to implement virtually any innovation it might choose. However, its attempts to innovate did not always succeed, and, so far, previous attempts to automate the Sales Force had failed miserably. Nevertheless, Jane had been charged with finding a way to get this particular innovation to work – to bring the Logico Sales Force into the twenty-first century by providing its salespeople with the first step towards attaining a worldwide Customer Relationship Management system.

This 'first step' had been defined as the 'Sales Force Automation' project – a two-year process of providing the Freight Management (FM) division sales force with company-supplied laptops, new and centrally-managed sales software, and an internationally-connected database of information about customers. Jane knew that this challenge should be relatively simple to accomplish, at least from a technological perspective. The question was, then, why had a comparatively simple project such as this been so hard for a company such as Logico to set its collective mind to achieve? What was so hard about getting a worldwide sales force to share information?

Jane's task was to explore this question. She and her team would act as internal consultants, studying the pilot Sales Force Automation project, which was being carried out by the European Marketing department in the UK, and extended to part of the USA, and Singapore, as it progressed.

After an initial analysis of previous failed attempts, where she and her team looked at the 'usual' attributions given to resources invested, contextual timing, internal politics, or quality of the technology available, she began to believe that there was a more pervasive and underlying mechanism that affected the company's ability to implement this strategic change. This, she thought, was rooted in the shared cognitive schemas (Gick & Holyoak, 1983; Balogun and Johnson, 2004) held within different groups in Logico, that could be fundamentally summarized or understood to be either 'inductive' or 'deductive' (Kase, Slocum, & Zhang, 2011). In the case of this particular technological innovation, Jane decided that one of the most important elements that top management needed to understand better were the two opposing approaches of inductive and deductive thinking typically carried out by different departments, in this case, those of Sales and IT (Information Technology). Jane was convinced that only by better understanding and synthesizing these different approaches would Logico be able to implement the changes it sought.

## Background and context

Though a worldwide leader in logistics, Logico had long struggled to gather and compare consistent data about its customers around the globe. In the ten years leading to 2002, various attempts to establish a central customer database had been made, with little success. These problems were only made worse by numerous mergers and acquisitions, differing cultures in the divisions and strategic business units, and worldwide information systems that were pieced together as the whole company grew.

Indeed, the complicated organizational structure of Logico at the time was a source of constant debate and change. The company had, only a year and a half previously, undergone a merger with another large logistics company, GLOBFREIGHT Global Logistics[3] (where the FM division originated), and the new organizational structure had now discarded its former geography-based organization in favour of what it considered to be a more customer-based structure. The current organization chart was a matrix which established its major divisions by customer industry first (that is, healthcare or retail), *then* by geography (the Americas, Asia and the Pacific, and Europe with the Middle East and Africa), and finally by type of customer product or service (warehousing usually was categorized under contract logistics; sea freight and airfreight were usually categorized under freight management).

Freight Management, which provided transportation services to customers in *every* industry, was already an exception within the new company's organizational structure, in that it did not focus only on one industry, but provided transportation services to all industries. In addition, however, it also serviced a predominant number of major clients that tended to be in what it called the 'High Technology' sector, accounting for about 35 per cent of its overall revenues. Technology and FM were therefore combined into one industry *and* service-type based division, now called 'Technology and Global Freight Management' (TGFM). However, this meant that FM customers in the other industries (healthcare, heavy industry, retail and fashion and so on) were managed by either international FM Key Account Managers (there were fewer than 50 of these worldwide) or local FM sales-people. This was at the root of why it was perceived within TGFM that many medium and large-sized accounts that crossed borders and used many types of services were being served on a disjointed basis and the sales force was unable to work together in developing them to their maximum potential. (See Figures A2.8.1, A2.8.2 and A2.8.3, Logico, TGFM Global and TGFM Europe Organization Charts).

The Freight Management division, where Jane worked, was a subunit of the larger company, providing global transportation services via air, sea and road, as well as accompanying value-added ground and delivery logistics services. Each country and region was a separate business unit, and coordination was achieved through global 'network behaviour', where each country and unit followed a unified set of procedures and processes to carry out tasks related to merchandise travelling from one place to another. Global FM coordination was also achieved through the use of a single global IT system integrating the operational tasks. However, no single system yet existed to integrate information on sales and customers worldwide. (See Figure A2.8.4, scope of customer information systems within TGFM).

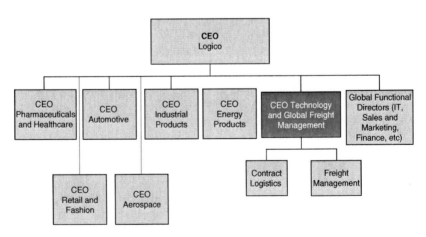

*Figure A2.8.1*  New Logico organizational structure
*Source*: Logico's Annual Report.

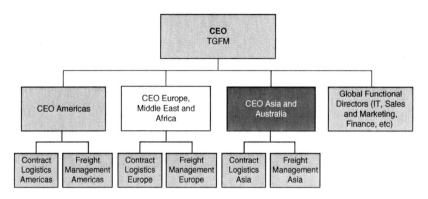

*Figure A2.8.2*  Global TGFM organizational structure
*Source*: Logico's Annual Report.

The international Freight Management division was therefore based upon a worldwide network of offices that necessarily had to work together, aiming for a seamless provision of services to all customers. To the company's credit, and for the most part, this was generally achieved, customers received a high level of service quality and value, and this led to the company ranking as the second biggest freight forwarder worldwide. This was the case in Europe as well, in the year 2003. (See Figure A2.8.5, Market rankings for Logico FM in Europe). The problem, however, was that each market was slightly different, and therefore had different competitive situations, different large customers, and different focuses on specific industries. The information that had to be shared, therefore, varied widely, and was important to others in differing degrees.

Integrated services were not achieved without a great deal of human effort, much of which was perceived to be less efficient or transparent than might otherwise have been. In an increasingly competitive landscape; 'integration' and 'information' became key buzzwords for both Sales and IT managers who wanted to 'direct' and 'measure' and 'control' these 'seamless' processes. Top Logico management, especially, was concerned about managing integrated products and services across many different divisions, and achieving a strategic objective of getting the different divisions to work more effectively together. They wanted information about what was going on in the company, regardless of the internal and external borders the information had to cross, and argued that this would help all managers to do their jobs more efficiently and effectively. Essentially, all Logico managers wanted an integrated view of the sales of FM products and services they were providing to customers worldwide.

Parallel to this in time was a general move, on the part of many theorists in the academic world, to question the positivist, linear and objective approach to strategic change that was prevalent in the Western world during

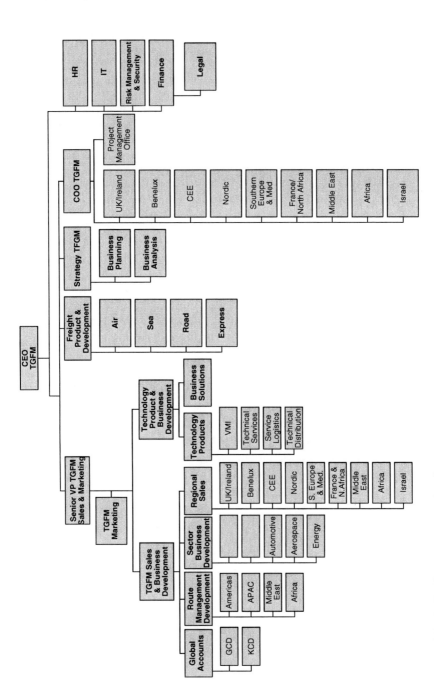

*Figure A2.8.3* TGFM Europe organizational structure

*Source:* Logico's Annual Report.

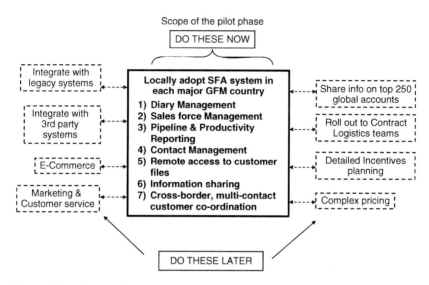

*Figure A2.8.4*  Scope of customer information systems within TGFM

*Source*: Prepared by the author based on Logico's information.

| | 1999 | 2000 | 2001 | Who's #1? |
|---|---|---|---|---|
| UK | 2 | 1 | 2 | Company A |
| Germany | 5 | 5 | 5 | Company B |
| Italy | 5 | 5 | 3 | Company A |
| Netherlands | 7 | 2 | 3 | Company A |
| Finland | 2 | 2 | ? | Company A |
| Sweden | 6 | 2 | 1 | Logico |
| Ireland | 5 | 5 | 1 | Logico |
| Belgium | 7 | 7 | 7 | Company A |
| France | 21 | 10 | 11? | Company C |
| Spain | 19 | 20 | 20? | Company D |
| Denmark | 9 | 7 | 6 | Company E |
| Norway | 16 | 10 | 8 | Company A |
| Portugal | 18 | 25 | 25? | Company C |
| Logico in Europe | | 5 | 3 | Comp A (1), Logico (2), Comp B (3), Comp D (4), Comp E (5) |

*Figure A2.8.5*  Market (IATA) rankings for Logico FM in Europe

*Source*: IATA data, ranking by IATA revenue.

the latter half of the twentieth century, and move towards a more socially constructed, continuous and open-ended approach to understanding management (Morgan, 1985/95). Tsoukas and Cummings, for example, called for a 'reconceptualization of management in terms of meaning, interpretation, ambiguity, conflict, context-dependence, and reflexivity' (Tsoukas and Cummings, 1997: p. 656). This new approach had begun to trickle into the consciousness of some managers in Logico, especially those in the Strategy or Sales departments, and created a perceived need to approach the employment of new technologies, and their uses for information, in a way that was different from what had been done in the past.

This, however, was in direct conflict with an ingrained and pervasive belief within the company, especially among senior IT managers, that any innovation, or action, or even simply a decision taken by managers, was ultimately one of many strategic mechanisms that needed to be 'harnessed' and controlled more effectively from the top down. Technology was seen as a tool to do this, and was therefore viewed as an object – as an external force which could be proactively used to represent and enact top-down strategic choices (Orlikowski, 1992). In the words of one senior IT manager, 'You tell us what you want, and we will configure the IT system to do that'. Technology was, therefore, considered to be one of many organizational tools which were defined in advance and programmed to represent and facilitate existing and desired processes, hierarchies and structures. The benefits of the new technology then would be proven with 'hard' numbers, comparing the costs of implementing and running the new programme with the new sales that it was assumed would accrue. In addition, the new technology would be used to measure the productivity of sales employees, in terms of their (demonstrated via the new system) benefits to the company. (See Figures A2.8.6a, A2.8.6b, and A2.8.6c).

However, while a quantitative and objective approach, that is, deductive, was valid and necessary in managing a large service organization, and certainly, a department as logical and structured as the IT department, it was, in many ways, anathema to the processes and structures in place to carry out direct and personal sales to large, and discerning, customers. IT managers who expected an immediate, objective and measurable result from the new technology tended to misunderstand the continuous nature of human interaction and communication required in the sales department. This led them, to some degree, to belittle what was unquantifiable or not yet proven, and essentially, 'inductive'. If it could not be understood via either very clear numbers, rigidly defined processes or very clear facts, it was considered to be badly managed and likely to lead to company failure.

One top IT manager, for example, insisted upon recounting (many times) his horror when a young member of an external consultancy, who had visited only three customers with one salesperson during one day, stated that he 'didn't think the sales force in Logico followed any definable processes in

## What Are We Measuring?

→ Most of what we have measured relates to sales force **PRODUCTIVITY**, although we have also identified trends for **INCREASED SALES**.

→ We have tailored a benefits analysis methodology from Capgemini and other sources, to arrive at numeric conclusions wherever possible.

| Objective | Lever | KPI | Method | |
|---|---|---|---|---|
| | | | Qualitative | Quantitative |
| | Increased sales time/ customer facing time **(B2)** | - Time allocation pre-/post-SFA<br>- Activity levels<br>- telephone calls per month | Surveys | Singapore tele-marketing |
| | Improved customer profiling & targeting **(B9)** | - Quality of calls & meetings<br>- Pre-call planning & research effectiveness | Surveys | |
| Improved productivity | Improved management of Business Development Executive turnover **(B4/B3)** | - Value & percentage of total lapsed opportunities not reassigned to a Business Development Executive<br>- Opportunities which have stayed with the company | | US Pipeline<br><br>UK Pipeline/ SFA |
| | Quicker effectiveness of new sales people **(B3)** | Apply value to efficient induction programme<br>- Start date to first activity<br>- Training hours | Anecdotal and surveys | SFA |
| | Reduced time in filing & retrieval of information **(B6)** | - Time saved in filing & retrieval time<br>- Telephone sales campaign time & resource | Surveys | Singapore example |
| | Positive/ collaborative & motivated sales team **(B8)** | - Positive feedback re SFA<br>- % and number of companies with team members | Surveys | SFA |
| Increased sales | Higher numbers attained by sales force **(B1)** | - Revenue<br>- Margin<br>- Number of opportunities | Control group comparison | Legacy/ SFA/ Pipeline |

*Figure A2.8.6a* Early attempts to measure productivity of the SFA

Source: Logico.

The Benefits Framework

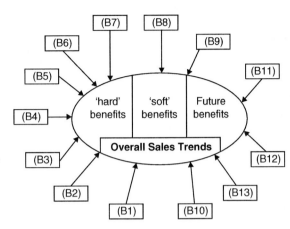

- Section one will cover the key 'hard' metrics used to determine the overall benefit of the SFA pilot

- Section two will cover the key 'soft' metrics used to determine the estimated additional benefits of SFA

- Section three will cover the potential 'future' benefits of the global deployment of SFA

*Figure A2.8.6b*    Early benefits framework
Source: Logico.

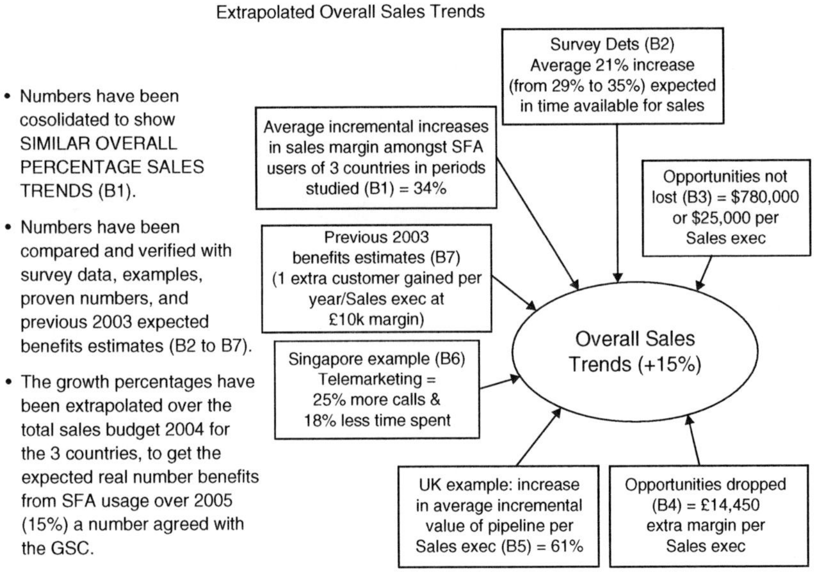

Extrapolated Overall Sales Trends

- Numbers have been cosolidated to show SIMILAR OVERALL PERCENTAGE SALES TRENDS (B1).

- Numbers have been compared and verified with survey data, examples, proven numbers, and previous 2003 expected benefits estimates (B2 to B7).

- The growth percentages have been extrapolated over the total sales budget 2004 for the 3 countries, to get the expected real number benefits from SFA usage over 2005 (15%) a number agreed with the GSC.

Survey Dets (B2)
Average 21% increase
(from 29% to 35%) expected
in time available for sales

Average incremental increases in sales margin amongst SFA users of 3 countries in periods studied (B1) = 34%

Opportunities not lost (B3) = $780,000 or $25,000 per Sales exec

Previous 2003 benefits estimates (B7) (1 extra customer gained per year/Sales exec at £10k margin)

Singapore example (B6) Telemarketing = 25% more calls & 18% less time spent

Overall Sales Trends (+15%)

UK example: increase in average incremental value of pipeline per Sales exec (B5) = 61%

Opportunities dropped (B4) = £14,450 extra margin per Sales exec

*Figure A2.8.6c*    Early productivity results
Source: Logico.

selling to customers'. This manager's perception, like that of many people in the IT department, was that if a process could not be written in detail and then programmed into an IT system, it was either incorrectly defined or badly designed. The fact that other well-respected members of the top management team began to repeat this story in various different settings was important. It created an insidious way of undermining the confidence of many employees in the sales team, and chipped away at Logico's ability to accept a structure based on tacit knowledge, fluid interactions between individuals and a lack of predictability.

Jane had come to the conclusion that this type of approach, one that attempted to 'force' a deductive system onto an essentially inductive process, had only resulted in casting aspersions on both the new system and the sales process itself, before anything had been launched. In doing so, she felt, many top managers from the company may have been rejecting a different, yet complementary, way to attain a dialectical balance between a seemingly tangible and 'deductive' structure such as technology and a more 'inductive' process of organizing an effective sales force. Jane therefore decided to approach the new project with a dialectical lens, in an attempt to facilitate a comparative view of *both* a deductive as well as a more inductive way of achieving strategic change.

In her MBA course, Jane had been taught that one way to deal with issues that crossed international borders and integrated people from different cultures was to identify her 'Self–Reference Criterion' (SRC), isolate it and put it aside, and then reincorporate her interpretation and analysis of what was happening around her, between countries and international individuals, from a less culturally-biased point of view (Cateora and Graham, 2008: pp. 15–17). She wondered, however, how this might be applied within the Logico SFA project to get the different departments to work together more effectively. Was there a way to redefine the objectives of this project, or even just the subconscious assumptions related to it, in such a way that IT and Sales could understand and work with each other more effectively?

It was within this context that the task for Jane was set, to study the piloting of a Sales Force Automation system (SFA) in Logico, where the company was seeking to both attain and maintain one central database for information about freight management customers, shared across borders. Her task would be to evaluate the method of implementation, as well as make a recommendation to the TGFM Board of Directors, about whether to continue to launch this project along these lines, and to specify the required budget throughout Logico if the project was successfully allocated the resources it would require to roll out the system worldwide. While various initiatives had been attempted earlier, each had been only a partial solution, or had failed. The new Sales Force Automation project had arisen as an attempt to combine the best of both the IT and the sales worlds, using a methodical and well-planned, yet open-ended and flexible approach to achieve a shared, worldwide customer database and sales automation system.

## The SFA project organization

The FM Board originally decided that the Sales Force Automation, or 'SFA project', as it was now known, would be managed as a half-time, special assignment by the European FM Marketing Director, Jim Jones, who was considered to be a knowledgeable but relatively impartial third party. Jim was a 45-year-old British citizen, who had grown up in Surrey. He nevertheless had spent many years abroad, first in Spain, then in Germany and then in South Africa, and he spoke three European languages well.

Jim was allocated a small, full-time team dedicated to the SFA project, where members would originate from both the IT as well as the Sales and Marketing departments, and one external consultant would be assigned from the software company. The team members would all take on the project as a two-year, but temporary assignment, with plans to return to their 'home' departments after the project was completed. Jim himself would continue to manage his regular marketing team for two years, dividing his own time between the SFA Project and his regular marketing tasks on a fifty-fifty basis. The SFA project team would be housed on the same floor as his department, and he would be responsible for their salaries and career evaluations during this time, although each person's 'source' department would be kept informed of their activities and expected to reemploy them again at some point in the future.

The internal team Jim put together consisted of five people. Aya, from the Marketing Department, was assigned as team leader for the sales and marketing side of the business. Aya had six years' experience as a Marketing Analyst, and had already launched two other, smaller, sales projection systems, that had been successful and were still in use. She was of Indian origin, and had immigrated to the UK as a child, with her family, although this wasn't immediately apparent from her rather 'posh' British accent. She was diligent, organized, knowledgeable about IT, and she understood the sales teams and processes well.

Aya's counterpart as team leader for the IT side of the project was Khor, of Malaysian origin, who had lived and studied all over the world (including India, Singapore and the USA) before settling in the UK. Khor was a rarity in the IT department – while he definitely considered himself to be 'an IT person', he nevertheless understood and communicated well with salespeople, and was surprisingly sensitive to different cultural approaches. When he first met Aya, for example, he was careful to ask her about her participation in the Divali festival, which was to take place that week. He immediately settled in well with the project team, and still maintained good relations with his colleagues in IT. Both Aya and Khor were allocated one assistant each.

There was also a full-time Project Manager, Linda (coming from a separate pool of internal consultants who were available to manage different projects for Logico anywhere in the world) who was allocated to 'drive' the project forward, using project management software and techniques.

In addition to the internal team, Peter, a top customer service manager from the software company, Axis, was assigned to work with the Logico team directly over the following months, helping them to understand and implement the new system, and also ensuring that the project flowed smoothly from starting as a pilot programme in three countries to eventually achieving strategic worldwide implementation after a few years. (See Figure A2.8.7, SFA project team organization chart).

The budget allocated to the pilot project over the first two years was approximately US$540,000, (see Table A2.8.1, Project budget and breakdown) which Jim considered to be rather tight in order to achieve this change in three

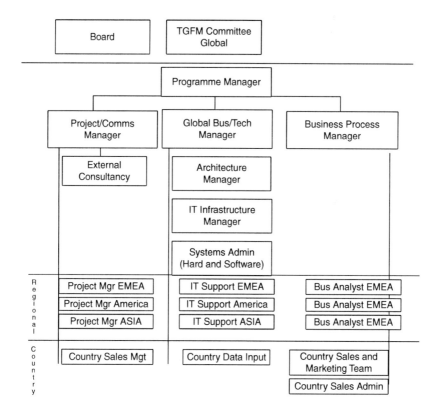

*Figure A2.8.7*   SFA project team organization chart
*Source*: Logico.

*Table A2.8.1* Project budget and breakdown per quarter, 2003

| External and cape costs | Q1 | Q2 | Q3 | Q4 | Total 2004 |
|---|---|---|---|---|---|
| Software licenses | £105,000 | | | | £105,000 |
| Hardware (servers) & applications | | £51,200 | | | £51,200 |
| External Supplier development and support | £10,000 | £54,400 | £51,200 | £20,000 | £135,600 |
| Additional infrastructure (capex) | | £10,800 | £33,000 | | £43,800 |
| External and Capex Subtotal | £115,000 | £116,400 | £84,200 | £20,000 | £335,600 |
| | | | Capex per Region | | £37,289 |
| Incremental internal costs | | | | | |
| Client install | | £1,875 | | £1,875 | £3,750 |
| Infrastructure maintenance | | £7,500 | | £12,044 | £19,544 |
| Workshops, training, travel, mtls | | £5,667 | £5,000 | £5,000 | £15,667 |
| Contracted resources | £3,000 | £9,750 | £25,250 | £25,250 | £88,375 |
| Incremental internal Subtotal | £3,000 | £24,792 | £30,250 | £44,169 | £127,336 |
| | | Internal Costs per Region | | | £42,455 |
| Estimated Recharge for central resource already budgeted | | £35,250 | £51,750 | £51,750 | £138,750 |
| | Rechanged Central Resource per Region | | | | £46,250 |
| | Total Costs per Region | | | | £125,984 |

*Source*: Logico.

different countries. All current costs had to be included in that total amount, and anything beyond that would have to be voluntarily paid for by the host countries, which were already indirectly paying for the project as part of their contribution to various cost centres established at a corporate level. The central budget had to include, therefore, the new hardware, software, travel, and the full salary costs of the non-incremental personnel. Even more importantly, the three countries involved in the initial pilot project would be obliged to pay all their own additional and ongoing costs for the project, such as additional laptops, IT support, training, and incremental and ongoing software costs after the system had been implemented. This meant that Jim constantly needed to 'sell' the project to the individual country managers, convincing them of the project's benefits before these had even been fully identified.

I take every opportunity I have to discuss the project with other senior and middle managers, and I always try to explain what I know and don't know about it to them. The problem is that this turns into a rather circular process – they then have to defend their projected future expenses to their bosses or the FM Board, and often they have to jump to conclusions about something that hasn't even happened yet, said Jim in September, 2003.

They received their budget packs just last week, for example, and one of the questions on it is, of course, how they expect to achieve their projected sales next year. We think that the new SFA will help generate and maintain new sales over the long term, of course, but not necessarily in a direct way, and certainly not immediately. The Country Managers of the UK, USA and Singapore know that, initially, the project will cost them money, because of the extra training and general expenses related to provoking a change of this magnitude. However, we don't project having much of an increase in sales next year, due to the new system, at all. I guarantee you that they will all be coming back to me next week, demanding my sales projections in their countries, which I will then have to turn around and ask their people for anyway. Then, the Board will contact me in about a month, asking me whether I think the Country Managers' projected sales are on the mark. It's like asking which came first – the chicken or the egg! (Jim Jones, 2003)

The Sales Force Automation project began in mid-January, 2003, after the Logico Board had officially approved the budget for piloting the programme in three countries worldwide, and after a decision was finally made to choose a supplier (Axis) of an 'off-the-shelf' system that would be configured to meet Logico's requirements. Already, and from the beginning, senior management concerns and high-level disagreement on the approach to be taken meant that the SFA Project team had some very fundamental paradoxes to deal with. The team was asked to prove the benefits of a global freight management, shared customer database and sales force automation system. However, at the same time, it was limited to a relatively low budget, a scarcity of qualified resources, a need to adapt to current (constantly changing) structures and infrastructure, a tendency on the part of top management to avoid or delay decisions, and perhaps most importantly, fundamentally conflicting IT, sales and management views on how to advance.

To deal with these, and a multitude of other seemingly unsolvable paradoxes, the project team chose to actively embrace an iterative, and collaborative, approach. It was made clear that they would start with understanding what an off-the-shelf program, backed by a supplier with considerable sales force automation expertise with hundreds of other companies of this size worldwide, could do. The team would then, at the same time, work very closely with representatives from sales and management, to document and agree the detailed sales processes they used.

At the end of this cycle, it would hold a task force meeting, with representatives from the country sales team, from the supplier, and from the core project team, to understand and agree upon common processes and requirements which would then form the basis for the IT department to program the new system.

At this meeting, and after two days of going through each detailed step in the country's potential usage of the demonstrated program, sales delegates were allowed to leave only after *committing* themselves to the requirements and plans for going forward. It was made absolutely clear that all participants would still form part of the overall project team, which could go no further without continued collaboration. It was also made clear, and accepted by the representatives, that this would continue to be an iterative process, where the ultimate 'answer' would only come through a great deal of participation and hard work, adapting back and forth between the existing programme and the existing processes in individual countries towards a system that could potentially be used in common around the globe.

The core SFA team was then tasked with ensuring that the program was configured to adapt to the agreed requirements, and the country teams were tasked with preparing data and structures, deciding business rules, making ad hoc decisions, setting up the infrastructure, and preparing for participant training and usage.

Once developed, the new program was tested and loaded with data, and the users were trained and asked to parallel their usage of it with manual processes and reports for a short period. Now, the sales force was being asked to begin to understand and play with how they could use the program in live situations, while still 'backed up' by either a training environment or parallel use of manual systems. They needed to learn the program, and understand the idiosyncratic ways in which it would begin to affect their daily work routines. They were also told that they should keep in mind that this project was still under evaluation, and that they were to expect, and inform the core project team of, any bugs or requested changes, throughout their usage.

The 'pilot implementation and evaluation phase' was expected to run for approximately six months, corresponding to the planned budget. At the end of this period, senior management would be presented with results and benefits, and a choice of whether to continue investing in this strategic initiative at a 'whole company' level. Crucially, the initial six months were expected to help the company define how, for how much money, and with what level of results, the project could be launched worldwide.

While there was clearly an unwieldy mix of tactical and strategic goals to deal with during the pilot project, what was even more difficult was finding a way to deal with the 'different set of understandings' about timings, budgets and results regarding how the project should progress and be measured, from and by the different managers, divisions and departments involved. What would it take to get everybody to work and think together?

## Sales force management in FM

The Logico Freight Management (FM) sales force in 2003 differed from that of its Contract Logistics (CL) counterparts in that it dealt with products that were fast-moving, often transactional, and rarely supported by a long-term contract. Each country sales force had been developed to support slightly different organizational structures, and hence, no single sales organization chart applied to every country in freight management. Processes existed, but were not necessarily uniform, nor traditionally written down. As there had often been a dichotomy between what was defined as good network behaviour and what was best for an individual business unit's profit and loss (P&L) account, there was often an underlying culture of not sharing information, especially regarding customers, because profits could be, and were often, lost that way.

Many of the most effective members of the three country sales forces studied (UK, Singapore and USA) had only recently learned to use personal computer (PC)-based sales and database technology, having only received laptops within the last few years. Others, generally younger ones with less freight management experience, were impatient with the lack of advances by Logico in this respect. Similar to the way the company was built (through a series of acquisitions, alliances and mergers), the information technology (IT) systems used in Sales were also varied and piecemeal, with unclear rules and reasons behind them. This in itself often led inexperienced users of IT systems to conclude that the system was at fault, when in reality what may have been at fault was the stopgap measure taken to keep it all working together. This, in turn, was often due to the piecemeal investments of a large conglomerate, and lack of clarity on how to share information, profits and costs.

During this period, (2002–2004) Logico's top managers had identified a need for the entire organization to more effectively 'work together' (Logico, 2003), as a necessary condition for more integrated services. However, by now, most of the profit and loss business units that had achieved successful growth within Logico Freight Management had done so because, to some degree, they had found a way of solving their own problems and advancing 'in spite of' the centre and its costs and rules. In addition, there were multiple natural barriers between countries and regions, including language, politics, culture, history, training, currency, company structure and so on. Many Logico managers considered this a typical 'recipe for disaster' that would lead to what was then a perceived average 70–75 per cent failure level in the market for the large majority of Customer Relationship Management (CRM) software or SFA implementation efforts. The managers of the SFA program, however, argued that these circumstances would only occur when 'the need to work together went unrecognised'.

At the same time, one of the major advantages that Logico was considered to have in launching anything new was a relatively flexible workforce that was able to cope with change, because it did so on a daily basis. One sales manager stated, for example, 'I am so used to change that when I go on vacation for longer than two weeks, I fully expect to have either a new organization structure to adapt to or a new acquired company to help integrate on my return' (Logico interviews, 2003).

With regards to the launch of the new SFA system, the launch team considered that many of the younger or newer members of the sales force, having come from other companies where an SFA system already existed, would recognize that there were great advantages to be had from using sales force automation software because other software had worked well for them in the past. Among the sales force, there was an increasingly voiced need to adapt the sales system to perceived changes in the environment (many of which were seen as being of a technological nature) as well as to improve collaboration within the network (Logico interviews, 2003).

There was a generally voiced recognition by members of the sales force, therefore, that they could clearly gain something from using SFA software. The challenge was in how this was to be done, and whether it was perceived to be, on balance, helping rather than hindering their work.

Aya was especially adept at communicating with *both* the sales department *and* the IT department. She was very logical about what was essentially a fluid and uncertain process, and was well able to communicate with temperamental, 'left or right brain' individuals. She spanned the gap between the two departments, although she 'spoke the language' of her own department best. Jim had worked with Aya for years, on various projects, many of which were 'mini' SFAs. He felt very fortunate to have her on his team, as she was both competent and trustworthy, and because she seemed well able to manage across any culture, and between the 'inductive' and 'deductive' camps.

## IT management in FM

The Information Technology department within Freight Management (FM) was considered to be crucial to the present and future viability of the organization, although it was a virtual behemoth in size and unwieldiness. When the first FM integrated operations system was developed, in the early 1990s, Logico (then GLOBFREIGHT) was considered to have strategically leaped ahead of many competitors. By 2003, however, it was still using the same basic operations system, and it had evolved into following a somewhat piecemeal policy of applying 'fixes' and 'add-ons' to already existing solutions, especially as a way to cope with and incorporate numerous newly acquired companies.

In deference to its strategic value to the company, however, by 2003 the IT department was represented at the most senior level of the organization by a Board-level director. Below this was a department that accounted for approximately 30 per cent of the company's overall annual expenses, and in which many hopes of further strategic advancement were placed. However, the company had also recently weathered the technological boom of the 1990s, the dot.com bust, the trend towards outsourcing, and the after-effects of '9/11' on the air transport industry, all of which had led to varying, pendulum-swinging policies in the overall direction of the IT department, and had led at different times to some rather large cutbacks in IT personnel.

Because of this, many of the IT staff who had been with the company for quite a few years had become rather cautious about large projects, tight deadlines and big investments. The perception among many IT employees was that things could change very quickly, and that no one wanted to be caught paying the price, in hours or effort or job loss, for budgets that had been underestimated. There had been a history in the department of rather sudden layoffs and redundancies. A perception grew from this that each year was a 'game' of being ensured employment for only another year or whatever the duration of a project came to be.

Overestimating a budget, however, with its resulting lack of competitiveness, was seen as a lesser evil by IT, (most considered that losing business was 'not our problem') because most of the major IT work was not directly customer-responsible. The IT department employees, in essence, began to feel that they were living in a world where technological and political change went much faster than budgeted implementation plans. Their response was to try to control this by elongating time periods, increasing budgets, and requiring iron-clad commitments and guarantees from co-workers.

At the same time, IT did not understand the sales department. 'What do they do all day, anyway? Probably just out having lunch at the company's expense!' was a comment often heard in reference to the sales department. The uncertainty associated with sales, as well as a lack of understanding of the processes involved, led IT workers to distrust and undervalue the customer-facing side of the business. And as the organization was increasingly pieced together from acquisitions and mergers, it became more and more difficult to encourage employees to share information, profits and costs.

By mid-2003, the IT department was deeply enmeshed in an attempt to wrest more and more control from the projects in which it was involved. One senior manager in IT even demanded that Jim leave her office when he suggested that his team would be capable of managing and defending the IT element of the project budget. She considered it a major offense, principally because her definition of her department's job included 'controlling' the timing, budgets and internal and external resources of any project it would be involved in. While Jim managed to arrive at a negotiated middle ground for this aspect of the project, it continued to cause strife and lack of trust.

Khor had originally joined Logico as a member of the IT department of a small acquired specialist-freight company, Smallfreight. He had successfully managed a team that implemented a new operations system for them, and had also successfully worked through many of the integration issues that arose when Logico bought them. Eventually, however, he was incorporated into the larger IT department of Logico Freight Management. It was there that he soon began to feel buried under innumerable rules, procedures and acquired interests. To extricate himself from what he referred to as the 'hard-core techies', and as he had already gained some experience in working on sales systems, he actively lobbied to be assigned to the core SFA project team. Jim jumped at the chance to hire him.

Khor was soon well accepted in his new project team, as someone with much expertise on the technical side. However, he soon found himself admitting that he had to fight, to some degree, to 'retain his legitimacy and acceptance' from his former IT colleagues, who placed him under strong pressure to make the budgets and plans conform to their way of thinking. Essentially, he had to work very hard to overcome the opposed way of working between his current and former departments, as well as deal with some of his older colleagues, many of whom he now outranked.

Added to this was the challenge that some of his initial decisions were also extremely difficult to make, to a large degree because they involved having an in-depth knowledge of the strategic direction of the entire company, information which he was often not sufficiently senior to be privy to. This included whether Logico should contract a hosted system, and/or whether to work with outsourced suppliers for some elements of the program. At this point in time, 2003, the wider environment of technology was very fluid and dynamic indeed. The internet was still 'new', information highways had not yet been tested, and cloud computing was still a theory. This, combined with the less fluid and somewhat defensive IT mentalities and ways of working that had developed, caused friction.

There were even different 'languages' spoken within the IT department itself, which were already creating a rift between 'those who created' new technologies and 'those who maintained and managed' the old technologies. This led to a perceived need to establish an 'ambidextrous' department, allowing creative IT managers to race ahead with new plans while the majority of the department focused on keeping the systems running. Making decisions about human resources for IT had become a real challenge, and was certainly the type of decision many of his colleagues sought to avoid.

## The strategy department's analysis

To try to address what to do, in the longer term, about the SFA Project, Jane and her team (two Assistant Strategy Analysts) undertook a study to look, in what they considered to be 'a new and different way', at how technological change was perceived and executed by participants in the change programme as it progressed. Over the year 2003, she and her team closely followed the progress of the pilot SFA program as it was communicated and tested with the members of the three FM country sales forces who were asked to use it. In addition to her usual approach of gathering and analysing quantitative and objective data, Jane decided to examine this change with an additional 'cognitive lens' in order to compare an 'IT'-oriented mentality with a 'sales'-oriented one. Her goal was to try to understand what the members of the sales forces involved were thinking, and also to observe and participate in the meetings of the project team and other departments as they went about implementing the trial program.

Jane wanted to apply Pettigrew's definition of contextualism,[4] and thereby sought to study change in the context of interconnected levels of analysis, taking into account temporal links, and exploring 'how context is a product of action and vice-versa' (Pettigrew, 1990: p. 269). Her goal was to identify the overall processes, structures, actions and synergies that might make this project succeed (Pettigrew, 1990). Ultimately, what she really wanted was to focus on the 'how' of implementing a new technological system, which she then hoped would lead to an understanding of its likely, longer-term strategic success.

To do this, Jane and her team first put together a timeline, presented in Figure A2.8.8, which summarizes the major events around which the project took place in the organization. This timeline shows a retrospective view of events as they occurred along a whole-organization continuum. It also shows how and when Jane's group was called upon to study the project's evolution, and to make recommendations for the future, as an 'additional' layer in a complex structure. (See Figure A2.8.8 Timeline.)

Jane also decided that it would be necessary to carry out a number of interviews, thereby trying to find out, in as much depth as possible, what people were thinking about the Sales Force Automation project as it progressed. She and her team talked with managers and SFA project members in the IT department, as well as those in sales who would be affected by

Timeline: SFA Launch in LOGICO

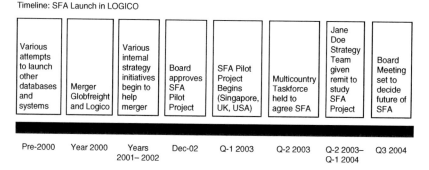

| Various attempts to launch other databases and systems | Merger Globfreight and Logico | Various internal strategy initiatives begin to help merger | Board approves SFA Pilot Project | SFA Pilot Project Begins (Singapore, UK, USA) | Multicountry Taskforce held to agree SFA | Jane Doe Strategy Team given remit to study SFA Project | Board Meeting set to decide future of SFA |
|---|---|---|---|---|---|---|---|
| Pre-2000 | Year 2000 | Years 2001–2002 | Dec-02 | Q-1 2003 | Q-2 2003 | Q-2 2003–Q-1 2004 | Q3 2004 |

*Figure A2.8.8*  Timeline

the implementation of the SFA, and also key members of the project team itself. Eventually, she and her team created brief summaries of what they thought each department was saying and thinking. (Logico Interviews, 2003). After looking them over, she arrived at a number of conclusions. (See Figure A2.8.9 for summarized interviews.)

1. The IT and sales departments seemed to be speaking very different 'languages', although many of the words they used were the same. For example, both groups used words such as 'pilot', 'structure', 'schema', 'budget', 'planning', 'measure', 'process'... and yet they often seemed to mean very different things. The project team members, on the other hand, generally tried to specify what they meant by each of their words and statements, and had put together a glossary of terms they would use during training. However, it seemed clear to Jane that the project team was the only group that came close to 'speaking both languages'.

2. Each department had a very different concept of how to plan for, and use, its time. It appeared that the IT department had had many difficult experiences in the past, where they had had to work a lot of overtime in order to deliver projects within the promised time frames. The IT department seemed to deal with this by setting out a linear model of how they thought the new SFA system could be implemented, based on adding up the estimated hours each IT person involved would require, planning what seemed like a reasonable amount of time to provide and receive work from the other departments, and then somehow, virtually doubling their original estimate to cover for contingencies. For them, once a plan or timing was set, it was a reference point for all subsequent deviations from it, and those deviations were what they measured and used to define the success or failure of their plan.

   The Sales Department, on the other hand, treated time in an almost circular way, always making any plan contingent upon customers, and yet assuming that once a decision was made, things would advance relatively quickly. In discussing their time planning, they were prone to use words such as 'inspiration' or 'motivation' or to recount stories of how they had reacted to pleasant or unpleasant surprises that had arisen with different customers. While the salespeople were able to perceive many elements that customers had in common, they nevertheless expected each customer to demonstrate a combination of traits that would make them unique, including how they made decisions, the products sent, or the size, destination or currency involved in each transaction. They considered it a fundamental part of their jobs to talk with customers and come to understand their unique needs, within the limiting framework of the overall services Logico was able to provide.

3. It was clear to Jane and her team that there was a fundamental difference in the way that the IT group vs. the sales group understood and dealt

**Highlights from Interviews of various IT and Sales personnel**

| Topic | Sales | IT |
|---|---|---|
| Logico should have a shared Sales Database | 'Yes, as long as it doesn't take time away from sales' | 'With time and money, we can programme anything Sales wants' |
| Processes | 'We have written them down a million times' | 'What are Sales' processes?' |
| What can SFA be used for | 'Sales come from having good information' | 'Garbage in, garbage out' |
| 'Ownership' of customers | 'Right now, it's all in my head. I own it because no one else has it' | 'This is company information, It should be held centrally' |
| Use of an IT tool | 'My idea of fun is not sitting playing with a new computer' | 'This will make it so much easier for them to work, if they all used it' |
| Control | 'Big Brother will be watching' | 'SFA should make Sales so much more productive' |
| Time | 'Takes up a lot of time' | 'Should save them a lot of time' |
| Measurement | 'You can't measure a customer that is about to buy but hasn't yet' | 'Will provide logical, useful facts at our fingertips' |
| Cost | 'How long is a piece of string?' | 'If they say it is a hundred, then we double it but try to make them stick to a hundred!' |

*Figure A2.8.9* Summarized interviews
*Source*: Author.

with the concept of control. While control was of deep-seated importance to the IT department, in the sales department it was virtually considered an illusion. The IT department sought more and more 'control' in almost everything they did, specifying, measuring and committing only to what were perceived to be tangible structures or concrete concepts. Indeed, one of IT's biggest fears seemed to be that most problems arose from elements of a project that were beyond their borders, and that the only logical way to deal with this was to take over more elements of a project, ensuring that they had even more control over all of its aspects. They were especially keen to have direct responsibility for money, human and technical resources, decision-making, and the reporting of results to senior management. What was more, if they did not have what they considered to be a comfortable level of control, they tended to refuse to work on a project.

Sales, on the other hand, appeared to have an innate assumption or understanding that 'everything was beyond their control anyway'. No one day was exactly like any other day and could not be expected to be, in relation to customers. Their attitude was, 'why try to control a human process that will change later on, anyway?' However, while this made them well able to improvise last-minute solutions, and very flexible in dealing with varying customer demands, it also meant that they tended to be very reactive to events, rather than strategically proactive about the longer-term future. Forecasts were approximate, and objectives were reprioritized on a regular basis.

4. Another element where Jane thought the two groups differed fundamentally was in their definitions of success or failure. The IT group sought provable, measurable, achievable endpoints, and wanted to be able to accumulate and 'look back on a steady stream of achievements'. The sales department, in contrast, seemed to be 'pacing' themselves for what was expected to be a long and continuous journey, full of surprises and yet easing towards a general direction.

5. With few exceptions, Jane thought that only those in the core project team were 'boundary spanners', able to work and feel comfortable in either IT or sales. Jane thought that Jim, Aya and Khor were especially good at adapting to what she began to see as 'different thought worlds' (Dougherty, 1992) in each department. She thought much of this had to do with their international backgrounds, as well as their ability to merge logic, and a scientific approach, with the understanding of what could be termed 'softer' human characteristics, such as the ability to deal with ambiguity and uncertainty, or a strong sense of values underlying their business actions. However, during meetings, it appeared to Jane that what the IT and sales people most lacked was a basic knowledge of how each department worked, and therefore what was missing was a basic level of trust when attempting to work together.

By the beginning of 2004, Jane had gathered almost a year's worth of both qualitative and quantitative information about the SFA Project. At this point, Jane was asked to present a recommendation to Logico's CEO as to whether to continue with the SFA global investment or not. He was not yet convinced that the project should continue, arguing that there was no consensus within the organization about what could really be gained from further expenditure in this area. In addition, he was aware that, within a year or so, bigger changes might even supersede this change within the organization. So far, the results had been indicative but inconclusive. (See Figure A2.8.6c: Results.)

According to the results that had been put together to date, sales were good, but sales by other groups NOT using the SFA had been almost as good. Processes were written down, but they still appeared to be more general than specific. Control was still elusive. 'Why'" said the CEO to Jane, 'after investing this amount of time and money, can't I have a clear picture of what sales are doing and how much we are likely to sell in the future? Why does the technology always have to cost so much and take so long?'

While it was clear that the sales force *was* adapting, the CEO and other top managers were now prioritizing many other projects into future expenditures, and were unsure how to categorize the SFA at this point. Was it a success or a failure? Qualitatively, the sales force was clearly very happy with the attention and tools they had been given, while the IT department had also, clearly, delivered their end of the bargain – it worked, and only needed to be used more to be really effective. Quantitatively, however, there was not a conclusive amount of new business that had been gained from having the system in place so far. Hence, in a rapidly changing world and company, where money and focus would be needed for other objectives, the SFA's strategic importance was a difficult decision.

Essentially, Jane's task was to develop a 'project within a project' as well as to help senior managers decide about 'the SFA project's fit' within the longer-term strategic goals and priorities of Logico FM as a whole. Was this an insurmountable task, and no further time or resources should be 'wasted' in getting two departments and three geographic regions to work together? Or, was it the beginning of a major change management programme, where Logico would soon be able to store and retrieve a large amount of very useful data on past and future Sales?

Jane thought about the many layers in what was a very complex Logico matrix organization. Was it even possible to peel back these layers of ingrained departmental culture to arrive at a commonly beneficial solution for all parties? If not, what was the alternative? And, if so, could this be done on a tight budget, for a finite period of time, with limited resources? Was it a possible and economically feasible project, which would eventually pave the way towards strategic and long-term-sales success for Logico as a whole?

## What next?

Jane had recently read Graham Allison's *Essence of Decision*,[5] about the three different ways that political scientists could study and understand the Cuban missile crisis in the USA. Allison asked that managers and politicians and scientists should carry out a 'new kind of case study...' looking at a whole new range of factors with which to refine and test propositions, and to explore 'a much larger space of possibilities than prediction requires' (Allison, 1971: p. 273).

In effect, what Jane realized that she must do was to combine and merge some of the inductive and deductive capabilities of Logico, into what Boisot and McKelvey call a 'more scalable abduction' (Boisot and McKelvey, 2010: p. 430).

In the final analysis, Jane needed to harness the excellent capabilities of those in IT who could manage the logic of a new technological system within a predictable fiscal year, while at the same time support and yet give more freedom to those in sales who needed to manage and nurture the complexities of human interaction over varying periods of time.

# Notes

## Foreword

1. Chandler, A. 1992. Organizational capabilities and the economic history of the industrial enterprise. *Journal of Economic Perspectives*, 6(3): 79–100.
2. Peter Cappelli, Harbir Singh, Jitendra Singh and Michael Useem, 2010. The India Way: Lessons for the U.S. *Academy of Management Perspectives*, May: 6–24.
3. Khanna, T. Yafeh, Y. 2007. Business Groups in Emerging Markets: Paragons or Parasites? *Journal of Economic Literature*, 45 (2): 331–372.
4. Moran, P. and S. Ghoshal, 1996. Bad for practice: A critique of the transaction cost theory. *Academy of Management Review*, 21(1): 13–47.
5. Hertel, G., S. Niedner and S. Herrmann. 2003. Motivation of software developers in open source projects: An internet-based survey of contributors to the linux kernel. *Research Policy*, 32(7): 1159.
6. Doktor, R., R.L. Tung, M.A von Glinow, 1991. Incorporating international dimensions in management theory building. *Academy of Management Review*, 16(2): 259–261.

## 1 Introduction

1. 洋務運動 or 自強運動.
2. In this book, we focus our attention on Eastern Asia, especially Japan, Korea and China (and Taiwan), as a perceived entity with a certain level of homogeneity in its basic cognition patterns. Confucianism and sinicized Buddhism such as Pure Land and Zen schools may have provided cohesion.
3. In a similar vein, we centre our study on the West, understanding as such Western Europe, namely, Germany, France, Italy, Spain, as well as the UK, Ireland, the US and Canada. Latin America, namely, the countries including Mexico and her Southern neighbours, ought to be included in this category as well, though we have not turned our attention to it because of time constraints.

## 2 Literature Review: Philosophical Perspectives on Knowledge and Cognition

1. flātus us, m. [flo], a blowing, breathing, snorting (Lewis, 1989).
2. vox vōcis, f. [voco], a voice, sound, tone, cry, call (Lewis, 1989).
3. http://en.wikipedia.org/wiki/Idealism (accessed 2 September 2010).
4. The contrast between reductionism and phenomenology may be added as another example of the dichotomy. Reductionism (Frisby) understood as 'an attempt or a tendency to explain complex phenomena or structures by relatively simple principles, as by asserting that life processes or mental acts are instances of chemical and physical laws' (American Heritage Dictionary), was superseded by phenomenology (Husserl, 1999; Merleau-Ponty, 1958, 2008) in an attempt to interpret the objective world based on one's own subjective

experience (Kida, 1970). Gestalt psychology (Brigandt, 2003; Hamlyn, 2005; Köhler, 1967; Lorenz, 1962; Wertheimer, 1924; Westheimer, 1999), *l'Ecole des annales* (Braudel, 1992), *structuralisme* in anthropology (Levi-Strauss, 1974), etc., are some examples.

5. 'Mind, as employed in perceiving and thinking, sense, wit' (Liddel and Scott, 1996).

6. 'The foundationalist's thesis in short is that all knowledge and justified belief rest ultimately on a foundation of non-inferential knowledge or justified belief.' (Stanford Encyclopedia of Philosophy, http://plato.stanford.edu/entries/justepfoundational/ (accessed 16 March 2010)).

7. 'Synderesis, keeping/understanding natural principles of moral law' (Lewis, 1989).

8. As to the effort to integrate Christianity and Aristotelian philosophy, especially relating to cognition, see the works by Thomas Aquinas (1993, 1995) and the commentaries on his works (Copleston, 1955; Kenny, 1980; Kretzmann and Stump, 1993; MacDonald, 1993).

9. 'A theory of substantial forms asserts that there are things called forms (or ideas), and that they are what organize matter and make it intelligible. Substantial forms are the source of order, unity, and identity of objects.' (http://en.wikipedia.org/ wiki/Substantial_form (accessed 23 March 2010))

10. This is called a 'dreaming argument' since 'there are no certain marks to distinguish being from being asleep' (Cottingham, 2005: p. 202).

11. Descartes (1968b) expresses his resolution to observe several principles, the first of which is never to accept anything as true that he does not know to be evidently so.

12. This is called Cogito argument (Cottingham, 2005: p. 20).

13. (Kim, 2005).

14. Russell (1995: p. 546) sees two merits in this: (1) it made the soul wholly independent of the body, since it is never acted on by the body; and (2) it allowed the general principle – 'one substance cannot act on another' – wherefore, they being so dissimilar, no interaction between mind and matter seems conceivable.

15. Therefore, in the West, we have developed a method that could be termed 'micro' while, as explained later, on the 'method' used in Asia could be termed 'macro'.

16. '[f]ive interrelated aggregates...five psycho-physical aggregates. These are the aggregate of consciousness, the aggregate of form...the aggregate of feeling, the aggregate of discrimination, and the aggregate of motivational tendencies' (Dalai Lama, 2005: p. xiii).

17. http://en.wikipedia.org/wiki/Buddhism (accessed 30 March 2010).

18. 'Tominaga Nakamoto (1715–46)...analysed the history of the three systems (that is, Confucianism, Buddhism and Shinto) and pointed out...how the notions of each were conditioned by the internal logic of ideas themselves...' (Kato, 1981b: p. 129).

19. Circa 150–250 AD (Nakamura, Fukunaga, Tamura & Konno, 2000: p. 830r).

20. Confused with a Bodhisattva of the same name, his historic existence is doubted (Nakamura, et al., 2000: p. 810r).

21. 1240–1321 (Japanese English Buddhist Dictionary, 1999: p. 104r).

22. (Eliade, 1958: pp. 11–12).

23. 'Xuanzang...a native of Henan, A.D. 600–664' (Soothill and Hodous, 2003).

24. Xuanzang in pinying.

25. (Soothill and Hodous, 2003).

26. (Japanese English Buddhist Dictionary, 1999).
27. http://6865.blogcindario.com/2007/11/04483-la-iglesia-catolica-en-espana-noviembre-de-2007-campana-de-comunicacion.html (accessed 3 April 2010).
28. http://www.stat.go.jp/english/data/jinsui/tsuki/index.htm (accessed 4 April 2010).
29. http://www.ine.es/jaxiBD/tabla.do?per=01&type=db&divi=EPOB&idtab=2 (accessed 3 April 2010).
30. 'Taoism is believed to be the inspiration for spiritual concepts in Japanese culture. Taoism is similar to Shinto in that it also started as an indigenous religion in China. However, it is more hermetic than shamanistic. Taoism's influence can be seen throughout the culture but to a lesser extent than Confucianism' (Wikipedia, 2010b).
31. 莊子
32. 淮南子
33. 躰用 in Buddhism is 'substance, or body, and function; the fundamental and phenomenal; the function of any body' (Soothill & Hodous, 2003); in Neo-Confucianism, 'a principle and its application' (Kenkyusha's New Japanese English Dictionary, 2004).
34. 気
35. 理
36. 'Not to be confused with New Confucianism.' Contemporary New Confucianism (dangdai xin Rujia 當代新儒家; dangdai xin Ruxue 當代新儒學; xiandai xin Rujia 現代新儒家; xiandai xin Ruxue 現代新儒學, hereafter, New Confucianism) is a movement promoted and/or researched by prominent Chinese intellectuals based in China, Taiwan, Hong Kong and the United States of America. (In English, the term 'New Confucian' is to be distinguished from 'Neo-Confucian', which refers to certain Confucian thinkers of the Song, Yuan and Ming dynasties, in particular.) New Confucianism has emerged as a neo-conservative philosophical movement, with religious overtones, which claims to be the legitimate transmitter and representative of orthodox Confucian values' (Makeham, 2003: pp. 1–2).
37. 宋學
38. 性理學
39. 心學
40. 理學
41. 朱熹1130–1200 AD (Kojien, 2008).
42. 周濂渓 1017–1073 AD (Kojien, 2008).
43. 程明道 1032–1085 AD, 程伊川 1033–1107 AD (Kojien, 2008).
44. 理気説
45. 性即理説
46. 居敬 窮理説
47. 'The yang and yin are thought to have originated in a process of differentiation from the taiji （太極）which is "the grand origin"' (Carus, 1902:p. 25).
48. 五行
49. 聖人
50. 格物致知
51. 王陽明（1472–1528）(Kojien, 2008).
52. 致良知
53. 良知
54. 良能
55. 心即理

56. 知行合一
57. Taylor (2004: p. 17) stresses the importance of Neo-Confucianism in Korea during the 14th–20th century Joseon (also Chosŏn, Choson, Chosun) Dynasty with such a figure as Yi T'oegye, who flourished in the 16th century.
58. 'Most significant early Chinese interpreter of Taoism, and the purported author of the Taoist classic that bears his name' (*Encyclopaedia Britannica*, 2004).

## 3   Literature Review: Epistemological Perspective – Inductive and Deductive Thinking

1. '[Socrates] And now, I said, let me show in a figure how far our nature is enlightened or unenlightened: –Behold! human beings living in an underground cave, which has a mouth open towards the light and reaching all along the cave; here they have been from their childhood, and have their legs and necks chained so that they cannot move, and can only see before them, being prevented by the chains from turning round their heads. Above and behind them a fire is blazing at a distance, and between the fire and the prisoners there is a raised way; and you will see, if you look, a low wall built along the way, like the screen which marionette players have in front of them, over which they show the puppets.
   [Glaucon] I see.
   [Socrates] And do you see, I said, men passing along the wall carrying all sorts of vessels, and statues and figures of animals made of wood and stone and various materials, which appear over the wall? Some of them are talking, others silent.
   [Glaucon] You have shown me a strange image, and they are strange prisoners.
   [Socrates] Like ourselves, I replied; and they see only their own shadows, or the shadows of one another, which the fire throws on the opposite wall of the cave?' (Plato, 1989: 514a–515a)

## 4   Literature Review: Cognitive Science Perspective

1. 'The principle that in explaining a thing no more assumptions should be made than are necessary. Also called law of parsimony' (*Shorter Oxford Dictionary*, 6th Edition).
2. Louis Quichierat's (1799–1884) *Gradus ad Parnassum* and Pliny's *Naturalis Historia*.
3. 'Exemplos de memoria: La memoria, bien tan necesario a la vida, quién la haya tenido mayor no es cosa fácil de juzgar entre tantos que han alcanzado su Gloria.
   El rey Cyro nombrava uno por uno todos los soldados de su exército; Lucio Scipión todos los del pueblo romano; Cyneas, Legado del rey Pirrho, los del senado y orden de cavalleros en Roma, otro día después de venido; Mythrídates, rey de 22 diferencias de gentes, les dio leyes a todos en otras tantas lenguas haziéndoles pláticas sin intérprete. Un Charmidas, en Grecia, refería en las librerías, como si lo fuera leyendo, los volúmines que havía compuesto cada uno. Y, en fin, se hizo [un] arte de [la] memoria, inventada por Simónides de Mélico y acabada por Methrodoro Scepsio para que no huviese cosa que, oída una vez, no se dixese de coro ...' (Cayo Plinio Segundo, 1999: pp. 326–327).

(N.B.: This is a 17th century Spanish translation by Francisco Hernández and Jerónimo de Huerta.)
4. 'Al caer, perdió el conocimiento; cuando lo recobró, el presente era casi intolerable de tan rico y tan nítido...' (Borges, 1989: p. 488).
5. 'En lugar de siete mil trece, decía (por ejemplo) Máximo Pérez; en lugar de siete mil catorce, El Ferrocarril... Yo traté de explicar que esa rapsodia de voces inconexas era precisamente lo contrario de un sistema de numeración.' (Borges, 1989: p. 488).
6. 'Le molestaba que el perro de las tres y catorce (visto de perfil) tuviera el mismo nombre que el perro de tres cuarto (visto de frente)' (Borges, 1989: p. 490).
7. http://en.wikipedia.org/wiki/Funes_the_Memorious (accessed 3 June 2009).
8. 'Deductive and inductive arguments' The Internet *Encyclopedia of Philosophy* www. iep.utm.edu (accessed 10 April 2008).
9. For further information on object individuation, see, for example, Tremoulet, Leslie and Hall (2000) and Wilcox (1999).

## 6 Theoretical Framework

1. In Islamic philosophy distinction is made of *māhīyah* and *huwīyah* regarding the essence or quiddity (the former corresponding to the essence found in the general or universal while the latter corresponding to the essence found in the specific) (Izutsu, 1991). It is possible that the Westerners' way of thinking follows the path of *māhīyah* and the Asians' way of thinking that of *huwīyah*.
2. This is a replication of Table 3.3 in Chapter 3. We reproduce it here for ease of understanding. It integrates the information contained in Tables 6.3 and 6.4.
3. See Stephen (1904) cited by Natsume (1985: p. 68), who expresses his belief about the English penchant for concreteness or perhaps inductive inference: 'The strong point of the English mind is vigorous grasp of facts: its weakness is its comparative indifference to logical symmetry.'
4. These concepts are explained in Confucius' Analects and other Confucian sacred books (Legge, 1986). Their exegesis ought to be done inductively because they are extremely context-dependent and sometimes even seem to be contradictory (Yoshikawa, 1971).
5. http://www.census.gov/eos/www/naics/ (accessed 13 October 2010).
6. The short-termism in the Asian context may not necessarily mean the pursuit of short-term profit maximization to the exclusion of the long-term vision (Fruin, 1992; Hamel & Prahalad, 1989; Kono, 1984; Nonaka, 1990; Pascale, 1988; Quinn, 1985; Yoshino, 1968).
7. This could be a moot point, though. Companies in the UK and the US (therefore, possibly more deductive than inductive) are often criticized because of their short-termism (Marginson & McAulay, 2008; Grinyer, Russell & Collison, 1998).

## Annex 1

1. The survey was conducted in May to July in 2010 by Kimio Kase (IESE Business School), José Antonio Ruiz (Universidad Complutense de Madrid), Lourdes Susaeta (IESE Business School) and Nuria Villagra (Universidad Complutense de Madrid) between March and July, 2010. A more detailed report on this survey is under preparation for journal publication.

## Annex 2.1

1. IESE Business School Case No. SM-1557-E. Written by Kimio Kase and Antonio Guerrero. Reproduced with IESE's permission.
2. http://www.time.com/time/asia/2006/heroes/bl_shih.html (accessed 28 March 2010).
3. http://www.um.es/docencia/barzana/DIVULGACION/INFORMATICA, (accessed 18 February 2010).
   http://duiops.net/hardware/micros/microshis,.htm, (accessed 18 February 2010).
4. http://apple2history.org (accessed 18 February 2010).
5. http://muycomputer.com/ (accessed 20 March 2010).
6. http://www.cmq.colmex.mx/docinvest/document/DI17118.pdf (accessed 18 February 2010).
   http://www.cad.com.mx/generacion_de_las_computadoras.htm (accessed 18 February 2010).
   http://www.monografias.com/computacion/Hardware, (accessed on 18 February 2010).
   http://www.sourcejuice.com/1269381/ (accessed 18 February 2010).
7. Fujimoto T. 2004. *Brush up the manufacturing industry's integrating skills: Strengthen its strategy-designing capability* (Seizogyo suriawaseryoku wo migake: senryaku kosoryoku mo kyoka), *Nihon Keizai Shimbun*: 16: 12 January: Tokyo.
8. Interview in the *San Francisco Chronicle* (Monday, 25 February, 2002).
9. http://es. wikipedia.org/wiki/Microprocessor (accessed 22 February 2010).
10. http://es. wikipedia.org/wiki/Microprocessor_II (accessed 22 February 2010).
11. http://es. wikipedia.org/wiki/Microprocessor_III (accessed 22 February 2010).
12. Founded in 1979 by Dave Jackson and Ron Conway in San José, California.
13. http://www.answers.com/topic/acer-inc (accessed 22 February 2010).
14. Acer's founder.
15. http://taiwaninfo.nat.gov.tw (accessed 22 February 2010).
16. http://www.fundinguniverse.com/company-histories/Acer-Inc-Company-History (accessed 22 February 2010).
17. *Business Week*, 2 July, 2004. Special Report, Stars of Asia.
18. http://www.c.enter.hu/Archive/News/june.2006/Acer's Channel Business Model (accessed 22 February 2010).
19. http://www.muymac.com/ accessed 27 March 2010.
20. http://www.crn.com/it-channel (accessed 6 November 2009).
21. Based on http://en. Wikipedia.org/stan_shih (accessed 6 November 2009).
22. http://www.crn.com/it-channel (accessed 6 November 2009).
23. http://www.sfgate.com (accessed 6 November 2009).
24. http://www.time.com /time/asia (accessed 6 November 2009).
25. See Kimura (2006).
26. http://www.crn.com/it-channel (accessed 6 November 2009).
27. http://www.crn.com/it-channel (accessed 6 November 2009).
28. http://www.crn.com/it-channel (accessed 6 November 2009).
29. (Shih, 2001).
30. http://www.crn.com/it-channel (accessed 6 November 2009).
31. http://www.crn.com/it-channel (accessed 6 November 2009).
32. http://blogs.bnet.com/salesmachine (accessed 6 November 2009).
33. http://blogs.bnet.com/salesmachine (accessed 6 November 2009).

34. www.acergroup.com (accessed 6 November 2009).
35. Acer 2008 Annual Report.

## Annex 2.2

1. IESE Business School case No. SM-1558-E. Written by Kimio Kase. Reproduced with IESE Business School's permission.
2. Unless specified otherwise, the explanation applies to the Imperial Japanese Navy too.
3. Based mainly on Tobe, Teramoto, Kamata, Murai and Nonaka (1991: pp. 268–339). Summarized with the authors' authorization.
4. 'The orientation of the Japanese economy toward war began in 1928, and continued with increasing emphasis during the Manchurian and Chinese campaigns. By 1940, total production had risen by more than 75 per cent; heavy industrial production by almost 500 per cent; and 17 per cent of Japan's total output was being devoted directly to war purposes and the expansion of her munition industries, as opposed to 2.6 per cent dedicated to these endeavours at that time in the United States. Construction of industrial facilities in these years assumed – for the Japanese conditions – gigantic proportions. Her aircraft, aluminum, machine tools, automotive, and tank industries were erected from almost nothing during this period.

   This industrial expansion was based, and heavily depended upon, the availability of raw materials. Great efforts were devoted to the increase of raw material output in the home islands. In some respects, major results were achieved. Coal production in Japan rose from 28,000,000 tons in 1931 to 55,600,000 tons in 1941. Domestic iron mining made considerable progress. Nevertheless, no country could have been farther from self-sufficiency, with respect to raw materials, than Japan. The development of basic materials sources on the Asian continent constituted almost the central issue of Japan's economic policy during this period.

   Although progress in Manchuria and China helped significantly to alleviate Japan's raw material shortages in coking coal, iron ore, salt and foods, insufficiency of raw materials continued to be the most important limiting factor on Japanese industrial output. Negligible quantities of oil and no bauxite sources existed within Japan's "Inner Zone." Output of aluminum ingots had risen from 19 tons in 1933 to 71,740 in 1941, 90 per cent of which was produced from bauxite imported from the Dutch East Indies. Plans to develop a synthetic oil industry failed to yield significant results and Japan was almost wholly dependent on oil imports from the United States or the Dutch East Indies. A similar dependence on imports existed for rubber, ferro-alloys such as manganese' (United States Strategic Bombing Survey, 1946: p. 13).
5. *Effective* is to be 'capable of bringing about an effect: productive of results' (*Webster's Third New International Dictionary*).
6. *Efficient* means to be 'marked by ability to choose and use the most effective and least wasteful means of doing a task or accomplishing a purpose' (*Webster's Third New International Dictionary*).
7. A Korean MBA student pointed out that the majority of these shortcomings might be applicable to the Korean Army since 'the Korean Army inherited some characteristics of the Japanese military and something I noticed while I served in the military is that the first five causes apply directly to our military system' (Che-Kwon Chung's personal communication to Kimio Kase on 1 June 2009).

8. Not discussed in this document.
9. 'Objectives are a description of what we want to achieve. They are the results to be reached, the ends that we direct our actions toward, those things that we want to obtain. It is highly advisable when stating an objective that we indicate, in some form, what has to be done in order to reach the future situation, dimension it quantitatively, and establish a determined time period. The use of generalities or the expression of mere desires on the part of management should be avoided' (Valero y Vicente and Lucas Tomás, n.d.).
10. By way of anecdote, we may refer to Haruki Murakami's *The Wind-Up Bird Chronicle* (1997), a popular Japanese novel in which the Nomonhan Incident is a recurring topic.
11. Another interpretation of the situation is less harsh on Nagumo: 'Admiral Nagumo, in accordance with Japanese carrier doctrine at the time, had kept half of his aircraft in reserve. These comprised two squadrons each of dive bombers and torpedo bombers, the latter armed with torpedoes, should any American warships be located. The dive bombers were, as yet, unarmed. As a result of the attacks from Midway, as well as the morning flight leader's recommendation regarding the need for a second strike, at 07:15, Nagumo ordered his reserve planes to be re-armed with general-purpose contact bombs for use against land targets. Some sources maintain that this had been underway for about 30 minutes when, at 07:40, the delayed scout plane from the cruiser *Tone* signalled the discovery of a sizable American naval force to the east; however, new evidence suggests that Nagumo did not receive the sighting report until 08:00, so that the rearming operation actually proceeded for 45 minutes. Nagumo quickly reversed his order and demanded the scout plane ascertain the composition of the American force. Another 40 minutes elapsed before *Tone's* scout finally radioed the presence of a single carrier in the American force, TF 16 (the other carrier being missed).

Nagumo was now in a quandary. Rear Admiral Yamaguchi Tamon, leading Carrier Division 2 (Hiryū and Sōryū), recommended Nagumo strike immediately with the forces at hand: 18 Aichi D3A2 dive bombers each on Sōryū and Hiryū, and half the ready Civil Air Patrol (CAP) aircraft. Nagumo's seeming opportunity to hit the American ships, however, was now limited by the fact his Midway strike force would be returning shortly and needing to land promptly or ditch (as is commonly believed). Because of the constant flight deck activity associated with combat air patrol operations during the preceding hour, the Japanese never had an opportunity to spot their reserve for launch. The few aircraft on the Japanese flight decks at the time of the attack were either CAP fighters, or (in the case of Sōryū) fighters being spotted to augment the CAP. Spotting his flight decks and launching aircraft would have required at least 30–45 minutes. Furthermore, by spotting and launching immediately, Nagumo would be committing some of his reserve to battle without proper anti-ship armament; they had just witnessed how easily unescorted American bombers had been shot down. (In the event, poor discipline saw many of the Japanese bombers ditch their bombs and attempt to dogfight interceptor F4Fs.) Japanese carrier doctrine preferred fully constituted strikes, and in the absence of a confirmation (until 08:20) of whether the American force contained carriers, Nagumo's reaction was doctrinaire. In addition, the arrival of another American air strike at 07:53 gave weight to the need to attack the island again. In the end, Nagumo chose to wait for his first strike force to land, then launch the reserve force, which would have by then been properly armed and ready. In the final analysis, it made no difference; Fletcher had launched beginning at 07:00, so the aircraft which would deliver the crushing blow were already on their way. There was nothing Nagumo could do about it. This was the fatal flaw of Yamamoto's dispositions: it followed strictly traditional battleship doctrine (http://en.wikipedia.org/wiki/ Battle_of_Midway (accessed 29 May 2009).

12. According to http://ja.wikipedia.org/wiki/ on the battle accessed 29 May 2009, the Japanese Army initially planned to fight on land in Luzon Island and by sea in Leyte and other areas, but the top officers at the Japanese Army mistook the result of the Aerial Battle of Taiwan–Okinawa between 12 and 16 October 1944 and believed that they had sunk four US aircraft carriers, and overruling General Yamashita's opinion against it, decided to fight the decisive battle near Leyte on land.

13. (Cohen, 1949).

14. 'War Plan Orange (commonly known as Plan Orange or just Orange) refers to a series of United States Joint Army and Navy Board war plans for dealing with a possible war with Japan during the interwar years. The plans were begun informally in 1919 and formally adopted by the Joint Army and Navy Board beginning in 1924' http://en.wikipedia.org/wiki/War_Plan_Orange (accessed 26 May 2009).

15. Akira Nakamura's 1990 book in Japanese entitled *The Way to Greater East Asia War*, widely popular among the conservatives in Japan, estimates the casualties in the USSR Army at 20,000 instead of the traditional figure of 8,000, which contrasts with 12,000 casualties in the Japanese Army, serving as a basis for his conjecture that Japan had not been defeated in the Incident, an opinion echoed in the Japanese version of Wikipedia on the Battle (http://ja.wikipedia.org/wiki accessed 30 May 2009).

16. The principle that decisions are taken not on the basis of systems, rules and so on, but of people and their relationships with others.

17. For a classic sociological study of the relationship structure in Japan, see Nakane (1973) and, for a political study, see Maruyama (2008).

18. (Kahane, 2007).

19. See Benedict, 2006); Doi, 2002; Imai, 2002; Imai and Gentner, 1997, for the analysis of Japanese ideas and thought processes.

20. Hastings (2008: 53) cited by http://en.wikipedia.org/wiki/Masanobu_Tsuji (accessed 28 May 2009).

21. http://en.wikipedia.org/wiki/Renya_Mutaguchi (accessed 30 May 2009).

22. For the differences between US/Western and Japanese management, see, for example, Kagono, Nonaka, Sakakibuar and Okumura (1985), various books by Professor Masao Aoki (1986, 1988, 1993, 2002, 2003; 1994; 1986, 1989), Abegglen (1958) Abegglen (1985) and Dore (1973, 1987).

## Annex 2.3

1. IESE Business School case No. DG-1521-E. Written by Kimio Kase and Fanqi Xu. Reproduced with IESE Business School's permission.

2. Based on Xu (2007) and Xu (2005).

3. For further information about the acquisition deal, see Siddhanta and Chakraborty (2007).

4. In an interview, Liu recognized that he did not have any great ambitions. He only wanted to raise more income, as it was unlikely that the Chinese Academy of Sciences would let him develop his business as much as he wanted. See Xu (2007: p. 257).

5. Xu (2007: p. 265). Start-up businesses by Beijing University, for instance, also fall in this category, namely, businesses outside the state's plan and protection.

6. LaMoshi (2006) argues that 'Lianxiang used government incentives to expand to Hong Kong' and that 'its partner in Hong Kong was a government company ... that gave Lianxiang access to offshore capital as well as contacts.'

7. Marukawa (2002b: p. 12 et seq) points out the following as Lenovo's success factors: 1) the PC's compatibility with a lower entry barrier, 2) the focus on sales, 3) the good image of its parent organization, 4) the flexibility of private companies, 5) the alignment of the company's and the employees' interests by the latter's 35 per cent share ownership.

8. 'Moore's Law is the empirical observation made in 1965 that the number of transistors on an integrated circuit for minimum component cost doubles every 24 months. It is attributed to Gordon E. Moore (born 1929), a co-founder of Intel.' (http://en.wikipedia.org/wiki/Moore's_law accessed 28 October 2007)

9. LaMoshi (2006) contends that 'by 2000, Lianxiang had a 30 per cent home-market share; but its government and business customers began to abandon it in favour of Compaq ... and, especially Dell" and that "with growth increasingly hard to achieve in China, Lenovo ... agreed to a ... deal to buy IBM's PC business in 2004 ... Liu approved the acquisition only after becoming convinced that his company could turn a profit on the business that was losing money for IBM.'

10. Drawn from Liu Chuangzhi's speech at Xi'an Electronic Science and Technology University on 28 October 2000, cited by Xu (2007).

11. For Liu, innovation requires 1) the ability to turn technology into merchandise, 2) the ability to get the better of foreign competitors by combining management and technology, and 3) shifting from state ownership to shareholder ownership (currently, 35 per cent is owned by Lenovo's employees – with Liu holding 1 per cent).

12. Marukawa (2002a: p. 22) emphasizes this point and attributes it to the fact that Lenovo's initial business consisted of commercializing products manufactured by others; he believes that this is deeply rooted in its DNA.

13. Liu in Xu (2007: pp. 256–7) stresses that in the high-technology industry, shortening the time in inventory is vital for reducing costs.

14. In his interview with Xu (2007: p. 254), Liu reminisced that at the beginning, the major factor for a hi-tech enterprise's survival was not to have staff, resources, and money, but to convince the staff that products must be sold and they must go to the market instead of waiting for the market to come to them.

15. Xu (2007: pp. 222–226).

16. Taken from Lenovo's annual report 2005/2006.

## Annex 2.4

1. IESE Business School case No. SM-1560-E. Written by Ying Ying Zhang and Kimio Kase. Reproduced with IESE Business School's permission.

2. Source: http://www.huawei.com/corporate_information/vision_mission.do (accessed 4 November 2009).

3. Ibid.

4. Yuan is the Chinese monetary unit. According to the exchange rate published in www.xe.com on 3 November 2009, 1 Euro was approximately equivalent to 10 Yuan.

5. *Chinese Entrepreneurs* (中国企业家) is one of the most well-known magazines in China focusing on Chinese entrepreneurs. More information can be found on http://www.iceo.com.cn
6. *The Winter of Huawei* (华为的冬天) is an article written by Zhengfei Ren published in February 2001 (Tang, 2004). In the article, Ren warned the company about the forthcoming winter (crisis) and suggested preparing for the crisis. The article is well known in the Chinese IT industry, and has been widely distributed by many top managers in the industry. More information about the article can been found on: http://www.tcnet.com.cn/tcsite/idnptech/41.asp

## Annex 2.5

Due appreciation is expressed for the permission given by the authors cited in the text, especially Ben Bland.

1. IESE Business School case No. SM-1548-E. Written by Kimio Kase and Ignacio Olivares. Reproduced with IESE Business School's permission.
2. Bland (2009).
3. *Berliner Zeitung* (http://www.berlinonline.de/berlinerzeitung/print/magazin/709927 accessed 28 December 2009).
4. 'The activity of Kantha Bopha I Hospital was initiated in 1992 by 16 European expatriates and 68 Cambodians. In 2008, the personnel working in all Kantha Bopha hospitals consists of 2100 Cambodians (including 180 doctors) with only two permanent European expatriates. Since 1992/93, the mortality rate has been reduced from 5.4 per cent to 0.75 per cent in 2008.' http://www.beat-richner.ch/Assets/richner_KBAP_Academy.html (accessed 29 October 2009.)
5. Based on Chandler (2000) and http://en.wikipedia.org/wiki/Cambodia (accessed 31 October 2009).
6. As to the splendours of Cambodia's past, refer to authors of travel books and chronicles such as Mouhot (2000), Zhou (2007), Quiroga de San Antonio (1998), Loti (1996).
7. For example, Chandler (2000).
8. Source: World Institute for Asian Studies.
9. Based on the 2009 CIA World Factbook.
10. Based, inter alia, on http://www.beatocello.com/Assets/richner_history.html accessed 28 October 2007
11. The three main objectives of the Foundation are to help sick children, support medical training in Cambodia and fight against corruption, according to the Foundation's 2006 Annual Report.
12. http://www.beatocello.com/Assets/richner_history.html (accessed 1 November 2009).
13. http://www.beat-richner.ch/Assets/richner_KBAP_Academy.html (accessed 29 October 2009).
14. Data updated to 2009, as provided by the institution.
15. *Berliner Zeitung* (http://www.berlineronline.de/berlinerzeitung/print/magazin/709927 accessed 1 November 2009).
16. http://www.beat-richner.ch/Assets/richner_present.html (accessed 15 December 2009).
17. Dr Beat Richner's inauguration speech of Kantha Bopha V on 28 December 2007.

18. http://www.beat-richner.ch/pdf/Reviews/BeatRichner_FTMAG_140309.pdf accessed 15 November 2009
19. Dr Beat Richner's article in the *Cambodia Daily*, 17 August 2007 (p. 7).
20. Based on the extract from the Kantha Bopha Foundation's 2006 and 2008 Annual Reports.
21. Une bonne action? Pensez au Dr med Beat 'Beatocello' Richner KANTHA BOPHA Children's Hospital http://www.lausannekendo.ch/modules/wordpress/category/friends/ (accessed 1 November 2009).
22. Donations can be made after each concert or through various bank accounts in Europe: Postal account in Switzerland, ZKB – Zürcher Kantonalbank, and UBS AG.
23. 1 CHF = €0.659 = $0.6222, as of 1 November 2009.
24. Aktion Zwaenzger Noetli 2004.
25. Source: www.beat-richner.ch.
26. http://lg-media.blogspot.com/2009/08/cambodian-clinic-twice-declares.html (accessed 1 November 2009).
27. Based on the Foundation's 2006 and 2008 Annual Reports.
28. Dr Richner is quoted as saying, 'In a government hospital, you have to pay under the table to see the doctor; you have to pay for an X-ray, you have to pay for the surgeon and the anaesthetist and then you have to find a doctor to look after the follow-up. Altogether, it would probably cost US$400 and there's no way a family could afford it' (Bland, 2009).
29. Extract from Doctor Beat Richner: Celebration address on the 175th anniversary of the Real-Gymnasium Zürichberg, given on-stage at the Schauspielhaus Zürich, 4 September 2008.
30. Bland (2009).
31. Bland (2009).
32. Extract from the speech of Dr Beat Richner addressed to Mrs Carol Bellamy, executive director of UNICEF at Siem Reap on 27 October 2004.
33. Extract from the appeal to the president of the International Court of Justice and Human Rights dated 10 December 1999 in Siem Reap by Dr Beat Richner and Kantha Bopha Children's Hospitals.
34. Dr Beat Richner's online newsletter dated 30 May 2008 (http://www.beat-richner.ch accessed 15 November 2009).
35. Dr Beat Richner's online newsletter dated 19 June 2009 (www.Beatocello.com).
36. *Berliner Zeitung* (http://www.berlinonline.de/berlinerzeitung/print/magazin/709927 accessed 15 November 2009).
37. Bland (2009).
38. *Berliner Zeitung* (http://www.berlinonline.de/berlinerzeitung/print/magazin/709927 accessed 15 November 2009).
39. Bland (2009).

## Annex 2.6

1. IESE Business School case No. SM-1534-E. Written by Kimio Kase and Federico Marinelli. Reproduced with IESE Business School's permission.
2. http://www.elpais.com (accessed 21 October 2008).
3. http://www.elpais.com (accessed 21 October 2008).
4. This section and others that follow it are based on Kase K, Jacopin T. *CEOs as Leaders and Strategy Designers: Explaining the Success of Spanish Banks*. Hampshire, UK: Palgrave Macmillan 2007.

5. In 1980, the banking regulation in Spain controlled 1) interest rates, 2) capital, 3) access to stock markets, 4) entry of foreign banks, 5) credits, 6) coefficients of investment, 7) insurances, and 8) leasing. This strongly contrasted with the situation in the UK where only access to stock markets was controlled. Belgium (1&2), the Netherlands (6&7), Ireland (1&2) were countries where regulation was not so severe, while France (1–7), Greece (1, 2 & 4–8), and Portugal (all items) and Italy as well as Spain were more interventionist where the banking business was concerned. See Kase K. and Jacopin, T., p. 18 as in footnote 3.

6. 'TFP growth is broken down into external, scale, and mark-up components. The external component is further dissected into deregulation and technical change components.' (A. Lozano-Vivas, S.C. Kumbhakar, 2005, Deregulation and productivity: the case of Spanish banks. *Journal of Regulatory Economics* 27(3)).

7. S.C. Kumbhakar and A. Lozano-Vivas. 2005, Deregulation and productivity: the case of Spanish banks. *Journal of Regulatory Economics* 27(3) pp. 331–51.

8. 'The 1999 merger between Santander and Banco Central Hispano (BCH) was designed to be a "merger of equals" in which the top executives of the two pre-existing firms would share control of the merged entity. Soon after the merger, former BCH executives accused Botín of trying to push his own agenda ... This post-merger squabbling was resolved when BCH executives José Amusátegui and Angel Corcóstegui agreed to accept severance payments, retire and renounce control to Botín, at an expense ... of €164 m.'

9. Upon his appointment as Chairman, Botín decided to drop "de" from the bank's name, thus it became Banco Santander.

10. According to the *Financial Times* Global 500 quarterly update for Q2 2008.

11. Santander Annual Report, 2007, p. 10.

12. *The Economist* , Nov. 8–14, 2008. "A special report on Spain", p. 18.

13. Kase K., Jacopin T. *CEOs as Leaders and Strategy Designers: Explaining the Success of Spanish Banks* (Hampshire, UK: Palgrave Macmillan, 2007: p. 233.)

14. http://www.elconfidencial.com/economia/ (accessed 13 November 2008).

15. http://revista.abatoliba.edu/ (accessed 31 October 2008). Interview with Emilio Botín, *Revista Universitaria*, No.15

16. An interview with Alfredo Sáenz, IESE's *Revista de Antiguos Alumnos*, Oct–Nov. 2004, pp.81–3.

17. K, Kase, F. Sáez, H. 2005, Riquelme. *Transformational CEOs: Leadership and Management Success in Japan*. Cheltenham, UK: Edward Elgar Publishing.

18. PIF (Proto-Image of the Firm) is a strategy pattern found in companies like Sony and Apple. It focuses more on the fit of decision options with the shared values, belief system, and so on. Immediate cash flow generation is not assigned the highest priority. See K. Kase, F. Sáez, H. Riquelme as in footnote 16.

19. http://www.computerweekly.com/Articles/2004/10/01/205635/it-successes-are-built-on-rock-of-partenon.htm (accessed 18 November 2008).

20. www.weforum.org/pdf/am_2006 (accessed 18 November 2008).

21. J.P. Moreno, E. Avendaño. 'Situación Competitiva de la Banca Española en el Marco Internacional', Accenture, 2006.

22. http://www.telegraph.co.uk/finance/2949796/It%27s-all-systems-go-at-Britain%27s-banks.html (accessed 18 November 2008).

23. S.C. Kumbhakar, A. Lozano-Vivas. 2005, "Deregulation and productivity: the case of Spanish banks", *Journal of Regulatory Economics* 27(3), pp. 331–351.

24. http://www.tmcnet.com on Banco Santander (accessed 11 November 2008).

25. http://www.telegraph.co.uk/finance/2949796/It%27s-all-systems-go-at-Britain%27s-banks.html (accessed 18 November 2008).

26. Price earning ratio.
27. EpS = (Net income – dividends on outstanding preferred stock)/Average outstanding stocks or shares.
28. BPR or Price-To-Book Ratio = stock price/(Total assets – Intangible assets and liabilities).
29. *Dinero*, No. 984, Nov. 2008, p. 25.
30. See RC. Koo, *The Holy Grail of Macroeconomics: Lessons from Japan's Great Recession*, (Singapore, Asia: John Wiley & Sons, 2008). Koo's thesis is that Japan's decade-long recession caused by real estate bubbles was due to 1) the plunging asset price triggering corporate balance sheet problems and 2) the Japanese companies moving collectively to repair balance sheets by paying down debt instead of using their cash-flows for new capital expenditures. Koo estimates the destruction in wealth at ¥ 1,500 trillion, equivalent to three years of Japanese GDP.
31. Based on UBS Annual Reports 2001–2007, Shareholder Report on UBS's Write-Downs, Thomson Reuters: 'UBS Rips up one-bank model as rich clients flee', 12 August 2008, Reuters: 'UBS universal bank model breaks', 13 August2008, Reuters: 'UBS One Bank U-turn intensifies speculation', and Swissinfo 13 August 2008.
32. UBS Archive, UBS to merge with PaineWebber, 12 July 2000.
33. 'Subprime lending (near-prime, non-prime, or second-chance lending) is a financial term that was popularized by the media during the 'credit crunch' of 2007 and involves financial institutions providing credit to borrowers deemed 'subprime' (sometimes referred to as 'under-banked'). Subprime borrowers have a heightened perceived risk of default, such as those who have a history of loan delinquency or default, those with a recorded bankruptcy, or those with limited debt experience. http://en.wikipedia.org/wiki/Subprime_lending (accessed 14 November 2008).
34. The risk related to how a portfolio will fare during a period of financial crisis.

## Annex 2.7

1. IESE Business School case No. SM-1559-E. Written by Bernardo Bátiz-Lazo and Kimio Kase. Reproduced with IESE Business School's permission.
2. Unless otherwise stated, the remainder of this section borrows freely from *Virgin Money deal paves way for own High Street bank*, BBC News http://news.bbc.co.uk/1/hi/business/8447560.stm (accessed 8 January 2010).
3. The strike ended in March 1971 when 200,000 postal men and women voted in favour of a new pay deal (see http://news.bbc.co.uk/onthisday/hi/dates/stories/march/8/newsid_2516000/2516343.stm (accessed 30 April 2010).
4. Virgin Records were sold to Thorn EMI in 1992 for £560m. This was used to help finance Virgin Atlantic, the airline established in 1984. In 1999, when Branson sold a 49 per cent stake of the airline to Singapore Airlines to relieve a financial squeeze, he valued the business at £1.2bn (Bower, 2005).
5. Directed by William Friedkin and adapted from the 1971 novel of the same name by William Peter Blatty. The story tells of the demonic possession of a young girl and her mother's desperate attempts to win her back. Released in December 1973, the film became one of the most profitable horror films of all time, grossing $440,000,000 worldwide (equivalent to $810m in 2010 after adjusting for inflation; see further http://www.boxofficemojo.com/movies/?id=exorcist.htm, accessed 28 April 2010). It won two Academy Awards (i.e. Oscars), one of them for Best Sound.

6. No-frills air travel took off in 1966 with the establishment of Laker Airways by British entrepreneur Freddie Laker. This venture went bankrupt in 1982 but received much attention during the 1970s. Other companies entered the field inspired by Laker. This included Branson (who eventually invited Laker to the board of Virgin Atlantic) and People Express, which between 1981 and 1987 continued with Lakeraker. This venture went bankrupt in 1982.

7. Following the purchase of Euro Belgian Airlines by Virgin Travel in 1996, a second flotation took place in 1997 for the benefit of Virgin Express, as the airline was renamed. Stock was quoted in Brussels, London and the electronic, US-based NASDAQ. See Dick (2007: p. 17).

8. The City is the historical core within central London from where financial activities grew. It houses the regulators (Bank of England and Financial Services Authority) as well as headquarters and offices of many international banks, Lloyds insurance market and related services (such as accounting, legal). The concentration of financial activities in the area also known as 'the square mile' dates back to the eighteenth century.

9. Queensway was a UK retailer specializing in the sale of carpets and furniture. Established in 1967 by Anthony Parish in Norwich, it was a pioneer of out of town shopping and one of the first retailers in the UK to sell directly to customers from a warehouse. After a boardroom coup the company was sold to Phillip Harris in 1977 and it became Harris Queensway plc. Valued at £450m in 1988, the company was sold to become Lowndes Queensway which then went bankrupt in 1993 due to the recession. See further http://www.gerryparish.co.uk/life_story.php (accessed 1 May 2010).

10. Unless stated otherwise, the remainder of this paragraph borrows freely from Grant (2004: p. 314).

11. In the US, venture capital is taken to mean a very particular form of finance in which specialized financial intermediaries invest in the equity of high-risk opportunities typical of the computer and biotechnology sectors. Firms such as Microsoft, Apple, Starbucks and Celegene benefited from venture capital finance at a crucial point in their development. Venture capitalists invest where banks find it difficult to lend because of a lack of track record, topped by the need to be prompt to market (or a competitor's idea will have first mover advantage). Some take an active role in helping to manage the company while others take a more 'hands-off' approach and step in only when called (for example, to help negotiate terms with banks) or when things are going bad. Venture capitalists often exit the firm through flotation on the stock market or by helping to sell the firm to a larger company in the same industry. In Britain, the term is used more loosely to encompass all forms of private equity investment.

12. The extent to which the proposed synergies materialized was questionable, given that the *Membership Miles* programme was open to 34 airlines (Webster, 1993). The programme was also vilified by the press as being more expensive than other alternatives for accruing rewards through *Virgin Freeway* (Anderson, 1995).

13. It is interesting to note that *Virgin*'s quick international launch of the credit card was also encouraged by Australia's central bank decision to shake up the credit card industry by increasing competition and reducing fees (Condie, 2003). This change in regulation also introduced a reduction in wholesale interchange fees banks charge each other to process credit card transactions and freed up the credit card network to new entrants.

14. In 2000, RBS engineered what at that point was the biggest takeover in the history of British banking, when RBS acquired National Westminster Bank plc (NatWest)

to create one of the three leading financial services providers in the UK and one of the top 10 global banks with a highly diversified portfolio of services for personal, business and corporate customers. Before the merger, RBS's subsidiaries included Citizen's Bank, a retail bank operation in North America.

15. The Virgin One account was launched internally to Virgin staff in October 1997 and rolled out to the public throughout 1998 (Branson, 2008: p. 162).

16. The sale of Virgin One to RBS in December 2006 included a clause whereby Virgin would not enter the mortgage market for two years (Branson, 2008: p. 164). Subsequently, the 2007–9 financial crisis limited market possibilities for these activities. Hence, Virgin had not been able to get back into the mortgage business since selling Virgin One (Branson, 2008: p. 165).

17. In 2005, Bank of America Corp. acquired MBNA Corp. for US$35 bn. The deal created one of the world's largest credit card issuers (called Bank of America Credit Card Services) but also resulted in a loss of 6,000 jobs of former MBNA employees (http://www.msnbc.msn.com/id/8414809/ (accessed 13 May 2010)).

18. Early in 2000, Rowan Gormley, the founder of the ground-breaking business, was replaced as chief executive by Mark Lund and moved to set up Virgin Wines, an internet wine retailer. Lund was the former managing director of Henderson Investors, which was part of AMP's activities in the UK. Lund was said to have been brought in with a mandate to turn Virgin Direct's losses into a profit (Treanor and Cassy, 2000). The move was also seen as abandoning the original plan for it to turn a profit within five years with an option for flotation by 2003 (Treanor and Cassy, 2000). However, Lund left the company after less than six months in the job and for reasons that remain obscure (Senior, 2000). There were no immediate plans to appoint a new CEO while the company was run by the managing directors of its three divisions (Virgin Direct, Virgin Money and Virgin One) (Senior, 2000). This set-up seems to have remained in place at least until the sale of Virgin One to RBS in 2001.

19. As is widely known, Elizabeth I (1533–1603), the last ruler of the Tudor dynasty, remained a maiden for all her reign (crowned 1558). But thinking that the original 'Virgin Queen' could take over 'the Rock' was inaccurate as that did not happen until 1704 when an Anglo–Dutch expedition first took control of the town Gibraltar during the War of Spanish Succession (1701–1714). Gibraltar was ceded for perpetuity to Britain with the signing of the Treaty of Utrecht (1713). Gadhia, however, was married to a former tax accountant who, as house-husband, took care of their five-year-old daughter.

20. The FTSE index tracks the movements in the price and volume of shares in the most highly capitalized companies in the London Stock Exchange. Capitalization is measured by multiplying price times the number of shares outstanding of a public company. It is typically used as a measure of business prosperity.

21. http://www.virgin.com/about-us/ (accessed 3 May 2010).

## Annex 2.8

1. IESE Business School case No. SM-1563-E. Written by Alesia Slocum. Reproduced with IESE Business School's permission.
2. A pseudonym.
3. A pseudonym.
4. (Pettigrew, 1990).
5. (Allison, 1971).

# Bibliography

Aamodt, A., & Plaza, E. 1994. Case-based reasoning: foundational issues, methodological variations, and system approaches. *Artificial Intelligence Communications*, 71(1):39–52.

Ackermann, R. 1966. Confirmatory models of theories. *The British Journal for the Philosophy of Science*, 16(64): 312–326.

Adam, B. 2003. Time. *Theory, Culture and Society*, 23(Special Issue on Problematising Global Knowledge): 8.

Adler, N. J. 1983a. A typology of management studies involving culture. *Journal of International Business Studies*, 14(2): 29–47.

Adler, N. J. 1983b. Cross-cultural management research: The ostrich and the trend. *Academy of Management Review*, 8(2): 226–232.

Allen, P. 2001. "What is the science of complexity?" *Emergence* 3(1).

Allison, G. T. 1971. *Essence of Decision: Explaining the Cuban Missile Crisis*. Boston, MA: Little, Brown and Company.

Allison, H. E. 2006. Kant's transcendental idealism. In G. Bird (Ed.), *A Companion to Kant* (pp. 111–124). Oxford: Blackwell Publishing.

Anagnostopoulos, G. 2009. Aristotle's methods. In G. Anagnostopoulos (Ed.), *A Companion to Aristotle* (pp. 101–122). Oxford: Wiley-Blackwell.

Andrews, K. R. 1983. Director's responsibility for corporate strategy. In R. G. Hamermesh (Ed.), *Corporate Planning – Addresses, Essays, Lectures* (pp. 512–521). John Wiley & Sons.

Apospori, E., & Papalexandris, N. 2008. HRM: Convergence, divergence, or a middle of the road (MOR) approach? Presented in 2008 Annual meeting of *The Academy of Management*, Anaheim, CA, USA, pp. 1–6.

Aquinas, T. 1993. *Commentary on Aristotle's Nicomachean Ethics* (C. I. Litzinger, Trans.). Notre Dame IN: Dumb Ox Books.

Aquinas, T. 1995. *Commentary on Aristotle's Metaphysics* (R. McInerny, Trans.). Notre Dame, IN: Dumb Ox Books.

Aquinas, T. 1997. De Ente et Essentia (on Being and Essence). http://www.fordham. edu/halsall/sbook2.html (accessed 6 February 2010).

Aristotle. 1984. Prior analytics. In J. Barnes (Ed.), *The Complete Works* (The Revised Oxford Translation ed., pp. 39–113). Princeton NJ: Princeton University.

Aristotle. 2001a. Analytica posteriora. In R. McKeon (Ed.), *The Basic Works* (pp. 110–187). New York: The Modern Library.

Aristotle. 2001b. Ethica Nicommachea (Nicomachean Ethics). In R. McKeon (Ed.), *The Basic Works of Aristotle* (pp. 935–1126). New York: The Modern Library.

Asanga. 2003. *The Summary of the Great Vehicle* (J. P. Keenan, Trans.). Berkeley, CA: Numata Center for Buddhist Translation and Research.

Aśvaghosha. 2001. *Discourse on the Awakening of Faith in the Mahāyāna* (D. T. Suzuki, Trans.). Fremont, CA: Asian Humanities Press.

Axelrod, R. 1976. *Structure of Decision*. Princeton, NJ: Princeton University Press.

Azumi, K. 1974. Japanese society: A sociological view. In A. E. Tiedemann (Ed.), *An Introduction to Japanese Civilisation*. New York: Columbia University Press.

Balogun, J., & Johnson, G. 2004. Organizational restructuring and middle manager sensemaking. *Academy of Management Journal*, 47(4): 523–549.

Baltes, P., Reese, H., & Lipsitt, L. 1980. Life-span developmental psychology. *Annual Review of Psychology,* **31**(1): 65–110.

Bandura, A. 1971. Analysis of modeling processes. *Psychological modeling: Conflicting theories,* 1–62.

Bandura, A. 1986. *Social Foundations of Thought and Action: A Social Cognitive Theory.* Englewood Cliffs, NJ: Prentice-Hall.

Bandura, A. 1989. Social cognitive theory. *Annals of Child Development,* **6**: 1–60.

Bandura, A. 2001. Social cognitive theory: An agentic perspective. *Annual Review of Psychology,* **52**: 1–26.

Barney, J. B., & Zhang, S. 2009. The future of Chinese management research: a theory of Chinese management versus a Chinese theory of management. *Management and Organization Review,* **5**(1): 15–28.

Baron, R. A., & Ward, T. 2004. Expanding entrepreneurial cognition's toolbox: potential contributions from the field of cognitive science. *Entrepreneurship Theory and Practice,* 28.

Bartlett, C. A., & Ghoshal, S. 1989. *Managing Across Borders.* London: Hutchinson Business Books.

Bartunek, J. M. 1984. Changing interpretive schemes and organizational restructuring: the example of a religious order. *Administrative Science Quarterly,* **29**: 355–372.

Bartunek, J. M., & Moch, M. K. 1987. First-Order, second-Order, and third-Order change and organizational development interventions: a cognitive approach. *The Journal of Applied Behavioral Science,* **23**: 483–500.

Basart Muñoz, J. M. 2004. Conocimiento y método en Descartes, Pascal y Leibniz. *Ciencia Ergo Sum,* **11**(March–June), 105–111.

Bermejo, V. J., & Rodríguez, P. 1987. Estructura sem·ntica y estrategias infantiles en la solución de problemas verbales de adición. *Infancia y aprendizaje,* **39**: 71–81.

Bettis, R. A., & Prahalad, C. K. 1995. The dominant logic: retrospective and extension. *Strategic Management Journal,* **16**: 5–14.

Biberman, J., & Altman, Y. 2004. Welcome to the new Journal of Management, Spirituality and Religion. *Journal of Management, Spirituality and Religion,* **1**(1):

Bird, G. 2006a. Introduction. In G. Bird (Ed.), *A Companion to Kant* (pp. 1–9). Oxford: Blackwell Publishing.

Bird, G. (Ed.). 2006b. *A Companion to Kant.* Oxford: Blackwell Publishing.

Blaikie, N. 1993. *Approaches to Social Enquiry.* Cambridge: Polity Press.

Bluedorn, A. 2002. *The Human Organization of Time: Temporal Realities and Experience.* Stanford, CA: Stanford University Press.

Boje, D. 1991. The storytelling organization: A study of story performance in an office-supply firm. *Administrative Science Quarterly,* **36**: 106–126.

Borges, J. L. 1989. Funes el Memorioso *Obras Completas* (Vol. 1). Buenos Aires: Emecé Editores. pp. 485–490.

Boroditsky, L. 2001. Does language shape thought? Mandarin and English speakers' conceptions of time. *Cognitive Psychology,* **43**(1): 1–22.

Branson, R. 2008. *Business Stripped Bare: The Adventures of a Global Entrepreneur.* London: Virgin Books.

Braudel, F. 1992. *The Mediterranean and the Mediterranean World in the Age of Philip II* (S. Reynolds, Trans. Abridged ed.). London: HarperCollins Publishers.

Brigandt, I. 2003. Gestalt experiments and inductive observations. Pittsburgh, PA: Department of History and Philosophy of Science, University of Pittsburgh.

Brislin, R. W., Lonner, W. J., & Thorndike, R. M. 1973. *Cross-Cultural Research Methods.* New York: John Wiley & Sons.

Carruthers, P. 2004. Reductive explanation and the 'explanatory gap'. *Canadian Journal of Philosophy*, **34**(2): 153–174.

Carus, P. 1902. *Chinese Philosophy*. Chicago: The Open Court Publishing.

Cayo Plinio Segundo. 1999. *Historia Natural: Trasladada y Anotada por el Doctor Francisco Hernández y por Jerónimo de Huerta (1624)*. Mexico, DF: Universidad Nacional de México.

Chalmers, A. F. 1999. *What is This Thing called Science* (3rd ed.). Maidenhead, Berkshire: Open University Press.

Chappel, T. 2009. Plato on knowledge in the Theaetetus. In E. N. Zalta (Ed.), *The Stanford Encyclopedia of Philosophy* (Fall ed.) http://plato.stanford.edu/entries/plato-theaetetus/ (accessed 16 March 2010) Stanford University.

Chen, M. 2002. Transcending paradox: the Chinese 'Middle Way' perspective. *Asia Pacific Journal of Management*, **19**: 179–199.

Chermack, T., & van der Merwe, L. 2003. The role of constructivist learning in scenario planning. *Futures*, **35** (5).

Chermack, T., Lynham, S., & Ruona, W. 2001. A review of scenario planning Literature. *Futures Research Quarterly*, Summer.

Chia, R. 2002. The production of management knowledge: philosophical underpinnings of research design. In D. Partington (Ed.), *Essential Skills for Management Research*.

Child, J. 1981. Culture, contingency and capitalism in the cross-national study of organizations. In L. L. Cummings, & B. M. Staw (Eds.), *Research in Organizational Behavior* (Vol. 3, pp. 303–356). Greenwich, CT: JAI Press.

Child, J., & Tayeb, M. 1982–83. Theoretical perspective in cross-national organizational research. *International Studies of Management and Organization*, **12**(4): 23–70.

Chinese Culture Connection. 1987. Chinese values and the search for culture-free dimensions of culture. *Journal of Cross-Cultural Psychology*, **18**(2): 143–164.

Clarke, T., & Clegg, S. 2000. *Changing Paradigm: The Transformation of Management for the 21st Century*. London: HarperCollins Pub Ltd.

Cook, F. H. 1999. Translator's introduction. *Three Texts on Consciousness Only* (pp. 1–6). Berkeley, CA: Numata Center for Buddhist Translation and Research.

Copleston, F. C. 1955. *Aquinas*. Hammondsworth, Middlesex: Penguin Books.

Cornelissen, J. P., & Clarke, J. S. 2010. Imagining and rationalizing opportunities: Inductive reasoning and the creation and justification of new ventures. *Academy of Management Review*, **35**(4): 539–557.

Coseru, C. 2010. Mind in Indian Buddhist philosophy. In E. N. Zalta (Ed.), *The Stanford Encyclopedia of Philosophy* (Spring 2010 ed.) http://plato.stanford.edu/entries/mind-indian-buddhism/ (accessed 30 March 2010) Stanford University.

Cottingham, J. 2005. Descartes, René. In T. Honderich (Ed.), *The Oxford Companion to Philosophy* (pp. 201–205). Oxford: Oxford University Press.

Crane, T. 2005. Cognitive science. In T. Honderich (Ed.), *The Oxford Companion to Philosophy* (p. 147). Oxford: Oxford University Press.

Crossan, M., Lane, H. W., & White, R. E. 1999. An organizational learning framework: from intuition to institution. *Academy of Management Review*, **24**(3), 522–537.

Dalai Lama. 2005. Introduction. *The Tibetan Book of the Dead*. London: Penguin Books.

Deal, T. E., & Kennedy, A. A. 1999. *The New Corporate Cultures: Realizing the Workplace after Downsizing, Mergers, and Reengineering*. Reading, MA: Perseus Books.

Deal, T., & Kennedy, A. 1982. *Corporate Cultures: The Rites and Rituals of Corporate Life*. London: Penguin Books.

Descartes, R. 1968a. Discourse on method and the meditations (F. E. Sutcliffe, Trans.). *Discourse on Method and the Meditations* (pp. 93–188). London: Penguin Books.

Descartes, R. 1968b. Discourse on the Method of properly conducting one's Reason and of seeking the truth in the sciences (F. E. Sutcliffe, Trans.) *Discourse on Method and the Meditations*. London: Penguin Books.

Descartes, R. 1968c. Meditations on the first philosophy in which the existence of god and the real distinction between the soul and the body of man are demonstrated. *Discourse on Method and the Meditations*. London: Penguin Books.

Descartes, R. 1996. Meditations on the First Philosophy http://www.iep.utm.edu/ (accessed 22 March 2010) Internet Encyclopedia of Philosophy.

Dolan, S. L., Díez, P. M., Fernández, A. M., Martín, P. A., & Martínez, F. S. 2004. Exploratory study of within-country differences in work-life values: The case of Spanish business students. *International Journal of Cross-Cultural Management*, 4(2): 157–180.

Dolan, S., Garcia, S., & Auerbach, A. 2003. Understanding and managing chaos in organizations. *International Journal of Management*, 20(1): 23–36.

Dunphy, D. 1987. Convergence/divergence: A temporal review of the Japanese enterprise and its management. *Academy of Management Review*, 12(3): 445–459.

Eisenberg, E. M., & Riley, P. 1988. Organizational symbols and sense-making. *Handbook of Organizational and Communication*. In M. Goldhaber & G. A. Barnet (Eds.), Norwood, NJ: Ablex Publishing Corporation.

Eliade, M. 1958. *Yoga: Immortality and Freedom* (W. R. Trask, Trans.). Princeton, NJ: Princeton University Press.

Encyclopaedia Britannica. 2004. (Standard Edition 2004 CD ed.). London: Encyclopaedia Britannica (UK).

Engstrom, Y., & Middleton, D. 1999. *Cognition and Communication at Work*. New York: Cambridge University Press.

Etzioni, A. 1961. *A Comparative Analysis of Complex Organization: On Power, Involvement, and Their Correlates*. New York: The Free Press.

Farh, J. L., Hackett, R. D., & Liang, J. 2007. Individual-level cultural values as moderators of perceived organizational support-employee outcomes relationships in China: Comparing the effects of power distance and traditionality. *Academy of Management Journal*, 50: 715–729.

Feng, M. 1989. *The Quashing of the Revolts (Jingluanlu/Seiranroku)*. Tokyo: Meitoku Shuppansha.

Ferejohn, M. 2009. Empiricism and the first principles of Aristotelian science. In G. Anagnostopoulos (Ed.), *A Companion to Aristotle* (pp. 66–80). London: Wiley-Blackwell.

Fernandez, J. A., & Willendrup Jenster, P. (Eds.) 2010. *Chinese Entrepreneurs: Lessons from the New Wave*. Shanghai: The Spanish Center of Entrepreneurship, CEIBS.

Filella, J. 1991. Is there a Latin model in the management of human resources? *Personnel Review*, 20(6): 14–23.

Fisher, A. V., & Sloutsky, V. M. 2005. When induction meets memory: evidence for gradual transition from similarity-based to category-based induction. *Child Development*, 76(3): 583–597.

Fogel, J. A. 1984. *Politics and Sinology: The Case of Naito Konan (1866–1934)*. Cambridge, MA: Council on East Asian Studies, Harvard University.

Frisby, W. 2005. The good, the bad, and the ugly: critical sport management research. *Journal of Sport Management* (19), 1–12.

Fruin, W. M. 1992. *The Japanese Enterprise System: Competitive Strategies and Cooperative Structures*. Oxford: Oxford University Press.

Fu, Y. (Ed.). 1995. *The Great Learning and the Doctrine of the Mean (Daxue, Zhongyong)*. Beijing: Huayu Jiaoxue.

Furuya, N. 2006. *Repatriation Management Effectiveness – a Mechanism for Developing Global Competencies through a Comprehensive Process of Repatriation*, Unpublished dissertation. University of Tsukuba, Japan.

Gannon, M. J., Locke, E. A., Gupta, A., Audia, P., & Kristof-Brown, A. L. 2005/2006. Cultural metaphors as frames of reference for nations: a six country study. *International Studies of Management and Organization*, **35**(4): 37–47.

Garfield, J. L. 1995. The text and commentary. *The Fundamental Wisdom of the Middle Way: Nāgārjuna's Mūlamadhayamakakārikā* (pp. 87–360). New York: Oxford University Press.

Gentner, D., Imai, M., & Boroditsky, L. 2002. As time goes by: evidence for two systems in processing-space→time metaphors. *Language and Cognitive Processes*, **17**(5): 537–565.

Gersick, C. J. G. 1994. Pacing strategic change: the case of a new venture. *Academy of Management Journal*, **37**(1): 9–45.

Gertler, B. 2002. Explanatory reduction, conceptual analysis, and conceivability arguments about the mind. *Noûs*, **36**(1): 22–49.

Ghoshal, S., & Nohria, N. 1989. Requisite variety versus shared values: managing corporate-division relationships in the M-form organization: INSEAD.

Giddens, A. 1984. *The Constitution of Society*. Berkeley: University of California Press.

Ginsberg, A. 1990. Connecting diversification to performance: a sociocognitive approach. *The Academy of Management Review*, **15**(3): 514–535.

Gómez, L. O. (Ed.). 1996. *The Land of Bliss: The Paradise of the Buddha of Measureless Light*. Honolulu: University of Hawaii Press.

Goodenough, W. H. 1971. *Culture, Language and Society*. Reading, MA: Addison-Wesley Modular Publications.

Grant, R. M. 1991. The resource-based theory of competitive advantage: implications for strategy formulation. *California Management Review* (Spring), 114–135.

Grant, R. M. 1996. Toward a knowledge-based theory of the firm. *Strategic Management Journal*, **17**(Winter Special Issue): 109–122.

Grant, R. M. 2007. *Contemporary Strategy Analysis* (6th ed.). Oxford: John Wiley & Sons.

Grinyer, J., Russell, A., & Collison, D. 1998. Evidence of managerial short termism in the UK. *British Journal of Management*, **9**(1): 13–22.

Grisson, T. 1987. The economic and scientific future of forensic psychological assessment. *American Psychologist*, **42**(9): 831–839.

Guthrie, W. K. C. 1986. *A History of Greek Philosophy: IV Plato: The Man and his Dialogues – Earlier Period*. Cambridge: Cambridge University Press.

Guthrie, W. K. C. 1990. *A History of Greek Philosophy: VI Aristotle: An Encounter*. Cambridge: Cambridge University Press.

Guyer, P. 2000. Absolute idealism and the rejection of Kantian dualism. In K. Ameriks (Ed.), *The Cambridge Companion to German Idealism* (pp. 37–56). Cambridge: Cambridge University Press.

Gyonen. 2006. The Essentials of the Eight Traditions (L. Pruden & R. Rhodes, Trans.) *The Essentials of the Eight Traditions and The Candle of the Latter Dharma* (New ed.). Berkeley, CA: Numata Center for Buddhist Translation & Research.

Hahn, U., & Chater, N. 1998. Similarity and rules: Distinct? exhaustive? empirically distinguishable? *Cognition*, **65**(2–3): 197–230.

Hall, E. T. 1976. *Beyond Culture*. New York: Anchor Publishing.

Hamel, G. 2001. Revolution vs evolution: You need both. *Harvard Business Review,* **79:** 150–156.

Hamel, G., & Prahalad, C. K. 1989. Strategic intent. *Harvard Business Review*(May-June), 63–76.

Hamilton, E. 1989. Note to Theaetetus. In E. Hamilton & H. Cairns (Eds.), *The Collected Dialogues of Plato* (pp. 845–846). Princeton, NJ: Princeton University Press.

Hamlyn, D. W. 2005. Gestalt theory. In T. Honderich (Ed.), *The Oxford Companion to Philosophy* (p. 338). Oxford: Oxford University Press.

Harris, S. 1994. Organizational culture and individual sensemaking: a schema-based perspective. *Organization Science,* **5**(3): 309–321.

Hart, C. 1998. *Doing a Literature Review.* London: Sage Publications.

Harvey, P. 1986. *The Oxford Companion to Classical Literature.* Oxford: Oxford University Press.

Hendry, J., & Seidl, D. 2003. The structure and significance of strategic episodes: social systems theory and the routine practices of strategic change. *Journal of Management Studies,* **40**(1): 175–196.

Herrigel, E. 1984. *The Japanese Archery (Nihon no kyujutsu)* (J. Shibata, Trans.). Tokyo: Iwanami Shoten.

Hesseling, P. 1973. Studies in cross-cultural organization. *Columbia Journal of World Businesses,* **Winter:** 120–134.

Hill, R., & Levenhagen, M. 1995. Metaphors and mental models: sensemaking and sensegiving in innovative and entrepreneurial activities. *Journal of Management,* **21:** 1057–1074.

Hofstede, G. 1980a. *Culture's Consequences: International Differences in Work-Related Values.* Beverly Hills, CA: Sage Publications.

Hofstede, G. 1980b. Motivation, leadership, and organization: Do American theories apply abroad? *Organizational Dynamics,* **Summer:** 42–63.

Hofstede, G. 1983. The cultural relativity of organizational practices and theories. *Journal of International Business Studies,* **14**(2): 75–89.

Hofstede, G. 1984. The cultural relativity of the duality of life concept. *Academy of Management Review,* **9:** 389–398.

Hofstede, G. 1993. Cultural constraints in management theories. *The Academy of Management Executive,* **7**(1): 81–94.

Hofstede, G. 1994. Management scientists are human. *Management Science,* **40**(1): 4–13.

Hofstede, G. 1996. Riding the waves of commerce: A test of Trompenaars' 'model' for national cultural differences. *International Journal of Intercultural Relations,* **20**(2): 189–198.

Hofstede, G. 2001. *Culture's Consequences: Comparing Values, Behaviors, Institutions, and Organizations across Nations* (2nd ed.). London: Sage Publications.

Hofstede, G. 2006. What did GLOBE really measure? Researchers' minds versus respondents' minds. *Journal of International Business Studies,* **37:** 882–896.

Hofstede, G., & Bond, M. H. 1988. The Confucious Connection: From Cultural Roots to Economic Growth. *Organizational Dynamics,* **16:** 5–21.

Hofstede, G., Neuijen, B., Ohavy, D. D., & Sanders, G. 1990. Measuring organizational cultures: A qualitative and quantitative study across twenty cases. *Administrative Science Quarterly,* **35:** 296–316.

Holland, J. H., Holyoak, K. J., Nisbett, R. E., & Thagard, P. R. 1987. *Induction: Processes of Inference.* Cambridge, MA: MIT Press.

Holland, R. F. 1954. The empiricist theory of memory. *Mind,* **63**(252): 464–486.

Holyoak, K. J., & P. Thagard 1997. *The Analogical Mind.* Waterloo, Canada, University of Waterloo.

Honderich, T. (Ed.). 2005. *The Oxford Companion to Philosophy* (New ed.). Oxford: Oxford University Press.

Honen. 1971. *Honen, Ippen.* Tokyo: Iwanami Shoten.

Hsüan-tsang. 1999. Demonstration of consciousness only (F. H. Cook, Trans.). *Three Texts on Consciousness Only.* Berkeley, CA: Numata Center for Buddhist Translation and Research.

Huang, H. J., & Dastmalchian, A. 2006. Implication of trust and distrust for organizations: Role of customer orientation in a four-nation study. *Personnel Review*, 35(4): 361–377.

Hume, D. 1969. *A Treatise of Human Understanding.* Harmondworth: Penguin.

Hunt, E. 1989. Cognitive science: definition, status, and questions. *Annual Review of Psychology*, 40: 603–630.

Hunt, E., & Agnoli, F. 1991. The Whorfian hypothesis: A cognitive psychology perspective. *Psychological Review*, 98(3): 377–389.

Huntington, S. P. 1993. The clash of civilizations? *Foreign Affairs*, 72(3): 22–49.

Husserl, E. 1999. *The Essential Husserl: Basic Writings in Transcendental Phenomenology.* Bloomington, IN: Indiana University Press.

Hutchings, K. 2002. Improving selection processes but providing marginal support: A review of cross-cultural difficulties for expatriates in Australian organizations in China. *Cross-Cultural Management*, 9(3): 32–57.

Hutchins, E. 1996. *Cognition in the Wild.* Cambridge, MA: MIT Press.

Imai, M. 2002. Constraint on word-learning constraints. *Japanese Psychological Research*, 41(1); 5–20.

Imai, M., & Gentner, D. 1997. A cross-linguistic study of early word meaning: universal ontology and linguistic influence. *Cognition*, 62: 169–200.

Itami, H. 1987. *Mobilizing Invisible Assets.* Cambridge, MA: Harvard University Press.

Izutsu, T. 1991. *Consciousness and Quiddity: In Search of the Spiritual Orient (Ishiki to honshitsu: seishinteki toyo wo motomete).* Tokyo: Iwanami Shoten.

Jacobs, C., & Heracleous, L. 2006. Constructing shared understanding: the role of embodied metaphors in organization development. *The Journal of Applied Behavioral Science*, 24: 207–226.

Japanese English Buddhist Dictionary. 1999. (Revised ed.). Tokyo: Daito Shuppansha.

Johnson, G. 1990. Managing strategic change: the role of symbolic action. *British Journal of Management*, 1(17): 183–200.

Jung, C. G. 1964. Foreword. *An Introduction to Zen Buddhism (Daisetz Teitaro Suzuki).* New York: Grove Press.

Kant, I. 2003. *Critique of Pure Reason* (J. M. D. Meiklejohn, Trans.). Mineola, NY: Dover Publications.

Kase, K. 1996. *The Corporate Centre in Japanese Management: An Analysis of its Size from an Information-Processing Perspective.* Doctor of Business Administration, Manchester University, Manchester.

Kase, K., & Jacopin, T. 2007. *CEOs as Leaders and Strategy Designers: Explaining the Success of Spanish Banks.* Hampshire, UK: Palgrave Macmillan.

Kase, K., Sáez, F., & Riquelme, H. 2005. *Transformational CEOs: Leadership and Management Success in Japan.* Cheltenham, UK: Edward Elgar Publishing.

Kato, S. 1981a. *A History of Japanese Literature: The First Thousand Years* (D. Chibette, Trans. Vol. 1). Tokyo: Kodansha International.

Kato, S. 1981b. *A History of Japanese Literature: The Years of Isolation* (D. Sanderson, Trans. Vol. 2). Tokyo: Kodansha International.

Kato, S. 1999. *A History of Japanese Literature (Nihon bungakushi josetsu).* Tokyo: Chikuma Shobo.

Katz, A., Paivio, A., & Marschark, M. 1985. Poetic comparisons: psychological dimensions of metaphoric processing. *Journal of Psycholinguistic Research,* **14**(4): 365–383.

Kaufman, B. E. 1990. A new theory of satisficing. *Journal of Behavioral Economics* (Spring) 16.

Keats, B. W. 1990. Diversification and business economic performance revisited: Issues of measurement and causality. *Journal of Management,* **16**(1): 61–72.

Keats, B. W., & Hitt, M. A. 1988. A causal model of linkages among environmental dimensions, macro organizational characteristics, and performance. *Academy of Management Journal,* **31**(3): 570–598.

Keenan, J. P. 2003. Translator's introduction. *The Summary of the Great Vehicle* (pp. xiii–xvii). Berkeley, CA: Numata Center for Buddhist Translation and Research.

Kenkyusha's New Japanese English Dictionary. 2004. (5th CD-ROM ed.).

Kenny, A. 1980. *Aquinas.* Oxford: Oxford University Press.

Ketokivi, M., & Mantere, S. 2010. Two strategies for inductive reasoning in organizational research. *Academy of Management Review,* **35**(2): 315–333.

Keyt, D. 2009. Deductive logic. In G. Anagnostopoulos (Ed.), *A Companion to Aristotle* (pp. 31–50). Oxford: Wiley-Blackwell.

Khanna, T., & Papelu, K. 1997. Why focused strategies may be wrong for emerging markets. *Harvard Business Review,* **75**(4): 41–51.

Kida, G. 1970. *Phenomenology (Genshogaku).* Tokyo: Iwanami Shoten.

Kim, J. 2005. Mind-body problem. In T. Honderich (Ed.), *The Oxford Companion to Philosophy* (pp. 613–614). Oxford: Oxford University Press.

Kim, Y. Y. 1977. Communication patterns of foreign immigrants in the process of acculturation. *Human Communication Research,* **4**: 66–77.

Kitayama, S., Duffy, S., Kawamura, T., & Larsen, J. T. 2003. Perceiving an object and its context in different cultures. *Psychological Science,* **14**(3): 201–206.

Knowlton, B. J., & Squire, L. R. 1996. Artificial grammar learning depends on implicit acquisition of both abstract and exemplar-specific information. *Journal of Experimental Psychology: Learning, Memory, and Cognition,* **22**(1): 169–181.

Köhler, W. 1947. *Gestalt Psychology: An Introduction to New Concepts in Modern Psychology.* New York: Liveright Publishing Corp.

Köhler, W. 1967. Gestalt psychology. *Psychological Research,* **31**(1).

Kojien. 2008 (DVD-ROM ed.): Iwanami Shoten.

Kondo, Y. 1972. Commentary *Sayings and Letters (Chuanxulu/Denshuroku)* (pp. 1–20). Tokyo: Meiji Shoin.

Kono, T. 1984. *Strategy and Structure of Japanese Enterprises.* London: The Macmillan Press.

Koriat, A. 1993. How do we know that we know? The accessibility model of the feeling of knowing. *Psychological Review,* **100**(4): 609–639.

Koriat, A., & Levy-Sadot, R. 2001. The combined contributions of the cue-familiarity and accessibility heuristics to feelings of knowing. *Journal of Experimental Psychology: Learning, Memory, and Cognition,* **27**(1): 29–37.

Kretzmann, N., & Stump, E. (Eds.). 1993. *The Cambridge Companion to Aquinas.* Cambridge: Cambridge University Press.

Kroeber, A. L., & Kluckhohn, C. 1952. *Culture: A Critical Review of Concepts and Definitions.* Cambridge, MA: Harvard University Peabody Museum of American Archeology and Ethnology.

Kuhn, T. S. 1996. *The Structure of Scientific Revolutions.* Chicago, IL: Chicago University Press.

Kukai. 1972. *Major Works* (Y. S. Hakeda, Trans.). New York: Columbia University Press.

Labianca, G., Gray, B., & Brass, D A. 2000. Grounded model of organizational schema change during empowerment. *Organization Science*, **11**(2): 235–257.

Lacey, A. 2005a. Empiricism. In T. Honderich (Ed.), *The Oxford Companion to Philosophy*. Oxford: Oxford University Press.

Lacey, A. 2005b. Rationalism. In T. Honderich (Ed.), *The Oxford Companion to Philosophy*. Oxford: Oxford University Press.

Laurent, A. 1983. The cultural diversity of management conceptions. *International Studies of Management and Organization*, **13**: 75–96.

Lawson, H., & Appignanesi, L. 1989. *Dismantiling the Truth: Reality in the Post-Modern World*. London: Weidenfeld and Nicolson.

Legge, J. (Ed.). 1986. *The Four Books (The Great Learning, The Doctrine of the Mean, Confucian Analects, and The Works of Mencius)*. Taipei: Wenhua Tushu.

Leonardi, P. M., & Barley, S. R. 2008. Materiality and change: challenges to building better theory about technology and organizing. *Information and Organization*, **18**(3): 159–176.

Leung, K., Bhagat, R. S., Buchan, N. R., Erez, M., & Gibson, C. B. 2005. Culture and international business: Recent advances and their implications for future research. *Journal of International Business Studies*, **36**(4): 357–378.

Lévi-Strauss, C. 1969. *The Elementary Structures of Kinship* (J. H. Bell, & J. R. v. Sturmer, Trans.). Boston: Beacon Press.

Lévi-Strauss, C. 1974. *Structural Anthropology*. New York: Basic Books.

Lewin, K. 1951. *Field Theory in Social Science*. Chicago, IL: University of Chicago Press.

Lewis, C. T. 1989. *A Latin Dictionary: Founded on Andrew's Edition of Freund's Latin Dictionary – Revised, Enlarged, and In Great Part Rewritten*. Oxford: The Clarendon Press.

Lewis, R. D. 2010. *When Cultures Collide*. London: Nicolas Brealey International.

Li, Z. 1994. *Conversing Again the Pragmatic Rationality*. Beijing: Chinese Social Science Publishing House. 李泽厚, 1994. 再谈实用理性. 北京: 中国社会科学出版社.

Liddel, H. G., & Scott, R. 1996. *Greek-English Lexicon* (9th ed.). Oxford: Clarendon Press.

Liu, L. A., Friedman, R. A., & Chi, S. C. 2005. 'Ren Qing' versus the 'Big five': The role of culturally sensitive measures of individual difference in distributive negotiations. *Management and Organization Review*, **1**(2): 225–247.

Locke, E. A. 2007. The case for inductive theory building. *Journal of Management*, **33**(6): 867–890.

Locke, J. 1997. *An Essay concerning Human Understanding*. London: Penguin Books.

Lorenz, K. 1962. Gestalt perception as fundamental to scientific knowledge. *General Systems Yearbook*, **7**, 37–56.

Losee, R. M. 2001. *Processing and Management*. Elsevier.

MacDonald, S. 1993. Theory of knowledge. In N. Kretzmann & E. Stump (Eds.), *The Cambridge Companion to Aquinas*. (pp. 160–195). Cambridge: Cambridge University Press.

Maddock, S. J., & Parkin, D. 1993. Gender cultures: Women's choices and strategies at work. *Women in Management Review*, **8**(2): 3–10.

Makeham, J. (Ed.). 2003. *New Confucianism: A Critical Examination*. London: Palgrave Macmillan.

Malcolm, N. 1963. *Knowledge and Certainty*. Englewood Cliffs, NJ: Prentice Hall.

March, J. G. 1978. Bounded rationality, ambiguity, and the engineering of choice. *The Bell Journal of Economics*, **9**(2): 587–608.

March, J. G. 1991. Exploration and exploitation in organizational learning. *Organization Science*, **2**(1): 71–87.

Marginson, D., & McAulay, L. 2008. Exploring the debate on short termism: A theoretical and empirical analysis. *Strategic Management Journal*, 29(3): 273–292.

Marías, J. 2008. *Historia de la Filosofía*. Madrid: Alianza Editorial.

Markides, C. C., & Wiliamson, P. J. 1994. Related diversification, core competences, and corporate performance. *Strategic Management Journal*, 15(Special Issue): 149–165.

Markus, H. R., & Kitayama, S. 1991. Culture and the self: Implications for cognition, emotion, and motivation. *Psychological Review*, 98(2): 224–253.

Martin, C. B., & Deutscher, M. 1966. Remembering. *Philosophical Review*, 75: 161–196.

Masuda, T., & Nisbett, R. E. 2001. Attending holistically versus analytically: comparing the context sensitivity of Japanese and Americans. *Journal of Personality and Social Psychology*, 81(5): 922–934.

Matilal, B. K. 1986. Buddhist logic and epistemology. In B. K. Matilal & R. D. Evans (Eds.), *Buddhist Logic and Epistemology: Studies in the Buddhist Analysis of Inference and Language* (pp. 1–30). Dordrecht: D. Reidel Publishing Company.

Matilal, B. K., & Masson, J. M. 1986. Preface. In B. K. Matilal & J. M. Masson (Eds.), *Buddhist Logic and Epistemology: Studies in the Buddhist Analysis of Inference and Language* (p. ix). Dordrecht: D. Reidel Publishing Company.

Mayer, R. 1992. *Gestalt. Thinking, Problem Solving, Cognition*. W H Freeman and Co.

McPhee, D. 2008. *The Science of Learning and the Art of Teaching*. J Feldman Publishers.

Meister Eckhart. (n.d.). *The Works of Meister Eckhart, Doctor Ecstaticus*. Whitefish, MT: Kessinger Publishing.

Merleau-Ponty, M. 1958. *Phenomenology of Perception* (C. Smith, Trans.). London: Routledge Classics.

Merleau-Ponty, M. 2008. *The Structure of Behavior* (A. L. Fisher, Trans.). Pittsburgh, PA: Duquesne University Press.

Mervis, C. B., & Rosch, E. 1981. Categorization of natural objects. *Annual Review of Psychology*, 32, 89–115.

Metcalfe, J., & Shimamura, A. P. (Eds.). 1994. *Metacognition: Knowing About Knowing*. MIT Press.

Miller, A. 2010. Realism. In E. N. Zalta (Ed.), http://plato.stanford.edu/archives/sum2010/entries/realism/ (accessed 2 September 2010, Summer 2010 ed.): The Stanford Encyclopedia of Philosophy.

Mintzberg, H. 1990. The design school: Reconsidering the basic premises of strategic management. *Strategic Management Journal*, 11: 171–195.

Mintzberg, H., & Waters, J. A. 1985. Of strategies, deliberate and emergent. *Strategic Management Journal*, 6: 257–272.

Mintzberg, H., Raisinghani, D., & Théorêt, A. 1976. The structure of 'unstructured' decision processes. *Administrative Science Quarterly*, 21: 246–275.

Montgomery, C. A. 1982. The measurement of firm diversification: Some new empirical evidence. *Academy of Management Journal*, 25(2): 299–307.

Montgomery, C., & Wernerfelt, B. 1988. Diversification, Ricardian rents, and Tobin's q. *Rand Journal of Economics*, 19(4): 623–632.

Morgan, G. 1997. *Images of Organization*. Sage Publications.

Mount, M. K., Judge, T. A., Scullen, S. E., Sytsma, M. R., & Hezlett, S. A. 1998. Trait, rater and level effects in 360-degree performance ratings. *Personnel Psychology*, 51(3): 557–576.

Nagao, G. 1967. Buddhist thought and history (Bukkyo no shiso to rekishi). In G. Nagao (Ed.), *Mahayananistic Sutras (Daijo butten)* (pp. 5–66). Tokyo: Chuo Koronsha.

Nagao, G. 1978. *Mādhyamika and Vijñapti-mātrtā (Chukan to Yuishiki)*. Tokyo: Iwanami Shoten.

Nāgārjuna. 1995. *The Fundamental Wisdom of the Middle Way: Nāgārjuna's Mūlamadhayamakakārikā* (J. L. Garfield, Trans.). New York: Oxford University Press.

Nagel, T. 2005. Dualism. In T. Honderich (Ed.), *The Oxford Companion to Philosophy*. Oxford: Oxford University Press.

Nakamura, H., Fukunaga, M., Tamura, Y., & Konno, T. (Eds.). 2000. *Iwanami Dictionary of Buddhism (Iwanami Bukkyo jiten)*. Tokyo: Iwanami Shoten.

Natsume, S. 1985. *Critique of Literature 1 (Bungaku Hyoron – Jo)*. Tokyo: Iwanami Shoten.

Newman, L. 2008. Descartes' epistemology. In E. N. Zalta (Ed.), *The Stanford Enclyopedia of Philosophy* (Fall 2008 ed.) http://plato.stanford.edu/entries/descartes-epistemology/ (accessed 22 March 2010) Stanford University.

Nisbett, R. E. 1992. The Case for Rules in Reasoning. *Cognitive Science*, 16: 1–40.

Nisbett, R. E. 1998. Race, genetics, and IQ. In C. Jencks, & M. Phillips (Eds.), *Black-White Test Score Differences*. Washington, DC: Brookings Institution.

Nisbett, R. E. 2003. *The Geography of Thought: How Asians and Westerners Think Differently ... and Why*. London: Nicholas Brealey Publishing.

Nisbett, R. E., Peng, K., Choi, I., & Norenzayan, A. 2001. Culture and systems of thought: holistic vs. analytic cognition. *Psychological Review*, 108: 291–310.

Nishida, K. 1987. *An Inquiry into the Good* (M. Abe & C. Ives, Trans.). New Haven CT: Yale University Press.

Nishitani, K. 1982. *Religion and Nothingness* (J. Van Bragt, Trans.). Berkeley, CA: University of California Press.

Nonaka, I. 1988. Toward middle-up-down management: accelerating information creation. *Sloan Management Review*, 9(Spring): 9–18.

Nonaka, I. 1990. Redundant, overlapping organization: a Japanese approach to managing the innovation process. *California Management Review* (Spring): 27–38.

Nonaka, I. 1991. The knowledge-creating company. *Harvard Business Review* (November-December): 96–104.

Nonaka, I., & Takeuchi, H. 1995. *The Knowledge-Creating Company: How Japanese Companies Create the Dynamics of Innovation*. New York: Oxford University Press.

Nonaka, I., & Toyama, R. 2003. The knowledge-creating theory revisited: Knowledge creation as a synthesizing process. *Knowledge Management Research &# 38; Practice*, 1(1): 2–10.

Nonaka, I., Toyama, R., & Hirata, T. 2008. *Managing Flow: A Process Theory of the Knowledge-Based Firm*. London: Palgrave Macmillan.

Nonaka, I., Toyama, R., & Konno, N. 2000. SECI, Ba and leadership: a unified model of dynamic knowledge creation. *Long Range Planning*, 33(1): 5–34.

Nonaka, I., Toyama, R., & Nagata, A. 2000b. A firm as a knowledge-creating entity: A new perspective on the theory of the firm. *Industrial and corporate change*, 9(1): 1.

Norman, D. A. 1980. Twelve issues for cognitive science. *Cognitive Science: A Multidisciplinary Journal*, 4(1): 1–32.

Nosofsky, R. M. 1992. Similarity scaling and cognitive process models. *Annual Review of Psychology*, 43(1): 25–53.

Oda, M. 2003. Distribution of Buddhism in Japan: an attempt to draw a map of the Buddhist-denominational regions (Nihon ni okeru bukkyo shoshuha no bunpu – bukkyo chiiki kubunzu sakusei no kokoromi). *Department of Geography Komazawa University* (39), 37–58.

Okhuysen, G. A., & Eisenhardt, K. A. 2002. Integrating knowledge in groups: how formal interventions enable flexibility. *Organization Science*.

Orlikowski, W. 2006. Material knowing: the scaffolding of human knowledgeability. *European Journal of Information Systems,* **15** (Oct): 460–466.

Orlikowski, W. J., & Gash, D. C. 1994. Technological frames: making sense of information technology in organizations. *ACM Transactions on Information Systems,* **12**(2): 174–207.

Orlikowski, W. J., & Yates, J. 1994. Genre repertoire: The structuring of communicative practices in organizations. *Administrative Science Quarterly,* **39**: 33.

Osherson, D. N., Smith, E. E., Wilkie, O., López, A., & Shafir, E. 1990. Category-based induction. *Psychological Review,* **97**(2): 185–200.

Otagi, M., & Terada, T. 1998. *Mongol and Great Ming Empires (Mongol to daimin teikoku).* Tokyo: Kodansha.

Pachur, T., Broder, A., & Marewski, J. N. 2008. The recognition heuristic in memory-based inference: is recognition a non-compensatory cue? *Journal of Behavioral Decision Making,* **21**(2): 183–210.

Paivio, A. 1991. Dual coding theory and education. *Educational Psychology Review,* **3**: 149–210.

Palich, L. E., Cardinal, L. B., & Miller, C. C. '2000. Curvilinearity in the diversification – performance linkage: An examination of over three decades of research. *Strategic Management Journal,* **21**: 155–174.

Park, C. 2003. Prior performance characteristics of related and unrelated acquirers. *Strategic Management Journal,* **24**: 471–480.

Pascale, R. T. 1988. The Honda effect. In J. B. Quinn, H. Mintzberg & R. M. James (Eds.), *The Strategy Process: Concepts, Contexts, and Cases.* Englewood Cliffs, NJ: Prentice-Hall International. pp. 115–123.

Pascale, R. T. 1996. Reflections on Honda. *California Management Review,* **38**(4): 112–117.

Pascale, R. T., & Athos, A. G. 1981. *The Art of Japanese Management.* New York: Simon & Schuster.

Pauleen, D.J., Rooney, D., & Holden, N.J. 2010. Practical wisdom and the development of cross-cultural knowledge management: A global leadership perspective. *European Journal of International Management,* **4** (4): 382–395.

Peñaloza, L., & Gilly, M. C. 1999. Marketer acculturation: The changer and the changed. *The Journal of Marketing,* **63**(3): 84–104.

Peng, M. W., Lee, S.-H., & Wang, D. Y. L. 2005. What determines the scope of the firm over time? A focus on institutional relatedness. *Academy of Management Review,* **30**(3): 622–633.

Peters, T. J., & Waterman, R. H. 1982. *In Search of Excellence: Lessons from America's Best-Run Companies.* New York: Harper & Row.

Pettigrew, A., Woodman, R., & Cameron, K. 2001. Studying organizational change and development: challenges for future research. *Academy of Management Journal,* **44**(4): 697–713.

Piaget, J. 1968. Genetic epistemology. http://www.marxists.org/reference/subject/philosophy/works/fr/piaget.htm (accessed 22 October 2010).

Piaget, J. 1999. *The Construction of Reality in the Child.* New York, NY: Routledge and Kegan Paul.

Piaget, J. 2008. *Intellectual evolution from adolescence to adulthood.* Paper presented at the La 3ème convention international Fomene sur l'education humaine de l'adolescence a l'age adulte.

Pierce, C. 1903. Lectures on pragmatism. In Turesi, P. (ed.), *Pragmatism as a Principle and Method of Right Thinking: the 1903 Harvard Lectures on Pragmatism.* Cambridge, MA: State University of New York Press.

Plato. 1989. Republic (P. Shorey, Trans.). In E. Hamilton & H. Cairns (Eds.), *The Collected Dialogues of Plato including the Letters* (pp. 575–844). Princeton, NJ: Princeton University Press.

Plato. 1989. Theaetetus (F. M. Cornford, Trans.). In E. Hamilton (Ed.), *The Collected Dialogues of Plato including the Letters* (pp. 845–919). Princeton, NJ: Princeton University Press.

Platt, J. R. 1964. Strong inference. *Science*, 146(3642), 347–353.

Polanyi, M. 1966. The logic of tacit inference. *Philosophy*, 41(155): 1–18.

Polanyi, M. 2003. *The Tacit Dimension (Anmokuchi no Jigen)*. Tokyo: Chikuma Shobo.

Pool, I. S. 1965. Effects of cross-national contact on national and international images. In H. C. Kelman (Ed.), *International Behavior: A Social-Psychological Analysis*. New York: Holt, Rinhart & Winston.

Popper, K. 1953, 1974. The Problem of induction. *Popper Selections*.

Popper, K. 1957. Science: conjectures and refutations http://cla.calpoly.edu/~fotoole/321.321/popper.html (accessed 18 June 2008): Cal Poly State University.

Popper, K. 2002. *The Logic of Scientific Discovery*. Abington Oxon: Routledge.

Porter, M. 1991. Towards a dynamic theory of strategy. *Strategic Management Journal*, 12(Winter Special Issue): 95–107.

Pothos, E. M., & Wolff, J. G. 2006. The simplicity and power model for inductive inference. *Artificial Intelligence Review*, 26(3): 211–225.

Powell, G. N. 1993. *Women and Men in Management*. Thousand Oaks, CA, London, and New Delhi: Sage Publications.

Prahalad, C. K., & Hamel, G. 1990. The core competence of the corporation. *Harvard Business Review* (May-June): 79–90.

Quine, W. V. O. 1960. *Word and Object*. Cambridge, MA: MIT Press.

Quine, W. V. O. 1968. Ontological relativity. *The Journal of Philosophy*, 65(7): 185–212.

Quinn, J. B. 1980. *Strategies for Change: Logical Incrementalism*. Homewood, IL: Irwin.

Quinn, J. B. 1985. Managing innovation: Controlled chaos. *Harvard Business Review*, May-June(May-June): 73–84.

Rahman, O., & Rollock, D. 2004. Acculturation, competence, and mental health, among Asian students in the United States. *Journal of Multicultural Counseling and Development*, 32: 130–142.

Ramanujam, V., & Varadarajan, P. 1989. Research on corporate diversification: A synthesis. *Strategic Management Journal*, 10: 523–551.

Reder, L. M., & Ritter, F. E. 1992. What determines initial feeling of knowing? Familiarity with question terms, not with the answer. *Journal of Experimental Psychology: Learning, Memory, and Cognition*, 18(3): 435–451.

Roberts, K. H. 1970. On looking at an elephant: An evaluation of cross-cultural research related to organizations. *Psychological Bulletin*, 74: 327–350.

Robichaud, D., Giroux, H., & Taylor, J. 2004. The metaconversation: the recursive property of language as a key to organizing. *Academy of Management Review*, 29(4): 1–18.

Rosener, J. B. 1990. Way women lead. *Harvard Business Review*, 68: 119–125.

Rowe, C. 2006. Interpreting Plato. In H. H. Benson (Ed.), *A Companion to Plato* (pp. 13–24). Oxford: Blackwell Publishing.

Rowlinson, M., Booth, C., Clark, P., Delahaye, A., & Procter, S. 2010. Social remembering and organizational memory. *Organization Studies*, 31(1): 18.

Rumelt, R. P. 1982. Diversification strategy and profitability. *Strategic Management Journal*, 3: 359–36.

Runciman, W. 1962. *Plato's Later Epistemology.* Cambridge: Cambridge University Press.

Russell, B. 1995. *History of Western Philosophy.* London: Routledge.

Safdar, S., Lay, C., & Struthers, W. 2003. The process of acculturation and basic goals: Testing a multidimensional individual difference acculturation model with Iranian immigrants in Canada. *Applied Psychology: An International Review,* **52**(4): 555–579.

Sahay, S. 1997. Implementation of information technology: a time-space perspective. *Organization Studies,* **18**(2): 229–260.

Salam, A. 1990. *Unification of Fundamental Forces: The First 1988 Dirac Memorial Lecture.* Cambridge.

Schein, E. 1992. *Organizational Culture and Leadership* (2nd ed.). San Francisco: Jossey-Bass.

Schönfeld, M. 2006. Kant's early dynamics. In G. Bird (Ed.), *A Companion to Kant* (pp. 33–46). Oxford: Blackwell Publishing.

Schwegler, A. 2010. *Handbook of the History of Philosophy* (J. Hutchison Stirling, Trans.). Charleston, SC: Bibliobazaar.

Schweiger, D. M., Sandberg, W. R., & Rechner, P. L. 1989. Experiential effects of dialectical inquiry, devil's advocacy, and consensus approaches to strategic decisionmaking. *Academy of Management Journal,* **32**(4): 745–772.

Schwenk, C. R. (1988). The cognitive perspective on strategic decision-making. *Journal of Management Studies,* **25**(1 January): 41–55.

Sellars, W. 1967. Some remarks on Kant's theory of experience. *The Journal of Philosophy,* **64**(20), 633–647.

Seo, M., & Creed, W. 2002. Institutional contradictions, praxis, and institutional change: a dialectical perspective. *Academy of Management Review,* **27**(2): 222–247.

Sharps, M., Hess, A., Casner, H., Ranes, B., & Jones, J. 2007. Eyewitness memory in context: toward a systematic understanding of eyewitness evidence. *Forensic Examiner,* **16**(3): 8.

Shimada, K. 2001. *China's Traditional Thought (Chugoku no dento shiso).* Tokyo: Misuzu Shobo.Shimada, K. 2004. *Neo-Confucianism and the Doctrines of Wang Yang-ming (Shushigaku to yomeigaku).* Tokyo: Iwanami Shoten.

Shimizu, T. 1994. Nominalism (yuimeron) *Nihon Daihyakkazensho.* Tokyo: Shogakukan.

Shinran. 1971. *Shinran – Kyogyo Shinsho.* Tokyo: Iwanami Shoten.

Silverman, A. 2008. Plato's middle period metaphysics and epistemology. In E. N. Zalta (Ed.), *The Stanford Encyclopedia of Philosophy* (Winter ed.) http://plato.stanford.edu/entries/plato-metaphysics/ (accessed 16 March 2010) Stanford University.

Singh, H., & Montgomery, C. A. 1987. Corporate acquisition strategies and economic performance. *Strategic Management Journal,* **8**: 377–386.

Skidd, D. R. A. (1992). Revisiting bounded rationality. *Journal of Management Inquiry* (Dec), 343–347.

Skirry, J. 2008. René Descartes (1596–1650): overview http://www.iep.utm.edu/descarte/#H6 (accessed 22 March 2010) Internet Encyclopedia of Philosophy.

Sloutsky, V. M., & Lo, Y.-F. 2001. Linguistic labels and the development of inductive inference. *Child development,* **72**(6): 1695–1709.

Smith, R. 2009a. Aristotle's logic. In E. N. Zalta (Ed.), *The Stanford Encyclopedia of Philosophy* (Spring ed.) http://plato.stanford.edu/entries/aristotle-logic/ (accessed 16 March 2010) Stanford University.

Smith, R. 2009b. Aristotle's theory of demonstration. In G. Anagnostopoulos (Ed.), *A Companion to Aristotle* (pp. 51–65). Oxford: Wiley-Blackwell.

Smith, W. K., & Tushman, M. L. 2005. Managing strategic contradictions: a top management model for managing innovation stream. *Organization science,* **16**: 522–536.

Soja, N. N., Carey, S., & Spelke, E. S. 1991. Ontological categories guide young children's inductions of word meaning: object terms and substance terms. *Cognition*, 38(2): 179–211.

Soothill, W. E., & Hodous, L. 2003. *A Dictionary of Chinese Buddhist Terms* (2nd ed.). London: Routledge.

Stadler, F. (2004a). Induction and deduction in the philosophy of science: a critical account since the Methodenstreit. In F. Stadler (Ed.), *Vienna Circle Institute Yearbook (2993)* (pp. 1–15). Dordrecht: Kluwer Academic Publishers.

Stadler, F. (Ed.). 2004b. *Induction and Deduction in the Sciences*. Dordrecht: Kluwer Academic Publishers.

Stadtler, F. 2004. *Induction and Deduction in the Sciences*. Vienna Circle Institute Yearbook. Dordrecht/Springer: Vienna.

Standifer, R., & Bluedorn, A. 2006. Time and the temporal imagination. *Academy of Management Learning and Education*, 5: 196–206.

Stening, B., & Zhang, M. 2007. Methodological problems confronted when conducting management research in China. *International Journal of Cross Cultural Management*, 7(1): 121–142.

Stephen, L. 1904. *English Literature and Society in the Eighteenth Century: Ford Lectures in 1903*. London: Duckworth and Co.

Suchman, L. A. 2007. *Human-Machine Reconfigurations: Plans and Situated Actions* (2nd ed.). New York, NY: Cambridge University Press.

Sueki, F. 2003. *Buddhist Thought (Bukkyo shiso)*. Tokyo: Hoso Daigaku Kyoiku Shinkokai.

Sutcliffe, F. E. 1968. Introduction *Discourse on Method and the Meditations* (pp. 7–23). London: Penguin Books.

Sutton, J. 2010. Memory. In E. N. Zalta (Ed.), *The Stanford Encyclopedia of Philosophy* (Spring ed.). http://plato.stanford.edu/entries/memory/ (accessed 21 April 2010). Stanford University.

Suzuki, D. T. 1949. *Essays in Zen Buddhism (First Series)*. New York: Grove Press.

Suzuki, D. T. 1964. *An Introduction to Zen Buddhism*. New York: Grove Press.

Suzuki, D. T. 2000a. *Essay in Zen Buddhism (Second Series)*. New Delhi: Munshiram Manoharlal Publishers Pvt.

Suzuki, D. T. 2000b. *Essays in Zen Buddhism (Third Series)*. New Delhi: Munshiram Manoharlal Publishers.

Suzuki, D. T. 2002. *Mysticism: Christian and Buddhist*. London: Routledge Classics.

Suzuki, S. 1995. *History of China (Chugokushi)* (2nd ed.). Tokyo: Yamakawa Shuppansha.

Swanson, R. A., & Law, B. D. 1993. Whole-part-whole learning model. *Performance Improvement Quarterly*, 6(1): 10.

Takada, S., & Goto, M. (Eds.). 2000. *Yijing (Ekikyo)*. Tokyo: Iwamani Shoten.

Taylor, R. L. 2004. *Confucianism*. Philadelphia, PA: Chelsea House Publishers.

Taylor, S. E., & Crocker, J. 1981. Schematic bases of social information processing. *Social Cognition. The Ontario Symposium*. Hillsdale: Erlabaum.

Taylor-Bianco, A., & Schemerhorn, J. 2006. Self regulation, strategic leadership, and paradox in organizational change. *Journal of Organizational Change Management*, 19: 457–475.

Thagard, P. R. 2008. Cognitive science. In M.-L. D. C. e. a. (eds) (Ed.), *The Stanford Encyclopedia of Philosophy*. http://plato.stanford.edu/cgi-bin/encyclopedia/archinfo. cgi (accessed 12 April 2010). Stanford University.

Thagard, P., & Shelley, C. P. 1997. Abductive reasoning: logic, visual thinking and coherence. In M.-L. D. C. e. a. (eds) (Ed.), *Logic and Scientific Methods*, (pp. 413–427): Dordrecht: Kluwer.

The World Great Encyclopaedia (Sekai Hyakka Jiten). 1998. Hitachi Digital Heibonsha.

Tjosvold, D., & Leung, K. (Eds.). 2003. *Cross-Cultural Management: Foundations and Future*. London: Gower.

Tolman, C. 1959. *Principles of Purposive Behavior*. In S. Koch (Ed.), *Psychology: A Study of Science: Vol 2. General Systematic Formulations, Learning, and Special Processes* (pp. 92–157). New York: McGraw Hill.

Tominaga, N. 1973. Words after Enlightenment (Shutsujo kogo). In N. Mizuta & T. Arisaka (Eds.), *Nihon Shiso Taikei* 43. Tokyo: Iwanami Shoten.

Tomoeda, R. 1971. Kumazawa Banzan to chugoku shiso (Kumazawa Banzan and Chinese thought) *Kumazawa Banzan* (pp. 535–580). Tokyo: Iwanami Shoten.

Toynbee, A. J. 1946a. *A Study of History: Abridgement of Volumes VII–X*. Oxford: Oxford University Press.

Tregaskis, O., & Brewster, C. 2006. Converging or diverging? A comparative analysis of trends in contingent employment practice in Europe over a decade. *Journal of International Business Studies*, 37(1): 111–126.

Tremoulet, P., Leslie, A., & Hall, D. 2000. Infant individuation and identification of objects. *Cognitive Development*, 15(4): 499–522.

Triandis, H. C. 1972. *The Analysis of Subjective Culture*. New York: Wiley-Interscience.

Trice, H. M. a. B., J M. 1984. Studying organizational cultures through rites and symbols. *Academy of Management Review*, 9(4): 653–669.

Trompenaars, F. 1993. *Riding the Waves of Culture: Understanding Cultural Diversity in Business*. London: The Economist Books.

Trompenaars, F. 2006. Resolving international conflict: Culture and business strategy. *Business Strategy Review*, 7(3): 51–68.

Trompenaars, F., & Hampden-Turner, C. 1997. *Riding the Waves of Culture: Understanding Cultural Diversity in Business* (2nd ed.). London: Nicholas Brealey Publishing.

Tsui, A. S. 2009. Editor's introduction – Autonomy of inquiry: shaping the future of emerging scientific communities. *Management and Organization Review*, 5(1): 1–14.

Tudge, J. R. H., & Winterhoff, P. A. 1993. Vygotsky, Piaget, and Bandura: Perspectives on the relations between the social world and cognitive development. *Human Development*, 361: 61–81.

Tung, R. L. 1998. American expatriates abroad: From Neophytes to Cosmopolitans. *Journal of World Business*, 33(2): 125–144.

Tylor, E. B. 1903/1988. Primitive culture: The science of culture. In P. Bohannan, & M.Glazer (Eds.), *High Points in Anthropology*. New York: McGraw-Hill.

Ui, H. 1974. *Outline of Buddhism (Bukkyo hanron)*. Tokyo: Iwanami Shoten.

Varenne, H. 2002. *The culture of culture*. Accessed on 10 May 2011 and available at http://varenne.tc.columbia.edu/hv/clt/and/culture_def.html.

Vasubandhu. 1999a. The thirty verses on consciousness only (F. H. Cook, Trans.) *Three Texts on Consciousness Only* (pp. 373–384). Berkeley, CA: Numanta Center for Buddhist Translation and Research.

Vasubandhu. 1999b. The treatises in twenty verses on consciousness only (F. H. Cook, Trans.) *Three Texts on Consciousness Only* (pp. 387–408). Berkeley, CA: Numata Center for Buddhist Translation and Research.

Wang, Y. 1972. *Sayings and Letters (Denshuroku or chuanxulu)* (Vol. 13). Tokyo: Meiji Shoin.

Watanabe, J. 2005. *The First Approach to Philosophy (Hajimete manabu tetsuaku)*. Tokyo: Chikuma Shobo.

Waxman, W. 2006. Kant's debt to the British empiricists. In G. Bird (Ed.), *A Companion to Kant* (pp. 93–108). Oxford: Blackwell Publishing.

Weaver, G., & Gioia, D. 1994. Paradigms lost: incommensurability vs structurational inquiry. *Organization Science*, 15(4): 565–590.

Webb, D., & Pettigrew, A. 1999. The temporal development of strategy: patterns in the UK insurance industry. *Organization Science*, 10(5): 601–621.

Weber, M. 1904/1949. *The Methodology of the Social Sciences* (A. d. E. A. Shils, & H. A. Finch, Trans.). New York: New York Free Press.

Weick, K. E. 1979, *The Social Psychology of Organizing*. New York: McGraw Hill.

Weick, K. E. 1979. Cognitive process in organization. In B. M. Staw (Ed.), *Research in Organizational Behavior*. Greenwich, CN: JAI Press. 1: 41–74.

Weick, K. E. 1995. *Sensemaking in Organizations*. Thousand Oaks, CA: Sage Publications.

Wertheimer, M. 1924 Gestalt theory. http://gestalttheory.net/archive/wert1.html (accessed 28 April 2010). The Society for Gestalt Theory and its Applications.

Wertheimer, M. 1959. *Productive Thinking*. New York: Harper and Row.

Westheimer, G. 1999. Gestalt theory reconfigured: Max Wertheimer's anticipation of recent developments in visual neuroscience. *Perception*, 28, 5–16.

Whorf, B. L. 1940. Science and linguistics. *Technology Review*, 42(April): 229–231, 247–248.

Whorf, B. L. 1955. Language and logic. In J. B. Carroll (Ed.), *Language, Thought and Reality* (pp. 233–245). Boston, MA: The MIT Press.

Whorf, B. L. 1962. *Language, Thought, and Reality* (5th ed.). Cambridge, MA: MIT Press.

Whorf, B. L. 1997. The relation of habitual thought and behavior to language. *ETC: A Review of General Semantics*, 197–215.

Wikipedia. 2010a. Korean confucianism http://en.wikipedia.org/wiki/Korean_Confucianism (accessed 6 April 2010).

Wikipedia. 2010. Zhu Xi. http://en.wikipedia.org/wiki/Zhu_Xi (accessed 1 April 2010).

Wikipedia. 2010a. Cognitive science. http://en.wikipedia.org/wiki/Cognitive_science (accessed 12 April 2010).

Wikipedia. 2010b. Developmental psychology. http://en.wikipedia.org/wiki/Developmental_psychology (accessed 13 April 2010).

Wikipedia. 2010b. Taoism in Japan http://en.wikipedia.org/wiki/Taoism_in_Japan (accessed 2 April 2010).

Wikipedia. 2010c. Metamemory. http://en.wikipedia.org/wiki/Metamemory (accessed 23 October 2010).

Wikipedia. 2010c. Wang Yangming http://en.wikipedia.org/wiki/Wang_Yang_Ming (accessed 2 April 2010).

Wikipedia. 2010d. Zhu Xi. http://en.wikipedia.org/wiki/Zhu_Xi (accessed 1 April 2010).

Wilcox, T. 1999. Object individuation: Infants' use of shape, size, pattern, and color. *Cognition*, 72(2): 125–166.

Wilensky, R. 1983. *Memory and inference*. Paper presented at the 8th International Joint Conferences on Artificial Intelligence, Karlsruhe, Germany.

Williams, R. (Ed.). 1981. *Contact: Human Communication and its History*. London, New York: Thames and Hudson.

Wong, D. 2009. Comparative philosophy: Chinese and Western. In E. N. Zalta (Ed.), *The Stanford Encyclopedia of Philosophy* (Winter 2009 ed.) http://plato.stanford.edu/entries/comparphil-chiwes/ (accessed 1 April 2010) Stanford University.

Wood, A. W. 2006. Kant's life and works. In G. Bird (Ed.), *A Companion to Kant* (pp. 10–30). Oxford: Blackwell Publishing.

Woolf. 1977. The Webster's Dictionary: Webster Publishing.

Woolhouse, R. 1997. Introduction *John Locke's An Essay concerning Human Understanding* (pp. ix–xxiv). London: Penguin Books.

Woolhouse, R. 2005. John Locke. In T. Honderich (Ed.), *The Oxford Companion to Philosophy* (pp. 525–529). Oxford: Oxford University Press.

Yakura, E. K. 2002. Charting time: timelines as temporal boundary objects. *Academy of Management Journal*, **45**(5): 956–981.

Yanagi, M. 1997. a *Nama Amitābhudhāya (Nama Amida Butsu)*. Tokyo: Iwanami Shoten.

Yin, R. K. 1989. The case study crisis: some answers. *Administrative Science Quarterly*, **26**(1): 58–65.

Yin, R. K. 1994. *Case Study Research: Design and Methods*. Thousand Oaks, CA: Sage Publications.

Yoshikawa, K. 1971. A discourse on the scholarship of Jinsai and Togai (Jinsai Togai gaku-an). In K. Yoshikawa & S. Shimizu (Eds.), *Ito Jinsai, Ito Togai* (Vol. 33). Tokyo: Iwanami Shoten.

Yoshino, M. Y. 1968. *Japan's Managerial System: Tradition and Innovation*. Cambridge, MA: The MIT Press.

Yu, Chong Ho 1994, April. Is there a logic of exploratory data analysis? Paper presented at the Annual Meeting of American Educational Research Association, New Orleans, LA.

Yunus, M. 2010. No going back. *IESE Insight*, **3**(6): 76.

Zemach, E. M. 1968. A definition of memory. *Mind*, **77**(308): 526–536.

Zhang, Y., Dolan, S., & Zhou, Y. 2009. Management by values: A theoretical proposal for strategic human resource management in China. *Chinese Management Studies*, **3**(4): 272–294.

Zhang, Y., Straub, C., & Kusyk, S. 2007. Making a life or making a living? Cross-cultural comparison of business students' work and life values in Canada and France. *Cross-Cultural Management: An International Journal*, **13**(4): 174–195.

Zhu, Y., & Han, S. 2008. Cultural differences in the self: From philosophy to psychology and neuroscience. *Social and Personality Psychology Compass*, **2**(5): 1799–1811.

Ziporyn, B. (n.d.). Form, principle, pattern, or coherence? Li 理 in Chinese philosophy: Northwestern University.

# Index